See Australia All Year

See Australia

All Year

Bruce Elder & Ivan Coates

Over 700 annual festivals, shows and sporting events

Publisher	Gordon Cheers
Associate Publisher	Margaret Olds
Art Director	Stan Lamond
Managing Editor	Dannielle Doggett
Senior Editor	Kate Etherington
Text Editors	Alan Edwards Erin King Janet Parker
Cover Design	Stan Lamond
Cartographer	John Frith
Map Editors	Louise Buchanan Heather McNamara Dee Rogers
Picture Research	Gordon Cheers Ivan Coates
Photo Library	Alan Edwards
Typesetting	Dee Rogers
Index	Heather McNamara
Publishing Assistant	Erin King
Production	Rosemary Barry Bernard Roberts

Photographers

Chris Bell, Rob Blakers, Ken Brass, Adam Bruzzone, Claver Carroll, Marcus Clinton, Frank Dalgity, Grant Dixon, Richard Eastwood, Bruce Elder, Stuart Owen Fox, Philip Gostelow, Ivy Hansen, Dennis Harding, Richard I'Anson, Ionas Kaltenbach, Colin Kerr, Mike Langford, Gary Lewis, John McCann, Richard McKenna, Ron Moon, Nolen Oayada, Lee Pearce, Geof Prigge, Don Skirrow, Steve Starling, Ken Stepnell, Oliver Strewe, J. Peter Thoeming, James Young

Published by
Gregory's Publishing Company
(A division of Universal Press Pty Ltd)
ACN 000 087 132

Marketed and distributed by Universal Press Pty Ltd
New South Wales: 1 Waterloo Road, Macquarie Park 2113
Ph: (02) 9857 3700 Fax: (02) 9888 9850
Queensland: 1 Manning Street, South Brisbane 4101
Ph: (07) 3844 1051 Fax: (07) 3844 4637
South Australia: Freecall: 1800 021 987
Victoria: 585 Burwood Road, Hawthorn 3122
Ph: (03) 9818 4455 Fax: (03) 9818 6123
Western Australia: 38a Walters Drive, Osborne Park 6017
Ph: (08) 9244 2488 Fax: (08) 9244 2554

Produced by Global Book Publishing Pty Ltd
1/181 High Street, Willoughby, NSW Australia 2068
Phone 61 2 9967 3100 fax 61 2 9967 5891

ISBN 0 7319 1443 0

National Library of Australia Cataloguing-in-Publicatio
Coates, Ivan.
See Australia all year.
ISBN 0 7319 1443 0.
1. Festivals - Australia - Guidebooks. 2. Carnival - Australia - Guidebooks. 3. Australia - Description and travel - Guidebooks. I. Elder, Bruce. II. Title.
(Series : See Australia (Sydney)).
919.4047

Printed in Hong Kong by Sing Cheong Printing Co. Ltd,
Film separation Pica Digital Pte Ltd, Singapore

Disclaimer
The authors and publisher disclaim any responsibility to any person for loss or damage suffered from any use of this guide for any purpose. While considerable care has been taken by the authors and the publisher in researching and compiling the guide, the authors and the publisher accept no responsibility for errors or omissions. No person should rely upon this guide for the purpose of making any business, investment or real estate decision. It is possible that dates and venues may change, and events may be cancelled. The authors and the publisher advise readers to check with event organisers as to the status of the event.
The representation on any maps of any road or track is not necessarily evidence of public right of way. Third parties who have provided information to the author and publisher concerning the roads and other matters did not warrant to the author and publisher that the information was complete, accurate or current or that any of the proposals of any body will eventuate and, accordingly, the author and publisher provide no such warranty.

Captions for preliminary pages
Page 1: Carnivale participants, Darling Harbour, Sydney, New South Wales..
Page 2: Melbourne Concert Hall at the Victorian Arts Centre, Melbourne, Victoria.
Page 3: Decorated tram, Moomba Festival, Melbourne, Victoria.
Page 4: Bungendore Rodeo, Australian Capital Territory.
Pages 6–7: Australia Day on Sydney Harbour, Sydney, New South Wales.

Photographers
Global Book Publishing would be pleased to hear from photographers interested in supplying photographs.

Key to Road Maps

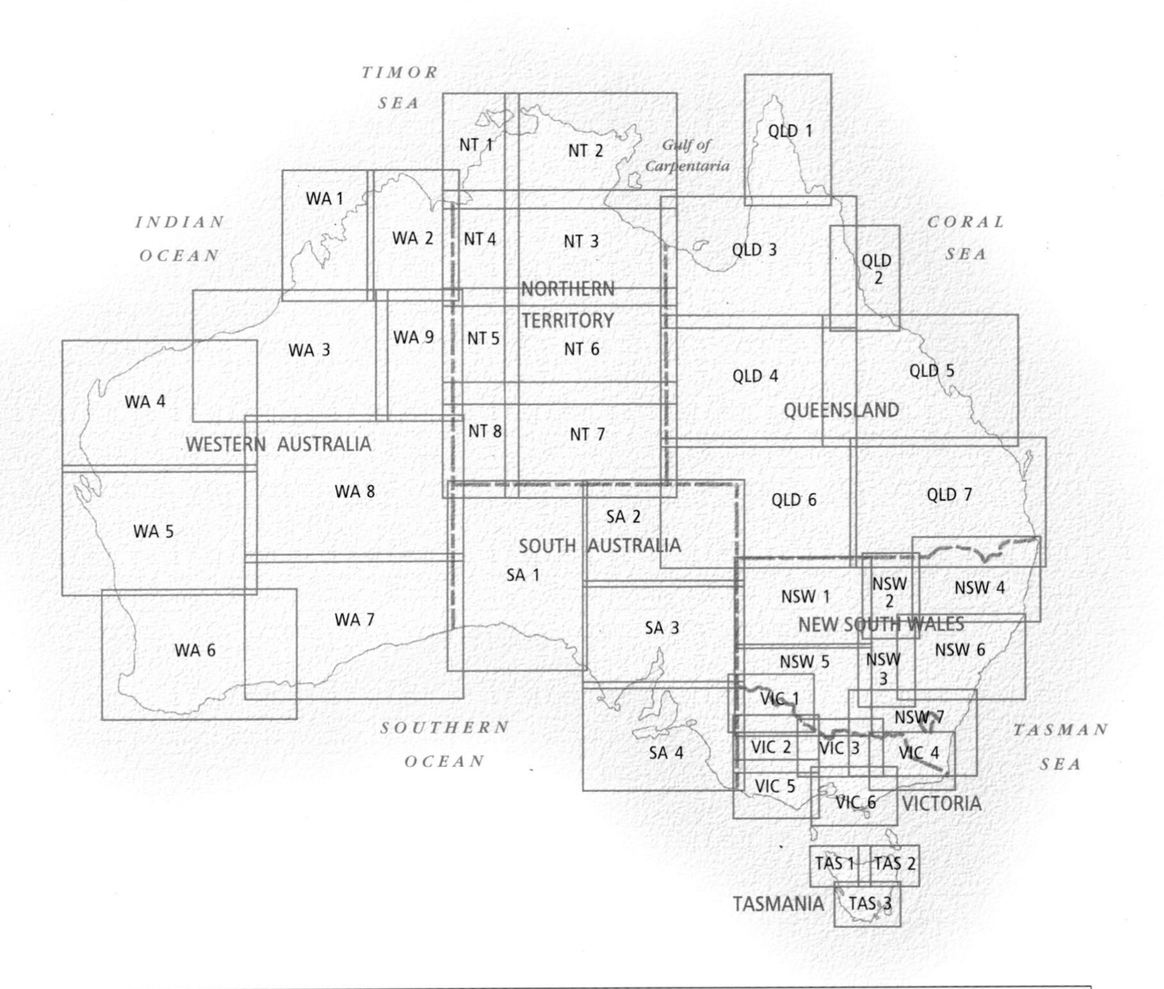

Legend to Road Maps

Freeway or motorway with national or federal route number	66 A8 1	Major linear feature (as noted)	Dog Fence
Freeway or motorway tunnel	M1	International airport	
Highway with state route numbers	69 A20	Major built up area, state or territory capital	
Major sealed road with metroad route number	5	Major city or town, other towns	
Minor sealed road, bridge		Homestead, ruin, mine,	
Major unsealed road, gate, grid		Landmark or tourist feature, mountain peak	
Minor unsealed road or track, 4WD where indicated	4WD	Bore, well or waterhole, tank or dam	
Walking track		Major river, other watercourse	
Road distances in kilometres, major and intermediate	12 18 30	Perennial lake, dry or intermittent lake	
Railway line with station	Watson	Boundary of prohibited area or military reserve	
Underground railway (city maps only)		State ot territory border	
Tramline with station (city maps only)		Marine park or reserve, coral reef	
Railway line, dismantled or abandoned (regional maps)		Aboriginal land	
Ferry route		National park, reserve, conservation area or state forest	

AMP

Contents

Introduction

See Australia: All Year is a compendium of more than 700 Australian events and festivals. It is not, by any means, a complete list as there are thousands of towns and cities in Australia and nearly all of them have local celebrations or sporting events that recur at regular intervals. Rather, this is an attempt to delineate some of the more significant social activities that occur annually or biennially.

In many outback towns, events such as rodeos and campdrafts reflect the importance of horsemanship skills in Australia's pioneering history.

With a coastline measuring 35 877 km in length, the ocean plays a vital role in the life and culture of most Australians. Surf-lifesaving carnivals, blessing of the fleet festivals and other seaside events occur regularly.

The range of social phenomena is broad. All are, at their core, a simple and fundamental expression of the desire to celebrate life or, to put it another way, to have fun. Karl Marx once suggested that what distinguishes human beings from other species is superfluity: production above and beyond that required for basic survival. In this sense, much of human culture is superfluous and it is this abundance, this fat upon the flesh, which we celebrate at the majority of our fiestas. Moreover, in these days of social atomisation and individualism, there is something reassuringly communal and giving about most festivals. Regardless of the particular motif or rubric they adopt, most are celebrations of the community itself: its survival, prosperity, productivity, skills and talents and its desire for self-expression, recognition and social contact. The word itself—'society'—derives from a Latin word for companionship. In this sense the more participatory regional festivals are perhaps most typical, whereas the major urban festivals are more likely to involve a relationship between the expert artist/performer and the passive viewer/consumer.

Right: *Australians are very patriotic, especially at events involving our national sporting teams. The country's colours of green and gold are often worn, and Australian flags of all sizes are proudly waved—sometimes they are even painted on faces.*

Perhaps the most common aspect of the modern festival is the consumption of food and beverages. 'Festival' derives from the Latin word for feast, and many of the regional festivals adopt as their theme some item, or items, of local produce, usually food, though sometimes this may involve local minerals or metals such as gold, which has played a vital role in Australian history. Often the timing of regional celebrations reflects the harvest, and it is this relationship between harvest and feasting that most clearly connects modern festivals to the oldest human celebrations, where abundance is at its most obvious.

However, the celebratory impulse takes many different forms and objects, and the festivals included in this volume also incorporate sporting competitions; cars and automobile culture; a variety of music genres; the visual arts; dancing; films and other elements of popular culture; spiritual ceremonies (such as the blessing of the fleet); celebrations of a way of life, a tradition or a particular community (highland gatherings, outback festivals, urban multicultural fiestas, gay festivities, alternative lifestyle events and ethnic festivals such as Chinese New Year); celebrations of the water, its bounty and the opportunities it offers for profit and play; major business events (Agfests); celebrations of Australiana (coo-ee festivals); and some that are simply humorous and/or satirical in the socially levelling and pretension-pricking manner that is acutely Australian, as is the case at the Henley-on-Todd Regatta near Alice Springs, the Winton Dunny Derby and the bong-throwing competition at the Nimbin Mardi Gras.

Right: *Being an island continent, sailing is a popular pastime in the bays and rivers of the state capital cities and coastal towns. One of the most famous events is the Sydney to Hobart Yacht Race.*

Below: *Australians are well known as sports fanatics. Australian Rules Football is one of the country's favourite sports, and the atmosphere at huge venues like the Melbourne Cricket Ground is electric.*

Vetta
TORY
TOYOTA
COLLAROY

January

January is the height of summer in Australia. All around the country children take a break from school and families attempt to reinvigorate themselves by seeking some fun, relaxation, a change of environment and a little adventure. Many search for a place less crowded and more scenic, with coastal locations proving the most popular in this month of typically high temperatures.

Of course, the year commences at a second after midnight on 1 January with the usual noisy revelries. The nation recovers from its celebrations with a public holiday to mark the start of the New Year. While many people choose, or are compelled, to spend the day doing as little as possible, there are some entertaining public events scattered around the country for those with some energy to spare.

January occurs during the middle of the Australian summer. Many families take advantage of the warm, sunny days and visit one of the nation's pristine national parks to enjoy a picnic.

Another nationwide holiday is Australia Day, which commemorates the occasion on 26 January, 1788, when Governor Phillip landed at Sydney Cove and proclaimed Britain's formal possession of the colony. In this sense Australia Day is a celebration of nationhood and Australian-ness, although recently an awareness of how this event affects the nation's indigenous peoples has led to a more complex and diverse perspective on its meaning.

January is also the month in which the daylong music festival known as the Big Day Out commences its annual circuit from Southport on the Gold Coast to Perth, stopping at Sydney, Melbourne and Adelaide on the way. It showcases national and international alternative rock music, offering live performances by around 50 bands.

Below: *The Big Day Out is a travelling music festival that features well-known alternative rock acts from Australia and around the world, plus a number of up-and-coming bands.*

Left: *Sport is an integral part of the Australian identity, and this is celebrated on Australia Day with many surf-lifesaving carnivals and triathlons along the nation's beaches.*

South Bank is the focus for the Brisbane Lord Mayor's Australia Day Celebrations. Adults and children alike enjoy the carnival-like atmosphere, with parades, performers and stunning fireworks.

Right: *Brisbane's Energex Australia Day Parade has a host of vibrant floats inspired by favourite icons of Australia, such as the kewpie doll and Vegemite.*

did you know?

Located less than 10 km from Coominya, Lake Wivenhoe was created in 1985 when a dam was built across the Brisbane River. When full, Lake Wivenhoe contains twice as much water as Sydney Harbour.

Queensland

BRISBANE

Brisbane's Australia Day festivities centre on South Bank where the Lord Mayor's Australia Day Celebrations offer family-orientated fun, and end with spectacular fireworks in the evening. South Bank is also the terminus for the colourful floats of the Energex Australia Day Parade, which weave their way through South Brisbane in the afternoon. On a different note the famous Australia Day Cockroach Races are held at the Story Bridge Hotel, and the 26th marks the start of the Lifeline Bookfest, the city's largest second-hand book sale.
Map: Qld 7 N7

The Grape and Watermelon Festival
Coominya

SECOND SATURDAY IN JANUARY

Coominya is a small but pleasant rural town in the Brisbane Valley, which has developed a reputation for its turn-of-the-century buildings, including the famous Bellevue Homestead. The nature of the area's economy is evident in the festival, which celebrates the grape and watermelon harvests with a day of contests relating to eating, weighing, throwing and running with watermelons. Stage entertainment, fireworks and children's rides are part of this family festival.
Map: Qld 7 M7

Magic Millions Summer Racing Carnival
Gold Coast

EARLY JANUARY

Queensland's biggest horseracing event features a 12-day calendar of fashionable social events and draws visitors from around the world. The main attractions are the Yearling Sales and the races for the 2-year-olds and 3-year-olds, which boast prize money of over $2.5 million.
Map: Qld 7 N8

Summer Solstice Light and Sound Spectacle at Olsen's Capricorn Caves

As the sun's angle shifts in mid-January, this unusual lighting phenomenon ceases (see the main entry in December).
Map: Qld 5 J8

Rocky New Year Bash and Ball at Rockhampton

Four days of festivities wind up on 3 January (see the main entry in December).
Map: Qld 5 J8

Speed in the Mountains
Stanthorpe

THIRD WEEKEND IN JANUARY

Stanthorpe's Storm King Dam hosts the Queensland Sprint Triathlon Championships (known as Speed in the Mountains) in which entrants amass points by competing in three events: the 1-km run, the 300-m swim and the 6-km cycle. Those with the most points advance to the final event—the 750-m kayak—that determines the champion.
Map: Qld 7 L9

Woodford Folk Festival

This folk festival ends on 1 January (see the main entry in December).
Map: Qld 7 M6

New South Wales

SYDNEY

For three weeks in January the New South Wales capital celebrates the arts during the Sydney Festival, with international and Australian figures and popular free concerts. It concludes amid the festivities associated with Australia Day, peaking with lasers, fireworks and performances in the evening at Cockle Bay. An alternative view of Australia Day can be enjoyed at Bondi's Aboriginal Survival Concert. Film lovers have their choice of the Flickerfest Short Film Festival at Bondi, the on-going Moonlight Cinema programme (see the main entry in November) and the Open-Air Cinema in the Botanic Gardens. Other events include the Adidas Tennis International and the Ferrython ferry races.

Map: NSW 6 J8

The Thursday Plantation East Coast Sculpture Show at Ballina

This annual event finishes in January (see the main entry in September).

Map: NSW 4 P3

The Festival of Fish and Chips

Brunswick Heads

MID-JANUARY

This quiet and pleasant holiday resort town is located at the mouth of the Brunswick River on the north New South Wales coast. The festival is a fun four-day family affair with sideshows, carnival rides, fishing contests, an art and photography competition, auctions, a surf carnival, model railway displays, live entertainment and a fireworks display. It incorporates the Brunswick Valley Woodchop Carnival, which sees axemen compete in first-class woodchop events.

Map: NSW 4 P2

don't miss

Visit the Rocks area of Sydney and step back in time. Take a tour of the old terrace houses and shop at Susannah Place, or go for a pleasant dinner cruise aboard the *Bounty* which leaves from Campbell's Cove.

The Sydney Festival takes place all over the city. It features a dazzling array of both Australian and international acts from the worlds of music and dance, plus films, art exhibitions and more.

The grand Victorian architecture of Forbes reflects the prosperity found in this goldmining town during the 1860s. When the gold ran out, Forbes became an agricultural and pastoral centre.

Forbes Jazz Festival
Forbes

FIRST WEEK IN JANUARY

Each year this substantial country town, located 387 km west of Sydney, launches its jazz festival with a popular street parade of musicians. The festival includes programmed concerts, a jazz picnic, winery tours with jazz music, a gospel service, a public concert and an original tunes competition. Many of the country's leading jazz bands drop into Forbes during the five days of fun and entertainment.

Map: NSW 3 E5

Gulgong Folk Festival

This folk festival ends on New Year's Day (see the main entry in December).

Map: NSW 6 E4

Right: *Located on the New England Highway, Tamworth, the Golden Guitar is a 12-m tall copy of the famous trophy given to the winners of the Country Music Awards of Australia.*

National Tomato Contest
Gunnedah

SECOND SUNDAY IN JANUARY

Gunnedah's farming heritage is reflected in the National Tomato Contest, which sees entries from all around Australia vying for the title of the biggest, the heaviest, the most unusual and, of course, the tastiest tomato. There are also other novelty events and fun family activities at the Gunnedah Services and Bowling Club, which hosts the event.

Map: NSW 4 E9

don't miss

Lake Keepit State Park is located 57 km northwest of Tamworth. It's a mecca for watersports enthusiasts during the summer months, with swimming, windsurfing, sailing, fishing, water-skiing and more.

The Shear Outback Festival
Hay

AUSTRALIA DAY WEEKEND

The Shear Outback Festival at Hay celebrates Australia's colourful shearing culture as well as outback life in general. The focus of the festival is the annual induction into the Shearing Hall of Fame. The Shear Outback complex showcases the stories, artefacts, technology and culture of the Australian shearing industry with humour, theatre, music, showmanship, shearing, competitions and a range of outback experiences for the whole family.

Map: NSW 5 K6

Carlton Country Music Festival
Tamworth

THIRD FRIDAY TO FOURTH SUNDAY IN JANUARY

Australia's largest and most famous country music event takes place every January in the nation's unofficial country music capital. Over 10 days, hundreds of Australian country music artists take to the streets, pubs and other venues of this substantial rural town. There are around 2500 separate events and activities. Highlights include the official opening concert, the Golden Guitar Awards, the Country Music Cavalcade and the competitions relating to busking, harmonica playing, newly emerging talent and bush poetry.

Map: NSW 4 G9

Australian Capital Territory

The Summernats Car Festival
Canberra

FIRST WEEK IN JANUARY

This popular four-day event is for enthusiasts of the street machine—a modified, customised or restored street car dating from after World War II. Held at Exhibition Park in Canberra, it is both a car show and a festival of the street machine lifestyle. Revheads can cruise the park's roadways or go for broke in the Burnout and Go-Whoa competitions.

Map: NSW 7 J4

Victoria

MELBOURNE

Sporting events are popular drawcards in Melbourne throughout the month of January. The two biggies in this respect are the Heineken Classic at the Royal Melbourne Golf Club and the Australian Open Tennis Championships. January also sees several one-day international cricket fixtures and numerous events on the horseracing calendar. On a very different note, January is the time of the unique Midsumma Festival, which is Melbourne's gay and lesbian cultural and arts festival.

Map: Vic 6 D3

Above: *The Australian Open Tennis Championships are the first Grand Slam title of the year. It draws the best tennis players in the world to Melbourne Park, as well as over 500 000 spectators.*

The Taste of Falls Creek Weekend

Falls Creek

SECOND WEEKEND IN JANUARY

Previously known as the Falls Creek Food, Wine and Flower Weekend, this is an opportunity to become acquainted with the wines and foods of Victoria's north-east and with the state's most exclusive ski resort. In summer the area is replete with blooming wildflowers and visitors can enjoy guided heritage and nature walks, gourmet food, live jazz and blues, cooking demonstrations, wine tastings, a champagne recovery breakfast, chairlift rides, bocce and mountain bike riding. Entry is free to all events throughout the weekend.

Map: Vic 4 B5

Above: *One of the most popular competitions in the Canberra's Summernats Car Festival is the Burnout, where competitors strive to burst both rear tyres simultaneously.*

don't miss

While you're visiting the Mornington Peninsula for the Summer of Wine festival, check out the many antique shops in the region. The town of Tyabb has Australia's biggest collection of old wares under one roof.

The Geelong Waterfront Festival

Geelong

AUSTRALIA DAY WEEKEND

Geelong is Victoria's largest provincial city. Despite its industrial reputation it is an elegant and attractive city, with delightful parks and gardens, historic architecture and a superb location on Corio Bay. The city's relationship with the ocean is celebrated during the Waterfront Festival at its newly developed waterfront leisure and recreation precinct. It offers live music performances, food and wine, water activities, parades, markets, sporting events and fireworks. Geelong's waterfront is also the location for The Bundaberg Rum Festival of Sail, Australia's largest keel boat regatta, with over 400 yachts, 4500 sailors and 25 000 visitors. First held in 1844, it was officially established in 1859 and is thus one of the oldest sporting events in the nation.

Map: Vic 5 P6

The Falls Festival at Lorne

The rainforest rock (see the main entry in December) ends on New Year's Day.

Map: Vic 5 M8

Geelong's coastal position has played a large part in the town's history, and this is celebrated during the Waterfront Festival. The city was the site of Australia's first submarine base.

The Maryborough Highland Gathering

Maryborough

NEW YEAR'S DAY

Now essentially an industrial town, Maryborough is a former goldmining town. The gold rushes of the 1850s and 1860s drew vast numbers of migrants to the Goldfields region of Victoria. Many came from Scotland, and the Highland Gathering was started by these migrants more than 130 years ago. The highlight is the running of the Maryborough Gift, although there are many other athletic events (including Scottish games such as caber tossing and sheaf tossing), highland dancing, brass bands, pipe bands, sideshows and a street parade.

Map: Vic 2 L10

Summer of Wine

Mornington Peninsula

ALL THROUGH JANUARY

The cooler, hilly terrain and quality soil in the eastern half of the Mornington Peninsula has proven to be a bonanza for the ancient art of oenology, making the Peninsula one of the state's principal wine-producing regions in recent years. Throughout January most of the area's innumerable vineyards are open every day, with extended opening hours, special programmes, festivals and entertainment on offer for visitors.

Map: Vic 6 C5

The Prom Country Summer Festival of Slow Food

Wilsons Promontory

FIRST TWO WEEKS IN JANUARY

The Festival of Slow Food (as opposed to fast food) was created to question the drift towards homogeneous, bland, mass-produced and thoughtlessly consumed food. It emphasises the appreciation of flavoursome, healthy, fresh, diverse, home-prepared and home-cooked provender. The result is a fortnight of gourmet food, wine, twilight races and special events in this scenic portion of the state's southern coast.

Map: Vic 6 J8

Sailing is a popular pastime along the Derwent River in Hobart, as it offers scenic views of Mount Wellington. Dinner cruises are especially enjoyable.

Tasmania

HOBART

The fine summer weather makes sport a popular pastime in Hobart during January. Not surprisingly, there are many boating activities, including the Australian Yachting Championships, the King of the Derwent Yacht Race and the Sailing South Race Week. The International Masters Golf Championship is for amateur golfers over the age of 35, while the Tasmanian International Women's Tennis Tournament is a prelude to the Australian Open. On a different note, visitors can enjoy the summer ambience at the very popular Downtown International Busker's Festival in Elizabeth Mall. It is part of the Hobart Summer Festival (see the main entry in December), which continues throughout the month, while the Taste of Tasmania (see the main entry in December) concludes in early January. The popular Hobart Cup horserace is run on Australia Day.

Map: Tas 3 K6

1875 ROYAL TENNIS COURT

Left: *Hobart has a long association with the game of tennis. In 1875, Samuel Smith Travers built the first royal ('real') tennis court here, and the city has the oldest royal tennis club in Australia.*

Cygnet Folk Festival

Cygnet

FRIDAY TO SUNDAY OF SECOND WEEKEND IN JANUARY

This small but locally important centre in Tasmania's pretty Huon Valley has, in recent years, become something of an alternative-lifestyle centre. The Cygnet Folk Festival is one of the premier events in Tasmania's musical calendar, as it presents an exceptional variety of music, dance and mixed media shows over three days.

Map: Tas 3 J7

South Australia

ADELAIDE

As the new year opens in South Australia, the state capital continues to host the AAPT Tennis Championship (see the main entry in December) and, later in the month, it provides the finishing line for the world-famous Jacob's Creek Road Cycling Tour Down Under. The area's Greek heritage is the focus during the Blessing of the Waters and Greek Festival at Glenelg, and South Australia's German heritage is celebrated at the world's second-largest Schutzenfest—at Hahndorf, just 25 km south-east of Adelaide—in which over 30 000 people enjoy German-style food and ales, oompah bands, folk dancing and a shooting competition. On a more serene note, the churches and wineries of the Adelaide Hills resound with *a cappella* ensembles, choirs, string quartets, jazz musicians and poetry readings during the Festival of 1000 Voices.

Map: SA 4 J3

Right: *Settled in 1839, Hahndorf is the oldest German village still surviving in Australia. The historic German Arms Hotel serves fine South Australian wines and imported German lagers.*

Below: *Sample the Cape Jaffa region's finest drops at the Seafood and Wine Festival. Local companies including Mount Benson Vineyards and Cape Jaffa Wines sell their products by the glass or bottle.*

Below: *Penola is the gateway to the Coonawarra wine-growing area. The Vignerons Cup Race day showcases the region's wineries, such as Bowen Estate, Leconfield, Lindemans and Balnaves.*

The Cape Jaffa Seafood and Wine Festival

Cape Jaffa

THIRD SUNDAY IN JANUARY

Cape Jaffa, on the south-eastern coast of South Australia, is noted for its nineteenth-century lighthouse, and every day around 1.00 p.m. the lobster fleet returns to the port with its catch. Its annual festival unfolds on the town's foreshore, offering visitors the chance to sample the finest wine, seafood and produce of the state's south-east. There are also boat rides, as well as live entertainment and children's activities.

Map: SA 4 L8

The Coonawarra Vignerons Cup Race

Penola

10 JANUARY

Cup Day, held at the Penola Racecourse, is an important social event on the South Australian calendar, as it mixes the thrill of the races with the opportunity to try a few of the wines from the 20-plus wineries along the road from Coonawarra to Penola. It offers plenty in the way of high fashion, fun, entertainment, food and fine local wines. The day starts with a sparkling breakfast in a large air-conditioned marquee, and there is a buffet lunch and an annual wine auction.

Map: SA 4 P9

John West Tunarama Festival

Port Lincoln

FRIDAY TO MONDAY OF AUSTRALIA DAY WEEKEND

This fishing port is the jewel of the Eyre Peninsula. Its lucrative tuna industry inspires the festival, which unfolds on the town foreshore. Attractions include the World Championship Tuna Toss competition, plenty of delicious local seafood, a parade and a spectacular fireworks display adjacent to Boston Bay.

Map: SA 4 D2

The Busselton Beach Festival

Busselton

CULMINATING IN SECOND WEEKEND OF JANUARY

This two-day event is designed to showcase local talent, with a focus on visual and performing arts. Children's workshops are held in the week before the festival, which attracts around 30 000 visitors and over 100 artists. There is also a beach party, attended by over 10 000 people, which provides a family environment with music and fireworks.

Map: WA 6 B7

don't miss

Kings Park in Perth is one of the world's largest city parks. Located less than 2 km from Perth's CBD, the 400-ha park encompasses 267 ha of bushland which is especially appealing when the wildflowers bloom in spring.

Western Australia

PERTH

The Hopman Cup (see the main entry in December) concludes in early January. This month sees the start of the Perth International Arts Festival, offering a variety of performances and art exhibitions, and the International Busker's Festival. The Perth Cup Horseracing Carnival at Ascot Racecourse on New Year's Day is popular, as is the Australia Day Carnival on the Swan River.

Map: WA 6 C4

Lancelin Ocean Classic

Lancelin

THURSDAY TO SUNDAY OF SECOND WEEKEND IN JANUARY

This famous windsurfing destination is 127 km north of Perth. The town's large bay is surrounded by shallow limestone reefs, and the waves around the passages are perfect for huge jumps. Consequently, it has become the home of the biggest windsurfing event in Australia, drawing a field of over 300 competitors.

Map: WA 6 B2

Left: *The Cullberg Ballet Company is just one of the many talented groups to appear at the Perth International Arts Festival over the years.*

Below: *Busselton sits on Geographe Bay, a lovely area of calm waters and long beaches ideal for seaside festivities. The 2-km jetty is the longest wooden jetty in the Southern Hemisphere.*

LINGUINE VONGOLE
FRESH JUMBO CLAMS IN
WHITE WINE SAUCE $11.50
FETTUCINE CARBONARA
$10.50

Western Australia

PERTH

The Perth International Arts Festival concludes in mid-February as does the International Busker's Festival (for both, see the main entry in January). There is a plethora of daily (or nightly) arts events throughout the Festival's duration, including popular, world, classical and avant-garde musical performances; theatre; fine arts displays; comedy; and dance and film. A festival highlight is the Margaret River Classic, which offers a world-class chamber music concert experience at the acoustically exquisite Vasse Felix Auditorium.

Map: WA 6 C4

Leeuwin Estate Concert

Margaret River

THIRD WEEKEND IN FEBRUARY

Margaret River is a fashionable South Coast tourist town in the heart of a well-established wine region. The Leeuwin Estate Winery, on Stevens Road, hosts an annual outdoor twilight picnic-concert amid the giant floodlit karri forest. Past drawcards here have included Michael Crawford, Dame Kiri Te Kanawa, George Benson, Dionne Warwick, Tom Jones, Shirley Bassey, James Galway and Diana Ross. The entertainment continues after the concert and there are numerous dining options (and wines to sample!).

Map: WA 6 B8

Above: *Margaret River's award-winning Leeuwin Estate has a majestic karri forest backdrop.*

Below: *Now attracting over 6000 guests, the Leeuwin Concerts began in 1985 with the London Philharmonic Orchestra.*

Mont Albert 109
The Home Buyer's Bank
298

March

The first of March heralds the official commencement of autumn in Australia. Throughout much of the nation, the unbearable heat and sometimes humidity of summer begins to slowly cool into some of the best and mildest weather of the year.

The feast day of Ireland's patron saint, St Patrick, is on 17 March. He was a missionary to the Emerald Isle in the fifth century who converted the Irish to Christianity. In Ireland it is the occasion of a religious holiday and special religious services. On the face of it, this would seem largely irrelevant to contemporary Australia. However, throughout the nineteenth century in particular, Australia received a very large number of Irish immigrants and, for this reason, St Patrick's Day is widely celebrated on these shores as a secular and festive occasion, marked by parties, parades, green clothing and copious amounts of Guinness. Many towns hold special picnic races to mark the day, where horseracing is combined with family entertainments. Others have special St Patrick's Day festivals.

Above: *The hotels in Sydney's historic Rocks area, such as the Fortune of War, are very popular on St Patrick's Day. Many hold special events to celebrate the day.*

The first Sunday in March of each year marks another special, but more industrious, occasion: Clean Up Australia Day. This is a recent and wholly Australian invention, which was initiated by noted yachtsman Ian Kiernan in 1989. On this day, individuals and community groups work together to remove tonnes of rubbish from the parks, waterways and roadways of Australia's cities and towns.

Below: *Sydney Harbour is probably the most famous waterway in the country to reap the benefits of Clean Up Australia Day.*

Left: *The streets of Melbourne are lined with deciduous trees forming a kaleidoscope of colour in autumn. Melbourne experiences more seasonal variation than the northern cities of Brisbane and Darwin.*

Queensland

BRISBANE

The *Courier Mail* Home and Garden Show is held early in the month at the RNA Showgrounds in Bowen Hills. On display are home-related products and services including do-it-yourself demonstrations. The St Patrick's Day Parade through the streets of Brisbane City and Fortitude Valley draws about 80 000 spectators. Other events are the Brisbane International Comedy Bonanza, featuring performers from around the world; the Queensland Bridal and Honeymoon Spectacular at the Brisbane Convention and Exhibition Centre; the Redlands Heritage Festival; the International Women's Day Fun Run/Walk and the Queensland Schoolboys Regatta at Lake Wivenhoe, in the north-west.

Map: Qld 7 N7

Right: *Enormous bales of cotton ready for transport. One of the most popular events at the Cotton Week Festival at Dalby is the Big Australian Bush Barbecue.*

don't miss

When in Brisbane, take the opportunity to travel south towards the Gold Coast and have some fun at the many huge theme parks. There is Warner Bros Movie World, Wet 'n' Wild Water World and Dreamworld.

The Australian Surf-Lifesaving Championships

Broadbeach

LATE MARCH

These national championships take place over five days at Kurrawa Beach. A celebration of the courage and athleticism of surf-lifesaving, this is the culmination of all preliminary competitions. There are more than 7000 competitors, including international entrants, across many events and age groups, providing much in the way of spectacle and entertainment. This is a major event with over 500 officials, nationally televised coverage and plenty of evening parties.

Map: Qld 7 N8

Below: *Surf-lifesaving is an integral part of Australian beach culture. The Australian Surf-Lifesaving Championships attract participants from around Australia and overseas.*

Australian Cotton Week Festival

Dalby

EARLY TO MID-MARCH

This large and prosperous Darling Downs town has the good fortune of being surrounded by rich, volcanic soil where cotton is grown in abundant supply. The link between local produce and local prosperity is celebrated annually with all manner of entertainments, including racing, fashion, fine food, art exhibitions, music and more than 30 sporting events conducted over the course of 11 days.

Map: Qld 7 K6

Gladstone Harbour Festival

Gladstone

LATE MARCH TO EARLY APRIL

Since 1960 this coastal town has undergone a remarkable transformation from a sleepy port to one of the largest, busiest and most successful seaports in Australia, due to its superb natural deepwater harbour. Gladstone has celebrated its harbour in an annual festival since 1963, and since then it has grown into one of this state's major community festivals. Over 11 days the celebrations include family fun days, a street parade, sporting and cultural

activities and a seven-day marina mardi gras, drawing thousands to the nightly on-stage entertainment and side shows.
Map: Qld 5 L9

Peanut and Harvest Festival
Kingaroy

LATE MARCH OR EARLY APRIL

Famously the home of controversial Queensland premier, Joh Bjelke-Petersen, this Central West town is known as the 'Peanut Capital of Australia'. The importance of this nut is evident in the town's many peanut silos, peanut signs and peanut vendors. Even the Tourist Information Office sells them. Not surprisingly, Kingaroy hosts an annual peanut festival. Highlights include the Peanut Ball, a heritage day, an art show, a thanksgiving service, concerts, trade fairs and open days.
Map: Qld 7 L5

The Apple and Grape Harvest Festival at Stanthorpe

This 10-day Granite Belt festival ends in March (see the main entry in February).
Map: Qld 7 L9

Chronicle Lifeline Bookfest
Toowoomba

FIRST WEEKEND IN MARCH

Held at Toowoomba Showground, this is the largest regional Bookfest in Queensland. It is Lifeline's major fundraising activity for the year, with more than 500 000 books and magazines on sale, spread out over 550 tables. There is the High Quality Priced section and a much larger General section, where all items are available at a minimal price. Also for sale are plants, pre-loved clothing, dolls, toys and food.
Map: Qld 7 L7

Left: *Kingaroy is not only the Peanut Capital of Australia, it also produces 75 per cent of the navy bean crop in the country that is used to make baked beans.*

Below: *Lake Wivenhoe, near Brisbane, was constructed in 1985. As well as being the site of the Queensland Schoolboys Regatta, it is popular for boating and swimming.*

New South Wales

SYDNEY

One of the biggest events on the calendar in Sydney is the now internationally famous Gay and Lesbian Mardi Gras Parade, which caps off the Gay and Lesbian Festival (see the main entry in February). The Italian Festa in Leichhardt celebrates the Italian flavour of Norton St with food, music and films. Horseracing fans can enjoy both the Golden Slipper (one of the major horse races on the New South Wales calendar), at Rosehill Racecourse near Parramatta, and the two-week AJC Autumn Racing Carnival at Royal Randwick Racecourse. Entertainment is also provided at Darling Harbour courtesy of the National Maritime Museum's Classic and Wooden Boat Festival, which features over 300 vessels both old and new, the Sydney Bridal Expo and the Commonwealth Bank Home Show. Other events are the Bargo Swap (the third-largest swap meet in Australia), held at Camden on the second weekend of the month, and the award-winning and scenic Mount Annan Challenge Walk at the Mount Annan Botanic Gardens.

Map: NSW 6 J8

Right: *Based on the Imperial Gardens in Kyoto, Japan, the Japanese Gardens at Cowra were designed by Ken Nakajima. Visitors to the Festival of Understanding can also see the World Peace Bell, a replica of the bell at the UN building in New York.*

did you know?

Charles Sturt University Goulburn Campus is the major provider of police education at tertiary level in Australia. The university offers a range of distance education programmes for students all around New South Wales.

Festival of Understanding

Cowra

MID-MARCH

Cowra is a country town famous as the site of the largest mass POW escape in British military history, during which 234 Japanese died and another 105 were wounded. Four Australian military personnel also died during the break-out. These events have prompted the town to pursue an agenda of internationalism, pacifism and multiculturalism, evident in the Japanese war cemetery, a student exchange programme, the Japanese Garden and Cultural Centre, the World Peace Bell and the Italy Friendship Monument. The Festival of Understanding celebrates world friendship by focusing on one guest nation, and features food and wine events, a spectacular parade and carnival, concerts, music and exhibitions.

Map: NSW 3 G6

Right: *The Big Merino at Goulburn is three storeys high and made from concrete. With this huge monument, it is fitting that this town holds the State Sheep Shearing Championships.*

Goulburn Show

Goulburn

THIRD WEEKEND IN MARCH

Goulburn is the commercial centre of a major pastoral and agricultural area. 'The Big Merino', located in Hume Street, is testimony to the importance of wool in the town's history and economy. The town's rural character is embodied in the annual show, which includes dressage, hack events, harness horse events, showjumping, pavilion exhibitions, sideshows, outdoor exhibitions and plenty of food. The New South Wales State Woodchop Championships and the New South Wales State Sheep Shearing Championships are also held during this weekend of activities at the Goulburn Showground.

Map: NSW 7 K2

Weekend of Heritage and Jazz

Goulburn

SECOND WEEKEND IN MARCH

Goulburn is the major rural centre of the New South Wales Southern Tablelands. Established in the 1820s, this was the first inland settlement in the state to be proclaimed a city. During the Heritage Weekend, Goulburn's restored heritage buildings are highlighted by interpretive sign-posting, open-house invitations and guided walking tours. There are dinners in historic properties, colonial markets and photographic displays, as well as celebrations featuring jazz bands and local wines. The Rose Festival is held concurrently.

Map: NSW 7 K2

Week of Speed Festival

Gunnedah

LATE MARCH

Held over two weekends, and the week in between, the Week of Speed Festival is a celebration of the Australian obsession with competitive racing. The festival is hosted by the wheat-belt town of Gunnedah, and the numerous events include go-kart racing through the streets, drag racing, burn-out competitions, motorcycle racing, a speedway competition, horse and dog racing, athletics as well as an enormous range of novelty events to amuse the whole family.

Map: NSW 4 E9

Blue Mountains Festival of Folk, Blues and Roots Music

Katoomba

THIRD WEEKEND IN MARCH

Katoomba is the major tourist attraction in the Blue Mountains, and this charming town combines spectacular views and beautiful environs with plenty of olde-worlde-style accommodation. Over three days in March visitors can also enjoy some fine acoustic popular music, courtesy of a variety of buskers, guitarists and other instrumentalists, both national and international. Attractions include concerts, the Poet's Breakfast, workshops, instrument-making classes, arts, crafts and a food fair.

Map: NSW 6 G8

don't miss

The Six Foot Track is a 46-km bushwalk through Blue Mountains National Park from The Explorer's Marked Tree at Katoomba to Jenolan Caves. The strenuous two- to three-day walk runs through the Megalong Valley.

Below: *As well as being home to the Week of Speed Festival, Gunnedah is the birthplace of poet Dorothea Mackellar. In 1908 she wrote the well-loved Australian poem 'My Country'.*

did you know?

The town of Shellharbour gets its name from the large number of historic Aboriginal middens situated in the area. These are listed by the Heritage Commission and are regarded as archaeologically significant.

John O'Brien Bush Festival

Narrandera

THIRD WEEKEND IN MARCH

In the Riverina region, the charming streets of Narrandera are lined with beautiful white cedar trees. It was here, during his 27-year stint as the local parish priest, that noted poet, John O'Brien, wrote his verse collection, *Around the Boree Log*, including such Australian bush classics as 'Said Hanrahan' and 'The Old Bush School'. O'Brien's verse and the Irish pioneer heritage he represents are both celebrated at this great festival through bush music, bush poetry and dance.

Map: NSW 7 B2

Kowmung Music Festival

Oberon

FROM THIRD SATURDAY IN MARCH

Oberon is an isolated highland township beyond the Blue Mountains, which was named after the King of the Fairies in Shakespeare's *A Midsummer Night's Dream*. Each year it hosts a nine-day international chamber music festival featuring traditional and progressive works. Interesting and exotic settings such as cattle sheds and limestone caves are selected in order to contribute to the atmosphere and to draw the audience's attention to the abundant natural beauty of the district. Acclaimed guests and international performers are included.

Map: NSW 6 F8

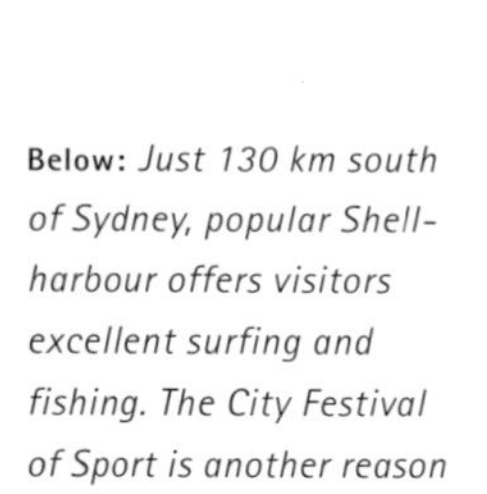

Below: *Just 130 km south of Sydney, popular Shellharbour offers visitors excellent surfing and fishing. The City Festival of Sport is another reason to visit this seaside town during March.*

National Fiddle Festival

Richmond

LATE MARCH

The National Fiddle Festival celebrates all four-stringed instruments, including violin, viola, cello and double bass, by exploring their usage across various musical genres. The National Fiddle Champion Award goes to winners in the categories of Classical, Bluegrass, Folk-Celtic, and Jazz, with the winner receiving cash, a trophy and a certificate. The Busking Competition winner also gets a cash reward, and any street act that uses the fiddle (big or small) is eligible. Concerts, workshops, eisteddfods and busking competitions also take place.

Map: NSW 6 H7

Shellharbour City Festival of Sport

Shellharbour

SECOND WEEKEND IN MARCH

The distinctive charm and character of Shellharbour township, on the Illawarra coast, has recently become the core of the larger concept of Shellharbour City. The second weekend of the month sees

Left: *The National Fiddle Festival includes many genres of music such as classical, jazz, bluegrass, Celtic, rock, fusion and pop, and celebrates not just the fiddle but all stringed instruments.*

plenty of opportunities to watch or participate in over 30 sports at the city's various sporting venues. Events include the International Karate Championships, a family fun day, a sporting expo, art and craft exhibitions, food stalls, entertainment, health and lifestyle displays, sporting demonstrations and sports for people with disabilities.

Map: NSW 6 H10

Tenterfield Show

Tenterfield

FIRST WEEKEND IN MARCH

Tenterfield is an historic and interesting inland town which claims to be the 'Birthplace of Federation', as it was here, in 1889, that Sir Henry Parkes made his famous Federation speech, which is credited with precipitating the movement that culminated in the formation of a national government in 1901. Tenterfield was also the birthplace of entertainer Peter Allen who wrote 'Tenterfield Saddler' about his grandfather. As it is located at the centre of a rich agricultural and pastoral economy, it is fitting that the town holds a big agricultural show each year, complete with fireworks and a demolition derby.

Map: NSW 4 K3

Left: *Tenterfield is well known for its saddlery thanks to singer Peter Allen. He brought the town to the attention of the world through his song 'Tenterfield Saddler'.*

Thirlmere Festival of Steam

Thirlmere

FIRST SUNDAY IN MARCH

Located 7 km south-west of Picton, Thirlmere is a tiny Southern Highlands settlement with the largest and oldest railway museum in the country. Steam engines relay passengers from Sydney to the event, where visitors can enjoy further steam-train rides along an otherwise disused rail line which was part of the original 1867 track that opened up the entire Southern Highlands. Attractions include chainsaw competitions, ferret races, steam train machinery and traction engines, line dancing, Australian music, market stalls and a model train exhibition.

Map: NSW 6 H9

Australian Capital Territory

Above: *The colour and flamboyance of participant's costumes, as well as entertainment and organised events, add to the fun of Canberra Day.*

Canberra Day

Canberra

THIRD MONDAY IN MARCH

This local holiday commemorates the founding of the Australian capital on 12 March, 1913. Canberra was created as a compromise when Sydneysiders and Melburnians could not agree on which city should become the national capital. The land was selected about halfway between the two state capitals in 1908, and the city was built according to the design of Walter Burley Griffin. Canberra Day is preceded by a 10-day community celebration, in which the Canberra Citizen of the Year is named.

Map: NSW 7 J4

Above: *Taste of Canberra and the Region is an annual exposition of the best food and wine in the area. Over 100 000 people usually fill Commonwealth Park for the fireworks display.*

Royal Canberra Show

The Royal Canberra Show concludes at the start of March (see the main entry in February).

Map: NSW 7 J4

Taste of Canberra and the Region

Canberra

SECOND SATURDAY IN MARCH

This is the major event on the calendar for the food and wine producers of the ACT and surrounding area. Commonwealth Park is the principal setting for lovers of gourmet provender to consume their fill to the accompaniment of live music, family activities, great cooking demonstrations, street theatre, grape stomping, a busking competition and cook-offs involving culinary celebrities. This event is run in conjunction with A Taste of the Arts Around Canberra, wherein local artists display their wares. In the evening there is a twilight concert and fireworks.

Map: NSW 7 J4

Victoria

MELBOURNE

The Australian Formula One Grand Prix concludes early in March while two of the month's major events, the Melbourne International Comedy Festival—one of the largest of its kind in the world—and the Melbourne Food and Wine Festival, get under way. The latter is considered Australia's premier food and wine celebration and incorporates more than 100 events, including the World's Longest Lunch on the banks of the Yarra. Melbourne has more people of Greek heritage than any city in the world, outside of Greece, and their culture and their contribution to Australia's arts, foods and culture are celebrated in the Antipodes Festival, which is considered the largest Greek festival in the entire world. Other events are the Brunswick Music Festival, which is regarded as Melbourne's biggest street party; the Melbourne Fashion Festival, which showcases the best of Australian fashion; the Melbourne Queer Film Festival; Altona's Bayside Festival; the Melbourne International Motor Show and the long-running Moomba Festival.

Map: Vic 6 D3

Right: *Flowers can bring a city to life with their vibrant colour. Thousands of people flock to Ballarat for the annual Begonia Festival that rightly adds to Ballarat's name as the Garden City.*

Apollo Bay Music Festival

Apollo Bay

THIRD WEEKEND IN MARCH

Outside the town's post office is an anchor that belonged to a steamer that sank in full view of the townsfolk in 1932, at the cost of 10 lives. It stands as testimony to a stretch of coastline which is very beautiful but treacherous. Fortunately, the beauty is all that matters to those who enjoy the delights of the annual music festival, which provides not only three days and two nights of great music but also dance, art and popular culture.

Map: Vic 5 L9

Ballarat Begonia Festival

Ballarat

EARLY MARCH

The state's largest inland city, Ballarat is a charming, elegant and historic former goldmining settlement which was the setting for the famous Eureka Rebellion

Left: *The street festival is a popular part of the Brunswick Music Festival. Performances are held at a number of venues in the Melbourne suburb of Brunswick, including the Town Hall, the Cornish Arms and the Lomond Hotel.*

of 1854. It is also known as the Garden City due to its many public and private floral displays. During the festival, the beautiful Botanical Gardens on Lake Wendouree host spectacular begonia displays, along with live music and informative talks, all in a festival atmosphere. The activities extend to many other attractions and entertainments in the city. This has been one of Victoria's most popular community festivals since 1953, attracting over 100 000 people annually.

Map: Vic 5 M4

Rip Curl Pro and Sun Smart Classic

Bells Beach and other nearby beaches

LATE MARCH TO EARLY APRIL

Bells Beach, a tiny bay sandwiched between two small headlands, is host to the longest-running surf contest in Australia. The consistency and excellence of the surf has seen Bells become a fixture on the world professional circuit. The men's contest is known as the Rip Curl Pro and the women's as the Sun Smart Classic. The contest unfolds over 11 days.

Map: Vic 5 P7

Castlemaine State Festival

Castlemaine

EARLY MARCH

Although the name of this historic town is associated with XXXX beer, it has a strong arts focus. The State Festival is a regional arts event using the town's heritage buildings and parks as settings for leading performers in a program of classical music, theatre, dance, jazz and folk music, comedy, workshops, visual art exhibitions and children's theatre. It is held biennially in odd-numbered years.

Map: Vic 3 C8

did you know?

In 1859 Nicholas and Edwin Fitzgerald, sons of an Irish brewer, established a brewery in Castlemaine in Victoria. In 1877 they bought a Brisbane distillery and it became the famous Castlemaine Brewery.

Below: *Bells Beach is one of Australia's most famous spots for serious surfers. This popular Australian sport has produced some great champions including the first World Champion, Bernard 'Midget' Farrelly.*

Above: *Established in 1879, Maffra is the service centre for the rich agricultural land that surrounds it. The town celebrates this with an annual Harvest Festival.*

Gippsland Harvest Festival
Maffra

SECOND SUNDAY IN MARCH

This large centre is in the middle of the productive West Gippsland district. Each year it hosts an annual daylong festival, which showcases the provender of that district. Attractions include fine gourmet foods, wines, arts and crafts, musical bands, artists and theatrical performances. It takes place in the splendid gardens of Powerscourt Country Homestead, which offers fine views from the courtyard and gardens across sweeping plains, the fertile Avon Valley and on to a mountainous backdrop.

Map: Vic 6 L4

Festival of the Southern Ocean
Mallacoota

THROUGHOUT MARCH AND APRIL

This attractive seaside holiday resort sprawls lazily along the East Gippsland coastline, amid the Croajingalong National Park. In the autumn it hosts an arts festival with a rather particular theme, celebrating the cultures and traditions of coastal communities that lie on the 38th parallel south. The popular and ambitious programme includes music, theatre, cabaret, circus acts, visual art, community events, workshops and a Youth Festival. There is a hands-on ethic, emphasising community involvement and audience participation.

Map: Vic 4 M8

High Country Harvest Festival
Mansfield

SECOND WEEKEND IN MARCH

Mansfield is a charming subalpine town of wide streets, old buildings and well-established trees. Because of its beautiful location near Lake Eildon and in the foothills of the Great Dividing Range, it is essentially a resort town and a winter base for those heading up to Mount Buller and Mount Stirling. The district's wine and gourmet food is the focus of the Harvest Festival, which starts on Saturday in High Street, moving to the Delatite Winery on Sunday. There is music on both days, petanque, art and the Great High Country Grape Stomping Championships.

Map: Vic 3 K8

Mildura–Wentworth Arts Festival
Mildura and Wentworth

THROUGHOUT MARCH

Mildura is something of an oasis in the desert. The formerly dry, brown land in the area was rendered lush and fertile by an ambitious irrigation scheme concocted by the Chaffey brothers–so much so that Mildura has become something of a riverside holiday resort. But when

don't miss

Mildura offers great opportunities to cruise the tranquil Murray River. A range of cruises are available, from a two-hour paddleboat cruise to a dinner cruise or even a five-day cruise on a houseboat.

Right: *Local produce stars at the Gippsland Harvest Festival. Harvest festivals and wine festivals, with their links to the land, have their origins in ancient times.*

most people think of Mildura they tend to think of fruit, not art. And yet the annual Arts Festival is steadily growing in stature, featuring 24 days of local and international performers, street theatre, world music, Australian authors, fine arts exhibitions, workshops, performances at the amphitheatre, jazz, food, wine, dance and carnival celebrations.
Map: Vic 1 F4

Tobacco, Hops and Timber Festival
Myrtleford

SECOND WEEKEND IN MARCH

This pleasant agricultural town on the Great Alpine Road is beautifully positioned in the northern foothills of the Mount Buffalo range. Tobacco and timber have long been central to the local economy, and the district has more recently become the largest hop-growing area in Australia. These three crucial economic mainstays of the district are celebrated in a three-day community festival which includes a film night, a ball, a street parade and market, a street party (with fun, food, wine and entertainment), a fun run, a family bike ride, beer brewing and fireworks. The Alpine Valley's Wine and Food Festival is also held on the Saturday at Myrtleford Recreation Reserve.
Map: Vic 3 M6

Above: *Folk music performers, My Friend the Chocolate Cake, play to crowds gathered at the Dandenong Ranges Folk Festival in Olinda.*

Dandenong Ranges Folk Festival
Olinda

THIRD WEEKEND IN MARCH

This small picturesque township, beautifully situated amid gardens, fern gullies, forests and outstanding views atop Mount Dandenong, offers one of the country's most scenic settings for a music festival. Presenting over 90 concerts in two days, this is a superb outing for the lover of acoustic, roots, blues, folk and world music. The venue is the National Rhododendron Gardens Hall.
Map: Vic 6 E3

Above: *Flowers of the tobacco plant,* Nicotiana tabacum. *Tobacco is a significant crop in the Myrtleford region.*

Above: *The quaint village of Port Fairy is one of the oldest ports in the state of Victoria, and has many delightful historic buildings. Many were built in the nineteenth century.*

Port Fairy Folk Festival
Port Fairy
SECOND WEEKEND IN MARCH

This delightful historic port on the south-west coast of Victoria offers many attractions but the most famous is the Folk Festival. First held in 1977, this four-day event is a premier festival of folk roots music and culture in Australia, winning Victorian and Australian tourism awards and being entered into the Australian Tourism Awards Hall of Fame. Major national and international guests share many stages with over 500 artists presenting a range of musical styles drawing on elements of Celtic, English, blues, country, bluegrass, jazz, rock, and ethnic music.

Map: Vic 5 F7

Red Gum Festival
Swan Hill
SECOND WEEKEND IN MARCH

In 1853 Francis Cadell made his famous steamer voyage along the Murray as far as Swan Hill, which became one of the first inland river ports. The town boasts a four-hectare, open-air heritage park that re-creates the nineteenth-century river port of old. This open-air historical museum is the venue for the three-day Red Gum Festival, which incorporates street theatre and a range of activities that would have been popular over 100 years ago, such as Clydesdale events, ploughing, log-snigging championships, horse-drawn vehicle rides and wood turning.

Map: Vic 2 L3

'Up the Creek' Discovery Festival
Swifts Creek, Hinnomunjie and Ensay
SECOND WEEKEND IN MARCH

This fun family weekend unfolds in the high country between Omeo and Bruthen. One event is the 4WD Discovery Rally—not a race but a prompt for participants, armed with a map and questionnaire booklet, to discover and enjoy the history and environs of the area. Other activities are a masquerade ball, mine tours, gold fossicking, market stalls, art exhibitions, the Ensay Cryptic Clue Bicycle Challenge, the Picnic Races at Swifts Creek and demonstrations of woodchopping, blade shearing and wool spinning.

Map: Vic 4 D6

Chinese Cultural Festival
All Saints Estate, Wahgunyah
FIRST SUNDAY IN MARCH

All Saints Estate was established in 1864 and is thus one of the state's oldest wineries. Indeed, the original owner was the first Australian to win an international gold medal for wine, in 1873. Chinese labour was essential to this early success, as evidenced by a large restored Chinese dormitory, built in 1869. This Asian influence is commemorated by this festival, which features lion dancers, tai chi, feng shui, Chinese food, kite flying, Chinese traders and all the colour of a Chinese festival.

Map: Vic 3 L4

Below: *All Saints Estate at Wahgunyah is one of Australia's oldest—in fact this winery won Australia's first international wine medal at the Vienna Exhibition in 1873.*

Frances Folk Weekend

Frances

FIRST WEEKEND IN MARCH

Frances is a small rural settlement one kilometre from South Australia's eastern border. Each year, from Friday to Sunday of the first weekend in March, it hosts a friendly, relaxed musical event featuring Victorian and South Australian folk singers, fine pub sessions and country dancing. A range of prizes is awarded, depending on age and experience, and there are competitions in musicianship, song, poetry and storytelling, with junior and senior sections.

Map: SA 4 P7

South Australian Wooden Boat Festival

Goolwa

THIRD WEEKEND IN MARCH

Goolwa is an unusual historic town that was once the main entry port on the Murray River. Now an upmarket holiday resort, it emphasises its past by restoring historic buildings and celebrating its nautical heritage in the Boat Festival. It features sailing and motor boat displays, steam launches, races for all types of craft, boat-building competitions, and nautical music.

Map: SA 4 K4

Kapunda Celtic Festival

Kapunda

FOURTH WEEKEND IN MARCH

Kapunda is a large, prosperous and historic copper mining town. Rich lodes of the metallic element were first discovered in 1842, with large-scale mining soon developing with the help of Cornish miners and Irish labourers. By no more than coincidence this Celtic theme was picked up in the 1970s with the establishment of what is now the longest-running Celtic festival in Australia.

Map: SA 4 K2

Quin's Blue Water Classic and Quin's Lincoln Week Regatta

Port Lincoln

EARLY MARCH

Sailing has always been part of Port Lincoln's way of life. Regattas involving fishing boats were recorded here back in the mid-1800s. This tradition culminated in the establishment, in 1950, of South Australia's major yachting event, which runs over the 150 nautical miles from Adelaide to Port Lincoln. The following week-long regatta in Port Lincoln includes presentation nights, dinners and a beach barbecue.

Map: SA 4 D2

Above: *The calm waters of the bay at Port Lincoln are a welcome shelter from the rough seas of the Southern Ocean. Port Lincoln is the finishing line for the Quin's Blue Water Classic.*

Riverland Greek Festival

Renmark

FIRST WEEKEND IN MARCH

Renmark is the oldest settlement on the Murray River in the heart of an orchard area partly fostered by Greek migrants. Their contribution is celebrated through music, dancing and traditional Greek food. It also involves Aboriginal and other cultures as part of its commitment to promoting a multicultural, reconciled and harmonious Australian society.

Map: SA 4 P1

Below: *The park at Renmark, on the banks of the Murray River. The oldest town in the Riverland region of South Australia, Renmark was the centre of Australia's first irrigation scheme which covered nearly 2830 ha.*

did you know?

During World War II up to 2500 military personnel were housed on Rottnest Island. Gun and military installations were built. Some, such as the Oliver Hill Battery, can still be seen on the island today.

Western Australia

PERTH

As autumn gets under way the West Australian capital hosts the Perth Sun Microsystems Australia Cup, which is the only match-racing yacht event in Australia to attain an official Grade One status. The challenging course along the picturesque Swan River attracts the world's finest competitors. The MS Moonwalk is a fund-raiser for multiple sclerosis sufferers, which engages participants in a 10-km moonlight walk around Perth, taking in some of the city's most popular sites. At the northern end of Perth, the vibrant Joondalup Festival offers many family activities.

Map: WA 6 C4

ASP World Professional Surfing Championship (Coca-Cola Masters)

Margaret River

FOURTH TUESDAY IN MARCH

A few kilometres from the town of Margaret River is the mouth of the river itself, and it is here that the World Championship surfers avail themselves of Western Australia's autumn action. The bluff above the bay is an excellent vantage point for taking in the beautiful scenery and observing the approach of the enormous breaks. This is considered an event for the stout-hearted—hence the $100 000 in prize money.

Map: WA 6 B8

Nannup Music Festival

Nannup

FIRST WEEKEND IN MARCH

Nannup is a quiet and rather attractive timber town of 500 people, situated amid rolling hills and tall stands of jarrah trees by the Blackwood River. The festival attracts some 4000 people each year, while maintaining a sense of community, place and intimacy. The organisers conscientiously provide venues and activities that allow families to participate in all aspects of the festival, and they make a point of encouraging new artists. The music is essentially contemporary folk and world music, with a good dollop of poetry, dance and street theatre occurring throughout the town.

Map: WA 6 C8

Below: *Rottnest Island is a favourite destination from Perth because of its beautiful beaches. It is also home to the Festa di Rottnest, which is a fun family event.*

Above: *The streets of the predominantly subterranean town of Coober Pedy—known as the Opal Capital of the World—are filled with colourful floats when the Opal Festival street parade takes place.*

Coober Pedy Opal Festival
Coober Pedy

THURSDAY TO EASTER SUNDAY

For those who know nothing of this fascinating and substantial outback town, which produces over 90 per cent of the world's opals, it comes as a surprise to find that most of the town's residents live underground, in order to escape the opressive heat. Nonetheless the town boasts a mixture of nationalities and offers sophisticated accommodation. There is a subterranean church and a diversity of recreational activities, including a grassless golf course that is the focus of a golf tournament during the Opal Festival. Other festival activities include dugout tours, street parades, craft stalls, stage acts, Aboriginal dancing, sideshows, marching bands, a sports day, a food festival, evening entertainment and a multicultural festival.

Map: SA 2 A8

Mediterraneo Festival
Port Lincoln

EASTER SATURDAY

Port Lincoln is on the same latitude in the south as the Mediterranean is in the north and, like Southern Europe, the region has a balmy moderate climate and produces an abundance of local seafood and wine. During the festival the Lincoln Cove Marina is organised so that visitors can move between specific sections that represent different Mediterranean countries, experiencing authentic traditional displays of national dress, music, dance, food, sport and fishing techniques. Festival highlights include the Long Lunch, the world's longest hand-to-hand Hellenic dance line, gondola excursions, a bocce competition, a Mediterranean cooking expo and the performance finale.

Map: SA 4 D2

Western Australia

Donnybrook Apple Festival
Donnybrook

EASTER SUNDAY

Located in the increasingly popular south-west of the state, Donnybrook is famous as the town in the centre of Western Australia's premier apple-growing area. It is particularly beautiful, and popular, when the apple blossoms are in bloom in October. However, Easter is the time of this annual community festival that showcases the area, its beauty and, centrally, its produce.

Map: WA 8 C7

Below: *While best known for its apples—most notably the Granny Smith—Donnybrook has an ideal climate for many fruit and vegetable crops.*

April

Above: *The old gambling game of two-up has long been an Anzac Day tradition—this is the only day on which it is allowed to be played in places other than casinos.*

The major nationwide holiday in April is Anzac Day. Troops from the Australian and New Zealand Army Corps who had fought at Gallipoli in World War I were known as Anzacs, though over time the term has come to apply to all Australian and New Zealand soldiers in the Great War. The heavy loss of life and the unquestionable bravery of the troops, in impossible circumstances—particularly at Gallipoli—led to the setting aside of 25 April as a public holiday for the purposes of remembering the dead, recognising their sacrifice and contemplating the cost of war.

Under heavy fire, the Anzac forces rushed across the beach at Gallipoli on 25 April, 1915, to take up positions on the steep ridges adjacent, experiencing substantial losses in the process. There they were pinned down by continuous fire and a stalemate ensued, although attempts to break the deadlock entailed tremendous loss of life, so much so that an armistice was arranged on 24 May to collect and bury the dead.

By the time the endeavour was abandoned and the peninsula evacuated in December the total Allied casualties, over the eight months, were 33 532 dead, 78 518 wounded and 7689 missing, of which 8587 of the dead and 19 367 of the wounded were Australian. Dysentery and paratyphoid made a major contribution to the death toll.

The nation's principal ceremony to mark this event occurs at the Australian War Memorial in Canberra with a dawn service, a guard of honour and a parade through the streets of the city with an emphasis on the remaining Anzacs, other war veterans or their surviving relatives. Similarly, dawn services and parades are a feature of many other Australian towns and cities. On a lighter note, the coin game known as two-up is traditionally played in pubs and clubs on Anzac Day.

Below: *Anzac Day around the country starts with moving dawn ceremonies. Street marches and dusk services also pay tribute to the courage and mateship of those who served their country.*

Left: *Today's Australian armed forces continue to uphold the Anzac tradition. Many Australians make the pilgrimage to Gallipoli in Turkey to honour the fallen on Anzac Day.*

Above: *The Mooloolaba Triathlon has steadily grown in stature since it first commenced in 1993 to become the second-largest Olympic Distance Triathlon in the country.*

Queensland

BRISBANE

The Australian Track and Field Championships are held at the ANZ Stadium, with both men and women competing in the open and under-20 age group divisions. Those keen on horse racing will be pleased to find that April also sees the start of the three-month Queensland Winter Racing Carnival, which attracts some of the nation's top thoroughbreds to compete for prize money and incentives of over $14 million. Many social and cultural events accompany the races. On another note, the *Sunday Mail* Escape Holiday and Travel Expo is held at the Brisbane Convention and Exhibition Centre each year in April.
Map: Qld 7 N7

Right: *Inland Ipswich is known as the 'Heritage City'. It has many fine examples of early architecture, including the Bremer Institute of TAFE which has been in use for over 100 years.*

Gladstone Harbour Festival

The Harbour Festival concludes early in April (see the main entry in March).
Map: Qld 5 L9

Ipswich Festival
Ipswich

SECOND WEDNESDAY TO THIRD SUNDAY IN APRIL

Once known as 'Limestone Hills', this attractive city near Brisbane has some of the most impressive domestic architecture in Queensland. Ipswich also made an important contribution to the early architecture of Brisbane by supplying lime for building construction. Coal was another early discovery, and today's coalmines still bear Welsh names, reflecting the origins of some of the early miners. The annual festival entails 10 days of fun and entertainment, including a street parade, fireworks and children's activities.
Map: Qld 7 M7

Mooloolaba Triathlon Festival
Mooloolaba

THIRD FRIDAY TO FOLLOWING MONDAY IN APRIL

Once a year this very popular seaside resort attracts 2500 competitors and over 15 000 spectators from all over Australia to a full weekend of sport and

fun. The main events combine distance swimming, cycling and running. However, there are also events for the general public, such as a 5-km Twilight Run for competitors of all abilities; the Mooloolaba Ocean Swim, catering for those aged seven and up; and the Superkidz Triathlon, held especially for children from 7 to 13 years. Other main attractions are the Queensland Beach Volleyball Championships, the sporting expo and the End of Season Awards Presentation Beach Party.
Map: Qld 7 N5

Toowoomba Royal Show
Toowoomba

SECOND WEDNESDAY TO FOLLOWING SATURDAY IN APRIL

Toowoomba has its origins as a hilltop stopover for teamsters and travellers that were heading west from Moreton Bay to the Darling Downs. It developed in the 1850s as a suburb of Drayton (the first Queensland town established west of the Great Dividing Range, and birthplace of Steele Rudd) and is known for its picturesque views, parks and gardens, clean air and bracing climate. The annual show is Queensland's oldest special event, attracting 50 000 people over four days. After the show, Toowoomba celebrates its horticultural base with Gardenfest, and its history with Heritage Day in Toowoomba.
Map: Qld 7 L7

New South Wales

SYDNEY

The Royal Easter Show and the AJC Autumn Racing Carnival at Royal Randwick Racecourse both conclude in April, while the Campbelltown City Show, known as the 'Mini Royal Easter Show' offers three days of entertainment at the Campbelltown Showground. The annual Anzac Day March starts at the Cenotaph in Martin Place and proceeds via George Street and Bathurst Street to the Anzac Memorial in Hyde Park South. On a very different note, Manly Beach is the venue of the ASP World Professional Surfing Championship, which is held on the final Friday of every April. On Buddha's Birthday (29 April) there are celebrations at the Chinese Garden Forecourt at Darling Harbour, and, on the last day of the month, the Golden Easter Egg—one of Australia's biggest coursing events—is held at Wentworth Park. It is open to the top 80 greyhounds in Australia and offers $100 000 in prize money.
Map: NSW 6 J8

Royal Bathurst Show
Bathurst

SECOND FRIDAY TO FOLLOWING SUNDAY IN APRIL

Australia's oldest inland city, Bathurst began as a depot for the team building the first road across the Blue Mountains. A government domain, established here in 1815, was used as the launching pad for explorations of the interior by John Oxley, Charles Sturt and Allan Cunningham. The site was opened to public settlement in the early 1830s, and it soon became the centre of a major pastoral area. This heritage, and the ongoing relevance of pastoral and agricultural pursuits in the area, is celebrated at the Bathurst Showground each year in the biggest regional agricultural show in New South Wales.
Map: NSW 6 E7

don't miss

Check out the night skies at Bathurst Observatory. Opened in 2000, it is a relatively recent addition to Bathurst's attractions. There are full viewing facilities and also a Visitors Centre housing displays and souvenirs.

Left: *One of the two bronze statues, this one of a soldier and the other, a sailor, placed at each end of the Cenotaph in Martin Place in Sydney. A dawn service is held at the Cenotaph on Anzac Day.*

Below: *Australia's earliest inland settlement, Bathurst was established in 1815. The major centre in the Central West during the gold rush, it has fine architecture, such as the Town Hall pictured here.*

don't miss

Bundanoon makes a great base for trips in the Southern Highlands. Interesting places to visit are the Glow Worm Glen, Morton National Park, picturesque Kangaroo Valley and the nearby Thai Buddhist monastery.

Bottom: *Surplus aircraft once stored at HMAS* Albatross *move to centre stage as displays at the Australian Naval Aviation Museum where the public can view the aircraft.*

Below: *Maitland boasts many heritage buildings—Saint Mary's Rectory, pictured here, was built in 1881.*

Bundanoon Is Brigadoon

Bundanoon

FIRST SATURDAY IN APRIL

This charming village in the Southern Highlands is noted for its delightful avenues of English trees and for the greenness, intimacy and elevation of the surrounding countryside. These landscape qualities probably suggested its suitability as a venue for this Highland Gathering, during which over 20 000 visitors come to witness the street parade; pipe band displays; Scottish country dancing; highland games such as haggis hurling, tug-o-war, the caber toss and the kilted dash; highland dress competitions; innumerable food, souvenir and information stalls; the lifting of the Bundanoon Stones of Manhood; and a traditional Celtic knees-up known as a ceilidh.

Map: NSW 7 M2

Marti's Canowindra Balloon Fiesta

Canowindra

THIRD FRIDAY TO FOLLOWING SUNDAY IN APRIL

This old-style country town describes itself as 'The Balloon Capital of Australia', as more flights are said to take place here annually than anywhere else. The association is due to the gentle winds and the availability of attractive open countryside, conveniently criss-crossed by roadways that make balloon recovery easy. First held in 1995, the award-winning Fiesta was the brainchild of Frank Hackett-Jones and was named in honour of his mother Marti, who was a local nurse. It has become a significant hot-air balloon event internationally, and features three days of fun and flying. The highlights include bush concerts, a country fair, a country-style party, bush poets, a night-time balloon glow and fireworks.

Map: NSW 3 G6

Hunter Valley Steamfest

Maitland

FOURTH WEEKEND IN APRIL

Maitland possesses one of the largest, most intact and most attractive nineteenth-century industrial complexes in the Hunter Valley. The Walka Waterworks Complex features fine architecture, ornate brickwork, a giant chimney and, when it opened in 1885, steam engines supplied by James Watt in England. It is open for exploration during Steamfest, which features public steam-train rides, a Newcastle–Maitland race between a steam locomotive and a Tiger Moth aircraft, a street fair, stalls, children's entertainment, historic coach tours, a performing arts and visual arts festival, vintage and veteran cars and motorbikes, steam traction engines and a woodchopping championship. April is also Heritage Month in Maitland, with several historic homes open to the public.

Map: NSW 6 K5

Australia's Museum of Flight Air Day

HMAS Albatross, *Nowra*

LAST SUNDAY IN APRIL

HMAS *Albatross* is a naval air base near Nowra. It is home to the Australian Naval Aviation Museum, which contains an impressive collection of historic military aircraft and memorabilia such as weapons, engines, models and uniforms. There is also a display on the history of

May

In most parts of Australia, other than in the far north of the country, the weather generally cools off during May, which is the final month of autumn. The first Monday in May is a public holiday in Queensland and the Northern Territory; in the former it is known as Labour Day and in the latter as May Day. Both states celebrate the successful struggle of trade unions for a shorter working week on this day.

Right around Australia, the second Sunday of the month is declared as Mother's Day. This day bears a resemblance to a seventeenth-century English tradition in which the fourth Sunday of Lent was known as 'Mothering Sunday', when in-house servants were encouraged to visit and honour their mothers, traditionally taking with them a cake. However, the modern event comes from the United States of America where Ana Jarvis began a letter-writing campaign to establish a national Mother's Day in 1907. President Woodrow Wilson made the official proclamation in 1914, choosing the second Sunday of May, and from there it made its way to other western nations. In Australia there is no public holiday associated with Mother's Day, however, many events occur on this day especially for mothers and their families. For example, there is a Mother's Day concert at Hawthorn, in Melbourne, and a Steam, Food, Wine and Jazz Racing Festival at Seymour in Victoria.

Above: *Flowers are a popular choice of gift to give on Mother's Day, with chrysanthemums traditionally being a favourite as they have a lovely meaning: 'you are a wonderful friend'.*

Left: *Spending the day on or beside Sydney Harbour—particularly at Watson's Bay where the world-famous seafood restaurant Doyles is located—is a splendid way to relax and enjoy an autumn day.*

Below: *Family picnics and barbecues are a great way to spend Mother's Day, especially in the north of the country where it is still quite warm in May.*

It's easy to get caught up in the spirit of the Paniyiri Festival in Brisbane, with the lively, infectious Greek music tempting visitors to join in the dancing.

Queensland

BRISBANE

May sees the continuation of the Queensland Winter Racing Carnival, and car-lovers can make their way to the Bowen Hills Showgrounds for the Hot Rod and Street Machine Spectacular. The Queensland Sacred Music Festival is held at the Brisbane Powerhouse Centre at New Farm, and the Paniyiri Festival—a celebration of Greek food, wine, dance, art, music and culture—is the largest one-day festival in Queensland. It unfolds at Musgrave Park in South Brisbane. Food and drink are also the focus of the Caxton Street Seafood and Wine Festival in Paddington. Finally, Kitefest is an award-winning family festival at Pelican Park at Clontarf.

Map: Qld 7 N7

Right: *The birdwing butterfly* (Ornithoptera priamus) *is the largest in Australia. The tropical rainforest around Cairns is the perfect place to catch a glimpse of these vibrant creatures.*

Cairns Tropical Garden Show

Cairns

SATURDAY TO MONDAY OF SECOND WEEKEND IN MAY

Famed for its tropical rainforest environs and its proximity to the Great Barrier Reef, this northern town appropriately runs an annual Tropical Garden exhibition at the Showgrounds. Attractions include 100 sq m of water gardens in the Rainforest Lagoon, awards for best photographic interpretation of a garden theme, the gardener of the year award, a floral art competition, talks by plant experts, a parade, food, a major flora and fauna exhibition, visual arts, street theatre, an orchestra, dance groups and the Tropical Garden Blitz, in which four specially designed tropical gardens have to be put together by four different construction teams in 30 minutes.

Map: Qld 2 B2

did you know?

Built in 1828, Brisbane's oldest building, Tower Mill Observatory in Wickham Terrace, was used as a grinding mill and later as a signal post. It has been restored and is one of the city's most popular tourist attractions.

Charters Towers Country Music Festival

Charters Towers

FIRST FRIDAY TO FOLLOWING SUNDAY IN MAY

Charters Towers is arguably the most beautiful inland city in Queensland. This is principally due to the decision of the nineteenth-century city fathers to plough goldmining profits into some superb public architecture. Each year the city conducts the largest amateur country music festival in Australia, with over 800 performances in the Amateur Competition. Other attractions are the special guest artists, a jamboree, a cabaret, a street procession, a bush poets' breakfast, a national 'Songs of the Outback' songwriting competition and the Grand Final concert on Sunday.

Map: Qld 5 B2

Goomeri Pumpkin Festival

Goomeri

LAST SUNDAY IN MAY

This is pumpkin country. Indeed, Murgon, the nearest major centre to Goomeri, even has a median strip named after Flo Bjelke-Petersen, the wife of the former Queensland premier, who turned the humble pumpkin into a *cause célèbre* through her famous pumpkin scones. A highlight of the festival is the Great Australian Pumpkin Roll, in which prizes are offered for the pumpkin that travels the greatest distance down Policeman's Hill. Other attractions include the award for the biggest pumpkin, a parade, children's activities, decorated pumpkins, a free open-air concert, markets, demonstrations, bush poetry, visits to historic homesteads and Cobb and Co rides.

Map: Qld 7 L4

Australian Italian Festival

Ingham

SECOND FRIDAY TO FOLLOWING SUNDAY IN MAY

This sugar town north of Townsville owes much to its Italian community, which began arriving in 1891. When the use of Kanakas in the cane fields was outlawed, the area experienced an influx of Italian labourers. The general culture and history of the region as well as the Italian contribution are celebrated with great Italian food and wine, arts, crafts, music, games, entertainment and cultural displays in the town's main street.

Map: Qld 2 C6

Julia Creek Dirt and Dust Triathlon

Julia Creek

SECOND MONDAY IN MAY

The oldest European settlement in north-western Queensland, Julia Creek has little in the way of conventional tourist attractions but, each year in May, it conducts the Dirt and Dust Triathlon. This event offers up to $15 000 in prize money, making it the richest triathlon in Australia. It is a highly challenging event involving an 800-m swim, a 25-km bicycle ride and a 2-km run in merciless outback temperatures.

Map: Qld 4 G3

Richmond Biennial Fossil Festival

Richmond

FIRST FRIDAY TO FIRST SUNDAY IN MAY

A service centre for the surrounding pastoral community, Richmond is most famous for the dinosaur skeletons that have been found in the area. This provides the concept for a biennial event, held in even-numbered years. It features fireworks, a parade, a rodeo, an iron-man competition, a four-wheeler derby, a billy-boiling competition and a moon-rock throwing contest.

Map: Qld 4 J3

Above: *The award-winning Australian Italian Festival at Ingham is a riot of colour. More than 20 000 people come to enjoy the traditional food, music and entertainment such as greasy pole climbing.*

Sanctuary Cove International Boat Show

Southport

LATE MAY TO EARLY JUNE

Attracting a field of over 350 exhibitors and 43 000 visitors from more than 20 countries, the exhibition has more than 180 boats on display. Product launches are a regular feature and sales valued at millions of dollars are arranged.

Map: Qld 7 N8

Below: *Marketed as the Asia-Pacific's premier marine event, the Sanctuary Cove International Boat Show takes place each year on Sanctuary Cove Marina, at Southport on the Gold Coast.*

New South Wales

SYDNEY

One of Sydney's premier events, the Biennale, gets under way in May during even-numbered years. This showcase for Australian artists unfolds in the city's leading galleries and museums. Darling Harbour's Exhibition Centre hosts the Mind Body Spirit Festival for fans of alternative therapies. The prestigious Sydney Writers' Festival unfolds at Walsh Bay, The Basement and the Seymour Centre, while Symphony in the Sand is held at Harbord and the Mudgee Food and Wine Fair at Balmoral Beach. Growing in popularity is the Sydney Sings series, in which a 450-strong choir gives voice to popular songs at the superb Town Hall. Fashion buffs can get their fill at Mercedes Australian Fashion Week, while thousands of athletes participate in the *Sydney Morning Herald* Half Marathon. Also not to be missed is the Australian Museum Open Day, when entry is free.

Map: NSW 6 J8

Above: *The fashion shows at Mercedes Australian Fashion Week give both big-name and up-and-coming Australian designers the opportunity to show the world their hot new outfits.*

Agfair
Broken Hill

FIRST FRIDAY AND SATURDAY IN MAY

Broken Hill is usually associated with mining but it is also the centre of the 16-million-hectare West Darling pastoral industry, which has 1.75 million wool-producing merino sheep protected by a 600-km dog-proof fence. It is this dryland agriculture of the region that is the focus of Agfair, a traditional agricultural trade fair and field day. Held biennially in even-numbered years at the Broken Hill racecourse, this well-attended event offers displays and demonstrations of horticultural and agricultural technologies and equipment. Also within the exhibition pavilion are rural merchandise, clothing and other items aimed specifically at rural women. Entertainment includes yard dog trials and novelty events for the whole family.

Map: NSW 1 B9

don't miss

While in the Glen Innes area, visit Gibraltar Range National Park. This scenic park provides a haven for many native animals, including rare species such as the parma wallaby, rufous rat kangaroo and long-nosed potoroo.

Casino Beef Week
Casino

THIRD FRIDAY TO LAST TUESDAY IN MAY

A pleasant and prosperous country town on the Richmond River, Casino's reputation as 'The Beef Capital' indicates its heavy reliance on the local cattle industry, which sends over 120 000 head of cattle through the Casino sale yards each year. This symbiosis of town and country is recognised in this 12-day regional community festival that celebrates the beef industry and promotes Casino and surrounding districts. It includes more than 80 distinct events such as displays of beef cattle breeds, a gala ball, a race day, a rodeo, a cabaret dinner, parades, a fashion show and a family day.

Map: NSW 4 M3

Australian Celtic Festival
Glen Innes

THURSDAY TO SUNDAY OF FIRST WEEK IN MAY

An interesting historic township located in the New England region, Glen Innes is known for its many attractive parks that are at their best in autumn. The area's Celtic heritage dates back to 1838 with the arrival of the first pastoralists, who were of Scottish descent. Irish settlers soon followed and Cornish miners came when tin was discovered. It was

Right: *Amazing rock sculptures can be seen at Broken Hill's Living Desert Sculpture Park. As well as being a famous artists' colony, Broken Hill holds an agricultural trade fair every two years.*

Bush Olympics, the Aboriginal and Local Art Show and the Diamond Hunt. Some of the events are held in, or pass through, Aboriginal land, which is off-limits to the public at other times due to its cultural heritage sites.
Map: WA 2 G5

Northern Territory

DARWIN

During odd-numbered years the biennial Arafura Games dominate the city for a week. This major multi-sport event for developing athletes in the Asia–Pacific region takes place across 25 venues and begins with a spectacular opening ceremony. The National Dragon Boat Race occurs on the last Sunday in May. Participants compete in traditional-style Chinese craft, and the event attracts local, interstate and overseas teams.
Map: NT 1 E4

Alice Springs Cup Carnival

This event ends early in May (see the main entry in April).
Map: NT 7 F5

Bangtail Muster
Alice Springs

MAY DAY

Cattle were once the main focus of the economy in and around Alice Springs, and the bangtail muster involved severing the ends of tails to keep track of the number of cattle mustered. Nowadays tourism is the main source of income and so this event neatly fuses past and present by drawing in contemporary visitors to witness an historical remnant. Activities include a parade down Todd Mall and a sports afternoon on Anzac Hill Oval.
Map: NT 7 F5

Pine Creek Gold Rush Festival
Pine Creek

FRIDAY TO SUNDAY OF FIRST WEEK IN MAY

Pine Creek is an historic town with links to both the Overland Telegraph Line and the railway line. The latter was built by 'coolie' labour from Singapore, Malaya and China. The Chinese later flocked to the local goldfields, which were established in 1871. Goldmining was the reason for the town's emergence, and mining remains its *raison d'être*. The heritage and culture of the Pine Creek area is celebrated during the Gold Rush Festival with trail rides, exhibitions, gold-panning championships and the Grand Bush Ball.
Map: NT 2 B7

Above: *Outdoor dining in Alice Springs can mean a plethora of choices—from the cosmopolitan cafés of Todd Mall to a old-fashioned bush barbecue.*

Left: *At the Pine Creek Gold Rush Festival there is an opportunity to hear the unmistakable sounds of the didgeridoo, as exponents of this traditional Aboriginal instrument showcase their talents.*

The town of Pine Creek has a long history of goldmining, and this industry is still the main employer in the area. Pictured here, a lake has been created by flooding an old open-cut goldmine.

June

The official start of winter in Australia occurs on 1 June. The second Monday of the month is set aside as a public holiday to celebrate the birthday of Queen Elizabeth II in all states except Western Australia, which commemorates the occasion with a public holiday at the end of September. Confusingly, however, the Queen was actually born on 21 April, 1926, to the future King George VI and Elizabeth, the Duchess of York. She was given the names Elizabeth Alexandra Mary after her mother (the late Queen Mother) and two earlier Queens. The separation of birthday and revelries began early in the twentieth century when Edward VII, born in November, celebrated the event in the more cheery English summer.

Australia's decision to honour the day reflects the British heritage of the majority. However, as Australia has incorporated more cultures, races and ethnicities, the resonance of the day has been diminished to the point where, for most, it is nothing more than a day of leisure divorced from its origins.

The earliest festivities associated with the Royal birthday occurred within five months of British settlement when, on 4 June, 1788, salutatory volleys were fired, bonfires burned into the evening and a band played while Governor Phillip dined with his officers amid toasts and hurrahs. Today, recipients of the Order of Australia, for outstanding services to the nation in a particular field, are announced twice a year: the first list on Australia Day and the second on the Queen's Birthday.

The statue of Queen Elizabeth II, at Parliament House, Canberra. The Queen opened the new Parliament House, which was built at a cost of over 800 million dollars, in 1988.

Below: *The Ah Toy family have run their family store, which was established in 1935, for three generations. Their story is typical of Australia's increasingly multicultural society.*

Left: *Skiing at Thredbo, near Mount Kosciuszko, one of the most popular skiing areas in New South Wales. Thredbo is renowned for its long runs of up to 5.5 km.*

Brisbane's city skyline and the Brisbane River at night. With a population approaching two million, Brisbane is a go-ahead, subtropical city offering many activities for visitors.

Queensland

BRISBANE

Queensland Day is 6 June—a celebration of the state's establishment as a separate colony in 1859. Family-style festivities are held throughout Brisbane (and the state) on the Saturday nearest to that date. The Brisbane Wine Festival occurs over three days in mid-June, offering jazz music, gourmet foods and wine tastings involving over 70 wine producers. On the arts and culture front, Out of the Box is a week-long arts festival at the Queensland Performing Arts Centre for children aged three to eight years, and the Southern Cross Music Festival features six days of concert bands, orchestras and choirs throughout Brisbane and the Sunshine Coast. Outdoor lovers can enjoy the Queensland Caravan, Camping and Touring Holiday Show at Bowen Hills. For anglers there is the Blue Water Classic—a game-fishing competition at Sandstone Point—and the Moreton Bay and Offshore Family Fishing Challenge at Redland Bay, which is open to all ages. The XXXX Sailing Gold Cup competition at Manly commences in June, and the Queensland Winter Racing Carnival continues throughout the month.

Map: Qld 7 N7

Right: *At the Brisbane Wine Festival people can enjoy sampling from 200 to 300 Australian and international wines. Each participant receives a sampling glass and tasting notes booklet.*

Coast to Coast Bike Ride

Atherton, Cairns and Other Towns of the Far North

FOURTH SUNDAY TO LAST SATURDAY IN JUNE

Open to participants of all ages, this unusual bicycle ride is a fund-raiser for children living in the remote rural areas of Far North Queensland. Participants need not be especially fit as the emphasis is on fun and raising money, not competition. They are entertained along the way with sporting activities, trivia nights, talent quests, bush dances and rodeos. Funds raised go to causes in the towns through which the event passes, and local communities are generous and supportive.

Map: Qld 3 N6

Cooktown Discovery Festival
Cooktown

FRIDAY TO TUESDAY OF SECOND WEEKEND IN JUNE

From 17 June to 4 August, 1770, Captain James Cook and his crew made camp on the shores of what is now called the Endeavour River after their barque struck the Great Barrier Reef off the coast. Cooktown was established here in the 1870s. Cook's landing is commemorated each year on the Queen's Birthday weekend. Events include a re-enactment of Cook's landing

Map: Qld 3 N2

Laura Aboriginal D
Cultural Festival
Laura

LATE JUNE

This tiny settlement
in the tropical north
is essentially an in

and it is the pastoral/agricultural environs that come to the fore during the annual show, which offers fun for all ages. Along with the cattle and horse events and the farm and garden displays, there are arts and crafts displays, kennel and cat club events, a sideshow alley, live entertainment and fireworks.

Map: Qld 5 J8

Sanctuary Cove International Boat Show at Southport

June sees the end of this well-attended expo (see the main entry in May).

Map: Qld 7 N8

Pine Creek Rainforest Festival
Townsville

FRIDAY TO MONDAY OF SECOND WEEKEND IN JUNE

Held at Mountain View Holiday Park, 40 km south of Townsville, this festival provides an opportunity for
ional folkies and other per-
formers of acoustic
music to demon-
strate their skills.

don't miss

Don't miss the James Cook Museum in Cooktown. Built in 1886 as St Mary's Convent, this impressive building was contructed at a time of optimism, when the town was the second largest in Queensland.

Left: *The Laura Aboriginal Dance and Cultural Festival draws participants from all over northern Queensland and celebrates traditional dance and culture .*

The Manly Food and Wine Festival features concert bands, jazz and world music, and camel rides, as well as quality foods and wines—and all at Manly's scenic beachside setting.

Right: *A participant in*

New South Wales

SYDNEY

Australia's oldest and most important international motion picture event, the Sydney Film Festival, takes place in June at the State Theatre, with some 200 films from nearly 40 countries. Other cul-

Harbour, on the New South Wales Mid-North Coast, it makes its way across the continent to Perth. As it is not a race, there are plenty of opportunities to take in the magic of the Outback. Entry is restricted to 2WD cars built before July 1971 and 4WD cars built before 1961.

Map: NSW 4 N7

Crescent Head Sky Show

Crescent Head

SECOND SUNDAY IN JUNE

This delightful village is one of the best-kept secrets on the northern New South Wales coast. It has beautiful beaches, nature reserves to the north and south and a headland with one of the most spectacular clifflines on the east coast. On the Queen's Birthday weekend the ... hosts a family fun day. ... reflected in a day of ... nd other activities, ... ompetitions, dem- ... ations, displays and games that continue during the day, and

and photography, competitions in song and short-story writing, poetry readings, a civic reception, a ball and a guided coach tour of Grenfell. Other highlights include a street parade, a carnival, competitions such as woodchopping, busking, guinea pig races and go-kart races.
Map: NSW 3 E7

Winter Magic Festival
Katoomba

FOURTH SATURDAY IN JUNE

Set in the heart of the magnificent Blue Mountains, Katoomba is a haven for artists, writers and those who are into alternative lifestyles and therapies. The community comes together in late June to celebrate the winter solstice, and thousands more from Sydney and the Mountains join in the fun. Live music in the form of the Great Busk-Off accompanies a very well-attended fancy dress morning parade, street entertainment, stalls and exhibitions of local artworks.
Map: NSW 6 G8

Australian Goanna-Pulling Championship
Wooli

SECOND SUNDAY IN JUNE

Wooli is a beach resort on the New South Wales Mid-North Coast, near the mouth of the Wooli River. It is surrounded by the Yuraygir National Park and retains pleasant clear waters and picturesque environs due to the lack of industry and low-key development. On the Queen's Birthday weekend it hosts a rather unusual event: a tug-of-war between pairs of goannas.
Map: NSW 4 N6

Australian Capital Territory

National Capital DanceSport Championships
Canberra

FOURTH WEEKEND IN JUNE

Each June about 800 of Australia's leading professional and amateur dancers compete in the DanceSport Championships. DanceSport is a team-based event that derives from ballroom dancing and incorporates elements of Latin American and New Vogue. It involves couples, or combinations of couples, presenting a strenuous dance performance with an artistic interpretation of the music. There is $30 000 in prize money, travel grants and awards on offer. The venue is the Australian Institute of Sport Arena in Leverrier Street, Bruce.
Map: NSW 7 J4

Bottom: *Located about 450 km north of Sydney, the magnificent headland at Crescent Head offers spectacular views.*

Below: *Katoomba is a popular place for winter weekend escapes for Sydneysiders. It is the gateway to many scenic attractions including the Three Sisters and the Katoomba Falls.*

don't miss

Cruise the Murray on a paddle-steamer at Echuca—the paddle-steamer capital of the country. Don't miss out on seeing PS *Pevensey*, which was used in the TV mini-series, 'All the Rivers Run'.

Victoria

MELBOURNE

Just as the St Kilda Film Festival comes to an end, the Pop Film Festival gets under way at the Frankston Cultural Centre. Further south, the wineries of the Mornington Peninsula run a special Wine Weekend on the Queen's Birthday weekend. The making, tasting, drinking and general savouring of the beverage is explored through face-to-face meetings with the winemakers of the region. On a more literary note, Bloomsday in Melbourne is a literary festival held each year on 16 June to celebrate James Joyce's great novel *Ulysses*. Each year the Bloomsday Players take elements of Joyce's work out into the community through enactments and readings. June also sees Victoria's ballroom dancers take to the floor in the Dancing Championships, which select Victorian representative couples for the Australasian Championships. Melbourne's gay and lesbian community takes the chill out of winter with June's excellent Winterdaze dance party.

Map: Vic 6 D3

Rotary Steam, Horse and Vintage Rally

Echuca

SECOND WEEKEND IN JUNE

An historic river port that has been carefully renovated, Echuca's appearance has proven sufficiently convincing to attract television productions looking for historic backdrops. This June rally features displays of vintage tractors, Clydesdales, classic cars and motorcycles, steam engines and oil engines. The rally also focuses on nineteenth-century bush skills with displays of bush cooking, wood sawing, threshing, chaff cutting, smithing and whip making.

Map: Vic 3 E4

National Celtic Folk Festival

Geelong

FIRST SUNDAY TO SECOND MONDAY IN JUNE

Located on Port Phillip, Victoria's second-largest settlement hosts the nation's principal Celtic music festival, with around 100 national and international performers. Attractions include traditional and contemporary music, traditional dancing, workshops, literary lunches, theatrical productions, a

Vines at Tuck's Ridge at Red Hill on Mornington Peninsula. During the Winter Wine Weekend, fine foods, and wines of course, are available at many of the wineries in the area.

Celtic dinner and a family ceilidh. Markets feature Celtic arts, crafts and food. The festival opens with an ecumenical church service and a lantern procession.
Map: Vic 6 A4

Rhapsody in June
Port Fairy

SATURDAY TO MONDAY OF SECOND WEEKEND IN JUNE

The first European settlers in this area were sealers and whalers whose bluestone cottages still stand in the town. Fishing is still one of the main sources of income, although tourism is now equally important. A family music festival held on the Queen's Birthday weekend gives regional performers a chance to strut their stuff. The styles include Celtic music, blues, acoustic folk, jazz, country, rock and rockabilly. There are workshops for children, a variety concert and an Irish dance performance.
Map: Vic 5 F7

Winery Walkabout
Rutherglen

FRIDAY TO MONDAY OF SECOND WEEKEND IN JUNE

Although Rutherglen is a former goldmining town, it is best known as the centre of one of Victoria's most important wine-producing districts. There are some 13 wineries in the district, and on the Queen's Birthday weekend they offer food, fun and entertainment that spills over into the town's main street. One of the highlights is Campbell's Winter Dinner at Tuileries, a food and wine event hosted by Campbell's Winery.
Map: Vic 3 L4

Tasmania

Suncoast Jazz Festival
St Helens

LAST WEEKEND IN JUNE

The largest town and holiday destination on Tasmania's east coast, St Helens is a remarkably warm town, given its location, due to a microclimate produced by the surrounding hills and warm ocean currents. Consequently, it is warmer than Melbourne in winter and is in a great position to host a wintertime jazz festival that takes place at the St Helens Hotel. Run by the Suncoast Jazz Club, the festival gives Tasmanian artists an opportunity to perform alongside musicians from the mainland.
Map: Tas 2 H6

Fishing boats at Geelong. Victoria's second largest city, Geelong is situated on Corio Bay, on the western side of Port Phillip Bay. It has always been an important port.

Left: *Rutherglen is one of Australia's oldest wine-producing regions. Many believe that the muscats and tokays represent the pinnacle of wine-making achievement in the area.*

South Australia

ADELAIDE

The Adelaide Cabaret Festival is a two-week event featuring the best of international, national and local artists performing both traditional and more experimental cabaret at the Festival Centre. On a different note, the Body, Mind and Psychic Expo features hundreds of stalls showcasing all things relating to alternative therapies. There are also lectures, demonstrations and workshops, tarot-card and tea-leaf readers, live musical entertainment and healthy foods.
Map: SA 4 J3

Tarot reading. The Mind, Body and Psychic Expo held at the Royal Adelaide Showground is thought by many to be the best alternative therapies weekend event in Australia.

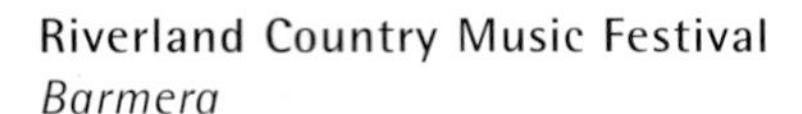

Riverland Country Music Festival
Barmera

FIRST SATURDAY TO SECOND MONDAY IN JUNE

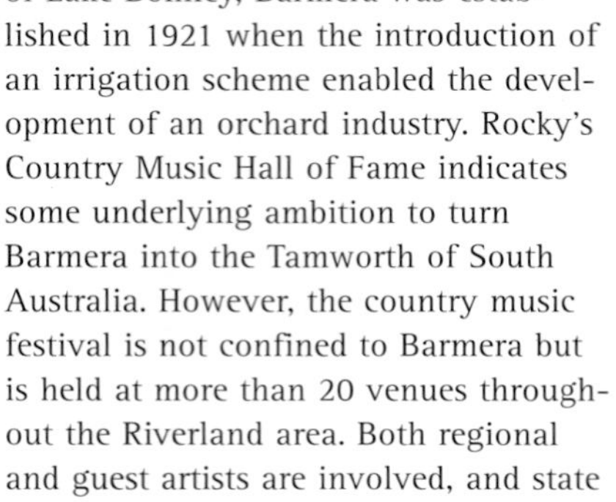

An attractive service town on the shores of Lake Bonney, Barmera was established in 1921 when the introduction of an irrigation scheme enabled the development of an orchard industry. Rocky's Country Music Hall of Fame indicates some underlying ambition to turn Barmera into the Tamworth of South Australia. However, the country music festival is not confined to Barmera but is held at more than 20 venues throughout the Riverland area. Both regional and guest artists are involved, and state awards are presented to the most promising new talent.

Map: SA 4 N1

Below: *Tasting room at Tatachilla Winery, McLaren Vale, a popular spot during the Sea and Vines Festival.*

The McLaren Vale Sea and Vines Festival
McLaren Vale Wine Region

SUNDAY AND MONDAY OF QUEEN'S BIRTHDAY WEEKEND IN JUNE

The McLaren Vale region has been producing wine since the 1850s. McLaren Vale itself is a charming township and, on the Queen's Birthday weekend, a superb seafood, wine and music festival takes place in many of the wineries. Gourmet food is supplied by top local and Adelaide restaurateurs.

Map: SA 4 J4

Western Australia

Albany Car Classic
Albany

FIRST SUNDAY IN JUNE

An attractive town on the south coast and the oldest European settlement in the state, Albany offers magnificent views across the harbour, a dramatic coastline and historic buildings. In June the streets buzz and roar as competitors test their skill in this time trial attended by about 10 000 spectators.

Map: WA 6 F10

Menzies to Kalgoorlie Cycle Classic
Menzies to Kalgoorlie

SECOND SUNDAY IN JUNE

Dating back to 1928, the Menzies to Kalgoorlie is now the richest handicap race in Western Australia and is one element of the Australian Road Race Cycling Championship. It is not for the faint-hearted, as it encompasses a strenuous 132 km in outback conditions.

Map: WA 7 B2

Bottom: *About 215 km east of Adelaide, Barmera is situated on the shores of Lake Bonney in the heart of the Murray Riverland. Lake Bonney has many sandy beaches and is popular for swimming and waterskiing.*

Northern Territory

DARWIN

Darwin experiences little cold weather, so outdoor events can be enjoyed year round. Local provender is up for grabs at the Myrniong International Food and Wine Festival while the Northern Territory Orchid Spectacular showcases the beauty of the Territory's orchids. The Northern Territory Expo is the largest annual international business and trade exhibition in Australia. It provides an opportunity for the businesses of the Territory to showcase their wares and expertise. More general participation is invited at the 11.75 km City To Surf Fun Run. Prize money is offered to the first male and female over the line.

Map: NT 1 E4

The Northern Territory Country Music Talent Quest
Adelaide River

SECOND WEEKEND IN JUNE

Adelaide River is a small township on the Stuart Highway, 114 km south of Darwin. It was first settled by telegraph workers who came to the area to build the Overland Telegraph Line and further profited from the Pine Creek Gold Rush and the arrival, in 1888, of the railway. Each June, Adelaide River attracts the Territory's best country music artists who perform and compete for prizes and prestige.

Map: NT 1 E6

Darwin, the capital of the Northern Territory and the country's only tropical capital, is situated on the eastern shore of Port Darwin. More than 50 ethnic groups are represented in the city.

Finke Desert Race
Alice Springs to Apatula and Return

SATURDAY TO MONDAY OF SECOND WEEKEND IN JUNE

This is considered the longest and most gruelling desert race in the Southern Hemisphere, encompassing 450 km of challenging outback terrain. The race offers a range of age categories, encouraging broad participation and an array of automobiles and motorcycles. It also offers the best prize money in the Southern Hemisphere for such an event, although a very sociable atmosphere is maintained. Many are happy enough to reach the finish line—an achievement in itself—rather than aspiring to win.

Map: NT 7 F5

Barunga Cultural and Sports Festival
Barunga

SECOND SATURDAY TO FOLLOWING TUESDAY IN JUNE

Situated 80 km south of Katherine, off the Arnhem Highway, Barunga is the venue for this family festival in which Aboriginal communities from all over the Top End compete in sports such as basketball, softball and football. Bands play at night and the event is also accompanied by traditional dancing with didgeridoo playing, a firestick competition, spear throwing and an exhibition of arts and crafts created by indigenous people from throughout the region. Camping facilities are provided, and food and drink are available.

Map: NT 2 D9

Merrepen Arts Festival
Daly River

SECOND SUNDAY IN JUNE

This is a single-day Aboriginal art and craft festival intended to showcase and sell the art and craft of the Ngauiyu Nambiyu and other regional communities. Items include paintings, screen prints, lino prints, batiks, silk weaving and other cultural artefacts. There is also entertainment such as music, dancing, bush tucker, hands-on tie dying, sports, an art auction, and the Darwin Symphony Orchestra gives an evening concert. The event is held in the Ngauiyu community on the banks of the Daly River, about 224 km south of Darwin.

Map: NT 1 E7

Miwulngini *(Nelumbo nucifera)* Lotus Lily, *by Marita Sambono Diyini, is representative of artwork displayed at Merrepen Arts Festival.*

La Renaissance
Café Patisserie
La Renaissance Café Patisserie
French Patisserie with Courtyard Café
Courtyard Café
NORMA COFFEE
NORMA COFFEE

July

As the chilly hand of Jack Frost reaches out into the gardens of the nation, so does the tax man thrust his hands into the pockets of all Australians as one financial year ends and another begins. Heedless of such worldly cares, many of Australia's school children enjoy a two-week mid-year break from their studies.

Although Australia has no national public holidays or nation-wide events in July, expatriates from the USA and France celebrate Independence Day (4 July) and Bastille Day (14 July) respectively. By and large these national days meet with what tend to be small, private celebrations, rather than major public events. Because the French language is pervasively taught in Australian schools, recognition of Bastille Day is small-scale but wide-spread, oft accompanied by the consumption of French provender in classrooms.

During winter, some regions celebrate 'Christmas in July', or Yulefest. European migrants and their descendants have long felt the anomaly of celebrating Christmas during the height of summer with foods and symbols that are more appropriate to the cold winter weather of Europe. Thus places that experience cooler European-like conditions and environs during July recreate the Northern experience with traditional Christmas foods in a celebratory atmosphere of party hats and streamers, log fires, snowmen, Santa Claus and snowball fights. These activities tend to be largely confined to inns, guesthouses, resorts, grand hotels and health farms in areas such as the Blue Mountains and Southern Highlands of New South Wales.

Top: *Leura is known as the 'Jewel in the Mountains' Crown'. It is worth a visit for its markets, fine shops and galleries, and during winter it occasionally has snow.*

Left: *Delectable French cakes and pastries can be enjoyed by expatriates, French culturalists and students of French as a way to mark Bastille Day.*

Above: *Students Australia-wide take a mid-year break from their studies in July. Families use this time for day trips and holidays.*

don't miss

When in Cairns take the Scenic Rail—over ravines and past waterfalls—to Kuranda's pretty station. Or you can take the world's longest gondola cableway above the rainforest, with views of the Coral Sea and mountains.

Queensland

BRISBANE

Held on the third weekend of July, the Queensland Masterclass at the Brisbane Hilton offers food seminars, cooking demonstrations and wine tastings. On the second Saturday, it is time to stop consuming and start dancing at East Brisbane's Colonial and Heritage Ball, where patrons dance traditional waltzes, quadrilles, polkas, jigs and reels to traditional accompaniment. Dance lessons are held in the month prior to the ball. Both the XXXX Sailing Gold Cup (see the main entry in June) and the Queensland Winter Racing Carnival (see the main entry in April) conclude in July.

Map: Qld 7 N7

Above: *Daintree National Park, near Cairns, covers much of Australia's true tropical rainforests. River cruises offer close-ups of the riverine fauna, which includes the fearsome saltwater crocodile.*

Boulia Camel Races
Boulia

FRIDAY TO SUNDAY OF THIRD WEEKEND IN JULY

Camels were introduced into Australia in the nineteenth century to facilitate desert travel. Boulia, a final outpost before the desert, has become part of Australian mythology through its association with the mysterious Min Min lights and the running of the Boulia Camel Races. The highlight of the event is a 2-km race drawing international competitors to the $30 000 purse. Other attractions include tandem skydiving, a ball, sideshows, fireworks, belly dancers, a concert and a camel-catching competition.

Map: Qld 4 D7

Cairns Annual Show
Cairns

THIRD WEDNESDAY TO THIRD FRIDAY IN JULY

Cairns is well known as a jumping-off point for the area's tropical rainforest and the Great Barrier Reef. Prior to the 1980s, the economy was heavily dependent upon sugarcane, beef and timber. It is from this era that the Cairns Show derives, celebrating local agriculture, industry and commerce. There are plenty of family activities, such as a Fun Park, ethnically diverse cultural presentations, a Heritage Park re-creating aspects of the past, rural sports, extreme sports displays, fireworks and the Queensland Pole Climbing Titles.

Map: Qld 2 B2

Camooweal Drovers' Festival
Camooweal

FRIDAY TO SUNDAY OF SECOND WEEKEND IN JULY

Located 13 km from the Northern Territory border, this small outback town shows its bush credentials during the Drovers' Festival, which celebrates all things outback. Activities include a street parade, country music, a bush dance, bush poetry, a bronco-branding competition, a truck-pull, the Last Great Mail Race, goat races and other novelty events. An art and photography competition is launched with a wine and cheese evening.

Map: Qld 4 A2

Great Matilda Camel Races and Festival
Charleville

TUESDAY TO THURSDAY OF FIRST WEEK IN JULY

An attractive town on the banks of the Warrego River, Charleville is a typical outback settlement that developed around a permanent watering hole

Right: *Charleville's Wills Street. At the end of the nineteenth century, this town had ten pubs servicing the 500 bullock teams that passed through each season.*

located on the old stock routes. It was also from here, in 1922, that the first regular Qantas airline service departed. Early in July the town kicks up the sawdust with three days of camel races, entertainment, novelty races, Fred Brophy's Boxing Tent, a gala ball and art exhibitions with the total prize money for the weekend surpassing the $20 000 mark.

Map: Qld 7 A5

Gold Coast Marathon

Gold Coast

FIRST SUNDAY IN JULY

Over 8000 athletes, including top international competitors, compete in one of Australia's best-attended marathon events. Established in the late 1970s, it includes a marathon (42.2 km), a half-marathon and a 10-km walk/run, with different age and gender categories throughout. There is also a 3-km junior event. Level ground and fine beaches characterise the course. The fastest male and female each win $10 000.

Map: Qld 7 N8

The Diamond Shears

Longreach

FRIDAY AND SATURDAY OF THIRD WEEKEND IN JULY

Perhaps the most prestigious shearing competition in Australia, this event cements the iconic Australian outback image of the shearer, drawing participants from around the nation. Held at the Civic and Cultural Centre, there are team and 'state of origin' competitions and a Shearers' Ball. Prize money is $20 000 plus a half-carat diamond to the champion.

Map: Qld 4 L8

Parkroyal Down Under International Games

Surfers Paradise

THROUGHOUT JULY

American college athletes compete with Australians in sports such as ice hockey, gridiron, basketball, golf, volleyball, handball, running and soccer. Independence Day (4 July) is celebrated with American cheerleaders, marching bands, American cars and fireworks.

Map: Qld 7 N8

Above: *The Gold Coast Marathon starts and finishes at the Southport Broadwater car park. Participants range in age from 18 to 84.*

Left: *Although the wool industry has been important in Longreach for a long time, shearing is not always done as carefully as it is under the eye of a Diamond Shears judge.*

did you know?

Goulburn is filled with National Trust-classified buildings, many of which are open to the public. St Saviour's Cathedral was designed by the famed colonial architect Edmund Blacket in Gothic Revival style.

Australian Festival of Chamber Music
Townsville

FIRST WEDNESDAY TO SECOND SUNDAY IN JULY

Located on Cleveland Bay, Townsville was established in the 1860s when the need for a port in north Queensland arose. A charming, elegant and sophisticated regional capital, Townsville's stylish architecture, tropical ambience (and weather) and lack of obtrusive tourism make a dignified setting for this major classical music festival, which was first established in 1991. Musicians are drawn from around the nation and overseas for 12 days of concerts and masterclasses. It is held at the Townsville Civic Theatre.

Map: Qld 2 D8

Right: *Many independent gourmet coffee roasters provide opportunities for tastings at the Aroma Coffee Festival in The Rocks in Sydney.*

New South Wales

SYDNEY

In July crowds of up to 75 000 are drawn to Darling Harbour for the Sydney International Boat Show, in which all manner of aquatic craft are on display, the Winter Music Program and the Our House Expo. Nearby, at the historic area known as The Rocks, Australia's best coffee makers ply their wares during the Aroma Coffee Festival. Accompanying entertainment is provided free for children, including street theatre and face painting. The Sydney to Gold Coast Yacht Classic takes place on the final Sunday of the month, and Magick Happens is a two-day forum at Sydney Town Hall for things related to witchcraft and paganism. In early July the Amphitheatre, in the Church Street Mall, Parramatta, hosts a display of foods, crafts, dances, art and music associated with NAIDOC Week, which celebrates the heritage of the Aboriginal and Torres Strait Islander peoples. South of Parramatta is the New South Wales Doll Collectors' Fair at Liverpool.

Map: NSW 6 J8

Below: *Sydney's International Boat Show has over 300 exhibitors and 120 vessels. It has fishing clinics, sailing expos and rigging competitions.*

A Classical Winter
Goulburn

EVERY WEEKEND IN JULY

Throughout the month of July, the inland town of Goulburn is treated to four weekends of classical music and theatrical performances at a variety of indoor venues. Most of the program consists of small ensembles or soloists performing at restaurants, cafés and also in club lounges. The highlight of the festival is a major orchestral or operatic concert.

Map: NSW 7 K2

Bridgestone International
Kempsey

THIRD OR FOURTH WEEKEND IN JULY

Located about halfway between Sydney and the Queensland border, right on the Pacific Highway, this large and vital rural centre near the coast is the home of the Akubra hat. Private farmland in the area has been used since 1981 to conduct one of five rounds of the Australian Off-Road Racing Championship. Competitors from around the world and approximately 10 000 spectators are drawn to this rugged 495-km event, which typically sees five out of six competitors withdraw before the end of the race.

Map: NSW 4 M9

Lightning Ridge Opal and Gem Festival

Lightning Ridge

FOURTH THURSDAY TO FOURTH SUNDAY IN JULY

The legendary town of Lightning Ridge came into existence for one reason only: opals. It is one of the few places in the world where black opals can be found and has turned up such prizes as the famous 822-gram 'Big Ben'. Once a very rough-and-ready outback settlement surrounded by mullock heaps, its core population of 1200 is now supplemented by around 80 000 tourists a year, and so it has acquired a veneer of civilisation in the form of quality motels and restaurants. The town's annual festival is a fun event, which features the Gala Opal Festival Awards Ball, plus an international jewellery design competition, street parades, markets, crafts and goat races, and you can also try out some tasty bush tucker.

Map: NSW 2 E3

Above: *A working opal mine at Lightning Ridge. Visit a mine and compare the mining methods and equipment (jackhammers and industrial vacuum cleaners) of today with those in the museum.*

International Brick and Rolling Pin Throwing Contest

Stroud

THIRD SATURDAY IN JULY

Since 1961, tiny historic Stroud has hosted a strange contest with three other Strouds—in England, Canada and the USA—in which bricks (for men) and rolling pins (for women) are hurled, discus-style. A street procession is followed by the opening ceremony and a variety of entertainments that change annually.

Map: NSW 6 L4

Above: *The Quambi School House Museum in Stroud, built in the 1830s, was an operating school until the 1890s and then a private home until 1976. It was bought, then restored and reopened as a local museum in 1988.*

don't miss

A great way to see the ACT is to watch the sun come up over the Brindabella Ranges from a hot air balloon, looking down over Canberra. Remember to dress warmly—it is likely to be quite cold.

Australian Capital Territory

The ANU Chess Festival

Canberra

THIRD SATURDAY TO THE FOURTH SUNDAY IN JULY

Considered to be the nation's most important chess festival, it certainly draws prestigious competitors. Hosted by the Australian National University, events include the National Computer Chess Championship, the ANU Primary Schools Championship, the ANU High Schools/Colleges Championship, the ACT Go Championship, the University Co-op Bookshop Simultaneous Match and the ANU Open.

Map: NSW 7 J4

Above: *Beautiful hand-made quilts feature at Melbourne's Needlework Craft and Quilt Fair. Here enthusiasts get a chance to meet, discover new products and learn more about a variety of crafts.*

The Australian National Bridge Championships

Canberra

SECOND TO FOURTH FRIDAY IN JULY

The primary event in the Australian bridge calendar, conducted under the auspices of the Australian Bridge Federation, it attracts competitors around Australia and includes the Australian international team trial. Competition is not restricted to the professional expert as the program is varied and incorporates a range of standards and competition categories, including women, teams, pairs, seniors and open events.

Map: NSW 7 J4

Victoria

MELBOURNE

Held over three weeks, the Melbourne International Film Festival is one of the city's principal art events. It screens about 350 features, documentaries and shorts, including the latest in Australian and international cinema, with English language and Asian cinema particularly well represented. Special events, such as retrospectives, focus on particular film-makers or regions. There is also an animation section, an international short film competition, a multimedia category and some fine speakers. Flemington Racecourse holds its Grand National Steeplechase Day on the first Saturday in July, while North Carlton's San Remo Ballroom is the venue for the Grand Prix Ballroom dancing competition on the second Saturday in July. The Needlework Craft and Quilt Fair is held over four days at the Melbourne Exhibition Centre on Southbank, and the Winter Show at the Maribyrnong Community Centre is a display of exotic orchids held on the first weekend of the month.

Map: Vic 6 D3

Australian Sheep and Wool Show

Bendigo

FRIDAY TO MONDAY AROUND THIRD WEEKEND IN JULY

Said to be the largest sheep and wool show in the world, it features over 2000 livestock entries. Major awards are issued relating to the National Fleece Competition, the National Merino Pairs, the Supreme Australian Long Wool Exhibit, the Supreme Australian Prime Lamb Breeds Exhibit and the Supreme British Breeds Group. Other features include a woolcraft competition with related displays, fashion parades, shearing and wool-handling competitions, sheepdog trials and over 100 stallholder sites. Held for 117 years in Melbourne, in 2000 the venue shifted to Bendigo.

Map: Vic 3 C7

Right: *The old adage 'Australia rides on the sheep's back' is true at the Australian Sheep and Wool Show in Bendigo. This event concludes with a ram sale.*

Winter Blues Festival
Echuca

LAST SUNDAY IN JULY

This former inland river port on the Murray River is enlivened each July by street theatre and buskers performing blues-based music along High Street, with its many specialty shops, and also in the historic port area. Both visitors and locals can vote for their favourites in the busking competition, with prize money and instruments up for grabs.

Map: Vic 3 E4

Red Cliffs Folk Festival
Red Cliffs

FRIDAY TO SUNDAY OF FIRST WEEKEND IN JULY

Created from irrigation schemes, this country town is surrounded by orchards, and vineyards. The annual folk festival features local and guest artists, busking and performing traditional and contemporary 'folk' music. There is also a bush dance, a poets' breakfast, street markets, workshops and competitions in poetry and storytelling. Events are held at many venues, including Lindeman's Winery and the local steam railway.

Map: Vic 1 F4

South Australia

Marree Camel Cup
Marree

FIRST WEEKEND IN JULY

A fascinating and famous old settlement right on the edge of Central Australia, Marree is truly a desert township, receiving only about 155 mm of rain each year. Established as a base for maintenance workers on the Overland Telegraph Line, it became an outpost for northward-bound expeditions and also a base for the Afghan camel drivers working camel trains that relayed wool and supplies around the outback. Marree became a major railhead between 1940 and 1980 and is now a jumping-off point for excursions along the Birdsville and Oodnadatta tracks. The Cup, with its races and gymkhana, is a highlight of the town's social calendar.

Map: SA 2 H9

Above: *Red Cliffs lies in the heart of Victoria's Sunraysia and boasts a true Mediterranean climate. A visit to this area will find endless rows of vineyards and large crops of citrus fruits and olives growing in the red sandy soil.*

Above: *Apart from watching the Camel Cup, you can explore a mosque, or visit an Aboriginal Heritage Museum in the Arabunna Aboriginal Community Centre in the township of Marree.*

Willunga Almond Blossom Festival
Willunga

LAST SATURDAY OF JULY TO EARLY AUGUST

This historic settlement was established just three years after the European settlement of South Australia. Largely unchanged since its glory days as a slate-quarrying area in the 1850s and 1860s, it retains many interesting old buildings and a distinctive European feel. Today the principal focus of the local economy is almonds, and the annual festival celebrates the nut and other forms of local produce with a week of family-orientated activities. They include fireworks, a street procession, a pageant, musical entertainment, arts and crafts, a market, a fair day, bus tours of historic sites and a gala ball.

Map: SA 4 J4

Below: *The Australian boab tree* (Adansonia gibbosa) *is restricted mainly to Western Australia. The Boab Prison Tree is said to have a girth of 14 m.*

Western Australia

Boab Festival
Derby

FIRST SATURDAY TO SECOND MONDAY IN JULY

The nature of the past is inscribed in the landscape. In this case, Derby's Boab (or Baobab) Tree, located 7 km south of town on the Derby Highway, is a reminder of the days when its internal cavity was used by police travelling back to Derby as an overnight lock-up for Aboriginal prisoners. The town now holds the 10-day Boab Festival during the July school holidays. Events include the mardi gras, a street parade with floats, a rodeo, races, mud football, a bush poets' breakfast, and the crowning of the Boab Quest Winner as well as the Charity Winner.

Map: WA 1 D8

Right: *The Camel Cup at Blatherskite Park, on the outskirts of Alice Springs. Races are held on a 400-m sand track. Camels start the race seated and jockeys get them to their feet at the starter's gun.*

Mowanjum Festival
Derby

WEDNESDAY TO THURSDAY OF SECOND WEEK IN JULY

Each year the Mowanjum Aboriginal community places its art and culture on display for two consecutive evenings. Artworks, such as paintings and shell carvings, as well as contemporary music are the focus of the first night, while traditional culture is celebrated on the second evening with traditional art displays and corroboree dancers coming from throughout the West Kimberley region to perform at this festival.

Map: WA 1 D8

Northern Territory

DARWIN

The Darwin Cup Carnival is the principal racing event in the Northern Territory, offering entertainment, fashion parades, an easy-going atmosphere and the feature race, the lucrative Darwin Cup. The Darwin Royal Show is the month's primary family event, incorporating an agricultural show; events; sideshows; competitions; and other entertainments; displays of arts, crafts and industry; and a giant fireworks display on the closing night. The Darwin International Guitar Festival, held at the Northern Territory University, explores the range of the guitar across many musical genres in a variety of settings, with international artists and a range of classes, workshops and concerts.

Map: NT 1 E4

Lions Camel Cup Carnival

Alice Springs

SECOND SATURDAY IN JULY

Noel Fullerton, who runs Camel Outback Safaris, was central to the inception, in 1971, of this huge fund-raiser, a major event on the Alice Springs social calendar. It is a fun day, with refreshments, novelty events such as rickshaw races, fireworks, the Miss Camel Cup, helicopter rides, preliminary races and Pocamelo (polo on camels), all culminating in the running of the Camel Cup.

Map: NT 7 F5

Katherine and District Show

Katherine

TUESDAY TO SUNDAY OF THIRD WEEK IN JULY

The third-largest town in the Northern Territory, Katherine is located far enough away from the ocean to avoid the usual coastal humidity and yet its northerly situation is beyond the grasp of the desert. Located to the south-west of the popular and spectacular Katherine Gorge, the town has hosted an annual rural show since 1966. The show is the most significant event for the Katherine region, attracting interstate and Territorian visitors from far and wide. The show is a showcase for the region's, and the Territory's, produce, skills, industries, and arts and crafts, and includes sideshows, equestrian events, a major rodeo and also campdrafting.

Map: NT 2 C9

NT Self-Government Day

Statewide

1 JULY

This date is of considerable importance to Territorians, who were given the right of self-government on this day in 1978. Paul Everingham became the first Chief Minister. The Territory had been governed under South Australia until 1911, when it passed to the Federal Government. The granting of full self-government is celebrated throughout the Territory with a range of events, including bonfires, government-sponsored sausage sizzles and fireworks displays.

Above: *Near Katherine lies Katherine Gorge within the Nitmiluk National Park. Thirteen sandstone gorges are separated by rock bars and rapids.*

Below: *The Darwin Cup Carnival—the biggest party of the year—runs for the entire month of July. There is the Darwin Cup, Grand Darwin NT Derby (2000 m) and the Darwin Guineas (1600 m).*

August

August in Australia is the last month of winter, although the country's size means that there is a considerable climatic variation across the continent. In the Northern Territory, for example, the weather is still of sufficient warmth to warrant festive outdoor celebrations such as the Mataranka Bushman's Carnival and the Harts Range Annual Races. On the other hand, in the north-east of Victoria, the slopes of Mount Beauty draw thousands of skiers to the Kangaroo Hoppet ski festival, while in Tasmania the cold bites into the events calendar with a discouraging severity.

Above: *Picnic Day in the Northern Territory is a public holiday, and with a day off work, there is the chance to catch-up over an informal lunch, as these two friends are doing in Darwin.*

Australia does not have any national public holidays occurring in August. However, in the Northern Territory only, the first Monday of the month is a public holiday known as Picnic Day. The same day in New South Wales and the Australian Capital Territory is a Bank Holiday, which means a day off work for many employees in the financial industry.

On the other hand, International Friendship Day, on 1 August, is not a holiday as such, but a time when we are encouraged to acknowledge the contribution that good friends have made in our lives, through some act of appreciation. Similarly, International Left-Handers Day, on 13 August, is a time when southpaws everywhere are encouraged to rejoice in their left-handedness. It is also meant to raise public awareness of the advantages and disadvantages of being left-handed in a right-handed world. On this day famous left-handers such as Michelangelo, Charlie Chaplin, Judy Garland, Charlemagne, Mark Twain, Alexander the Great, Queen Elizabeth II, Allan Border and Nicole Kidman are celebrated.

Left: *Around 10 per cent of Australians are left-handed, and there are twice as many males as females. In August, they celebrate their sinistral nature on International Left-Handers Day.*

Left: *There is still plenty of snow during August in Victoria's Alpine National Park, for the many skiers who converge on the slopes to celebrate their winter sport.*

Above: *Brisbane's Royal Queensland Show is a fun and educational family outing. It offers many city children their first hands-on experience of farm animals.*

Queensland

BRISBANE

Queensland's biggest annual event is the 'Ekka', otherwise known as the Royal Queensland Show. Held over 10 days at the RNA Showgrounds, Bowen Hills, this is the state's largest and most prestigious presentation of its agricultural and related industries, and its most famous family event. Riverfestival is a citywide celebration both of Brisbane and the river that encouraged the first European explorers to view the area as a potential settlement site. The city's history is also an important part of the Festival in Ruins, in which the public can view performances of drama, song, mime and comedy amid the evocative and historic prison ruins on St Helena Island. On a cultural note, the International Gala is a dance-fest that allows Australian audiences to see Queensland Ballet Company perform with international artists, in a variety of short contemporary works. Finally, the public can combine fitness and community spirit in the *Sunday Mail* Suncorp Metway Bridge to Bay Fun Run, which is open to all comers.

Map: Qld 7 N7

did you know?

The Royal Queensland Show has been held every year since 1876, except 1919, due to a Spanish influenza epidemic, and 1942, when the showgrounds were a staging post for troops moving north.

Gemfest

Anakie

TUESDAY TO FRIDAY OF FIRST WEEK IN AUGUST

Electricity only arrived at Anakie in 1977. Perhaps this could be seen as a sign of the area's remoteness. Located 300 km west of Rockhampton, for the lover of gems, it is a good town to visit in early August when the local sapphire industry celebrates Gemfest. There are fun events, such as music performances and street theatre. The major expo of gems draws traders, merchants, miners and enthusiastic amateurs from around the country.

Map: Qld 5 E9

Caboolture Air Spectacular

Caboolture

LAST SUNDAY IN AUGUST

Located just 45 km north of Brisbane, Caboolture is now considered a commuter area, although it still services the surrounding district where dairying, fruit-growing, mixed farming and pastoral industries predominate. The town boasts a superb Historical Village and a warplane museum at the local airfield, which is the venue for what is touted as Australia's largest biennial air show. Every odd-numbered year in August crowds of over 40 000 are drawn to the aerial acrobatics and the vintage planes.

Map: Qld 7 N6

World Lizard Racing Championships

Eulo

LAST WEEKEND IN AUGUST

At Eulo's famous Paroo Racetrack a sign memorialises 'Destructo', a champion racing cockroach killed after beating the champion racing lizard. This provides some insight into the character of this charming one-pub outback town. The Championships commence with a lizard auction and feature a five-race program at the end of a three-day festival of entertainment, rural competitions, dances, a street fair, a market, a grand parade and novelty events.

Map: Qld 6 N8

Mount Isa Rodeo Festival

Mount Isa

FRIDAY TO SUNDAY OF SECOND WEEKEND IN AUGUST

The biggest and richest rodeo in the Southern Hemisphere, it has grown to a festival drawing 20 000 spectators to one of Australia's most remote cities. Celebrations include a Mardi Gras, live country music, the Rodeo Queen Quest, a cowboys' and cowgirls' reunion, sideshows as well as a country music event. The rodeo offers $200 000 in prize money and attracts competitors from all around the world.

Map: Qld 4 C3

don't miss

While in Mount Isa, visit the Riversleigh Fossil Museum. The World Heritage-listed Riversleigh is described by Sir David Attenborough as one of the three most significant fossil records in the world.

Left: *In August's second week, get yourself and your family to Mount Isa in time for the Friday night Mardi Gras, before settling in to a more traditional weekend of rodeo events such as the rope and tie, seen here.*

Toyota National Country Music Muster

Gympie

LATE AUGUST

At the centre of a major agricultural district, Gympie hosts one of Australia's biggest country music events at local Amamoor Creek State Forest Park. The agenda incorporates blues, bluegrass and rock as well as some of the nation's best-known country music performers. A talent quest is a regular part of the 'Muster', with categories for traditional and contemporary country music, folk, Australian bush music and country rock.

Map: Qld 7 M4

The Noosa Half Marathon

Noosa Heads

LAST SUNDAY IN AUGUST OR FIRST SUNDAY IN SEPTEMBER

This upmarket, chic, seaside resort town on the Sunshine Coast holds one of only 10 Gold Class events in Australia. Incorporating the Australian Half Marathon Championships, it includes the major 21.1-km event, as well as 10- and 5-km runs. The flat course traverses Noosa Sound and Gympie Terrace, beginning and ending at Noosa Heads Lions Park.

Map: Qld 7 N5

Below: *On Queensland's Sunshine Coast, Noosa's name is said to derive from an Aboriginal word for 'shade' or 'shadow'. Enter the Noosa Half Marathon, and do some 'shadowing' of your own!*

Australian Heritage Festival

Jondaryan

LATE AUGUST TO EARLY SEPTEMBER

The Jondaryan Woolshed, once the largest shearing shed in Queensland, holds a nine-day festival that re-creates the rural heritage of the area through displays of pioneering practices, technologies, vehicles, machinery, music, arts and crafts with demonstrations of traditional skills by 300 volunteers in period dress. Events include the shearing of 4000 sheep and the Grand Parade.

Map: Qld 7 K7

World and Australian Cooee Contest
Yeppoon

EARLY AUGUST

A cooee is a loud, clear, prolonged call in which the second syllable rises rapidly in pitch. It is used in the bush as a signal or to attract attention. Cooee Beach is one of the attractive strands that surround the holiday town of Yeppoon. Each year, it hosts a competition for the best and the longest cooee and the finest team cooee. A distinctly Australian event, it includes contests such as husband-calling, bottle-top flicking, gum-leaf blowing, thong-throwing, billy-boiling, the Up Hill Bullpat Shovelling Challenge, kookaburra laughing and cow-horn blowing. Entertainment continues into the night.

Map: Qld 5 K8

New South Wales

SYDNEY

The City to Surf Fun Run is a 14-km event extending from Park Street in the city along the edge of the harbour to Bondi Beach. Attracting around 30 000 participants, it is held on the second Sunday of August. Culture vultures will enjoy the Manly Arts Festival, which unfolds around the beach in Manly. The works of local artists are showcased in the Manly Art Gallery, with other activities occurring in associated venues. The Adventure Show, held at Olympic Park, is a three-day expo of adventure-related activities, products, services and ideas, while the 'Our House' Home Improvement Expo showcases over 1000 different products, together with seminars, advice and live make-overs involving decorator and renovation techniques. August is also time for the Australian Jewellery Fair at Darling Harbour, the Sydney Teapot Show at Glebe, the Camden Antique Fair, the Goulburn to Camden Cycle Classic, the National Winter Sleepout Rock Concert at Mosman and Australian Design Week at Ultimo.

Map: NSW 6 J8

Below: *The 'Jazz Capital' of the Bellinger Valley hosts the Bellingen Jazz Festival. Bellingen began in the mid-1800s as a cedar-getting and ship-building community.*

Bottom: *Macquarie Street runs through the heart of Dubbo, a wheat and wool producing area. Every year locals join visitors in celebrating the Dubbo Jazz Festival.*

Bellingen Jazz Festival
Bellingen

FRIDAY TO SUNDAY OF THIRD WEEKEND IN AUGUST

This attractive inland town on the Bellinger River is a rather substantial rural service centre that has gained a more cosmopolitan air in recent years due to the numbers of people fleeing from the cities for greener pastures. The scenic qualities of the area and the town's heritage environs make a pleasant backdrop for the annual jazz festival, which unfolds in churches, hotels, a country club, the Old Butter Factory, on the streets and by the river. There are also community markets.

Map: NSW 4 M7

Dubbo Jazz Festival
Dubbo

FRIDAY TO SUNDAY OF SECOND WEEKEND IN AUGUST

Dubbo conducts one of New South Wales' major regional jazz festivals with performances taking place at various venues, including two of its outstanding tourist attractions—Old Dubbo Gaol and Western Plains Zoo. Some 20 bands are involved, with participants coming from around the country. One of the highlights is the piano competition.

Map: NSW 3 G2

Northern Rivers Herb Festival
Lismore

MID-AUGUST

The Lismore district has elements of a university town, rural industry and alternative lifestyles. This confluence is expressed in the town's week-long celebration of medicinal and culinary herbs. It explores regional cuisine, horticultural approaches, education about herbs and an information exchange between all players through debates, seminars and other forums. It also showcases local culture through a gourmet food market, restaurant participation in the HerBBQ, a Lantern Parade, concerts, a Youth Skate event, the Spaghetti Circus and the Hot 'n' Spicy Ball.

Map: NSW 4 N3

Australian Capital Territory

Australian Science Festival
Canberra

THIRD SATURDAY TO FOURTH SUNDAY IN AUGUST

With about 180 different events, this is one of the world's biggest and most innovative science festivals. Its aim is to promote a wider understanding and appreciation of science, technology and also the latest in research. It is also great fun. There are plenty of colourful, publicly staged activities in the city centre and most are free. These include fun and interactive science-themed displays, amusing but searching debates, behind-the-scenes tours of scientific institutions and industries, films, workshops, forums, theatrical presentations and other creative events.

Map: NSW 7 J4

Victoria

MELBOURNE

Founded in 1986, *The Age* Melbourne Writers Festival is one of the city's, and the nation's, most prestigious cultural events, attracting an impressive line-up of national and international literary minds for a 10-day celebration featuring an opening address at the Town Hall, separate youth and adult programmes, readings, interactive classes, conferences, workshops, talks, book sales and signings and *The Age* Book of the Year Award. Most of the festival programme takes place at the CUB Malthouse on Southbank. The Melbourne International Orchid Spectacular held at Melbourne Garden World in Keysborough is Australia's biggest orchid show. It features thousands of flowering orchids plus demonstrations and talks by experts. Meanwhile, Midwinta offers both cultural and fun events for the gay and lesbian community, including a dance party, a drag performance by an international figure, film screenings, performing arts and readings of homosexual literature.

Map: Vic 6 D3

Above left: *The ActewAGL Amazing World of Science is the centrepiece of the Australian Science Festival held in Canberra.*

Top: *Take a side trip after Canberra's science fest to nearby Mount Stromlow Observatory, which has a 188-cm telescope and offers guided tours.*

Left: *There are estimated to be up to 30 000 species of orchid in the world. At the Melbourne International Orchid Spectacular, you can see many examples such as* Cymbidium *Rosa Rita 'Stu's Surprise'.*

Above: *After the Hamilton Sheep-vention, wander through this historic town. The charming Uniting Church Manse was built in 1913, and is beautifully preserved.*

Top: *Tasmania's Derwent River scenery is only a blur for drivers of the Australian Rally Championships. After the rally experience the countryside at a slower pace.*

Ararat One-Act Play Festival
Ararat

FIRST WEEKEND IN AUGUST

Ararat's drama fest takes place over a weekend. Performances usually occur from Friday evening to Sunday. It is an opportunity for the public to view new plays, up-and-coming playwrights, actors and directors and for others to network and to test their skills before both the public and critics.

Map: Vic 5 H2

Hamilton Sheep-vention
Hamilton

FIRST MONDAY AND TUESDAY IN AUGUST

Located on a volcanic basalt plain in western Victoria, Hamilton calls itself the 'Wool Capital of the World'. It holds the Sheep-vention, a regionally significant field day promoting sheep, wool and other rural industries. Events include a sheep show, ram sales, cattle-dog trials, cooking demonstrations, a ewe-weaner competition, fashion and an inventions competition.

Map: Vic 5 E4

Kangaroo Hoppet
Mount Beauty

LAST SATURDAY IN AUGUST

The Bogong High Plains, in Victoria's Alpine National Park, hosts Australia's most significant cross-country ski festival, culminating in the 42-km Kangaroo Hoppet—the only event in the Southern Hemisphere to be included in the 14-race Worldloppet series of marathon ski races. It is also the final race of the Australian Cross-Country Skiing Continental Cup. There are shorter 21- and 7-km events. Kangaroo Hoppet is accompanied by plenty of social, sporting and festive activities at Falls Creek Alpine Village in the run-up to the final event. Attendance is typically around the 50 000 mark.

Map: Vic 4 B4

Tasmania

HOBART

The Tasmanian round of the Australian Rally Championships is known as Saxon Safari Tasmania. It is also regarded as the coldest leg, as it takes place right in the middle of winter. This classic event involves both inter-state and local drivers in high-speed races through the heart of the Tasmanian bush. The route for the rally changes each year but it begins in Hobart Mall and ends at the Entertainment Centre, exploring countryside such as the Derwent, Florentine, Styx and Plenty Valleys.

Map: Tas 3 K6

South Australia

ADELAIDE

The Royal Adelaide Show is the state's premier entertainment event. It features displays of South Australia's finest animals and produce, trade expos, a consumer goods fair, rides, carnival games, sideshows, sample bags, arts and crafts and motor vehicle displays, as well as sporting events, stunt acts, fireworks and arena events at the Wayville Showgrounds.

Map: SA 4 J3

Festival of the King
Victor Harbor

FRIDAY TO SUNDAY OF THIRD WEEKEND IN AUGUST

On the Fleurieu Peninsula, Victor Harbor was once the main port of the South Australian coast. It is now a holiday destination with attractions such as the horse-drawn tram ride along the old causeway out to Granite Island, where you can watch the fairy penguins at dusk. Recently it has taken up a festival in honour of all things Elvis, involving musical events and impersonation contests spread across 13 venues.

Map: SA 4 J4

Western Australia

Balingup Medieval Carnivale
Balingup

FOURTH SATURDAY IN AUGUST

August is tulip month, and their blooms in Balingup beckon visitors to a medieval theme day. This fancy dress affair commences with a costume parade around the Village Green. Entertainment and children's activities start at midday. These include jousting, a medieval jester, puppetry, dragons, drummers and other medieval-style musical entertainment, morris dancing, storytelling and a circus skills workshop for children. It is also possible to enjoy a steam-train ride on the Hotham Valley Tourist Railway.

Map: WA 6 C7

Carnarvon Mainstreet Party
Carnarvon

FRIDAY TO MONDAY OF FIRST WEEKEND IN AUGUST

Carnarvon once served as a port for local sheep stations, which transported wool via 12-foot-high (3.6 m) drays pulled by double teams of camels. The space required for them to turn around dictated the width of Carnarvon's main street. Here the annual street party takes place, which incorporates a children's festival, sideshows, consuming local produce and seafood, iron-man and iron-woman competitions, a rodeo and a two-day ride along the old stock route.

Map: WA 4 B9

Above: *A proud prize-winning cow, and an even prouder owner, at the Royal Adelaide Show, which has been held, in one form or another, since 1840.*

Left: *Victor Harbor has a 1.6 km section of reconstructed track, which is the only remaining seven-day per week horse-drawn public tramway in the world.*

did you know?

Australia has eight species of fruit-bats or flying foxes (they feed only on flowers and fruit). Four are among the world's largest and may weigh up to 1 kg, with wingspans of more than a metre.

Karratha Fenaclng Festival

Karratha

FIRST WEEKEND IN AUGUST

Lovers of the comedian John Clarke, and his alias Fred Dagg, will be familiar with the term Fenaclng but they may be surprised to find that the mining town of Karratha actually has a Fenaclng Festival. Indeed, mining is the key to the concept, as Fenaclng is an acronym of the chemical symbols for iron (Fe) and salt (NaCl), plus the abbreviation for liquefied natural gas (LNG). These are the objects of local industrial attention and the namesake for this fundraising event, which involves equestrian and canine events and displays of community crafts, cooking and knitting.

Map: WA 4 H1

Right: *About an hour from Perth, Northam is the commercial hub for the Avon Valley's farmlands, and hosts the thrilling Avon Descent.*

The Avon River Festival and The Avon Descent

Northam

FIRST WEEKEND IN AUGUST

Established in the early 1830s, Northam is one of the oldest European settlements in the Central Wheatbelt area. The beautiful Avon River winds its way through the town, passing parks, walkways and a population of white swans. The river is the focus of the festival, which is an evening of fun and entertainment prior to the Avon Descent—the nation's longest and most important whitewater race. The race attracts over 600 competitors from around the world to the extremely challenging 135-km course, which conveys them from Northam to Perth.

Map: WA 6 D3

The York Country Festival

York

FIRST TO SECOND SATURDAY IN AUGUST

One of Australia's better preserved and restored nineteenth-century towns, York is full of beautiful old buildings and has become a major tourist attraction with plenty of shops and entertainment designed for the visitor. The York Country Festival is a major regional event with a rodeo, a living expo, a fashion show of country clothing, rural youth and seniors' programmes, a country fair, a bush dance and Heritage Ball, an equestrian and field day, sports, rural competitions and other entertainment.

Map: WA 6 D4

Below: *In York, the experience of the well-preserved architecture is only heightened when combined with the music, bush dance and Heritage Ball of the York Country Festival.*

Northern Territory

DARWIN

The Darwin Cup Carnival (see the main entry in July) reaches its conclusion in early August with the running of the Darwin Cup race. The principal Top End event in August is the Festival of Darwin, which is a tribute to the city's multicultural population with a grand parade and a varied programme of family entertainment, arts and cultural events drawn from Aboriginal, European, Asian and Pacific traditions. The accompanying Fringe Festival explores less mainstream aspects of theatre, film, comedy, music and dance. The Darwin Beer Can Regatta is a popular charity event that involves various fun activities on the waterfront, notably the attempt by competitors to build and

race a boat made out of drink cans. Children are at the centre of the Beat Goes Wild, which involves over 1000 school students in open-air performances of dance, drama and music, while indigenous art is the focus of the prestigious National Aboriginal and Torres Strait Islander Art Awards.
Map: NT 1 E4

Harts Range Annual Races
Harts Range

SATURDAY TO MONDAY OF FIRST WEEKEND IN AUGUST

This traditional bush meet is one of only two bush races still held in the Territory. The Harts Range Racecourse is located 200 km north-east of Alice Springs. The fun kicks off on the Saturday with horse racing, followed by a formal ball in the evening. Sunday is a family sports day with a gymkhana, the Lizard Race, bull riding and a tug of war. That evening there is a family bush dance and talent quest for all the family. Monday is Picnic Day (a public holiday in the Northern Territory) and this is set aside for the clean-up. There is no official accommodation but plenty of camping space with toilet and shower facilities.
Map: NT 7 H3

Flying Fox Festival
Katherine

LATE AUGUST

During late winter the trees along the Katherine River abound with large bats that can be clearly seen (and heard) in the evenings. This seems as good a reason as any to have a local festival, and there is plenty of fun and much entertainment in the form of a family fun day, along with the Dragon Boat Challenge, the Grand Street Parade, the Mayoral Debutante Ball and community awards for entries in the youth and adult art and craft competitions.
Map: NT 2 C9

Mataranka Bushman's Carnival
Mataranka

FRIDAY TO SUNDAY OF SECOND WEEKEND IN AUGUST

This outback town is located over 1000 km north of Alice Springs and over 400 km south of Darwin. In fairness it is little more than a couple of roadhouses and a pub, but it does have a superb thermal pool in a 4-ha park to the east of town and strong associations with Jeannie Gunn's popular novel *We of the Never-Never.* In August the town hosts a genuine old-style bush carnival, featuring a campdraft, gymkhana, rodeo and live music on the Saturday night.
Map: NT 3 E2

Left: *Flying foxes are very sociable creatures, and congregate in large colonies. Come to the Flying Fox Festival in beautiful Katherine, and experience how sociable humans can be when having a great time!*

Below: *After a rousing day at the Mataranka Bushman's Carnival, have a dip in the crystalline waters of the nearby 34°C thermal pool.*

September

Above: *Spring flowers are used to beautify civic areas in many communities, adding freshness and colour to the streetscape. A little care and attention prolongs the effect.*

The first of September marks the official start of spring in Australia. On cue, many communities around the country welcome orchids, daffodils, camellias and a host of annuals as they burst into blossom, with a range of floral festivals.

The first Sunday in September is reserved as Father's Day, although it is not a public holiday. The Father's Day tradition dates back to 1909, when the idea was suggested by Sonora Smart Dodd of Washington State in the USA, who was inspired by the Mother's Day movement then in progress in the United States. She wanted to express her admiration for the love, selflessness and courage shown by her father, a Civil War veteran who raised his six children on a remote rural farm after his wife died in childbirth. At Mrs Dodd's prompting, the town of Spokane in Washington was the first to observe the day but the idea soon spread. By 1924 it had built up so much momentum that even President Calvin Coolidge supported the idea of a national day. However, the official declaration was not made until 1966 when President Johnson set aside the third Sunday in June. In Australia, Father's Day was officially recognised in 1972.

At the other end of the month, Western Australia celebrates the Queen's Birthday holiday on the Monday closest to 30 September. This reflects the tendency of Western Australians to see themselves as separate from, and independent of, the rest of Australia, which celebrates the Queen's Birthday early in June.

Left: *Spring's warmer weather encourages people to visit delightful gardens like the National Rhododendron Gardens in Olinda, Victoria.*

Below: *A family picnic is one of the most popular ways to celebrate Father's Day in Australia, as this wonderful celebration of fatherhood occurs just as the days are beginning to get warmer.*

Above: *The Energex Brisbane Festival offers a smorgasbord of visual arts, theatre, drama, music and many other activities, including face-painting, a tradition at festivals and fairs.*

did you know?

Out of the Box is an innovative cultural event for children aged 3-8 years. Part of the Energex Brisbane Festival, it embraces multiculturalism with a range of interesting activities, performances and exhibitions.

Queensland

BRISBANE

The principal event in September is the Energex Brisbane Festival, a major arts event incorporating the children's Out of the Box Festival. More localised is the Spring Hill Fair, which is Brisbane's oldest, biggest and probably best-loved market fair. Another local event is the Redlands Strawberry Festival, which includes the World Strawberry Eating Competition, while at Laidley there is the Chelsea Flower Show. Traditional Chinese music, dancing, costumes, foods, firecrackers, lanterns, arts and culture accompany the Chinese Moon Festival in Chinatown and the Brunswick Street Mall. The Queen Street Mall hosts the Summer in the City fashion showcase and the Spring Flower Show, while Sunset Cinema in the Botanical Gardens is an outdoor film programme that runs throughout spring. Less family-orientated, but still very popular, is the National Festival of Beers at the Story Bridge Hotel. Meanwhile the Riverfestival and Festival in Ruins (see the main entry in August) both come to a conclusion in September.

Map: Qld 7 N7

Beaudesert Show
Beaudesert

FIRST FRIDAY AND SATURDAY IN SEPTEMBER

Beaudesert is a pretty town nestled in the Logan River Valley behind the Gold Coast. It is a thriving agricultural centre producing dairy products and beef for the nearby state capital. In the early spring the community conducts one of the state's more substantial agricultural shows, featuring a very sizeable horse program, along with alpacas, a championship dog show, fireworks displays and plenty of family entertainment.

Map: Qld 7 N8

Right: *A milking yard in one of Beaudesert's dairy farms. Irrigation has made it a productive region, and this is celebrated at the Beaudesert Show.*

Birdsville Races
Birdsville

FIRST WEEKEND IN SEPTEMBER

Located on the edge of the Simpson Desert, 1600 km west of Brisbane and 10 km from the Queensland–South Australia state border, this tiny and isolated outback township lies at the northern end of the notorious and dangerous Birdsville Track, much beloved by those who enjoy 4WD treks. In September it experiences a population surge from 90 to over 6000 during the famous annual horse races, which offer over $100 000 in prize money. However, it is also a major outback social event with the Friday dance, the Saturday ball and ample social lubrication courtesy of over 100 000 cans of beer. Proceeds benefit the Royal Flying Doctor Service.

Map: Qld 6 C4

Festival of Cairns
Cairns

FIRST THREE WEEKS IN SEPTEMBER

This is the major event on the Cairns calendar and the largest community festival in regional Queensland. A celebration of the community and the local lifestyle, the Festival of Cairns is characterised by informality, a festive atmosphere, a Grand Parade, pool and beach parties, and fireworks. There are many

Above: *Birdsville, a dusty outback town near the Diamantina River, takes on a carnival atmosphere during the Birdsville Races. Crowds come from all over the country; here some watch celebrity TV chef Iain Hewitson demonstrate his skills.*

free activities, including a cultural night of traditional music and dancing, evening concerts and a children's night.

Map: Qld 2 B2

Goondiwindi Bachelor and Spinster Ball

Goondiwindi

SECOND-LAST SUNDAY IN SEPTEMBER

The home of famous racehorse Gunsynd, Goondiwindi is a prosperous service centre sprawling along the Macintyre River, on the New South Wales border. By the river the former Customs House is a reminder of the days when a tariff was incurred for the transportation of goods across the border. Each year Goondiwindi hosts a huge old-fashioned Bachelor and Spinster Ball, which attracts 3000 people from around New South Wales and Queensland. On the morning after the ball there is a free breakfast as well as a Recovery Party.

Map: Qld 7 H9

Australian Heritage Festival at Jondaryan

Celebrations at the Jondaryan Woolshed come to an end in early September (see the main entry in August).

Map: Qld 7 K7

National Road Cycling Championships

Mooloolaba

SECOND WEEK IN SEPTEMBER

Located on the Sunshine Coast, about an hour's drive north of Brisbane, Mooloolaba is a major holiday resort that, during September, hosts a week-long programme of major cycling competitions, including the National Road Cycling Championships which incorporates the Individual Road Time Trial, the Pairs Time Trial and the Road Races. There are numerous categories based on age and gender. The Masters competitions are open to women aged 30–59 and men aged 30 and over.

Map: Qld 7 N5

Left: *Apex Park in rural Goondiwindi is home to this statue of local hero, Gunsynd, one of Australia's most notable racehorses. The big grey won 29 of his 55 races and in the process charmed his way into the hearts of the racing fraternity.*

Right: *Mount Tamborine Vineyard sits about 560 m above the hinterland. Apart from wineries there are rainforests, waterfalls, bushwalks and a wealth of flora and fauna in the area.*

Gold Coast Hinterland Wine Country Crawl

Mount Tamborine Area

SECOND SATURDAY IN SEPTEMBER

The Gold Coast hinterland is something of a boutique winery area. Each year several of the vineyards participate in this event, which combines wine-tasting with guided tours of the vineyards and a lunch. A coach service operates from Brisbane to Albert River Wines, Canungra Valley Vineyards, Springbrook Mountain Winery and Vineyard and Mount Tamborine Vineyard and Winery.

Map: Qld 7 N5

Noosa Jazz Festival

Noosa Heads

WEDNESDAY TO SUNDAY OF FIRST WEEK IN SEPTEMBER

Noosa is a get-away-from-it-all coastal resort town. The upmarket boutiques, chic restaurants and beautiful surroundings make it a pleasant setting for the annual jazz festival, which attracts around 100 musicians performing traditional jazz, swing, modern jazz, funk and rhythm and blues in around 25 participating restaurants. There are also three major open-air concerts and jazz cruises on the water.

Map: Qld 7 N5

Tin Can Bay Bush to Bay Seafood Fun Day

Tin Can Bay

LAST SATURDAY IN SEPTEMBER

Tin Can Bay is a pleasant fishing and holiday resort on an inlet behind Wide Bay, south-west of Fraser Island. On the last Saturday of the month there is a

Below: *Dolphin Point at Noosa Heads is a spectacular stop on the walking track through the national park. From here you may see dolphins and even migrating whales.*

community fun day on the foreshore offering a tagged fishing competition with a $20 000 first prize, helicopter rides, a skateboard demo and competition, seafood cooking demonstrations, a sand modelling exhibition and competition, music and an art and craft show. There is also a sideshow with children's rides, street theatre, market stalls, family games, food stalls and fireworks.
Map: Qld 7 N4

Ag-Show
Toowoomba

TUESDAY TO THURSDAY OF FIRST WEEK IN SEPTEMBER

Toowoomba is the principal service centre of the productive agricultural and pastoral region known as the Darling Downs, which is also a major producer of agricultural machinery. Fittingly, it hosts Queensland's largest agricultural and machinery field days event, with displays of the latest in machinery and technology by over 500 exhibitors at the Toowoomba Showgrounds. The Farm Inventor of the Year offers substantial prize money to those who have not yet achieved commercial production. Other elements are the vintage machinery expo, Queensland's largest stud cattle sales, stud pigs, an alpaca display, the Best Exhibit Award and live demonstrations.
Map: Qld 7 L7

Carnival of Flowers
Toowoomba

LATE SEPTEMBER

The strength of horticulture in Toowoomba, the civic pride taken in the cultivation of private gardens and the presence of some fine and very substantial public parks and gardens have earned it the title of 'The Garden City'. The centrality of these elements to local culture and industry are recognised and celebrated in a week-long carnival. It takes the form of a major mardi-gras style float parade with extensive street entertainment, children's activities, a home garden competition, floral window displays, the crowning of the Carnival Queen and the international flower show in Queens Park.
Map: Qld 7 L7

Above: *A stockman sits at Combo Waterhole, located between Winton and Kynuna. It is believed to be the billabong that is featured in the famous Banjo Paterson poem 'Waltzing Matilda'.*

Outback Festival
Winton

LATE SEPTEMBER

Historic outback Winton has numerous claims to fame. The birthplace of Qantas, it also boasts 95-million-year-old dinosaur footprints, an old-style general store, ancient Aboriginal relics and one of only two remaining open-air picture theatres in Australia. Most famously, however, it is here that 'Banjo' Paterson penned the words of Australia's most famous of poems, 'Waltzing Matilda'. It was written just 14 weeks after an armed battle at a local station between striking shearers and station owners, and it is believed to be based on an actual incident involving the police and one of the insurrectionists. Considered one of Australia's finest non-metropolitan festivals, the biennial Outback Festival is a five-day celebration of bush culture held in odd-numbered years. Major events include the Australian Dunny Derby, in which 'dunny jockeys' are enthroned and pulled along in outhouses on wheels; the World Crayfish Derby; and Dunny Door Painting.
Map: Qld 4 J6

Left: *The madcap Dunny Derby at Winton's Outback Festival is accompanied by the hilariously irreverent Dunny Door Painting competition, which often involves well-known artists.*

Above: *Manly Arts Festival embraces and promotes art in all forms, such as this Living Statue. More traditional events include art exhibitions, theatre, film and music.*

New South Wales

SYDNEY

Those looking for something to do in Sydney would soon be exhausted trying to keep up with the city-wide smorgasbord of happenings in September. One event that pervades the city is the Carnivale Festival, which is widely considered the state's major multicultural arts festival. On the beachfront, the pleasant spring weather beckons people to the outdoor events—there is the Manly Arts Festival and, at Bondi Beach, the annual Festival of the Winds. This is perhaps Australia's largest and most renowned international kite festival, and draws crowds of more than 40 000 people. Darling Harbour hosts the Malaysian Festival early in the month and the Darling Harbour Fiesta at its end. September is also time for the all-important National Rugby League and Rugby Union Grand Finals.

Map: NSW 6 J8

The Thursday Plantation East Coast Sculpture Show

Ballina

MID-SEPTEMBER TO END OF JANUARY

About 40 000 people each year visit Thursday Plantation, which grows tea trees for their antiseptic oils. The major drawcard is the Sculpture Show that runs throughout spring and most of summer. The setting for this outdoor exhibition is 2.8 hectares of botanical gardens. At the centre, in a rainforest setting, are the headquarters. Scattered throughout the park are some 80 contemporary works, in addition to the permanent collection by artists from the East Coast and, in particular, from the local Northern Rivers region. This is the largest outdoor exhibition of contemporary sculpture in regional Australia.

Map: NSW 4 P3

Right: *Ballina's Thursday Plantation East Coast Sculpture Show is a celebration of art and nature where works such as Window by Matthew Harding may be viewed.*

The Bellingen Global Carnival

Bellingen

LATE SEPTEMBER TO EARLY OCTOBER

This fresh, new and somewhat unusual event offers three days and nights packed with varied and innovative performances from non-mainstream Australian and international guest artists in the fields of traditional, contemporary and classical music; dance; the visual arts; crafts; street theatre; and formal theatre. The goal is to enhance the understanding of the diversity and complexity of Australia's social and cultural tapestry and its elusive, plural and fluid identity by drawing artists from a range of ethno-cultural and linguistic backgrounds. The performances are spread over multiple stages and arenas. There are also workshops, a market bazaar and special children's concerts, workshops and activities, as well as child-care facilities.

Map: NSW 4 M7

Tulip Time

Bowral

THIRD WEEKEND IN SEPTEMBER TO FIRST WEEKEND IN OCTOBER

Deriving its name from the Aboriginal word *bowrel*, which the local indigenous population used to refer to the giant rock that towers over the town, Bowral is a quite delightful and pretty Southern Highlands town with an English ambience. For over 40 years the town has celebrated Tulip Time—one of the biggest floral festivals in Australia—with breathtakingly beautiful displays of tulips and other flowers in colourful Corbett Gardens. Many private gardens are open for visitors, and there are music performances, markets, dancing and other activities during the festival.

Map: NSW 6 G10

Above: *The highlight of Tulip Time festivities in Bowral is the massed display of over 80 000 tulips in bloom, complemented by flowering trees in Corbett Gardens. Many other activities also occur in these gardens.*

The Galston Country Music Festival
Galston

FRIDAY TO SUNDAY OF FIRST WEEKEND IN SEPTEMBER

Located in the Sydney hinterland, 9 km north-west of Hornsby, Galston offers a pleasant setting on the rural fringe of the state capital that is readily accessible for city-based country music fans. A safe family environment in Fagan Park is offered for this fundraising event, which draws talent from around the nation. The Festival Patron is singer Frank Ifield of 'I Remember You' fame.

Map: NSW 6 J8

Above: *The Coopers Golden Saddle Awards are an initiative of the Rotary Club of Galston for the Galston Country Music Festival. These awards are based on the Rotary Club of Galston awards for excellence.*

Henty Machinery Field Days
Henty

TUESDAY TO THURSDAY OF LAST WEEK IN SEPTEMBER

This rural service centre for the surrounding grain and sheep-producing landscape is known as the 'Home of the Header' because, in 1914, a local farmer named Headlie Taylor invented the header harvester that revolutionised the grain industry worldwide. Henty is thus an ideal setting for what is arguably the Southern Hemisphere's largest and most varied agribusiness event. Established in the 1960s, this outdoor supermarket now attracts more than 60 000 people and $300 million dollars worth of the latest in equipment and technology relating to dry-land agriculture, horticulture, viticulture, aquaculture and forestry. There are also displays of livestock and Australian wool, as well as emus, ostriches and alpacas.

Map: NSW 7 D4

did you know?

The Wagga Wagga Regional Gallery is home to the National Art Glass Collection. This is an impressive collection of glass made by artists using techniques such as blowing, casting and kiln-working.

Illawarra Folk Festival

Jamberoo

WEDNESDAY TO SUNDAY OF SECOND WEEK IN SEPTEMBER

This small and particularly charming village is located in a green valley a mere 7 km inland from Kiama on the New South Wales South Coast. Surrounded by nature reserves, Jamberoo has a quaint English feel that arises, in part, from the Mock Tudor façade of the local pub. This is but one of the venues for the annual folk festival that mostly unfolds across the road in the large town park. Over 250 local, national and international musicians, street artists, dancers, poets and storytellers perform for five days in 12 different venues. Participation is encouraged through a variety of jam sessions, music workshops and themed concerts. There are also concerts and activities especially for children, plus food stalls.

Map: NSW 7 N2

Right: *Toe-tapping music fills the air during the Wagga Wagga Jazz Festival. As well as outdoor concerts, there are performances in venues such as Romano's Hotel and the Commercial Club.*

Mudgee Wine Celebration

Mudgee

THROUGHOUT SEPTEMBER

An interesting, important and historic rural town on the New South Wales Central Tablelands, Mudgee is a very attractive settlement in the picturesque and fertile Cudgegong River Valley. Long noted for its quality wool and sheep studs, Mudgee also has an association with vineyards extending back to the 1850s. The district now has some 20 vineyards, and the pleasant spring days of September are dedicated to the promotion of local wines through special events at the local wineries.

Map: NSW 6 E5

Wagga Wagga Jazz Festival

Wagga Wagga

FRIDAY TO SUNDAY OF SECOND WEEKEND IN SEPTEMBER

The unofficial capital of the Riverina district, Wagga Wagga is one of the largest inland cities in Australia. A town of fine buildings, tree-lined streets, parks and gardens, it is a service centre for the abundant agricultural and pastoral properties of the area and is also a major regional education centre, due to the presence of Charles Sturt University. The annual jazz festival boasts a number of events including musical performances at several venues, street activities including a massed band performance at the amphitheatre, a gospel service in the main marquee and a jazz breakfast.

Map: NSW 7 D3

Below: *Poets Corner Winery in Mudgee was established in 1974 as Montrose Winery. As well as a name change, the vineyard has upgraded its wine-making technology and facilities.*

Wollombi Festival

Wollombi

THURSDAY TO SUNDAY OF LAST WEEK IN SEPTEMBER

A very small but charming, cosy and historic rural village, Wollombi's modest size is offset by its substantial old sandstone buildings and by its idyllic location within a pretty valley ringed by imposing tree-lined mountains. Located 4 km away, but within this same valley, is

Yanteen, an Aboriginal-owned property on the banks of Wollombi Brook. This is the venue for an annual folk festival featuring national and international performers, concerts, jam sessions, workshops, food stalls, a poets' breakfast, parades, displays and alternative health therapies. There is also a corroboree event that expresses the gratitude of the local indigenous people for the support they received from the community in making their land claim.
Map: NSW 6 J6

White Waratah Festival
Wollondilly Shire

LAST SATURDAY IN SEPTEMBER TO EARLY NOVEMBER

The White Waratah Festival is the umbrella name for a variety of events and activities that take place throughout Wollondilly Shire in the spring. These include the Picton Music Festival, the Ferret Derby and Billy Cart Derby at The Oaks (with speeds adjudicated by police radar clocks), the DingoFest and Dingo Parade at Bargo, the Food and Winefest, Halloween at Picton, the Greater West Games Carriage Driving Classic and New South Wales Driven Dressage Championships, railway heritage at the excellent Rail Transport Museum in Thirlmere, art exhibitions, an open gardens scheme and tours of heritage buildings and properties in this historic area.
Map: NSW 6 H9

Viva La Gong Wollongong Festival
Wollongong

MID- TO LATE SEPTEMBER

The presence of the University of Wollongong and the proximity of Sydney have both contributed to the growth of a lively community arts scene in the Illawarra. Viva La Gong explores the skills and imagination of the community through an eclectic presentation of innovative activities, ranging from street theatre, food fairs and parades to music, dancing and concerts.
Map: NSW 6 H10

Above: *Visitors to the Viva La Gong Wollongong Festival can take advantage of the area's other attractions, including walking tracks along the coastline that offer magnificent views.*

don't miss

Visual arts buffs will find Wollongong's northern suburbs a treasure trove. Well-known Articles Fine Art Gallery in beautiful Stanwell Park exhibits works by some of the country's finest artists and craftspeople.

Above: *Canberra's major attraction in spring is Floriade, which covers about 10 000 sq m of Commonwealth Park. Volunteers are on hand to inform visitors about the different plants used in the displays.*

Right: *Visit the Australian Cymbidium Orchid Show in Ararat to learn about these showy plants. There are over 40 species of cymbidiums, which are native to south-east Asia and eastern Australia.*

Australian Capital Territory

Floriade
Canberra

MID-SEPTEMBER TO MID-OCTOBER

The national capital heralds the arrival of spring when over one million bulbs and annuals–both Australian natives and exotic species–burst into bloom from the flowerbeds that line the shores of Lake Burley Griffin. First held in 1988 as part of Australia's bicentennial celebrations, Floriade has a different theme each year that determines the form of the floral layout; in the past these themes have included history, poetry and a tribute to the countries of the world. Hundreds of thousands of people from Canberra, interstate and overseas come to survey the horticultural masterpieces in Commonwealth Park each year.

Map: NSW 7 J4

Victoria

MELBOURNE

September is time for the state's largest and most popular event, the Royal Melbourne Show, a showcase of the state's agriculture and a huge family fun day. However, few events on the annual calendar possess as much frenetic charge as the Australian Football League Grand Final, which is passionately watched around the nation but especially in 'Aussie Rules' obsessed Victoria. Melbourne is also the departure point for the Melbourne to Warrnambool Classic cycling event, which attracts some renowned international competitors for a single-day, 275-km trek along the Great Ocean Road. Back in the city, a world away from sweat and strain, is the Spring Fashion Week. On the cultural front *The Age* Melbourne Writers Festival (see the main entry in August) comes to a conclusion, but the end of the month sees the start of Melbourne's Fringe Festival, an excellent opportunity for independent artists to showcase new and contemporary work.

Map: Vic 6 D3

Australian Cymbidium Orchid Show
Ararat

EARLY SEPTEMBER

Each year this former goldmining town in the foothills of the Pyrenees Mountains hosts the state titles for orchid cultivation at the local performing arts centre, which is also the town hall. Over the course of a weekend there is an outstanding display of classic orchids, exhibition plants and hybrids. Periodically the same venue is used for the national orchid cultivation championships, which rotate around different venues across Australia.

Map: Vic 5 H2

Spring into the Grampians
Halls Gap

LATE SEPTEMBER TO EARLY OCTOBER

Since the 1930s the local community has organised a comprehensive annual display of every known wildflower species in the Grampians, all labelled for visitors. This tradition continues today in Centenary Hall,

did you know?

In the 1850s philanthropist Caroline Chisholm lived in Kyneton. The terrible conditions for miners' families heading to the goldfields inspired her to develop a scheme to build shelters en route; one is still at Kyneton.

where there are also arts and crafts relating to plants and relevant books for sale. To coincide with this event, the National Parks and Wildlife Service conducts guided walks through the bushland around this attractive tourist village, gateway to the spectacular Grampians National Park. The Grampians mountain range marks the southern end of the Great Dividing Range, which extends to Cooktown in Cape York.

Map: Vic 5 G2

Left: *Old mill wheels sit outside what was once the G. W. Willis Corn Mill, which was built in 1862. This is just one of several nineteenth-century buildings found in the historic town of Kyneton.*

Kyneton Daffodil Festival

Kyneton

EARLY SEPTEMBER

The settlement of Kyneton has, in recent years, adopted the daffodil as a town symbol. Extensive plantations are at either end of town; daffodils adorn local gardens and shop windows, and they serve as the motif for an annual floral festival which takes place over 10 days, usually between the first and second weekends in September. The daffodil display, at Watts Pavilion in the Showgrounds, is held on the first weekend when there is also an antique fair. On the second weekend there is a spring fair featuring a parade, street entertainment, the naming of the Festival King and Queen, stalls, rides and sideshows.

Map: Vic 3 C9

Below: *Australian Football League supporters at the Melbourne Cricket Ground. The largest AFL crowd seen at the MCG was 121 696 at the 1970 grand final between Carlton and Collingwood.*

Rutherglen Wine Show
Rutherglen

MID- TO LATE SEPTEMBER

Australia's oldest known wine show, dating back to the late nineteenth century, takes place in Henderson Pavilion at the Rutherglen Showgrounds. This is a chance for the public to sample award-winning wines from every Australian wine-growing region. Epicurean delights from throughout the district are on offer, and the affair culminates in a gourmet presentation dinner at the Rutherglen Memorial Hall in which the wine judges nominate the year's winners.

Map: Vic 3 L4

Right: *A barrel from the rustic Chambers Rosewood Winery, featured at the Rutherglen Wine Show. Established in 1859, it is acclaimed for its fortified wines.*

Tesselaar Tulip Time Festival
Silvan

MID-SEPTEMBER TO MID-OCTOBER

East of Melbourne, in the Dandenong Ranges, is a 'Little Holland in the Hills'. Every year Tesselaar's Farm hosts a European-style celebration of spring featuring an abundance of colourful flowers—tulips, daffodils, anemones, hyacinths, ranunculi and many others. The Dutch theme is reflected in the music, clog dancing, costumes, specialty food and cakes, barrel organ, wandering accordionist and horse-and-buggy rides. There are special seniors' days; a Food, Wine and Jazz weekend; and children's days with puppet shows, clog walks, Dutch games, a scarecrow workshop, a storybook mobile, an animal farm and a guest fairy.

Map: Vic 6 E3

Below: *Many springtime flowers are on show at the Tesselaar Tulip Time Festival, including masses of bright yellow daffodils. Visitors can also pick their own tulips or have a picnic in the grounds.*

Werribee Orchid Society Spring Show
Werribee

THIRD WEEKEND IN SEPTEMBER

A city and suburb near Port Phillip Bay, 31 km south-west of the heart of Melbourne, Werribee has become part of the vast residential/industrial sprawl of the outer Melbourne metropolitan area. The 'for profit' horticultural preoccupations of the community are visible in the patchwork quilt of market gardens in Werribee South, while their 'for pleasure' exhibits are on display at the annual spring orchid show. Held at the Werribee Racecourse, it features hundreds of orchid species. Sales, potting demonstrations and talks relating to the cultivation of orchids are included.

Map: Vic 6 B3

Tasmania

HOBART

The cool climate of Tasmania is well suited to the propagation of tulips, daffodils and camellias, and September is the time when the new shoots thrust out into the welcoming arms of spring. Consequently, Hobart has many springtime floral festivals. Perhaps the biggest is the Tulip Festival of Tasmania, which offers the chance to see 12 000 tulips and 4000 daffodils set among other spring flowers in the beautiful Royal Tasmanian Botanical Gardens. The festivities include free entertainment, food, wine, and art and craft stalls, and this event takes place on the last weekend of the month. On the same weekend, and on the Friday and Monday surrounding it, the Tasmanian Orchid Society's Spring Orchid Show unfolds at the Hobart Town Hall. Earlier in the month the Hobart Horticultural Society's Spring Flower Show is held at the Hobart City Hall. It also features daffodils, camellias and other spring blossoms, along with

many horticultural displays, beautiful floral art, as well as sales of plants and gardening products.
Map: Tas 3 K6

Launceston Horticultural Society Spring Show

Launceston

SECOND WEEKEND IN SEPTEMBER

The Launceston Horticultural Society is the oldest in Australia, dating back to 1838. It was established by Ronald Campbell Gunn who, following in the footsteps of Joseph Banks, sent much new information back to Great Britain. Held in St Albie's Hall, the Spring Show features camellias and daffodils, floral art, specialist nurseries with stalls, cut flowers, container-grown plants, fruit, vegetables and children's exhibits.
Map: Tas 2 C7

Table Cape Tulip Farm Open Days

Wynyard

LATE SEPTEMBER TO MID-OCTOBER

A volcanic plug rising 190 m above sea-level, Table Cape is a beautiful headland located just 7 km north of Wynyard that offers outstanding views up and down the coast. The promontory is adorned with a lighthouse built in 1888 and a tulip farm that opens its doors to the public when the beautiful and richly coloured tulip fields are in bloom. Visitors can wander through the fields then head indoors where there are refreshments, displays, an art exhibition, educational elements, sales of potted bulbs and cut flowers and a chance to arrange the delivery of a particular bulb variety to your home in autumn.
Map: Tas 1 J4

Above: *While in Hobart, take a tour of Parliament House or go for a stroll around the neighbouring Parliament Square lawn, which features pretty floral borders.*

Below: *A graceful suspension bridge straddles the South Esk River at Launceston's Cataract Gorge, which can also be crossed by chairlift.*

South Australia

ADELAIDE

The three outstanding events associated with the state capital in September are the Royal Adelaide Show (see the main entry in August) that finishes early in the month, the Bay to Birdwood Run and the Bay to Birdwood Classic. The latter two are both biennial events with the former held in even-numbered years and the latter in odd-numbered years. Both follow a 64-km route that tends to be well lined with appreciative onlookers. They start at West Beach, on Holdfast Bay, and pass through the western and north-eastern suburbs of Adelaide, continuing on into the Adelaide Hills and finishing at the National Motor Museum in Birdwood. The Bay to Birdwood Run is open to cars manufactured before 1950 that are roadworthy and in largely original condition. Between 1500 and 2000 cars are typically involved, with the drivers in period costume. The Bay to Birdwood Classic is open to cars built between 30 and 55 years ago and substantially to manufacturer's specifications. The best car is announced at the Museum, where the entertainment includes live music, from swing to early rock 'n' roll.

Map: SA 4 J3

Right: *A life-saving flying doctor service was established by Reverend John Flynn in 1928, 17 years after his first appointment at Beltana mission.*

Below: *A visit to Adelaide must include a trip to Glenelg Beach, a short ride away on the original 1929 Glenelg tram.*

Beltana Picnic Races and Gymkhana
Beltana

SECOND WEEKEND IN SEPTEMBER

A superb semi-ghost town on the edge of the desert, Beltana is one of the truly remarkable outback settlements found in South Australia. It was from Beltana Station that many of the major explorations of South and Central Australia started. Camels bred at Beltana Station were of great use in the construction of the Overland Telegraph Line from Adelaide to Darwin, and Reverend John Flynn is said to have dreamt up the Flying Doctor Service while working at an inland mission at Beltana. People travel vast distances to enjoy the social atmosphere of the picnic races and gymkhana on the Saturday and the motorcycle gymkhana on the Sunday.

Map: SA 3 J3

Clayton Farm Vintage Field Day
Bordertown

END OF SEPTEMBER

The birthplace of Australian prime minister Bob Hawke, Bordertown is a substantial service centre located near the state border between South Australia and Victoria. The Clayton Farm Village at Bordertown is a particularly interesting

historic farm in this part of the country. Between 1872 and 1985 it was owned and operated by August Gottfried Wiese and his family. It now houses an amazing collection of historic farm machinery and buildings—all erected either by the owners or by local tradesmen from traditional materials such as limestone, grasses and a variety of gums. During the Vintage Field Day there is a rally of old tractors and other machinery, along with a host of other fun events such as a tractor pull.
Map: SA 4 P6

Above: *A collection of old farm equipment at Heritage-listed Clayton Farm. It also houses records, relics and a variety of other memorabilia assembled by the Bordertown District Museum.*

Heysen Festival
Hahndorf

LAST SATURDAY IN SEPTEMBER TO FIRST SUNDAY IN OCTOBER

Driving through very typical Australian countryside, it comes as a great surprise to enter Hahndorf and find a town that appears to have been transplanted directly from Central Europe. A remarkably well-preserved settlement, it was established in the late 1830s by German Lutherans fleeing persecution in their homeland. Hahndorf's most famous son was painter Hans Heysen, whose life and work is honoured during the annual nine-day arts festival that bears his name. It includes art competitions, the Heysen Art Prize, street entertainment, music, food and wine, exploring the Artist's Trail and 'The Cedars' open day (Heysen's former home and studio).
Map: SA 4 K3

Yorke Peninsula Field Days
Paskeville

TUESDAY TO THURSDAY OF LAST WEEK IN SEPTEMBER

Probably the principal event on the state's rural calendar, this is Australia's oldest and one of its largest field days. Over 50 000 visitors and 700 exhibitors of the latest in rural technologies and equipment attend the exhibition site at Paskeville. The multimillion dollar display is accompanied by demonstrations, a wool and sheep pavilion, working sheepdog trials, historical displays and motorcycle trials.
Map: SA 3 H10

Left: *The German Arms Hotel in Hahndorf was established in 1839. It was completely renovated in 1990 using very old recycled timbers from a Port Adelaide wool store, with excellent results.*

Above: *Perth is arguably Australia's most modern city, with the mining boom of the 1970s and 1980s—and the associated profits—transforming the skyline forever.*

Western Australia

PERTH

King's Park offers a superb view both of Perth's CBD and the graceful Swan River. One of the jewels in the crown of the city, it is especially beautiful in the early spring when it hosts the marvellous King's Park Wildflower Festival, which is large and varied in its displays. Later in the month the Perth Royal Show gets under way at the Claremont Showgrounds. The city's most popular and biggest festival, it draws about 400 000 people each year who come for the fun rides, showbags and sideshows, as well as the agricultural and business displays. Late September sees the opening, in Hyde Park, of the Pride Festival, a celebration of gay and lesbian theatre, film and music. There are forums, community events and sporting events, as well as an associated writers' festival.

Map: WA 6 C4

Below: *Dating back 1500 years, Wandjina art is the most distinctive style of rock art in the Kimberley. It is this traditional art—as well as modern Aboriginal works—that is celebrated during Broome's Stompem Ground Festival.*

Beverley Duck Race

Beverley

SECOND SUNDAY IN SEPTEMBER

The Avon River provides the inspiration for the town's quirky annual duck race in which interested parties aim to take home the Gold Duck Award. Plastic ducks are purchased, decorated, then entered in what is billed as 'the longest white-water Duck Race in the World'. There are no rules, so any method of getting a duck from start to finish is legal. Prizes are awarded for the best-dressed public duck. For those who like to wager, Australian dollars can be converted into duck bills at the 'Duck Burg Bank', which claims to offer punters the best exchange rates in the world.

Map: WA 6 E4

Stompem Ground Festival

Broome

LAST WEEKEND IN SEPTEMBER

Aboriginal communities have lived in the Kimberley district of Western Australia for thousands of years. Although many traditional folkways survive, culture is a dynamic process of adaptation and contemporary indigenous culture reflects the realities of modern circumstances. The Stompem Ground Festival, which focuses exclusively on indigenous art forms, encompasses both the traditional and the contemporary in the worlds of music, dance, visual arts and storytelling. The positive promotion of indigenous health is another aim of the festival, and so healthy food and drink is provided at this alcohol-free event.

Map: WA 1 A9

Coolgardie Day

Coolgardie

THIRD SUNDAY IN SEPTEMBER

This fascinating and beautifully maintained goldmining town declares itself to be a 'ghost town', although it now has around 2000 citizens and makes a healthy living promoting its status as a living relic of the past.

Certainly Coolgardie retains quite a few nineteenth-century buildings, a fully operational gold battery, an interesting museum and plenty of plaques explaining the history of different buildings and sites. Coolgardie Day is a family celebration of the town, with camel rides, goldpanning, rock-drilling, handbogging, wood-chop events, street parades, stalls and live entertainment.

Map: WA 7 B4

Bushies vs Townies Cricket Match

Derby

SATURDAY TO MONDAY OF LAST WEEKEND IN SEPTEMBER

One of the classic divisions in the Australian psychic and cultural landscape is that between country and city, bush and town. This divide still informs the politics of contemporary Australia, and at Meda Pastoral Station, situated near Derby, this rivalry between bushies and townies is played out, quite literally, on a cricket pitch. Fortunately good humour characterises the proceedings, with the match supplemented by an auction, a fun run, night-time entertainment and also a campout.

Map: WA 1 D8

Gascoyne Junction Race Weekend

Gascoyne Junction

LAST WEEKEND IN SEPTEMBER

Those who wish to explore the Australian outback should make the journey to Gascoyne Junction Racecourse, 180 km east of Carnarvon, where a classic bush race meeting is held close to the stunning countryside of the Gascoyne River and Kennedy Range National Park. Events include a tug of war with a $300 prize and a $1000 barrel race. Camping facilities are available, along with live music, a canteen, two-up games, a bar and plenty of country hospitality.

Map: WA 4 E10

Bottom: *Kennedy Range National Park, just north of Gascoyne Junction, has spectacular sandstone gorges with an immense plateau of ancient dune fields atop the range.*

Below: *Camel rides are popular on Coolgardie Day. The importance of camels to Coolgardie is seen in the design of the town: its main street is wide enough so a camel train can turn around.*

Right: *There are several places to discover Kalgoorlie gold, including the Western Australia Museum at Kalgoorlie-Boulder which has an underground gold vault.*

don't miss

Kalgoorlie's Super Pit is an enormous mining project, which is best viewed from the Super Pit Lookout. So large is it that this is one of the few man-made structures in the world that can be seen from space.

Right: *Poultry judging is a serious business at the annual Northampton Agricultural Show. The Shire of Northampton is an agricultural region best known for its quality citrus fruit.*

Kalgoorlie–Boulder Race Round
Kalgoorlie

EARLY TO MID-SEPTEMBER

Kalgoorlie is one of the country's most famous, important and impressive gold-mining towns, and it is the site of what was known as 'the richest goldfield in the world'. Horse-racing has always been popular in towns and cities throughout Australia, and Kalgoorlie is no exception. In September the Kalgoorlie–Boulder Race Club conducts what many people regard as the region's premier sporting and social event. The Race Round incorporates the running of the Coolgardie Cup, the Boulder Cup, Hannan's Handicap Cup and the Kalgoorlie Gold Cup. There is also a fun Fashions on the Field competition with a first prize valued at approximately $2500.

Map: WA 7 C4

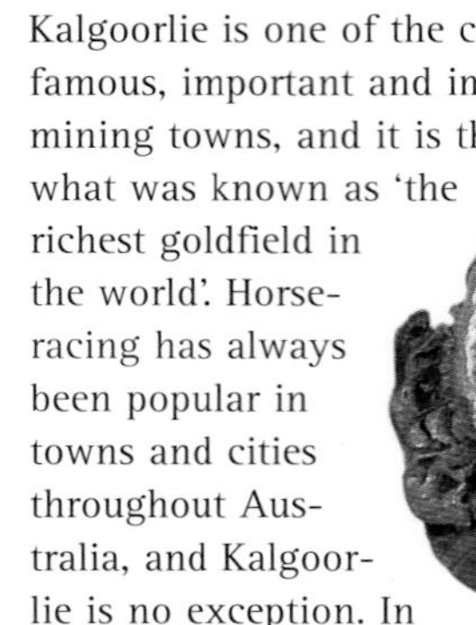

Balzano Barrow Race
Kalgoorlie/Kanowna

FOURTH SUNDAY IN SEPTEMBER

This unusual event is a fund-raiser that commemorates Italian prospector James Balzano, who pushed his wooden barrow about 900 km to the goldfield at Kanowna in 1896. As they are participating for charitable purposes, today's entrants are spared the enormity of such an undertaking—they simply have to run or walk their barrow from the Old Kanowna Cemetery to Centennial Park in Kalgoorlie, a distance of 21 km.

Map: WA 7 C4

Laverton Outback Celebration Weekend
Laverton

FRIDAY TO MONDAY OF LAST WEEKEND IN SEPTEMBER

Laverton once had the dubious reputation of being the wildest town in Western Australia. Formerly propped up by gold-mining, its economic mainstay is now a major nickel-mining operation. At the end of September this town of just over 1000 residents kicks up its heels with a country music concert, a fireworks display at the Windarra Heritage Site, a triathlon, markets, a ball, a golf competition, a day at the races, traditional two-up games, an enjoyable music night at Laverton Sports Club and an outback bush cricket match at the Old Lancefield townsite.

Map: WA 8 D10

Northampton Agricultural Show
Northampton

SECOND SATURDAY IN SEPTEMBER

Located about 470 km north of Perth and 50 km north of Geraldton, Northampton is a small and attractive town situated in undulating country on the edge of the wheat belt. Lead and copper mining in the area date back to the 1840s, but it is agriculture that now dominates in the region. Established in the 1910s, the annual agricultural show is a popular regional affair featuring ring events; the judging of sheep,

wool, grain, fodder, cattle and poultry; exhibition hall displays; an animal nursery and other entertainments for young children; the Ride the Mad Cow event; demonstrations in whipcracking expertise; a fashion parade; a tug of war; sideshows; rides; live music and fireworks.
Map: WA 5 D7

Above: *Wheat-growing is the mainstay of Trayning. To the north-east of the town there is an unusual finger-like projection of white quartz known as Whiteman, which was unearthed by gold fossickers.*

Toodyay Highland Games and Festival of the Celts

Toodyay

FRIDAY TO SUNDAY OF THIRD WEEKEND IN SEPTEMBER

The Celtic origins of many of Toodyay's first settlers come to the fore during this annual festival. A variety of celebrations include a ceilidh, a tartan ball, a tattoo, a pipe band, solo piping and highland dancing and drumming competitions. There are also displays by a drum major, a Scottish country dancing display and Celtic folk music. The sheepdog performances and men's heavy Highland athletics such as caber tossing add further interest. There is also some tasty traditional food to revive visitors and competitors alike, as well as a host of community and craft vendors.
Map: WA 6 D3

Stockman's Games

Trayning

FIRST WEEKEND IN SEPTEMBER

Located deep in the heart of Western Australia's wheat belt, the tiny township of Trayning came into existence because of a natural well that quenched the thirst of prospectors en route to the goldfields. During the two-day Stockman's Games, teams of three compete in a variety of different events that replicate and draw on the skills of the traditional bush stockman. Most of these involve interactions with horses, cattle and sheep. Camping sites are available for visitors, and there is plenty of music provided for entertainment. If you like to join in, spectator involvement is encouraged in some of the events.
Map: WA 6 F2

Northern Territory

DARWIN

The Festival of Darwin (see the main entry in August) spans the city's gentle transition from winter to spring. Concluding in mid-September, it continues to offer a diverse multicultural program of arts, culture and family entertainment, including the popular Teddy Bears' Picnic that is held on a Sunday in the Coconut Grove area of the Botanic Gardens.
Map: NT 1 E4

Left: *Buskers entertain passers-by by playing traditional Aboriginal music at the Mindil Beach Market. This colourful Darwin institution is held every Thursday night from May to October.*

don't miss

West of Alice Springs is the magnificent West MacDonnell National Park. The 220-km Larapinta Trail links the park's most beautiful natural features, including Ormiston Gorge, the Ochre Pits and Standley Chasm.

Centre Rocks

Alice Springs

EARLY TO MID-SEPTEMBER

Held over 10 days in Blatherskite Park, Centre Rocks is a new and very substantial gemstone and fossicking event that offers professional Australian and international dealers and amateur collectors a chance to get together, display, trade and sell their jewellery and other wares, plus sit in on lectures by internationally recognised experts and enjoy themselves. Entertainment includes evening speedway events, horse races, golf days and bush poetry. An optional extra is a three-day trip to the mineral museum at Tennant Creek, where evening entertainment is also provided.

Map: NT 7 F5

Henley-on-Todd Regatta

Alice Springs

THIRD SATURDAY IN SEPTEMBER

The Henley-on-Todd Regatta combines the fun, the satirical, the futile and the ridiculous, mocking the upper-class associations of English rowing competitions and humorously indicating the futility of attempting to transplant the culture of Britain to an utterly different landscape. Competing in traditional eights, fours, pairs etc, the costumed participants launch a motley assortment of 'boats', including bathtubs, into the dry bed of the waterless Todd River. The bottomless craft are driven to the finish line by foot power. At the end of the day comes the Battle of the Boats, in which the vessels fire water and flour mortar at each other until all are suitably loaded with dough. There are also iron sandman and sandwoman competitions. All proceeds from the event go to humanitarian projects.

Map: NT 7 F5

Daly Waters Campdraft

Daly Waters

SECOND WEEKEND IN SEPTEMBER

This tiny township of about two dozen people is best known for its famous pub. Built back in 1893, it is one of the oldest

Below: *The dry bed of the Todd River where the Alice Springs' madcap Henley-on-Todd Regatta is held. The event once had to be cancelled as the 'river' actually had running water in it.*

surviving buildings in the Northern Territory. Thought to have seen some wild times in its day, it originally served as a stopover for drovers seeking to replenish their supplies and spirits before continuing on the next leg of the journey between Queensland and the Kimberleys in Western Australia. The outback spirit is celebrated with the annual campdraft at the Daly Waters Rodeo Grounds. A gymkhana, an evening rodeo under lights, a live band and entertainment for the whole family are all part of the experience.

Map: NT 3 E5

Left: *The Daly Waters Pub, where visitors often leave interesting calling cards. This township has attracted many international travellers over the years, and was a stop-off for the 1926 London to Sydney air race.*

Jabiru Wind Festival

Jabiru

EARLY SEPTEMBER

Jabiru is a small centre that was built to house uranium-mine workers. It has excellent facilities, and is a good base from which to explore Kakadu National Park. The Wind Festival is a family-orientated cultural/musical/artistic event that seeks to attract quality performers and to provide exposure for local artists. During the week there are displays of photography, arts and crafts—including Aboriginal contributions—and exhibitions of basket-weaving. However, the climax of the festival is on the weekend when there are live bands, food stalls, a community market, sporting events, a formal youth ball, fireworks, fun rides, sideshows and exhibitions.

Map: NT 2 D5

Arnhem Land Open Day

Oenpelli

EARLY SEPTEMBER

Arnhem Land is located in the north-eastern corner of the Northern Territory. Now private property, it is inhabited by Aboriginals and controlled by the Northern Land Council. Generally it is not that easy to get permission to visit Arnhem Land, but once a year there is an open day that permits free access to Oenpelli. This is a chance to see some Aboriginal dancing, football and paintings, as well as the fine undeveloped landscape. Visitors must drive across the East Alligator River at low tide to get to Oenpelli, so the timing of the event can vary.

Map: NT 2E4

Desert Harmony Art and Cultural Festival

Tennant Creek

SECOND TO THIRD FRIDAY IN SEPTEMBER

This is the major cultural event of the year in Tennant Creek. It provides an opportunity for local artists and other Territorians to present their skills as visual and performing artists. It also gives the local community a chance to experience, participate in, and learn about aspects of culture that would not usually be available in such a remote location. Photography, multimedia works, comedy acts, poetry and festival dinners are all part of the affair.

Map: NT 6 G4

did you know?

About 100 km south of Tennant Creek are the Devils Marbles, a spectacular natural landmark. Although the gigantic boulders seem to be precariously balanced on top of each other, they can be climbed, with care.

Below: *This Aboriginal artwork at the Central Lands Council in Tennant Creek is an example of the type of indigenous visual art that can be seen at this town's Desert Harmony Art and Cultural Festival.*

October

October is a superb month. The last chills of winter have worn off, even in the coolest parts of Australia, and a gloriously temperate climate—neither too hot nor too cold—is the rule of thumb before the arrival of the summer swelter.

There are no nationwide holidays in October, although New South Wales, the Australian Capital Territory and South Australia celebrate Labour Day on the first Monday of the month. Labour Day is essentially a proletarian holiday which celebrates the Union achievement of the eight-hour working day. Many people do not realise that this idea first emerged in Australia where, in 1856, workers downed their tools for a day, marched, held meetings and enjoyed some entertainment as a demonstration in favour of the eight-hour day.

With an average of 12 hours of sunlight a day—providing plenty of time for outdoor fun and activities—Queensland does not need to put its clocks forward for daylight saving.

The final Sunday of October is also the day on which many Australian states put their clocks forward one hour under the scheme known as Daylight Saving. American Benjamin Franklin was the first to put the idea forward. His rationale—of saving both resources and expenses by decreasing the number of energy-consuming evening hours—re-emerged when energy consumption became a more pressing issue. This was especially the case during the two world wars when many countries, including Australia, introduced temporary daylight saving schemes to conserve important resources for the war effort. Following the initial example of Tasmania, three other states—New South Wales, Victoria and South Australia—plus the Australian Capital Territory adopted a permanent daylight saving scheme in 1971.

The last Friday in October is the time when Reclaim the Night marches are held in many Australian towns and cities, in order to protest the physical abuse of women and children.

Below: *Many families in New South Wales spend the Labour Day long weekend out in the sunshine, enjoying picnics in the park or taking in the amusing street theatre at Sydney's Circular Quay.*

Left: *On the last Friday in October, women and children take to the streets of cities such as Perth for Reclaim the Night rallies and marches. There are also candlelit vigils, entertainment and speakers.*

(see the main entry in September) winds up in October, but all is not lost as the RAQ Australian Fashion Design Awards continue the season of fashion and glamour. The Colonial George Street Festival is a popular outdoor event, while the Energex Brisbane Festival (see the main entry in September) reaches its conclusion in October.

Map: Qld 7 N7

Emerald Heartland Festival
Emerald

EARLY OCTOBER

This Central West town, located 260 km west of Rockhampton, is a major rural centre in an area noted for its rich, black clay soils. It seems an appropriate setting for one of Australia's bigger country music jamborees, drawing around 20 000 spectators. Other attractions of the event include bullriding, a Wine and Food Festival, children's entertainment, fashion parades, a gathering of hot-air balloons and fun competitions.

Map: Qld 5 E8

Gympie Gold Rush Festival
Gympie

SECOND TO THIRD SATURDAY IN OCTOBER

Located 166 km north of Brisbane, Gympie describes itself as 'The Town That Saved Queensland'. This unusual claim is not without foundation as the local gold rush (the state's first) did save a virtually insolvent Queensland from bankruptcy. This history is the motivation for a week-long festival which includes a twilight street procession with lantern sculptures, a Gold 'n' Steam Day at the Mining Museum, a steam-train ride to Imbil and back, the Mayoress's Command Performance, art and photographic exhibitions and competitions, special children's activities, a Gold Rush Street Party and, on the final weekend, competitions such as the Queensland

The Riverside Precinct of Brisbane offers visitors a choice of enjoyable activities. River cruises leave from the wharf, and on Sundays there is a craft market at the Riverside Centre.

Queensland

BRISBANE

The Queensland Cultural Centre, on South Bank, is the venue for the annual Brisbane Writers Festival, which attracts about 25 000 people. Music-lovers can get their fill at the Livid Festival, where national and international rock acts are the primary focus, but there are also extreme sports and market stalls down at the RNA Showgrounds. On a rather different arts front, the Dame Mary Durack Outback Craft Awards is a national competition held at the Queensland Museum. The Summer in the City fashion show

Warrumbungle Festival of the Stars

Coonabarabran

MID-OCTOBER TO EARLY NOVEMBER

Coonabarabran is known as the place where the 'Warrumbungles Meet the Stars'. This is a reference to the town's two greatest attractions: a mountainous national park and the Siding Springs Observatory. The latter is an astronomical complex of international importance, which boasts the largest optical research telescope in Australia. There are a number of activities at the festival, including an open day at the Observatory, Science in the Pub with a guest speaker, Astrofest (involving three days of star-gazing), an arts-and-crafts exhibition, the very popular Coonabarabran Cup, the Skywatch Concert (featuring a special guest musical performer), children's activities and a great concert featuring Aboriginal music and dancing.

Map: NSW 6 D1

The Cootamundra Show

Cootamundra

THIRD SATURDAY IN OCTOBER

The birthplace of Sir Donald Bradman, Cootamundra is a railway junction town and service centre that is also associated with the Cootamundra Wattle, made famous in a song by John Williamson. Lovers of 'The Don' can visit his birthplace, the adjoining memorabilia cottage and the 'Captain's Walk' in Jubilee Park, which features busts of the Australian cricketing captains. The annual show features competitive sections in fields such as livestock, produce, handicrafts and cooking, plus educational events and entertainment including whip-cracking, pet shows, talent quests, woodchopping and an excellent fireworks display.

Map: NSW 3 E9

Sakura Matsuri

Cowra

SECOND WEEKEND IN OCTOBER

During World War II, Japanese prisoners of war broke out of the camp at Cowra, with 4 Australian guards and 247 prisoners dying in the process. Rather than creating lasting racial enmity, this important historical event has made Cowra one of the most tolerant towns found in New South Wales. The town celebrates many different Japanese festivals, including Sakura Matsuri—the cherry blossom festival. Activities to watch or take part in include Japanese tea ceremonies, kite flying, and martial arts and calligraphy demonstrations.

Map: NSW 3 G6

A tranquil place to visit is the Cowra Japanese Garden, created by Ken Nakijima in 1979. It features an authentic teahouse, a working pottery house, plus a cultural centre and art gallery.

Warrumbungle Festival of the Stars at Coonabarabran gives visitors the opportunity to check out Siding Springs Observatory, 24 km from town. It has interactive exhibits and a café.

Grafton is a magical place in October, when its wide, tree-lined streets and 24 attractive parks become an ocean of magnificent purple flowers. The first jacaranda trees were planted here in 1907.

Gilgandra Cooee Festival

Gilgandra

SATURDAY TO MONDAY OF FIRST WEEKEND IN OCTOBER

This pleasant service town on the Castlereagh River is known as the 'Home of the Cooees'. This is a reference to the first World War I recruiting march from Gilgandra to Sydney, when 35 local men walked to the city gathering others along the way with the traditional bushman's cry of 'cooee'. Held on the Labour Day long weekend, the festival incorporates the New South Wales Cooee Calling Championships, market stalls, a parade, Clydesdale rides, novelty events such as watermelon-eating and broom-throwing, and a Sunday service with a brass band in St Ambrose Anglican Church.

Map: NSW 2 G9

did you know?

St Ambrose Anglican Church in Gilgandra was built with money given to the town by the parish of St Ambrose in England. The sum of £1200 was awarded for Gilgandra's contribution to the war effort in World War I.

Jacaranda Festival

Grafton

LAST WEEKEND IN OCTOBER TO FIRST WEEKEND IN NOVEMBER

Known as 'The Jacaranda City', Grafton is renowned for its 7000 magnificent jacaranda trees. During October, the trees put on a stunning display of lilac-hued flowers—just in time for the city's famous Jacaranda Festival. First held in 1935, this is Australia's oldest floral festival, and is still held today as a celebration of nature's bountifulness in the region. Thousands of interstate and international visitors flock to Grafton during the festival to enjoy a mix of cultural and sporting events, parades, art and craft exhibitions, and the crowning of the Jacaranda Queen for the year.

Map: NSW 4 M5

Griffith Festival of Gardens

Griffith

FRIDAY TO MONDAY OF THIRD WEEKEND IN OCTOBER

Griffith is a town that emerged out of the construction of the Murrumbidgee Irrigation Area early in the twentieth century. The abundance of water and the Mediterranean climate have produced a wealth of citrus fruits, wine grapes, rice and some beautiful gardens. About a dozen of the town's finest, ranging from cottage gardens to grand homesteads, are open to the public in October. The festival is convened with bell-ringing and music in the cathedral. Other activities include guided walks of the natural environs, a scarecrow trail, performances by local groups, a festival dinner, flower shows and floral arts displays.

Map: NSW 5 N5

Australasian Bullriding Titles

Kundabung

FIRST SUNDAY IN OCTOBER

Kundabung is a small settlement located just south of Kempsey on the Mid-North Coast. In early October, it hosts a cracking bullriding show characterised by non-stop frenetic action. This event has become the most prestigious of its kind in Australia, attracting around 10 000 spectators. With $15 000 in prize money up for grabs, contestants are drawn from around Australia, New Zealand and from Canada and the USA. The arena comes to life with music, dancing girls, clowns and special events such as champions attempting to ride unconquerable bucking bulls. There are also rides and other entertainment for children.

Map: NSW 4 M10

Leura Gardens Festival

Leura

FIRST SATURDAY TO SECOND SUNDAY IN OCTOBER

In many ways, Leura is seen as the most urbane and sophisticated of all the villages in the Blue Mountains. Its mall is full of chic coffee houses and delightful eateries; its streets are tree-lined and elegant. The charming old houses in the small township are attractive and commonly surrounded by English and European-style private gardens full of colourful azaleas, rhododendrons, camellias, flowering shrubs and annuals, set against the scenic backdrop of the mountains. As such it is in an ideal position to host the largest and best known of the Blue Mountains spring garden displays, attracting visitors from around Australia and the world.

Map: NSW 6 G8

Fly Kites for Peace

Narrandera

SECOND SUNDAY IN OCTOBER

Declared an urban conservation area due to its large number of heritage buildings, Narrandera is an elegant Riverina town that has taken up an idea initiated by an American woman known as Jane Parker Ambrose. She urged people all over the world to fly a kite for peace on the same day each year, in order to make a personal commitment and a public statement summed up in the slogan 'One Sky, One World'. The event is held at the Narrandera Showgrounds from 11.00 a.m.

Map: NSW 7 B2

Left: *One of the highlights of the Griffith Festival of Gardens is the sculptures incorporating local citrus fruits. Valencia oranges are the main citrus fruit grown in this fertile irrigation area.*

Mattara—Festival of Newcastle

Newcastle

FIRST SATURDAY TO SECOND SUNDAY IN OCTOBER

Located at the mouth of the Hunter River, Newcastle is the second-largest city in the state and the sixth-largest in Australia. Once an industrial centre, it is now an elegant and attractive destination full of historic buildings and interesting walks. Held in the heart of the city in leafy Civic Park, Mattara is the city's principal annual festival, involving family entertainment, sporting events, food, wine, arts and crafts exhibitions, market stalls, rock concerts and other music performances—and all events are free.

Map: NSW 6 L6

Held annually for almost 40 years, the Leura Gardens Festival is the oldest continuously run charity garden display in Australia, and attracts visitors from countries such as New Zealand and Japan.

Right: *More than 50 per cent of the 30 000 visitors to the Australian National Field Days own a farm, and view the event as a chance to see the very latest in machinery and methods.*

Australian National Field Days

Orange

SECOND TUESDAY TO FOLLOWING THURSDAY IN OCTOBER

Established in 1952, the Australian National Field Days at Orange is the oldest, and arguably the principal, annual agricultural exhibition in Australia. Drawing exhibitors from around the world, it showcases the latest products, services, ideas and technologies in agriculture. To give you some idea of its scale, the displays cover 40 hectares, the steer competition another 120 hectares and a further 40 hectares is set aside just for car parking.

Map: NSW 6 D7

Jazz in the Vines

Pokolbin

LAST SATURDAY IN OCTOBER

Pokolbin is less a town than an area of the Hunter Valley given over, almost exclusively, to vineyards. Each year about 10 000 people gather in Tyrrell's Long Flat Paddock to sample the wines of Tyrrell's, Tamburlaine, Terrace Vale, Drayton's and the Hunter Valley Wine Society. Leading local restaurants supply a range of gourmet foods, and the carnival ambience is enhanced by the upbeat sounds of numerous jazz bands.

Map: NSW 6 J5

After enjoying the ambience created by music and wine at Pokolbin's Jazz in the Vines, take a drive through the scenic vineyards or get a bird's eye view from the basket of a hot-air balloon.

White Waratah Festival in the Wollondilly Shire

The Wollondilly Shire continues to celebrate the White Waratah Festival (see the main entry in September).

Australian Capital Territory

Floriade at Canberra

The national capital's famous floral celebration of spring reaches its conclusion in October (see the main entry in September).

Map: NSW 7 J4

National Gospel Happening

Canberra

FRIDAY TO SUNDAY OF FIRST WEEKEND IN OCTOBER

This outdoor music festival provides three days of free spiritually orientated music. The bulk of the performers, whether solo, in bands or choirs, are drawn from local and national talent with a major guest artist or two and international performers.

Ceduna Oyster Fest
Ceduna

SATURDAY TO MONDAY OF FIRST WEEKEND IN OCTOBER

Over 20 000 oysters are consumed during this festival, which is held in the only major township on the eastern side of the Great Australian Bight. It promotes, celebrates and supports the town's links with the sea, especially its oyster industry, which employs many local people. The festival incorporates elements of Aboriginal culture, plus events such as the South Australian Oyster Opening Championships, the crowning of the Festival Queen, cooking demonstrations, a parade, gourmet food tasting, fireworks and sandcastle-building competitions.

Map: SA 1 M9

Curdimurka Outback Ball
Curdimurka

FIRST SATURDAY IN OCTOBER

Thousands attend this black-tie event, which is held in the open air at an old railway siding in the middle of nowhere. Despite its isolated location, this is a major event with exceptional light and sound production, live bands, full bar facilities and food. There is no hotel or motel but camping is free. A creche is available. Buses depart from Adelaide or participants can drive up via Roxby Downs or Marree. The trip takes about ten hours. Curdimurka also has an airstrip for light aircraft.

Map: SA 2 F9

Beyond and Back—Gawler Ranges Outback Challenge
Gawler Ranges

LAST WEEKEND IN OCTOBER

The Gawler Ranges Outback Challenge is an amateur team race involving cross-country running, cycling and horseriding. Teams are chosen at random on the evening before the race, with one competitor from each event placed together. The venue is Spring Hill on Thurlga Station, 95 km north of Kimba on the Eyre Peninsula. Cash prizes are offered for the best competitor in each discipline and for the overall winning team.

Map: SA 3 C6

Bottom: *The Ceduna jetty is excellent for crabbing and fishing. Anglers are likely to catch a variety of fish species, including whiting and garfish.*

Below: *Max Owen urges his mount along in the Gawler Ranges Outback Challenge. Horseriders face a 15-km trek, while runners tackle a 10-km course and cyclists ride for 20 km.*

don't miss

Kuitpo Forest, 20 km east of the town of McLaren Vale, is an outdoor recreation area in the Mount Lofty Ranges. Camping and picnic sites are available, and the forest is a popular place to bushwalk and ride horses.

Located next to the Onkaparinga River estuary, Port Noarlunga is a great place for picnics and swimming. It is believed to be the most popular land-based scuba diving area in Australia.

Heysen Festival at Hahndorf

This festival finishes in early October (see the main entry in September).

Map: SA 4 K3

McLaren Vale Bushing Festival

McLaren Vale

FRIDAY TO SUNDAY OF LAST WEEKEND IN OCTOBER

This attractive and historic town is in the heart of one of South Australia's premier grape-growing areas. To celebrate the start of the grape harvest, the 45 wineries of the region throw a harvest bash in the main street of McLaren Vale featuring decorated floats, street theatre, novelty events, the crowning of the Bushing Festival King and Queen, foods, crafts and regional wines. A carnival atmosphere prevails throughout a weekend of fun.

Map: SA 4 J4

Christies Beach Celtic Festival

Port Noarlunga

SECOND SUNDAY IN OCTOBER

This pleasant holiday resort and fishing destination is located just 35 minutes south of Adelaide. Five minutes from the old port is Christies Beach, which hosts the largest festival of its kind in South Australia and, what is more, it is entirely free. The entertainment takes the form of English, Scottish, Irish and Welsh music and culture; highland dancing; pipe and drum bands; broadsword duels; street theatre; a street market in crafts and wares; and children's activities. Quality wines, beers and food are available, and browsing through the stores along Beach Road is a must.

Map: SA 4 J3

Renmark Rose Festival

Renmark

THIRD TO FOURTH SUNDAY IN OCTOBER

A town of very wide streets with attractive central plantations, Renmark became an important and productive centre when the Chaffey brothers introduced an irrigation scheme in the 1880s. A beneficiary of that scheme is the town's rose bushes, 50 000 of which are located in a pleasant landscaped setting in Rustons

Rose Garden in Moorna Street. These, and the town's other roses, are at full bloom in October, and Renmark celebrates with a nationally recognised Rose Festival that involves an official opening, tours of private gardens, an awards presentation and entertainment such as live musical performances.
Map: SA 4 P1

Tanunda Brass Band Competition
Tanunda

THIRD SATURDAY IN OCTOBER

Truly the cultural heart of the Barossa, Tanunda is a large rural settlement with tree-lined streets that is completely surrounded by vineyards. Settled by German Lutherans, it retains a distinctly German feel with sausage shops, German bread shops, German-style restaurants and lots of wine. Brass bands have been a part of Teutonic culture since the nineteenth century, and each year Tanunda hosts what is widely regarded as one of the oldest continuously run brass band contests in the world at the Barossa Arts and Convention Centre.
Map: SA 4 K2

Western Australia

PERTH

The Perth Royal Show (see the main entry in September) concludes in October. So too does the Pride Festival (see the main entry in September), which climaxes with the Pride Street Parade in Northbridge and a dance party. As October folds into November Perth hosts the Telstra Rally Australia, which is the second-last round of the FIA World Rally Championship. Attracting some of the world's best drivers, it takes place over three nights in Langley Park and through regional areas in front of some 50 000 people. Competitors race against the clock and each other. Those who prefer to put fuel in their stomachs, rather than their cars, can attend the Taste of the Nation fund-raiser, in which local restaurants prepare their best dishes in marquees and the public pay for the food, wine and beer with all monies going directly to Community Aid Abroad. There is always plenty of colourful live entertainment.
Map: WA 6 C4

Fremantle Fishing Fleet Festival
Fremantle

THIRD SUNDAY IN OCTOBER

The traditional blessing of the fishing fleet, prior to the opening of the fishing season, is essentially an Italian Catholic tradition. After the mass at St Patrick's Basilica in Fremantle, a procession carries statues of Our Lady of Martyrs and Our Lady of Capo D'Orlando to the Fishing Boat Harbour, accompanied by a large number of children in traditional Italian costume, religious banners and brass bands. At the harbour the boats are decked out with colourful flags and flowers and a leading representative of the Catholic Church blesses the fleet. The procession then returns to the basilica and fireworks are held on the Esplanade at 4.00 p.m. and 8.00 p.m.
Map: WA 6 C4

Above: *The award-winning Renmark Hotel, overlooking the Murray River, was established in 1897 as the first community hotel in the British Empire.*

Left: *Turbo-charged cars competing in Telstra Rally Australia cover 1395 km in 21 stages, from the Langley Park Super Stage in Perth through the forests of the state's south-west and back again.*

did you know?

Fremantle was founded in 1829 when Captain Charles Howe Fremantle formally took possession of the entire west coast of what was then called New Holland in the name of King George IV. It became a city in 1929.

Above: *Kalgoorlie's York Hotel (1900) on Hannan Street is a marvellous example of Edwardian splendour. The carved staircase is a must-see.*

Top: *The Sacred Heart Convent, built in 1919 by Monsignor John Hawes and now a backpackers' hostel, is one of the historic buildings in Northampton to participate in the Airing of the Quilts.*

Spring Festival
Kalgoorlie

THIRD SUNDAY IN OCTOBER

Kalgoorlie was built on gold more than 100 years ago. A city full of extraordinary history (and historic buildings), it is truly one of Australia's great goldmining towns. In October the community celebrates spring with a family-orientated day in Hammond Park, featuring all-day entertainment, live performances, children's activities, specialty foods, fast foods and craft stalls.

Map: WA 6 M2

Kulin Bush Races
Kulin

FIRST WEEKEND IN OCTOBER

Kulin is a typical wheat-belt town in an area known for its beautiful springtime wildflower displays and for the Kulin Bush Races, which have become a major drawcard. The race weekend incorporates children's entertainment, novelty events, live bands, country-style food, camel races, foot races, a gymkhana and, of course, horseracing. It is held at the base of a huge granite monolith that overlooks a 1214-ha lake, 16 km east of town along the 'Tin Horse Highway'. The latter is named after the many artificial horses that are manufactured locally from a variety of materials and placed along the route as the weekend approaches.

Map: WA 6 G5

The Airing of the Quilts
Northampton

SECOND SATURDAY IN OCTOBER

This unusual open-air display sees more than 300 decorative quilts, of all sizes and designs, cast over lines which have been strung between the historic buildings of the town centre. Hand-made by the women of Northampton and the surrounding districts, they are the focal point for a day of festivities that includes an art exhibition at Chiverton House Museum, music, food stalls, crafts and produce stalls.

Map: WA 5 D7

Bibbulmun Eco Team Challenge
South-West Western Australia

MID-OCTOBER TO MID-NOVEMBER

The Bibbulmun Track is an award-winning walking trail that extends for 1000 km from Perth to Albany. The Eco Team Challenge is not a race. Instead the aim is for 16 teams of four to compete to gain the highest score by undertaking environmental activities and other challenges along the route. The winning team from each of four heats moves into the final. Each heat includes team-building and competitive activities, with a strong emphasis on outdoor skills, safety, environmental awareness and interpretation, physical and mental challenges, as well as bushwalker etiquette. Prizes are awarded to winners of the heats and the finals.

Spring in the Valley
Swan Valley

SECOND WEEKEND IN OCTOBER

Vineyards in the Swan Valley date back as far as 1829, although the first substantial vineyard was not established until 1859. It remained a low-key industry until the 1920s, when an influx of Yugoslav migrants from the Dalmatian coast applied their skills locally. Today the heirs of these settlers still run many of the Valley's vineyards, which tend to be smaller family affairs rather than bulk producers. Spring in the Valley celebrates the grape harvest with wine, food, music, stalls, art and children's activities.

Map: WA 6 C4

Northern Territory

DARWIN

As the temperature increases in Darwin thoughts turn to getting out and about, particularly by the water. On the first weekend in October anglers can participate in the Corroboree Park Challenge, which is a barramundi fishing competition drawing substantial interstate interest. The maximum line to be used is 10 kg, and there are worthwhile prizes on offer. Also by the waterside, in the Wharf Precinct, is the Darwin Food and Wine Festival, which proffers the best in local foods and wines to the general public while entertainment is provided.

Map: NT 1 E4

Alice Springs Masters Games
Alice Springs

THIRD TO FOURTH SATURDAY IN OCTOBER

This biennial sporting event (held in even-numbered years) is one of the premier events on the Alice Springs sporting and social calendar. Designed for athletes aged over 30, it is intended to encourage mature-aged people to participate in exercise and good-natured competition, offering opportunities in over 30 different sporting events. The socialising that accompanies the games, and the amiability of the entire town, is seen as equally vital to an event known as the 'Friendly Games'. Over 5000 athletes attend from all over the world, so make sure that you book accommodation more than two years in advance if you plan to visit Alice Springs during the Masters Games.

Map: NT 7 F5

don't miss

Aquascene at Doctors Gully, Darwin (phone 08 8981 7837), is a great place to take the kids. At high tide, hundreds of mullet, bream, catfish, barramundi and other fish species come close to shore to be hand-fed.

Left and below: *The Alice Springs Masters Games incorporates a variety of different sports, from hockey and basketball to darts and tenpin bowling. The small size of the town and the proximity of the venues to each other adds to the fun atmosphere.*

Left: *The Bibbulmun Track is one of the world's most scenic walking trails. There are 48 shelters along the track providing pit toilets, picnic tables, rainwater tanks and sites for tents.*

VICTORIA UNIVERSITY

November

The anniversary of the Armistice of World War I occurs on 11 November. Although Australia was legally bound to enter the war along with Great Britain, it did so willingly and with overwhelming popular support. The main military force was the Australian Imperial Force (AIF), which was a volunteer army, and there was no shortage of volunteers. Men rushed to enlist, selling their business interests or leaving them in the control of others. The only women to join were qualified nurses.

Three-quarters of those Australians who fought overseas were aged between 21 and 40. One-third were tradesmen and one-third were labourers; 80 per cent had worked in the country. In all, 330 000 men fought overseas in a theatre of war, and 68.5 per cent of these were to become casualties (the highest percentage of any British Empire country) with almost 60 000 killed or missing. On 11 November, Australians pause to remember these men, and, by extension, all who have fought and died in wars. It is a time for sober reflection on international conflict, and at 11.00 a.m. a minute's silence is still generally upheld in public institutions such as schools. Solemn parades are held all over Australia, although the nation's most famous symbol of war remembrance, the Australian War Memorial in Canberra, is the site of the country's central commemorative ceremony.

The first Tuesday of November is a public holiday in the metropolitan area of Melbourne, due to the running of the Melbourne Cup.

Above: *Almost every place in Australia has a memorial to those who gave their lives in World War I. This one is in the small town of Sorell, north-east of Hobart in Tasmania.*

Below: *Melbourne Cup Day is considered one of the most important fashion events in the country, and includes the Myer Fashions on the Field Competition.*

Left: *Flinders Street Station, Melbourne (foreground). The elegant and cosmopolitan city of Melbourne has a population of over 3 million people. However, even this bustling metropolis comes to a standstill on Melbourne Cup day, as the city enjoys a public holiday.*

don't miss

The Whitsunday Islands lie just off the east coast, inside the Great Barrier Reef. For an idyllic escape, hire a yacht and cruise the clear waters between the islands or take a seaplane out to the reef and go snorkelling.

Queensland

BRISBANE

The suburb of Chermside is the setting for the Queensland Country Music Festivals Champion of Champions, which is the state's most prestigious event for non-professional country music performers. It is essentially a grand final for winners of affiliated Country Music Club Festivals around Queensland, as well as an opportunity for young competitors to build friendships and gain self-confidence. The Dame Mary Durack Outback Craft Awards (see the main entry in October) reach their conclusion at the Queensland Museum in November, while late November sees the commencement of one of Australia's leading golf tournaments, the Australian PGA Championship, at the Royal Queensland Golf Club, Eagle Farm. At the end of the month Christmas celebrations get under way throughout Brisbane, with the decoration of the Queen Street Mall and King George Square.

Map: Qld 7 N7

Right: *The endangered loggerhead turtle* (Caretta caretta), *at the Mon Repos Conservation Park, one of the Southern Hemisphere's most significant turtle rookeries.*

The Whitsunday Reef Festival

Airlie Beach

FIRST FRIDAY TO SECOND SATURDAY IN NOVEMBER

Airlie Beach is the administrative centre for the complex of islands, small coastal villages and resort towns that constitute the Whitsunday Group. The Whitsunday Reef Festival is a celebration of the Great Barrier Reef, the balmy weather of the tropics, and the culture and lifestyle of the 74 Whitsunday Islands. The activities include beach volleyball, a family fun day, a lantern parade, a multicultural mardi gras, a beach party, live entertainment, a market day with a carnival and rides, community processions, yachting races, a fashion parade, a treasure hunt, fireworks, a golf competition, displays, cabaret night cruises and dinners.

Map: Qld 5 F2

Below: *Airlie Beach, gateway to the Whitsunday Islands, is an attractive holiday destination in its own right, with its beautiful beach, superb restaurants and a wide range of accommodation.*

Coral Coast Turtle Festival

Bundaberg

FIRST SATURDAY TO SECOND SUNDAY IN NOVEMBER

This community bash celebrates the commencement of the turtle season at Mon Repos Conservation Park. Each year people make the trip to this research and tourist facility to watch loggerhead, green and flatback turtles nesting at their rookery in the evenings. Back at Bundaberg the festivities take the form of a parade, entertainment, sporting competitions, art displays, a family fun day, shows, markets, beach activities and wine and food events.

Map: Qld 7 M2

Caloundra Surf Classic Carnival

Caloundra

SECOND WEEKEND IN NOVEMBER

When they are not scanning the beaches, surf lifesavers tend to enjoy a bit of competitive rivalry. The Caloundra Carnival represents the first round in the State Premiership Series and attracts over 1200 entrants in 74 events, both individual and team, in board, boat, beach, swim and ski disciplines. It is held at Dicky Beach, an outstanding surf beach at the beautiful holiday resort town of Caloundra, which offers excellent patrolled strands, sheltered family areas, plenty of greenery and some fine fishing, all within 100 km of Brisbane.

Map: Qld 7 N5

Above: *The Gold Coast region lays claim to being the tourist capital of Australia, with several million Australians and about a million overseas visitors each year—its permanent resident population is 334 000 people.*

Red November and the Legacy Flanders Poppy Festival of Faith

Glen Aplin

THROUGHOUT NOVEMBER

Glen Aplin is a tiny village amid vineyards and small family farms near Stanthorpe. In November the region uses the colour red as its motif in celebrating its produce—red wine, strawberries and cherries—and encourages visits to its wineries and orchards. The theme is deepened by the Legacy Flanders Poppy Festival of Faith, in which a field adjacent to Das Helwig Haus B&B is planted with red poppies. The Remembrance Field commemorates the fields of Flanders where so many died in World War I. On the weekend nearest Remembrance Day, there is a memorial service and the field is accessible to the public as part of an open garden scheme.

Map: Qld 7 L9

Schoolies Week

Gold Coast/Sunshine Coast

MID-NOVEMBER TO MID-DECEMBER

Each year Queensland is inundated with about 50 000 interstate Year 12 students. They are drawn to the bright lights of the Gold and Sunshine coasts, to celebrate the end of school. Attempts are made to channel the chaos by organising special events such as free beach concerts and sporting activities. One of the biggest is the Sunco Hyundai Sunshine Coast Schoolies Festival, which takes place at Kawana. It offers quality alcohol- and drug-free dance parties and concerts by live bands, plus movie nights, surfing lessons and other events, only open to 16–18 year olds.

Map: Qld 7 N8

Left: *Rowers head out into the surf to compete in the Caloundra Surf Classic Carnival. Caloundra is at the southernmost end of the 150-km stretch of coastline known as the Sunshine Coast.*

Above: *In places like Home Hill, where sugar is a mainstay of the economy, the canefields may be fired before the harvest to remove leaves and weeds and make the harvesting process easier.*

Home Hill Harvest Festival
Home Hill

FIRST FRIDAY TO SECOND SATURDAY IN NOVEMBER

This sugar town on the Burdekin River is linked to its twin town of Ayr by the remarkable 1-km Silver Link Bridge, which is the longest bridge of its type in the Southern Hemisphere. Every year in November, Home Hill celebrates the harvest, not only of sugar, but also of the other produce of the Lower Burdekin region that has greatly benefited from an irrigation scheme. The entertainment and activities, which include balls, street parades and special events related to cane-cutting, cater to all ages, and most of them take place in the central shopping area.

Map: Qld 2 E9

Noosa Triathlon Multi Sport Festival

The athletes of the Multi Sport Festival (see the main entry in October) wind up their competitions and festivities in November.

Map: Qld 7 N5

Right: *The Moonlight Cinema in Sydney's Centennial Park shows the latest movies and old favourites in an outdoor setting. Pack a picnic and rug for the main feature.*

New South Wales

SYDNEY

Sculpture By The Sea is a free exhibition of about 100 sculptural works along the Tamarama Coastal Walk. Featuring both national and international artists, it attracts around 200 000 visitors over 10 days. Darling Harbour is also abuzz with the Japanese Matsuri Festival (a celebratory festival with ritual elements derived from the Shinto religion), the Songwriters' Annual Performance Concert, and the Christmas Tree Lighting. In the city there is the Sydney Women's Festival, the Thai Food Festival and Loi Krathong (a Thai Buddhist festival). Three months of evening cinema commences with Moonlight Cinema at Centennial Park, while, nearby, there is fun at the Glebe Street Fair and the Newtown Festival. Further afield there is Britfest, which features British foods, beers and entertainment at the Blacktown Showground; Parramatta's Foundation Day Festival; the Heavy

Horse and Heritage Weekend at historic Belgenny Farm near Camden; and the popular Sydney to Wollongong Bicycle Ride, which is Australia's largest one-day recreational cycling event.
Map: NSW 6 J8

The Thursday Plantation East Coast Sculpture Show at Ballina

This impressive outdoor art show (see the main entry in September) continues throughout the month.
Map: NSW 4 P3

Blackheath Rhododendron Festival

Blackheath

FIRST WEEKEND IN NOVEMBER

One of the more substantial and interesting settlements, and the highest town in the Blue Mountains, Blackheath is noted for Govett's Leap Lookout, beautiful bushwalks, guesthouses and gardens. In spring it seems as though everyone in Blackheath has planted their gardens with rhododendrons—the Rhododendron Garden in Bacchante Street being a highlight. The annual festival, which dates back to the early 1950s, features garden inspections, a procession, distinguished art shows, the Festival of Flowers, a barbecue and bush dance, Mountain Link Trolley Tours, a model train exhibition, stalls and crafts, the Australian roof-bolting and coal-shovelling championships, sporting competitions, dancing, music, folk singing and carnival-style street entertainment.
Map: NSW 6 G8

Snowy Mountains Trout Festival

Cooma

FIRST SATURDAY TO SECOND SUNDAY IN NOVEMBER

The principal town of the Snowy River region, Cooma became the headquarters, in 1949, of the Snowy Mountains Hydro-Electric Scheme, which saw the construction of several dams in the area. These have been stocked with trout and are very popular with anglers. The Trout Festival, established in the early 1970s, is considered the largest inland fishing competition in New South Wales, and it attracts between 500 and 800 anglers. Separate prizes are offered for the largest brown trout and the largest rainbow trout caught in the following categories: trolling, spinning, bait-fishing, flyfishing and juniors. There are also prizes for the largest Atlantic salmon and the largest brook trout (on any tackle).
Map: NSW 7 J6

Warrumbungle Festival of the Stars at Coonabarabran

This astronomical event (see the main entry in October) concludes in November.
Map: NSW 2 G8

Exeter Olde English Village Fayre

Exeter

THIRD SATURDAY IN NOVEMBER

A quiet settlement 7 km north of Bundanoon in the Southern Highlands, Exeter is known as 'Little England' due to its trees, climate and gardens. It hosts an Olde English Village Fayre that features English music, maypole and morris dancing, seventeenth-century pike drills and musket firing, English ales, English foods (pork pies, pasties), games, rituals and 'Medieval'-style feasting.
Map: NSW 7 M2

Left: *Rhododendrons vary from tiny, ground-hugging and miniature plants to small trees. Many different rhododendrons can be seen at the Blackheath Rhododendron Festival.*

Below: *The Snowy Mountains Trout Festival attracts anglers from all over Australia for the week-long event. Recently the rules have been modified to promote the 'catch and release' ethos.*

Land of the Beardies Bush Festival
Glen Innes

FIRST FRIDAY TO SECOND SUNDAY IN NOVEMBER

The first white people in the Glen Innes area were two hirsute convict stockmen who did a great deal to open up the area for European settlement by advising and guiding prospective settlers. For this reason the district became known as the 'Land of the Beardies'. The citizenry of Glen Innes use this unusual motif to celebrate their town with a family-orientated festival, which incorporates a range of activities such as a beard-growing contest, Australia's richest bull ride, a shopping-trolley derby, a street parade, a mardi gras-style carnival, the announcement of the Festival Queen, art and craft displays, dances, a motor show, competitions and many other exciting events.

Map: NSW 4 J5

Above: *Many buildings in Glen Innes date from the mid- to late nineteenth century. Some have been redeveloped with careful attention to maintaining their heritage value.*

Jacaranda Festival at Grafton

The colourful festivities in the Jacaranda City conclude early in November (see the main entry in October).

Map: NSW 4 M5

Dog on the Tuckerbox Festival
Gundagai

FRIDAY TO SUNDAY OF FOURTH WEEKEND IN NOVEMBER

Settled in 1826, over the years Gundagai has been the subject of numerous songs, such as 'Along the Road to Gundagai', as well as many verses. One such poem that was penned by an anonymous writer, known only as 'Bullocky Bill', introduced the Dog on the Tuckerbox to Australian folklore back in the 1880s, and the legendary dog was immortalised in a bronze statue and placed by the roadside 'five miles' (8 km) from Gundagai in 1932. The legend is that the dog sat on the tuckerbox, refusing to assist his owner when his bullock team was bogged in a creek. The statue's 'birthday' is celebrated with a weekend of festivities including the Snake Gully Cup, which is one of the principal events of the country racing calendar, along with street parades, markets and a variety of other forms of entertainment.

Map: NSW 7 F3

Right: *The Dog on the Tuckerbox Festival includes the Snake Gully Cup, in honour of the family in Steele Rudd's* On Our Selection. *This statue in Gundagai also pays tribute to the characters in the book.*

Celebrate Lithgow
Lithgow

FOURTH SUNDAY IN NOVEMBER

Development of the Lithgow Valley really began with the construction, back in the 1860s, of the Zig Zag Railway. It was at that time acclaimed worldwide as a major engineering feat. Still a very popular tourist attraction, it enabled the industrialisation of the valley and thus the establishment of the city that was home to the nation's first modern blast furnace. The ironworks is gone but heavy industry still dominates employment in the valley. The whole community celebrates in November with street entertainment, singing, dancing, fashion parades and children's concerts, as well as some excellent displays featuring delicious local produce.

Map: NSW 6 F7

White Waratah Festival at the Wollondilly Shire

This collection of local shire celebrations (see the main entry in September) ends at the beginning of November.

National Cherry Festival
Young
LATE NOVEMBER TO EARLY DECEMBER

Young is the commercial centre of an agriculturally diverse area famous for its luscious cherries and a variety of other stone fruits. Along with Orange, it provides 80 per cent of the nation's cherry crop. Cherry picking season lasts about six weeks and generally starts in the first week of November. The town's celebrations include the announcement of the Cherry Queen; a market day; exhibitions of arts, crafts and quilts; a food and wine day; a fun run; and Kid's Week, which includes a carnival with rides and entertainment. There is a Heritage Day with traditional stalls and crafts, buggy rides and gold-panning. Also on offer are a fishing competition, entertainment, re-enactments, buskers, a pie-eating competition, shearing demonstrations, camel rides, a bush barbecue, sheepdog trials, a campfire with a bush dance and bush poetry readings, greyhound races and the Cherry Festival Cup.

Map: NSW 3 F8

Australian Capital Territory

Canberra's Pet Expo
Canberra

FRIDAY TO SUNDAY OF FIRST WEEKEND IN NOVEMBER

Held at Exhibition Park, this popular event attracts over 16 000 pet lovers. Indoor and outdoor exhibition areas offer a host of different activities and demonstrations. There are horse and bird pavilions; a live birthing centre; cats and dogs; displays of pet products and services; an arena showcasing the activities of various animals; a baby animal farm; a pavilion for larger animals such as sheep, cattle and alpacas; a display of reptiles, insects and aquatic creatures; plus competitions and seminars on a range of pet-related matters.

Map: NSW 7 J4

Above: *Cherry blossoms in Young, the site of Australia's first commercial cherry tree orchard. These beautiful flowers appear in spring.*

Below: *Sulphur-crested cockatoos* (Cacatua galerita) *live 30 to 50 years and crave attention. You can learn more about cockatoos at Canberra's Pet Expo.*

don't miss

The Melbourne Zoo is just 10 minutes from the heart of the CBD. It has more than 350 species of animals. On some summer evenings it opens for Zoo Twilights, offering fine food and musical entertainment.

Right: *Roses are one of the most widely grown and best loved of flowers. The large-flowered 'Just Joey' is one of many to see at the Alexander and District Rose Festival.*

Victoria

MELBOURNE

Certainly one of the most famous events on the entire Australian calendar is the Melbourne Cup, which dates back to 1861 and takes place at Flemington Racecourse on the first Tuesday of November. Adults all over the country, including many who never otherwise gamble, place a bet or enter a sweep then huddle around radios and televisions to hear the outcome of what has become the biggest horse-race in the Southern Hemisphere. Trackside is the place for the rich and famous to be seen in the most fashionable clothes—and the most stunning hats—that money can buy. The race is televised to over 300 million people around the world, while more than 90 000 attend the racecourse for the main race and for other events in the week-long Cup Carnival. Every second November (in odd-numbered years) Equitana Asia-Pacific occurs, which is the largest non-racing equine event in the Southern Hemisphere. It attracts over 75 000 spectators to eight days of competition, dressage, horse-dancing and entertainment. Wine Australia (which is a biennial event held in even-numbered years) is the largest national public gathering of the Australian wine industry and its produce.

Map: Vic 6 D3

Alexandra and District Rose Festival

Alexandra

THIRD WEEKEND IN NOVEMBER

Held at St Andrew's Uniting Church in Alexandra, the delightful annual rose festival is a winner of the Murrindindi Regional Tourism Best Festival and Event Award. Affiliated with the Rose Society of Victoria, there is a rose show, which is open to all, plus talks by well-known rosarians on the history and culture of roses. Also on offer are numerous displays and sales of potted roses, market stalls selling gardening paraphernalia, plus great entertainment, mouth-watering gourmet food, a church service, an open garden day featuring eight district gardens, an awards presentation ceremony and exhibitions of quilting, furniture making, children's books, T-shirt painting, music and Irish dancing.

Map: Vic 3 H9

Pyrenees Vignerons Petanque Weekend

Avoca

FOURTH WEEKEND IN NOVEMBER

This former goldmining town is in a region with nine wineries. To start the wine harvest, vineyards band together to host what is billed as the country's biggest wine and petanque festival. Just why this European game has developed an association with wine is a mystery, but perhaps it is related to petanque's dignified and gentlemanly air. No experience is necessary as there are clinics for beginners. Qualifying rounds are held on Saturday, with social competition on Sunday. Non-qualifiers can soothe themselves with a glass of wine.

Map: Vic 5 L2

Below: *For a change from the Family and Local History Expo, take a look at the Italian marble statues in the delightful Ballarat Statuary Pavilion.*

The Family and Local History Expo

Ballarat

FIRST WEEKEND IN NOVEMBER

Many people are interested in investigating their family history, but are unsure of where, and how, to look for evidence.

The considerable, and ever-growing, popularity of family history research has encouraged the Central Highlands Historical Association to proffer an expo that responds to these kinds of queries. There are around 50 stallholders, talks, workshops, displays, and experts to consult, with much practical information on subjects such as how to use the Internet. Food is available and there is a backdrop of entertainment at the Australian Catholic University Aquinas Campus.
Map: Vic 5 M4

Above: *Take a tour of Beechworth in style—on board a horse-drawn stagecoach.*

Beechworth Celtic Festival
Beechworth

FRIDAY TO SUNDAY OF THIRD WEEKEND IN NOVEMBER

This beautiful town in the north-eastern part of Victoria makes a fabulous venue for a major Celtic Festival that trebles the population over the weekend. It opens with a traditional Celtic dinner, featuring music and humour, and a fire and light procession from the post office to nearby Lake Sambell. Starting on Saturday, the entertainment consists of folk music; massed pipe-and-drum marches; family activities; historical re-enactments; buskers; dramatic performances; comedy shows; highland and country dancing; plus workshops in song, dance and musical instrument making. There is also a fabulous Welsh choir, clan and genealogy groups, an ecumenical service, whisky tastings, highland athletic competitions and sheepdog displays.
Map: Vic 3 M5

Below: *The pleasant surroundings of the Pyrenees wine district is a delightful setting for their petanque weekend.*

Three Peaks Classic Car Rally

Bright and District

SATURDAY TO MONDAY OF FIRST WEEKEND IN NOVEMBER

Based in the beautiful north-eastern town of Bright, this annual rally invites owners of rare and classic sports cars to undertake a tour of the Alpine region. Between Bright and Mansfield there are some closed road stages for navigation, driving and speed tests, although there are plenty of opportunities for spectators to view the 120-plus cars. At the end of the rally, after all the cars have reached Beechworth, they are placed on display.

Map: Vic 3 N7

Above: *In Castlemaine many significant buildings were erected during its gold-rush heyday. Buda, pictured, was the home of gold- and silversmith Ernest Leviny.*

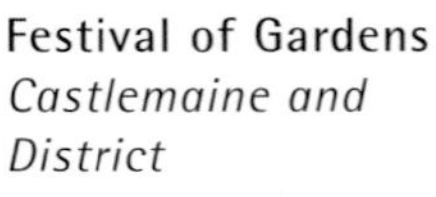

Festival of Gardens

Castlemaine and District

FIRST SATURDAY TO SECOND SUNDAY IN NOVEMBER

A biennial event (which is held in even-numbered years), this festival opens up about 50 of the most outstanding local gardens in Castlemaine and the surrounding district, which includes the towns of Maldon, Newstead, Harcourt, Sutton Grange and Chewton. All of these towns came into existence as goldmining settlements, and some of the open gardens, which vary greatly in size and style, surround houses that were built from the profits of goldmining. Events associated with the festival include the Castlemaine Agricultural Show, a street parade, an art exhibition, a guided tour of the Castlemaine Botanical Gardens, an antique fair, Devonshire teas, dinners and picnics, a flower and plant show and a gardeners' market.

Map: Vic 3 C8

Dimboola Rowing Regatta

Dimboola

THIRD SATURDAY IN NOVEMBER

This quiet and attractive wheat-belt town is situated on an especially fine stretch of the Wimmera River, close to Little Desert National Park. This riparian location gave birth to the rowing regatta back in 1884. Widely thought to be the best regional regatta in Victoria, it draws some of the state's finest rowing crews and features a full day's programme, including both the men's and women's Victorian Four-Oared Sprint Championship.

Map: Vic 2 E7

Harrietville Old-Timey and Bluegrass Weekend

Harrietville

FRIDAY TO SUNDAY OF THIRD WEEKEND IN NOVEMBER

A small town with access to the Mount Hotham ski fields in the winter as well as a number of excellent bushwalking tracks in the summer, Harrietville hosts an annual festival that, a little unusually for an Australian music festival, focuses specifically on bluegrass and old-timey music. Despite the overtly American nature of these songs and traditions, the festival will be enjoyed by those who prefer something a little more rootsy and musically skilful than the average country music concert. Each year there are usually a few players from the United States of America.

Map: Vic 4 B5

Right: *Apart from the Rowing Regatta, one of the highlights of a visit to Dimboola is a walk along the Wimmera River; you can also fish on this river year-round.*

Above: *The tasting room at Brown Brothers vineyard at Milawa. Visit the Milawa Epicurean Centre for a chance to sample food created especially to match certain wines.*

Meredith Country Festival

Meredith

LAST SUNDAY IN NOVEMBER

This tiny settlement, located on the Midland Highway, developed on the old gold route between Geelong and Ballarat. Situated amid a large dairying and agricultural district, it retains a couple of historic homes, including 'Durdidwarrah', which was built in 1842 by Charles Augustus von Steiglitz, after whom the nearby ghost town of Steiglitz is named. Meredith hosts a fine annual family festival on the town's recreation reserve featuring toe-tapping country music, fun rides in either a hot air balloon or a helicopter, local wines, wool crafts, country foods and free children's entertainment.

Map: Vic 5 N5

Brown Brothers Wine and Food Weekend

Milawa

THIRD WEEKEND IN NOVEMBER

Milawa has long been known as The Crossroads, as it is here that the Snow Road (to Mount Hotham) and Factory Road (to Wangaratta) meet. Today it is a centre for a range of craft activities, interesting food industries and vineyards—the most famous of which is Brown Brothers. Established in 1889, the oldest winery in the district hosts a gourmet food weekend in which the best dining establishments in the region supply excellent meals to complement the fine wines from the King Valley. It is the company's biggest event and one of the most popular in the region.

Map: Vic 3 L6

Sunraysia Wine and Jazz Festival

Mildura

FRIDAY TO TUESDAY OF FIRST WEEK IN NOVEMBER

Mildura has been hosting a jazz festival since 1979, although competition from the Wangaratta Festival of Jazz led the organisers to seek to differentiate themselves by introducing the wine theme in the early 1990s. This has proven to be a successful strategy that has preserved the popularity of the festival. Now jazz is played at all the local wineries, as well as in the streets, on riverboats, at the races, and in churches, hotels, clubs and restaurants. There are also Jazz Breakfasts, plus a Jazz Brunch, a Jazz Cabaret and also a Jazz Jamboree. Most, but not all, events are free.

Map: Vic 1 F4

Left: *If fine wine, delicious food and jazz played in idyllic surroundings is your idea of heaven, go to the Sunraysia Wine and Jazz Festival.*

Monbulk Jazz 'n' Blues Festival

Monbulk

THIRD FRIDAY TO FOLLOWING SUNDAY IN NOVEMBER

A small and attractive town located 47 km east of Melbourne, Monbulk is situated in rolling timbered country noted for its vegetable, fruit and tulip cultivation. The annual jazz and blues festival sees a range of styles performed at three different venues over three days. Activities cater for the whole family and include street entertainment, a billy-cart derby, a quilting exhibition, a street parade and the jazz 'n' blues church service.

Map: Vic 6 E3

Right: *Monbulk is known for its fruit cultivation as well as its Jazz 'n' Blues Festival. At nearby orchards you can pick strawberries, raspberries, cherries and more.*

Portland Three Bays Marathon

Portland

FIRST SUNDAY IN NOVEMBER

Portland is located on Portland Bay, part of the exceptionally beautiful south-west coast of Victoria. If you're feeling fit, the Three Bays Marathon offers a unique opportunity to explore the coast up close. The course heads west to Nelson Bay, through Cape Nelson State Park—with its high rugged cliffs, soap mallee and historic lighthouse—to Bridgewater Bay, which is bounded to the west by Cape Bridgewater. The latter overlooks the largest colony of Australian fur seals on the mainland. From Bridgewater Bay the event returns to Portland.

Map: Vic 5 C7

American double-bass player Curtis Lundy at the Wangaratta Festival of Jazz. The festival offers world-class performers, and also runs workshops for young musicians.

Queenscliff Music Festival

Queenscliff

FRIDAY TO SUNDAY OF LAST WEEKEND IN NOVEMBER

Popular and sophisticated, Queenscliff is a delightful seaside resort at the mouth of Port Phillip Bay. It hosts a dynamic, non-profit, award-winning, annual music festival aimed at presenting the best in original Australian contemporary music across any number of musical genres, including blues, jazz, soul, folk, Latin, acoustic, gospel, rock, rockabilly, world and dance music. There are also some special children's and youth programmes.

Around 80 artists perform in nine venues around central Queenscliff. These include famous acts and new talent. Aside from the music itself there is also plenty of enjoyable street entertainment. However, audience capacity is strictly limited and the tickets sell quickly—so book early.

Map: Vic 6 B5

Rosebud Family Festival

Rosebud

FOURTH WEEKEND IN NOVEMBER

With its pleasant foreshore and choice of three golf courses, Rosebud is a busy holiday resort and commercial centre located on the southern shore of Port Phillip, opposite Melbourne. During November Rosebud celebrates the commencement of the summer holiday season with a weekend of family fun on the foreshore at the Village Green. Activities include a grand parade, demonstrations, a fireworks display on Saturday night, a street carnival with rides, market and food stalls and free live entertainment, including bands, country music, line dancing, an animal farm and kite flying.

Map: Vic 6 C5

Wangaratta Festival of Jazz

Wangaratta

FRIDAY TO MONDAY OF FIRST WEEKEND IN NOVEMBER

This regional centre in the state's north-east hosts what is arguably Australia's most highly regarded jazz festival. The biggest event on the local calendar, it attracts artists of international stature and incorporates the National Jazz Awards, which are intended to reveal, encourage and nurture previously undiscovered new talent. Musically, a diverse range of jazz and blues is performed, and there are also jazz master-classes and public forums. The venues are quite diverse and they include Holy Trinity Cathedral, a couple of the local wineries, a golf course and even a cheese factory.

Map: Vic 3 L5

King Valley Virgin Wine, Food and Arts Festival

Whitfield

SECOND WEEKEND IN NOVEMBER

Whitfield is a quintessentially small and very picturesque country town situated in the highly scenic region of the King River Valley. Here the lush river flats are surrounded by some rather magnificent high country. Wine grapes are now the main produce of the valley, along with gourmet foods, apples and berries. This local produce is showcased during an annual festival that features food, wine and craft stalls. There is also some live musical entertainment. Associated events include an art prize, craft competitions, a children's art display and a flower show. The Sicilian flavour of the gourmet foods reflects the heritage of many of the vineyard owners.

Map: Vic 3 L7

Right: *The King Valley is one of Victoria's premium cool-climate wine areas, and 29 wine companies now operate from this region.*

Below: *Sergio Beresovsky drums in the jazz band Snag at the Wangaratta Festival of Jazz. Wangaratta (population 16 000) is in close proximity to the wine country, where some of the jazz events are held.*

Tasmania

HOBART

Early November is time for the Hobart Horticultural Society Rose, Iris and Floral Art Show at the town hall. Besides the main floral features, there are plenty of other flowers, along with fruit, vegetables, pot plants and other displays. Entry is free. Every second year, in odd-numbered years, the City Hall plays host to the Spirit of Gondwana, displaying the evolution of Australian native plants. Also included is floral art and craft and book sales. The Hobart Christmas Pageant is a parade of floats, costumed participants and marching bands that passes through the city.

Map: Tas 3 K6

Right: Iris sibirica *'Tropic Night'. As well as the displays, there are dahlia tubers, iris rhizomes and chrysanthemums for sale at Hobart's annual rose and iris show.*

Tasmanian Craft Fair at Deloraine

This enormously popular craft fair (see the main entry in October) concludes in November.

Map: Tas 1 N7

Pearn's Steam World Festival

Westbury

SATURDAY TO MONDAY OF FIRST WEEKEND IN NOVEMBER

Lovely beyond belief, Westbury is the most English of all villages in Australia, with all the charm the notion implies. There is a village green, tree-lined avenues, elegant old inns and courtyards, rustic stables and a bevy of beautiful old buildings. The antique air is underscored by Pearn's Steam World, which is said to have the largest collection of steam engines in Australia, ranging from trains to complex pieces of agricultural

Below: *Leisure Day in the Park focuses attention on Adelaide's beautiful parklands, an integral part of Colonel Light's original plan of the city.*

equipment. Each year it hosts a festival featuring working displays, free rides on trains and larger steam engines, together with family entertainment.
Map: Tas 1 N7

South Australia

ADELAIDE

The International Rose Festival concludes in November (see the main entry in October). But more entertainment is on offer. The Adelaide International Horse Trials are the only equestrian event in the Southern Hemisphere to attain a top ranking on the international equestrian calendar. Held in Adelaide's parklands, this three-day event features some of the world's best in dressage, showjumping and cross-country. The City of Adelaide Carnival Sprint Regatta and Leisure Day in the Park are annual events that have been combined to form a two-day free family event. The former features competition and novelty boat races and other water-based events on Torrens Lake, while the latter incorporates a vast array of family activities and entertainment involving over 150 organisations at the parklands adjacent to the lake. The French Festival entails three days of French food, wine, fashion, education, travel and entertainment in the grounds of the historic Carrick Hills mansion.
Map: SA 4 J3

Clare Valley Spring Garden Festival
Clare Valley

FIRST WEEKEND IN NOVEMBER

The Clare Valley is known for its rich vineyards. The annual festival combines a program of open gardens with new release rieslings and superb roses. The open gardens scheme showcases some of the region's best gardens, and is accompanied by music and regional provender. The Spring Affaire, at the historic mansion known as Martindale Hall, offers live musical entertainment, wine tastings, gourmet food, craft stalls and floral displays. Music, food and art also feature at local wineries. Guided heritage walks are conducted around some of the smaller villages.
Map: SA 3 J10

Above: *The tasting room at Knappstein Wines in the Clare Valley. This family winery specialises in red and white table wines, including riesling, which are showcased in the Clare Valley Spring Garden Festival.*

Gawler Country Music Festival
Gawler

FOURTH WEEKEND IN NOVEMBER

Located 44 km north of Adelaide, and with a population of nearly 20 000, Gawler is one of South Australia's largest towns. The second country town to be established in the state, it is also a significant historic settlement. In late November it hosts an annual country music festival that includes a talent quest, an awards presentation, a cabaret, a gospel concert at the Zion Lutheran Church and the Gawler Country Music Club Show.
Map: SA 4 J2

Goolwa to Meningie Sailing Classic
Goolwa to Meningie

FOURTH SATURDAY IN NOVEMBER

This is considered the longest freshwater yacht race in the Southern Hemisphere. It starts at Goolwa, at the western end of the Murray River, and finishes at the charming holiday destination of Meningie on the eastern shore of Lake Albert, behind Coorong National Park. The race's conclusion is accompanied by celebrations and festivities at Meningie.
Map: SA 4 K4

Below: *Meningie is the end destination of the Goolwa to Meningie Sailing Classic. The Pink Lake is about 15 km from Meningie—its unusual colouring is caused by algae in the salty water.*

did you know?

Mount Gambier is the highest point of an extinct volcanic crater. At its heart are a number of lakes including Valley Lake, Browne Lake and nearby Blue Lake, which turns a deep cobalt blue in November.

Mount Gambier Brass Band Festival

Mount Gambier

FOURTH WEEKEND IN NOVEMBER

The jewel of the state's south-east, Mount Gambier is a large rural centre noted for its many attractive and historic buildings and for the stunning Blue Lake. Each year the town hosts a brass band festival, which includes street marches, participation in the Mount Gambier Christmas Parade, and performances at a range of venues, including a major outdoor public concert for the general public.

Map: SA 4 P10

Australian Speed Shearing Competition

Naracoorte

EARLY NOVEMBER

A prosperous and thriving service centre in the state's south-east, Naracoorte is home to the award-winning Sheep's Back Wool Museum that documents the Australian history of wool and sheep, particularly in the local area. This ovine tradition renders Naracoorte ideal as a host venue for the country's (and allegedly the world's) richest speed-shearing competition, which draws competitors from around Australia and New Zealand. Shearers are given a single opportunity to shear a lamb as rapidly as possible before the judges assess the quality of the endeavour. The record is in the vicinity of 18 seconds.

Map : SA 4 N8

Robe Village Fair

Robe

FOURTH WEEKEND IN NOVEMBER

One of the most attractive historic towns in South Australia, Robe combines a sophisticated and charming town centre, a dramatic, rocky, windswept coastline and a number of picturesque and very secluded beaches. In late November, the Robe foreshore becomes the venue for an enjoyable village celebration featuring seafood, quality wines, live musical performances and a fireworks display. There is also a film festival, art, craft and photography exhibitions, a petanque competition and a golf tournament.

Map: SA 4 M8

Below: *The Victorian mansion Straun House in Naracoorte, the service centre for the surrounding fat lamb and wool-producing area.*

Western Australia

PERTH

The Telstra Rally Australia (see the main entry in October) concludes in November. However, the Perth International Golf Tournament ensures a continuation of the major sporting events. Held at Lake Karrinyup Country Club, 15 km from Perth, it is part of the Australasian PGA tour and attracts golfers on the international circuit. As a sign of its significance it is televised nationally and internationally. A very different kind of event is the Awesome Festival, an arts festival for young people, incorporating visual arts, theatre, music, dance, street theatre, literature and film at the Art Gallery of Western Australia, the Western Australian Museum, the State Library, the Perth Cultural Centre and other venues.

Map: WA 6 C4

Family fun at the Busselton Agricultural Show. Sideshow alley and fireworks offer entertainment for all ages, and there are also exhibitions of cattle, sheep, goats, poultry and farm produce as well as arts and crafts.

Jalbrook Balingup Classic Concert
Balingup

LAST SATURDAY IN NOVEMBER

Jalbrook is a 4-hectare alpaca farm with excellent accommodation adjacent to the Bibbulmun Walking Track. Each year it holds an outdoor light classical concert featuring noted Australian artists. In the past these have included Tommy Tycho, Marina Prior and Marcia Hines. The amphitheatre is a natural bush setting with quite an outstanding backdrop. Hampers can be ordered in advance and quality wines, beer and soft drinks are available.

Map: WA 6 C7

Blues at Bridgetown
Bridgetown

FRIDAY TO SUNDAY OF SECOND WEEKEND IN NOVEMBER

A picturesque settlement nestled amid timbered hills on the banks of the Blackwood River, Bridgetown is a perfect spot for this three-day festival of blues music. Numerous venues are provided to ensure a smorgasbord of music, which includes a wide range of blues artists, Australian and international, established and novice. Over 15 000 fans attend what is essentially a huge street party, as much of the action occurs in the main street.

Map: WA 6 C8

Left: *Blues at Bridgetown features many free performances in parks, clubs, restaurants and campgrounds, as well as ticketed events presenting some of the world's best blues performers.*

Busselton Agricultural Show
Busselton

FRIDAY AND SATURDAY OF FIRST WEEKEND IN NOVEMBER

The Agricultural Show is a reminder that, although Busselton is a coastal holiday destination, it has long been in existence as a service centre for the rural hinterland. This is especially apparent when one considers that the annual agricultural show has been held for over 140 years. Held in Churchill Park, the whole affair gets under way with ring events and sheepdog trials on Friday morning. The family entertainment starts on Friday afternoon at sideshow alley. The pavilions exhibit arts, crafts, cookery, produce, wool, woodwork and metalwork, children's school displays and animals.

Map: WA 6 B7

don't miss

If you are an avid angler, try the coast between Dongara and Geraldton. Shore angling is among the best on the west coast and you can catch tailor, mulloway, tommy rough (herring), whiting and silver trevally.

Larry Lobster Festival and Mid-West Boat Show

Dongara

FRIDAY AND SATURDAY OF FIRST WEEKEND IN NOVEMBER

A charming and pretty fishing village and holiday resort, Dongara boasts some beautiful historic buildings and a main street adorned by some of Australia's finest stands of Moreton Bay fig trees. The main catch along this part of the coast is the Batavia Coast rock lobster, which gives its name to this fun street festival. There is a boat expo; a variety of live performers in the fields of comedy, music and circus-style skills; an art exhibition; interesting displays; lots of market stalls; a family concert; fireworks; and a variety of activities for young children, including balloon modelling, novelty events, puppetry, face-painting, pantomimes, rides and creative workshops.

Map: WA 5 D8

Fremantle Festival

Fremantle

THIRD FRIDAY TO FOURTH SUNDAY IN NOVEMBER

The major event for this historic port, the Fremantle Festival is fundamentally a grassroots community event that is held over 10 days. It attracts around 120 000 people to what is essentially a very vibrant street festival, with music, drama, acrobatics, sport, comedy, visual arts, Latin dance, craft fairs and exhibitions. A small number of national and international performers are asked to participate each year, and most events are free to the public.

Map: WA 6 C4

Sunday Times Margaret River Wine Region Festival

Margaret River and District

SECOND FRIDAY TO THIRD SUNDAY IN NOVEMBER

The Margaret River region is noted for the vineyards that lie between Busselton and Augusta. In November the wineries

Below: *The Fremantle Festival reflects the city's multicultural community and showcases the local theatre, many innovative artists and café culture.*

host a collective celebration of local wines, foods and entertainment. There are informative wine masterclasses and other educational events; displays at the region's many art, craft and photography galleries; craft demonstrations; a film festival in the town of Margaret River; banquets; local carnivals; the Margaret River District Show; markets; and fairs all over the region. The Hogshead Handicap is an event in which competitors must push a hogshead (a 236-litre barrel) in a wheelbarrow or other wheeled contraption for nearly 10 km, while under fire from water bombs and other missiles.

Map: WA 6 B8

Bibbulmun Eco Team Challenge in South-West Western Australia

During the month of November, the competitors on the Bibbulmun Track (see the main entry in October) move into the finals.

Northern Territory

Alice Prize

Alice Springs

FRIDAY TO MONDAY OF FIRST WEEKEND IN NOVEMBER

First held in 1970, the Alice Prize attracts entrants from around Australia with a very substantial monetary reward and a residency in Alice Springs. An impressive panel of judges oversees the Prize, which was originally held in a corrugated iron shed with walls covered by hessian. There is no restriction on the number of admissible works, although no artist can enter more than one work, and anyone can win in this competition without categories. Airfreight is paid for by the overseeing foundation. Opening night is a major event on the social calendar.

Map: NT 7 F5

World Solar Challenge

Darwin to Adelaide

MID-NOVEMBER

This unusual and interesting biennial event (held in odd-numbered years) attracts competitors from around the world, including those from universities, research establishments and industries. Their task is to make their way, within five days, from Darwin to Adelaide—a distance of 3000 km—using solar-powered vehicles. The concept was conceived by Danish-born adventurer, Hans Tholstrup. A related event uses solar power-assisted pedal cycles, which undertake the course in seven daily stages.

Map: NT 1 E4

Dundee Beach Gamefish Classic

Dundee Beach

SECOND SUNDAY TO FOLLOWING SATURDAY IN NOVEMBER

This small but popular coastal village on Fog Bay is a weekend holiday spot for those seeking to escape Darwin, which is 120 km away. It has proven attractive to those who enjoy reef and gamefishing and, late in the year, it hosts a gamefishing competition that is open to all comers, although only members of the Dundee Beach Anglers Club can officially claim the record. There are billfish and gamefish divisions in various line classes.

Map: NT 1 D5

Left: *The Margaret River Wine Region Festival is the showpiece of the events in this region in November. Margaret River is recognised as one of Australia's top-quality wine-producing areas.*

Below: *The Alice Prize is a national contemporary art award, and works involving any medium can be submitted. The Alice Springs Art Foundation acquires and exhibits the winning artwork.*

December

December in Australia is time for Christmas; it is the start of the year's major school holiday break and, in a suitably circular fashion, we return to our starting point: the celebrations associated with the transition to the New Year. As December marks the start of summer in Australia, the weather is ideal for outdoor events: parties, picnics, barbecues, trips to the beach, or public events such as carol nights, fireworks displays and concerts.

Christmas Day (25 December) and Boxing Day (26 December) are both public holidays in Australia. The essentially English tradition of Boxing Day is only celebrated in countries that were once part of the British Commonwealth. On this day churches would open their collection boxes for the poor, while merchants and lords, as a sign of gratitude, filled boxes with fruit and other goods for social inferiors who had served them throughout the year. Some people continue to see the day as an opportunity for social benevolence, although most simply take it in gratitude as a day of leisure.

Above: *In some streets in our towns and cities, Christmas decorations and lighting displays have become such a tradition that people come from kilometres around to see them.*

Christmas (or 'Christ's Mass') is a celebration of the birth of Jesus Christ. No positive date can be assigned for Christ's birth, and it is thought that the early Christian church fixed on 25 December because it was already the occasion of a celebratory pagan feast. This is just one example of how celebrations and symbolic acts associated with pagan festivals (many to do with the winter solstice) have merged into Christian Christmas traditions. These include the decorating of evergreen trees, carolling, holly wreaths, mistletoe and the notion of beneficent patron saints from the icy north descending from the sky and distributing rewards and punishments. Most such wintry associations have little relevance to Australian conditions, but the European roots hold fast and perspiring Santa Clauses still appear in shopping malls and at Christmas parties.

Below: *Rowers waiting for their event to start. Rowing competitions are a popular event in surf-lifesaving carnivals, which are an important part of the summer beach holiday scene.*

Left: *The 24-m tall Christmas tree in Martin Place, Sydney, holds about 19 500 lights over a length of 6.5 km. If laid out straight, they could stretch from Bondi Beach to Martin Place!*

The beach at Surfer's Paradise. Christmas and New Year is a busy time on the Gold Coast, with holiday-makers visiting from all over Australia. The New Year's Eve festivities at Southport are a popular attraction.

Queensland

BRISBANE

A Christmas Lighting and Lantern Display adorns the 16-hectare Parklands site at South Bank throughout December, while the Night the River Sings is held at South Bank's Clem Jones Promenade on the second Sunday in December. This event features a beautiful parade of boats, which are adorned with imaginative lighting displays. The pageant is accompanied by fireworks and broadcast music, and it is possible to book a meal on one of the boats. South Bank's Parklands are also the venue for live performances and fireworks from 18 December to Christmas Eve and for the city's main New Year's Eve celebrations, which feature live music, a lot of dancing and hourly fireworks capped off by the major display at midnight.

Map: Qld 7 N7

Cathedral Cave is the largest cave in the system at Olsen's Capricorn Caves. Weddings, concerts and the annual 'Carols in the Cave' are held in this cave.

New Year's Eve Family Festival

Broadbeach and Southport

NEW YEAR'S EVE

Throughout Australia there are both Christmas carol-singing nights and New Year's Eve fireworks and entertainment evenings. The Gold Coast is no exception. A carols night is held at Broadbeach on the second Saturday in December, while people from around the entire Gold Coast area gather at Southport on New Year's Eve for an evening of free entertainment with music, food and fireworks.

Map: Qld 7 N8

Schoolies Week at the Gold Coast/Sunshine Coast

By mid-December the 'schoolies' (see the main entry in November) have generally had enough and, it is time to go home.

Map: Qld 7 N8

Summer Solstice Light and Sound Spectacle, and Carols in the Caves

Olsen's Capricorn Caves, near Rockhampton

START OF DECEMBER TO MID-JANUARY

Located 23 km north of Rockhampton, the caves, formed from an ancient coral reef, were opened to the public in 1884. For about six weeks in the year, a hole in the cave roof allows a beam of light in at midday that creates a dazzling light show of reflected colours. On the second Sunday in December the Cathedral Cavern is the venue for a traditional carol-singing event.

Map: Qld 5 J8

Rocky New Year Bash and Ball

Rockhampton

NEW YEAR'S EVE TO 3 JANUARY

Callaghan Park Racecourse is the venue for a black-tie ball on New Year's Eve. It kicks off a four-day event that incorporates a picnic race day, a rodeo, a beach party, live bands and a recovery day at offshore Great Keppel Island.

Map: Qld 5 J8

Woodford Folk Festival

Woodford

27 DECEMBER TO NEW YEAR'S DAY

This is surely the biggest folk festival in Australia. Over six days 85 000 people come to watch about 400 separate acts, from a vast array of cultural and musical backgrounds, perform at 20 different venues. The festival includes street theatre, an Aboriginal programme, a children's festival, films, and dance. Stallholders sell a diverse range of foods and crafts, with an emphasis on the alternative. The highlight and finale is the extraordinary Closing Ceremony, featuring a cast of a thousand.

Map: Qld 7 M6

New South Wales

SYDNEY

December is a time for carnivals and celebrations. At The Rocks there are wandering carollers and festivities throughout the month, while the Domain is the venue for both Homebake (a celebration of Australian rock music) and Carols in the Domain. The latter is a gigantic, outdoor, candle-lit carol service attended by about 100 000 people on the Sunday before Christmas. On Christmas Eve, Cockle Bay at Darling Harbour hosts Carols on the Bay, performed by the Sydney Concert Orchestra and Chamber Choir with special guests. Boxing Day sees the start of the Sydney to Hobart Yacht Race. Huge crowds turn out for the big send-off as the yachts depart for Tasmania. The real extravaganza unfolds at Sydney Harbour on New Year's Eve. At midnight all eyes turn to the Sydney Harbour Bridge, which is the launching pad for one of the biggest pyrotechnic displays seen anywhere in the world.

Map: NSW 6 J8

The Thursday Plantation East Coast Sculpture Show at Ballina

This impressive outdoor art show (see the main entry in September) continues throughout the month.

Map: NSW 4 P3

Left: *Run by the Cruising Yacht Club of Australia, the gruelling Sydney to Hobart Yacht Race is Australia's most famous ocean race and covers 630 nautical miles.*

Below: *Spectacular fireworks on Sydney Harbour and the finale featuring the Sydney Harbour Bridge are a major part of Sydney's New Year's Eve celebrations.*

Melbourne's fireworks festivities centre on the Yarra River, where barges set off their displays at midnight. Melbourne hosts over 1000 exciting events each year.

Gulgong Folk Festival
Gulgong

29 DECEMBER TO NEW YEAR'S DAY

Gulgong is a superb old goldmining town with many heritage buildings set on narrow winding streets. Each year it hosts a small but popular folk festival featuring traditional British music, blues, dance workshops for many traditions, a children's festival and a street dance.

Map: NSW 6 E4

Tuggerah Lakes Mardi Gras Festival
The Entrance

FIRST WEEKEND IN DECEMBER

This popular holiday resort and retirement centre at the mouth of Tuggerah Lake boasts a child-friendly open-air mall called The Waterfront where pelicans are fed every day at 3.30 p.m. The attractive foreshore parkland known as Memorial Park is the location of the Tuggerah Lakes Mardi Gras Festival. Established in the mid-1950s, this is a family event that welcomes the tourist season with a weekend of entertainment, starting with a parade that winds its way through Long Jetty to Memorial Park. Santa arrives before the fireworks at 9.00 p.m.

Map: NSW 6 K7

Right: *The Australian pelican* (Pelecanus conspicillatus) *can be found by the sea and in all parts of Australia where there are significant wetlands. Conditions are ideal at Tuggerah Lakes.*

don't miss

Brisbane Waters National Park and Bouddi National Park are both easily accessible from The Entrance. Commercial ecotours are available, with local guides offering wide knowledge of the flora and fauna.

National Cherry Festival at Young

This noted rural festival comes to a conclusion early in December (see the main entry in November).

Map: NSW 3 F8

Victoria

MELBOURNE

Since the late 1950s the residents of The Boulevarde in Ivanhoe have taken to adorning their houses and gardens in spectacular fashion with Christmas lights. This institution is now formally kicked off with Carols on The Boulevard on the second Friday night in December. The major carols event, however, is Carols by Candlelight at the Sidney Myer Music Bowl on Christmas Eve. This fund-raiser for the Royal Victorian Institute for the Blind was established in the 1930s and features major Australian acts. It is attended by 30 000 people and is telecast throughout the nation to an audience of over 1.5 million. On the sporting front Melbourne hosts the Summer Xtreme Games at the Melbourne Docklands and the Boxing Day Test Cricket match at the Melbourne Cricket Ground, which is attended, over five days, by more than 160 000 fans. General New Year's Eve festivities in Melbourne centre on the Yarra River, while the gay and lesbian community come together at the Prince of Wales complex, St Kilda, with major DJs, performers and dancers.

Map: Vic 6 D3

Mount Avoca Mountain Bike Race
Avoca

FIRST WEEKEND IN DECEMBER

This historic former goldmining town is notable for its extraordinarily wide main

street, its heritage buildings and its wineries. Mount Avoca Vineyard, in the foothills of the Pyrenees mountains, hosts a two-day mountain bike challenge that attracts cyclists of international standing. Quality food and wine are also part of the attraction.
Map: Vic 5 L2

National Eureka Sunday
Ballarat

FIRST SUNDAY IN DECEMBER

The Eureka Rebellion is one of the most famous events in the history of colonial Australia. Ending on 3 December 1854, with an attack by military and police forces on a stockade set up by the goldminers, it manifested deep-seated grievances in a rapidly changing Australian society regarding an obligatory licensing fee, the inability to vote, the lack of political representation and the absence of land for settlement. The upshot was a commission of inquiry that initiated a greater democratisation of the government. To celebrate the anniversary of the Rebellion, Ballarat hosts a range of related events at Sovereign Hill, the Eureka Stockade Centre and the art gallery, including a dawn lantern-lit walk over the historic site.
Map: Vic 5 M4

Daylesford Highland Gathering
Daylesford

FIRST WEEKEND IN DECEMBER

A pleasant former goldmining town noted for its mineral springs, Daylesford is a resort town situated on an elevated ridge and surrounded by mountain scenery, forestry and recreation areas. It is a fine setting for the annual highland gathering that kicks off with a march along Vincent Street featuring all participating pipe-and-drum bands. The march concludes in Victoria Park, where events include musical performances, highland dancing, Scottish country dancing and highland games such as caber tossing. There are market and food stalls.
Map: Vic 3 B9

The Falls Festival
Lorne

30 DECEMBER TO NEW YEAR'S DAY

An important holiday destination on the Great Ocean Road, Lorne is a popular and fashionable seaside resort. Rearing up behind the town are the slopes of the Otway Ranges. A farm within this scenic rainforest hinterland has been the setting for an annual rock music event since 1993. A bus provides access, and there are surfing safaris and nature walks to various waterfalls.
Map: Vic 5 M8

Bottom: *Mount Avoca Vineyard, the hosts of the Mountain Bike Race. The winery was founded by John Barry; over 30 years later it remains a family-owned producer of great Victorian wine.*

Below: *The Eureka Stockade Centre is located on the site of the original Eureka Stockade and is the focus of many activities on Eureka Sunday.*

Above: *Pretty lavender* (Lavandula angustifolia). *Yuulong Lavender Estate holds the National Collection of Lavenders for the Melbourne Royal Botanic Gardens, making its collection the best in Australia.*

Top: *The Murray Downs homestead and property, located 2 km east of Swan Hill, was established in the 1840s. Swan Hill is the finishing point for the Murray Marathon.*

Yuulong Music and Farming Festival

Mount Egerton

SECOND SUNDAY IN DECEMBER

Located 28 km south-east of Ballarat, on a hilltop overlooking a valley, the Yuulong Lavender Estate celebrates the start of the lavender harvest with a festival incorporating jazz, highland dancing, free sampling of lavender skin-care and culinary products, wine tasting and sales (courtesy of the Mount Buninyong Winery), a gourmet sausage sizzle and special one-off events. The Estate is set in picturesque bushland and incorporates a retail nursery, a craft and tearoom complex, a large garden and, of course, spectacular contoured hills of lavender that are harvested between December and March.

Map: Vic 5 N4

Moyneyana Festival, and New Year's Eve Procession

Port Fairy

CHRISTMAS EVE TO NEW YEAR'S EVE

The holiday season draws substantial numbers of visitors to this pleasant port in south-western Victoria. Over the Christmas period it hosts a family festival incorporating fun events, sporting activities, the opening up of historic homes to the public, the firing of cannons, garden parties and other entertainment. The New Year's Eve procession is another fun family night. Anyone can enter and prizes are offered for the best-decorated floats.

Map: Vic 5 F7

Melbourne to Devonport Yacht Race

Portsea

26 DECEMBER TO 31 DECEMBER

This popular, famous, and rather exclusive, holiday resort at the tip of the Mornington Peninsula sits at the mouth of Port Phillip. The long wooden pier is popular with anglers and bathers, and it is an excellent point for viewing the start of the Melbourne to Devonport Yacht Race, which runs concurrently with the Sydney to Hobart Yacht Race (see the main entry in Sydney). The competitors make their way around Point Nepean and through the rather treacherous mouth of Port Phillip before heading across Bass Strait to Tasmania. Forming the second leg of the Rudder Cup, this is one of Australia's oldest yacht races.

Map: Vic 6 C5

Murray Marathon

Yarrawonga to Swan Hill

27 DECEMBER TO 31 DECEMBER

Covering a little over 400 km in just five days, this tough sporting event is believed to be the world's longest internationally accredited canoe race. Established in 1969, when there were only eight entrants, it is managed for charity by Red Cross Victoria. The Murray Marathon now attracts more than 1000 competitors from around the world, together with over 5000 crew members, officials and supporters, and large numbers of spectators who line the banks of one of the longest navigable rivers in the world. There are different age categories and the event is open to all canoeists aged over 17, although there is a shorter course for juniors.

Tasmania

HOBART

December witnesses the start of a major two-month celebration known as the Hobart Summer Festival, which celebrates the state's talent, creativity and wonderful produce. More than 200 000 people typically attend over 130 events, including the Festival of Southern Lights lantern parade on the slopes of Mount Wellington, the City of Hobart Art Prize, the Hobart Cup Carnival at Elwick Racecourse, the International Buskers Festival, a film festival, music, street theatre, an antique fair and outdoor concerts. These events occur in a range of venues around Hobart, including the waterfront, and parks and gardens. The festival kicks off after Boxing Day with Taste of Tasmania, a showcase and celebration of the state's best gourmet food and beverages at Sullivans Cove, accompanied by fine entertainment. This coincides with the arrival, at Constitution Dock, of the fleet completing the gruelling and dangerous Sydney to Hobart Yacht Race.

Map: Tas 3 K6

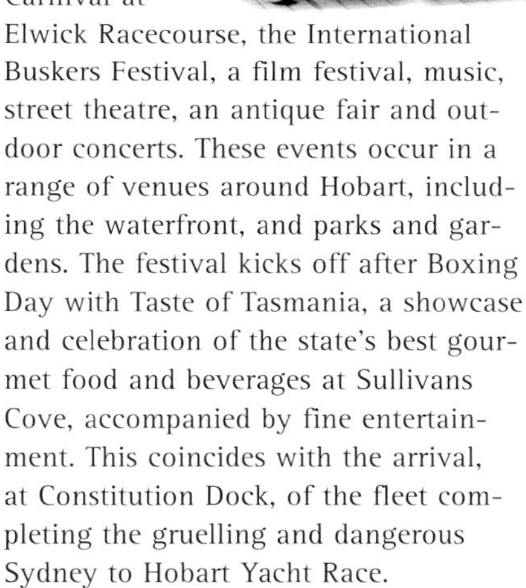

Left: *Theatre Alfresco are regular performers at the Hobart Summer Festival. The main event at this renowned lifestyle festival is the popular Taste of Tasmania.*

Beaconsfield Gold Festival
Beaconsfield

FIRST SUNDAY IN DECEMBER

Beaconsfield is a small town in the heart of a rich apple-growing district, located 39 km north-west of Launceston. Alluvial gold was found in the area in 1869 and, by 1881, Beaconsfield was known as the richest gold town in Tasmania. At its peak there were 53 companies working the local goldfields. In recent years a major goldmining operation has recommenced, and so the town has adopted the precious metal as the motif for an annual celebration that revisits the gold-rush era with period costumes, a colourful street parade, street theatre, 'goldmining' for children, carnival rides and other family entertainment.

Map: Tas 1 N5

The Bushranger Festival
Sorell

FIRST SUNDAY IN DECEMBER

Ironically William Sorell, who gained renown for suppressing bushranging in Tasmania, gave his name to a town that was subsequently held up by the bushranger Matthew Brady. Brady's gang caught local soldiers unawares and placed them in the lock-up and freed the prisoners. Sorell celebrates with a period festival featuring a grand parade, music, art, dancing and food.

Map: Tas 3 L5

Below: *Constitution Dock adds a maritime air to Hobart's Summer Festival. The Sydney to Hobart Yacht Race finishes here, allowing an intimate look at the some of the world's best ocean-racing yachts.*

South Australia

ADELAIDE

The first Saturday in December is the occasion of the Credit Union Christmas Pageant, which is one of the biggest Christmas pageants in the Southern Hemisphere. It features costumed characters and decorative fairytale floats that pass through the inner city streets. Carols by Candlelight is held on the third Sunday of the month at Elder Park with recognised acts and fireworks, while the Christmas Twilight Meeting at Victoria Park Racecourse is one of the most popular events on the horseracing calendar. Between Boxing Day and New Year's Eve Glenelg hosts the Bay Sports Festival, which is the second-largest sports festival in Australia. On 28 December 1836, the government of the province of South Australia was inaugurated, and Proclamation Day is celebrated annually in South Australia although, to avoid an additional public holiday, the authorities have simply renamed Boxing Day Proclamation Day. Celebrations involve a major day of entertainment on the banks of the Torrens River. New Year's Eve sees the AAPT Tennis Championships get under way, while general New Year's celebrations take place at Moseley Square and the Glenelg foreshore with party festivities, live music and fireworks.

Map: SA 4 J3

If you are visiting Lobethal, don't miss the many historic buildings, including the Lobethal Woollen Mill. The mill is now the Lobethal Costume Museum and displays many interesting items dating from 1812.

Lights of Lobethal

Lobethal

SECOND SUNDAY IN DECEMBER TO 31 DECEMBER

Located 33 km from Adelaide, this pleasant village in the Adelaide Hills was settled in the late 1830s by German Lutherans. Since around 1950 a tradition has emerged of collectively adorning homes, gardens and streets with a spectacular display of Christmas lights. The official Lighting Up Ceremony, complete with fireworks, takes place on the second Sunday in December, following a carols service at the Lutheran Church. From then until Christmas there are a number of events including markets and street stalls, the Christmas Tree Festival, the Living Nativity display and a Christmas pageant on 23 December. The lights stay on until 31 December.

Map: SA 4 K3

The beach at Glenelg. Held between Boxing Day and New Year's Eve, the Bay Sports Festival was held for the first time in 1886. It now offers something for everyone, including a beach fun run and beach volleyball.

Western Australia

PERTH

Perth's RAC Christmas Pageant attracts crowds of 300 000 to the city for one of the country's biggest Christmas events, featuring floats, street theatre, entertainment and Santa Claus. On the sporting side there is plenty to see and do with the annual Rottnest Swim Thru, held at Army Jetty Beach, and two venerable horseracing events at Ascot Racecourse. The Western Australian Turf Club Derby, established in 1890, is held on Boxing Day. It attracts a quality field of three-year-olds. The Railway Stakes, established in 1887, are run on 28 December. The Hopman Cup, which draws some of the world's finest tennis players, is another major sporting event.

Map: WA 6 C4

East Fremantle Festival

Fremantle

FIRST OR SECOND SUNDAY IN DECEMBER

A major one-day community celebration, the East Fremantle Festival unfolds in George Street with four performance and activity areas, a plethora of craft stalls, street theatre and artists, camel rides and children's play facilities. There are also rides, a food and drink area at the Sewell Street intersection, novelty competitions such as the waiters' race, activities such as wheelie-bin painting, and games and prizes.

Map: WA 6 C4

Broome Mango Festival

Broome

22 DECEMBER TO 24 DECEMBER

Located 2200 km north of Perth, Broome is a town with an unusual and remarkably cosmopolitan history, due to its past as a port and a centre of the pearling industry. In the days before World War I thousands of Japanese, Malay, Chinese, Filipino and Aboriginal divers all rubbed shoulders with Europeans in the town. This multicultural heritage is the focus of the annual Mango Festival, which features entertainment, mango tastings, a mango cocktail party and the Great Chefs of Broome Mango Cook-Off.

Map: WA 1 A9

Above: *Decorated for Christmas in Kalgoorlie. St Barbara's Festival honours the patron saint of mining with a festival that celebrates life in a mining community.*

St Barbara's Festival

Kalgoorlie

FIRST FRIDAY TO SECOND SUNDAY IN DECEMBER

Kalgoorlie is, and always was, a goldmining town. Each year the importance of the industry is saluted in a major festival that takes as its namesake St Barbara, who is patron saint of miners. The festival embraces many events, although the centrepiece is St Barbara's Street Parade, in which the town turns out to see a dazzling array of floats and a surreal-looking drive-by of gigantic mining equipment. Other events include a black-tie ball, the Concert in the Park, the Christmas Carnival complete with fireworks, sporting and novelty competitions, international food and music, a market day and Carols by Candlelight. About 20 000 participants and spectators are involved over the course of the 10 days.

Map: WA 6 M2

Left: *Named after legendary Australian Davis Cup player and coach Harry Hopman, the Hopman Cup showcases top international tennis talents, including Australia's own Lleyton Hewitt.*

Northern Territory

DARWIN

Darwin celebrates the prospect of the New Year at the Wharf Precinct with live entertainment, a major fireworks display and open-air dining under the stars. This is considered a family event.

Map: NT 1 E4

did you know?

The Fremantle Arts Centre is home to one of the state's most dynamic arts organisations, and offers contemporary exhibitions and workshops. Built by convicts in the 1860s, it originally served as the local asylum.

Map 1

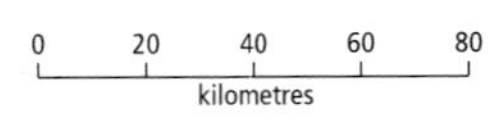
0
20
40
60
80
kilometres

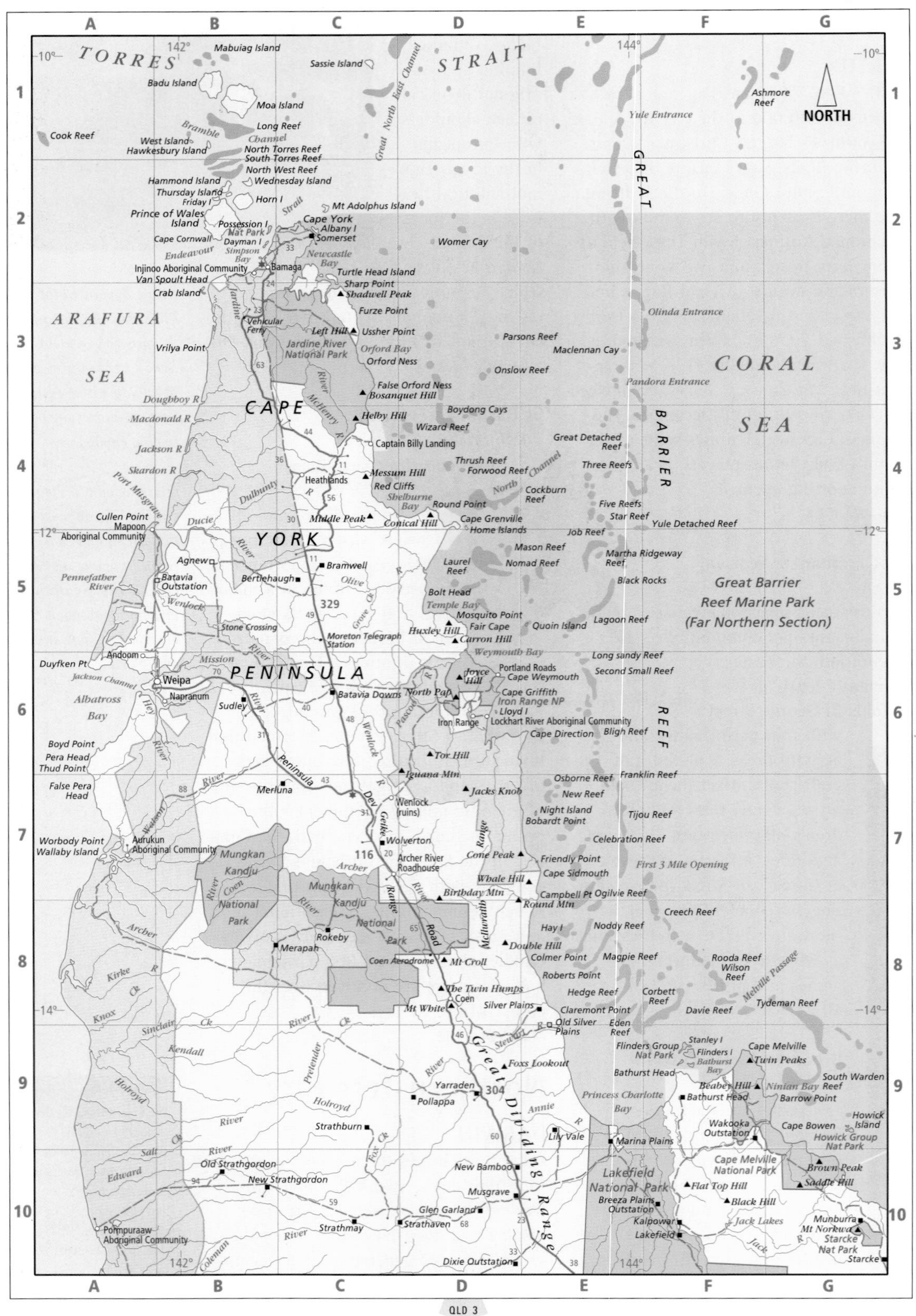
A
B
C
D
E
F
G
1
2
3
4
5
6
7
8
9
10
10°
12°
14°
142°
144°
NORTH
TORRES
STRAIT
ARAFURA
SEA
CORAL
SEA
GREAT
BARRIER
REEF
CAPE
YORK
PENINSULA
Great Barrier
Reef Marine Park
(Far Northern Section)
Mabuiag Island
Sassie Island
Great North East Channel
Badu Island
Moa Island
Bramble
Channel
Long Reef
Cook Reef
West Island
Hawkesbury Island
North Torres Reef
South Torres Reef
North West Reef
Hammond Island
Wednesday Island
Thursday Island
Friday I
Horn I
Prince of Wales
Island
Possession I
Nat Park
Mt Adolphus Island
Cape York
Albany I
Somerset
Cape Cornwall
Dayman I
Simpson
Bay
Endeavour
Strait
Newcastle
Bay
Womer Cay
Injinoo Aboriginal Community
Bamaga
Van Spoult Head
Turtle Head Island
Sharp Point
Shadwell Peak
Crab Island
Jardine
Furze Point
Vehicular
Ferry
Left Hill
Ussher Point
Jardine River
National Park
Orford Bay
Orford Ness
Parsons Reef
Maclennan Cay
Olinda Entrance
Vrilya Point
Onslow Reef
Pandora Entrance
False Orford Ness
Bosanquet Hill
McHenry
River
Doughboy R
Macdonald R
Helby Hill
Boydong Cays
Wizard Reef
Captain Billy Landing
Great Detached
Reef
Jackson R
Skardon R
Thrush Reef
Forwood Reef
Three Reefs
Port Musgrave
Heathlands
Messum Hill
Red Cliffs
Shelburne
Bay
North
Channel
Cockburn
Reef
Dulbunty
R
Round Point
Five Reefs
Star Reef
Cullen Point
Mapoon
Aboriginal Community
Ducie
Middle Peak
Conical Hill
Cape Grenville
Home Islands
Yule Detached Reef
Job Reef
Mason Reef
Martha Ridgeway
Reef
River
Agnew
Bramwell
Laurel
Reef
Nomad Reef
Pennefather
River
Batavia
Outstation
Bertiehaugh
Olive
Black Rocks
Bolt Head
Temple Bay
Wenlock
329
Grove Ck
Mosquito Point
Fair Cape
Huxley Hill
Carron Hill
Quoin Island
Lagoon Reef
Stone Crossing
Moreton Telegraph
Station
Weymouth Bay
Long sandy Reef
Andoom
Mission
River
Duyfken Pt
Jackson Channel
Weipa
Joyce
Hill
Portland Roads
Cape Weymouth
Second Small Reef
Napranum
Batavia Downs
North Pap
Cape Griffith
Iron Range NP
Lloyd I
Albatross
Bay
Sudley
Pascoe
Iron Range
Lockhart River Aboriginal Community
Cape Direction
Bligh Reef
Hey
River
Boyd Point
Pera Head
Thud Point
Wenlock
R
Tor Hill
Peninsula
Iguana Mtn
Osborne Reef
Franklin Reef
False Pera
Head
River
Merluna
Dev
Wenlock
(ruins)
Jacks Knob
New Reef
Watson
Geikie
Night Island
Bobardt Point
Tijou Reef
Worbody Point
Wallaby Island
Aurukun
Aboriginal Community
Wolverton
Range
Celebration Reef
Mungkan
Kandju
Coen
National
Park
116
Archer River
Roadhouse
Cone Peak
Friendly Point
Cape Sidmouth
First 3 Mile Opening
Archer
Mungkan
Kandju
National
Park
River
Whale Hill
Birthday Mtn
Campbell Pt
Ogilvie Reef
Round Mtn
Creech Reef
Rokeby
Road
Range
McIlwraith
Hay I
Noddy Reef
Archer
Merapah
Double Hill
Colmer Point
Magpie Reef
Rooda Reef
Wilson
Reef
Kirke
R
Coen Aerodrome
Mt Croll
Roberts Point
Melville Passage
Hedge Reef
Corbett
Reef
The Twin Humps
Coen
Silver Plains
Tydeman Reef
Mt White
Claremont Point
Davie Reef
Knox
Ck
River
Ck
Old Silver
Plains
Eden
Reef
Sinclair
Kendall
Stewart
R
Flinders Group
Nat Park
Stanley I
Flinders I
Cape Melville
Twin Peaks
Bathurst
Bay
Pretender
River
Foxs Lookout
Bathurst Head
South Warden
Reef
Holroyd
Yarraden
304
Beabey Hill
Ninian Bay
Barrow Point
Great
Dividing
Range
Pollappa
Holroyd
Annie
R
Princess Charlotte
Bay
Bathurst Head
River
Strathburn
Wakooka
Outstation
Cape Bowen
Howick
Island
Howick Group
Nat Park
Salt
Ck
Fox Ck
Lily Vale
Marina Plains
River
Old Strathgordon
Cape Melville
National Park
Brown Peak
Saddle Hill
Edward
New Strathgordon
New Bamboo
Lakefield
National Park
Flat Top Hill
Musgrave
Breeza Plains
Outstation
Black Hill
Glen Garland
Kalpowar
Jack Lakes
Munburra
Pormpuraaw
Aboriginal Community
River
Strathmay
Strathaven
Lakefield
Jack
R
Mt Norkwa
Starcke
Nat Park
Coleman
Dixie Outstation
Starcke

Map 2

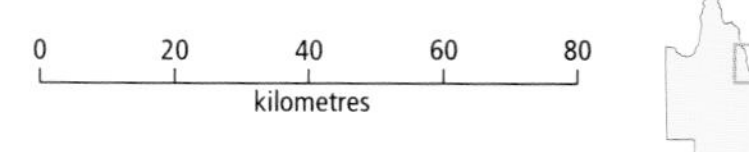
0
20
40
60
80
kilometres

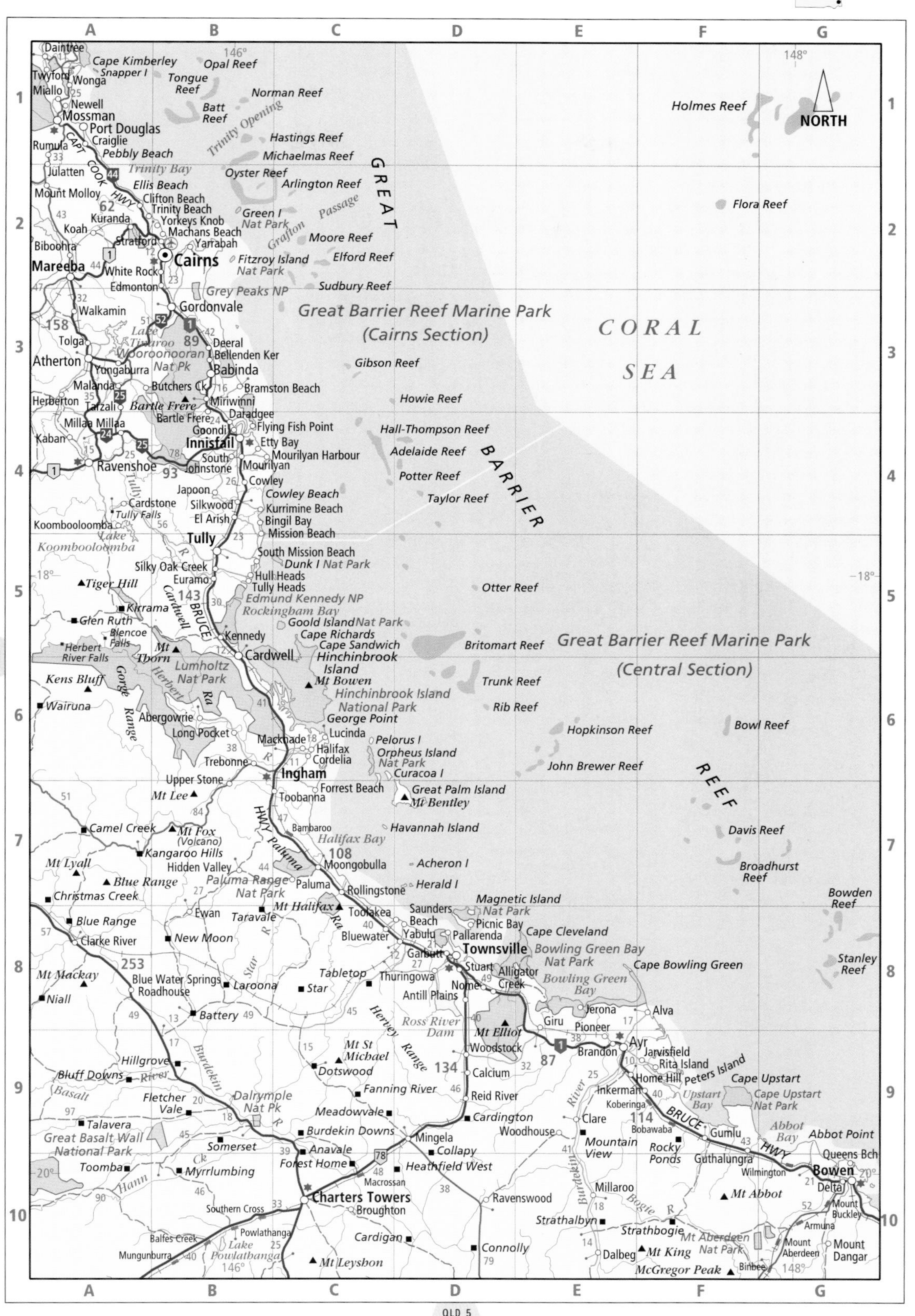
A
B
C
D
E
F
G
1
2
3
4
5
6
7
8
9
10
NORTH
QLD 3
QLD 5
CORAL
SEA
GREAT
BARRIER
REEF
Great Barrier Reef Marine Park
(Cairns Section)
Great Barrier Reef Marine Park
(Central Section)
Daintree
Cape Kimberley
Snapper I
Opal Reef
Tongue
Reef
Twyford
Wonga
Miallo
Norman Reef
Newell
Mossman
Batt
Reef
Trinity Opening
Port Douglas
Craiglie
Rumula
Hastings Reef
Pebbly Beach
Michaelmas Reef
Trinity Bay
Julatten
Oyster Reef
Ellis Beach
Arlington Reef
Mount Molloy
Clifton Beach
Trinity Beach
Green I
Nat Park
Kuranda
Yorkeys Knob
Koah
Machans Beach
Grafton Passage
Moore Reef
Biboohra
Stratford
Yarrabah
Mareeba
Cairns
Fitzroy Island
Nat Park
Elford Reef
White Rock
Edmonton
Sudbury Reef
Grey Peaks NP
Walkamin
Gordonvale
Lake Tinaroo
Tolga
Deeral
Atherton
Wooroonooran
Nat Pk
Bellenden Ker
Yungaburra
Babinda
Gibson Reef
Malanda
Butchers Ck
Bramston Beach
Herberton
Miriwinni
Howie Reef
Tarzali
Bartle Frere
Millaa Millaa
Daradgee
Goondi
Flying Fish Point
Hall-Thompson Reef
Kaban
Innisfail
Etty Bay
Mourilyan Harbour
Adelaide Reef
Ravenshoe
South Johnstone
Mourilyan
Potter Reef
Cowley
Japoon
Cowley Beach
Taylor Reef
Cardstone
Silkwood
Kurrimine Beach
Tully Falls
El Arish
Bingil Bay
Koombooloomba
Lake Koombooloomba
Mission Beach
Tully
South Mission Beach
Dunk I Nat Park
Silky Oak Creek
Euramo
Hull Heads
Tully Heads
Otter Reef
Tiger Hill
Edmund Kennedy NP
Kirrama
Rockingham Bay
Glen Ruth
Goold Island Nat Park
Blencoe Falls
Cape Richards
Herbert River Falls
Mt Thorn
Kennedy
Cape Sandwich
Britomart Reef
Cardwell
Hinchinbrook Island
Lumholtz Nat Park
Kens Bluff
Mt Bowen
Trunk Reef
Wairuna
Hinchinbrook Island National Park
Rib Reef
Abergowrie
George Point
Bowl Reef
Long Pocket
Lucinda
Hopkinson Reef
Macknade
Pelorus I
Orpheus Island Nat Park
Halifax
Trebonne
Cordelia
John Brewer Reef
Curacoa I
Upper Stone
Ingham
Forrest Beach
Great Palm Island
Mt Lee
Toobanna
Mt Bentley
Camel Creek
Mt Fox (Volcano)
Bambaroo
Havannah Island
Davis Reef
Halifax Bay
Kangaroo Hills
Mt Lyall
Hidden Valley
Moongobulla
Acheron I
Broadhurst Reef
Blue Range
Paluma Range Nat Park
Paluma
Herald I
Rollingstone
Bowden Reef
Christmas Creek
Magnetic Island Nat Park
Mt Halifax
Toolakea
Saunders Beach
Ewan
Taravale
Picnic Bay
Blue Range
Cape Cleveland
New Moon
Bluewater
Yabulu
Pallarenda
Clarke River
Townsville
Bowling Green Bay Nat Park
Stanley Reef
Garbutt
Mt Mackay
Blue Water Springs Roadhouse
Tabletop
Thuringowa
Stuart
Alligator Creek
Cape Bowling Green
Laroona
Star
Nome
Bowling Green Bay
Niall
Antill Plains
Battery
Jerona
Alva
Ross River Dam
Giru
Pioneer
Mt St Michael
Mt Elliot
Ayr
Hillgrove
Woodstock
Brandon
Jarvisfield
Rita Island
Bluff Downs
Calcium
Home Hill
Peters Island
Cape Upstart
Basalt
Dotswood
Fletcher Vale
Dalrymple Nat Pk
Fanning River
Inkerman
Upstart Bay
Cape Upstart Nat Park
Reid River
Kooberinga
Talavera
Meadowvale
Cardington
Clare
Bobawaba
Gumlu
Abbot Bay
Abbot Point
Great Basalt Wall National Park
Burdekin Downs
Woodhouse
Mingela
Mountain View
Somerset
Anavale
Collapy
Rocky Ponds
Guthalungra
Queens Bch
Toomba
Myrrlumbing
Forest Home
Heathfield West
Wilmington
Bowen
Macrossan
Millaroo
Delta
Charters Towers
Ravenswood
Mt Abbot
Southern Cross
Broughton
Mount Buckley
Strathalbyn
Armuna
Balfes Creek
Powlathanga
Strathbogie
Mt Aberdeen Nat Park
Mount Aberdeen
Mount Dangar
Mungunburra
Lake Powlathanga
Cardigan
Connolly
Dalbeg
Mt King
Mt Leysbon
McGregor Peak
Binbee
CAPT COOK HWY
BRUCE HWY
Cardwell Ra
Herbert Ra
Gorge Range
Paluma Ra
Hervey Range
Star R
Burdekin R
Burdekin River
Bogie R
Hann Ck
Tully R
Herbert R
146°
148°
18°
20°

Map 3

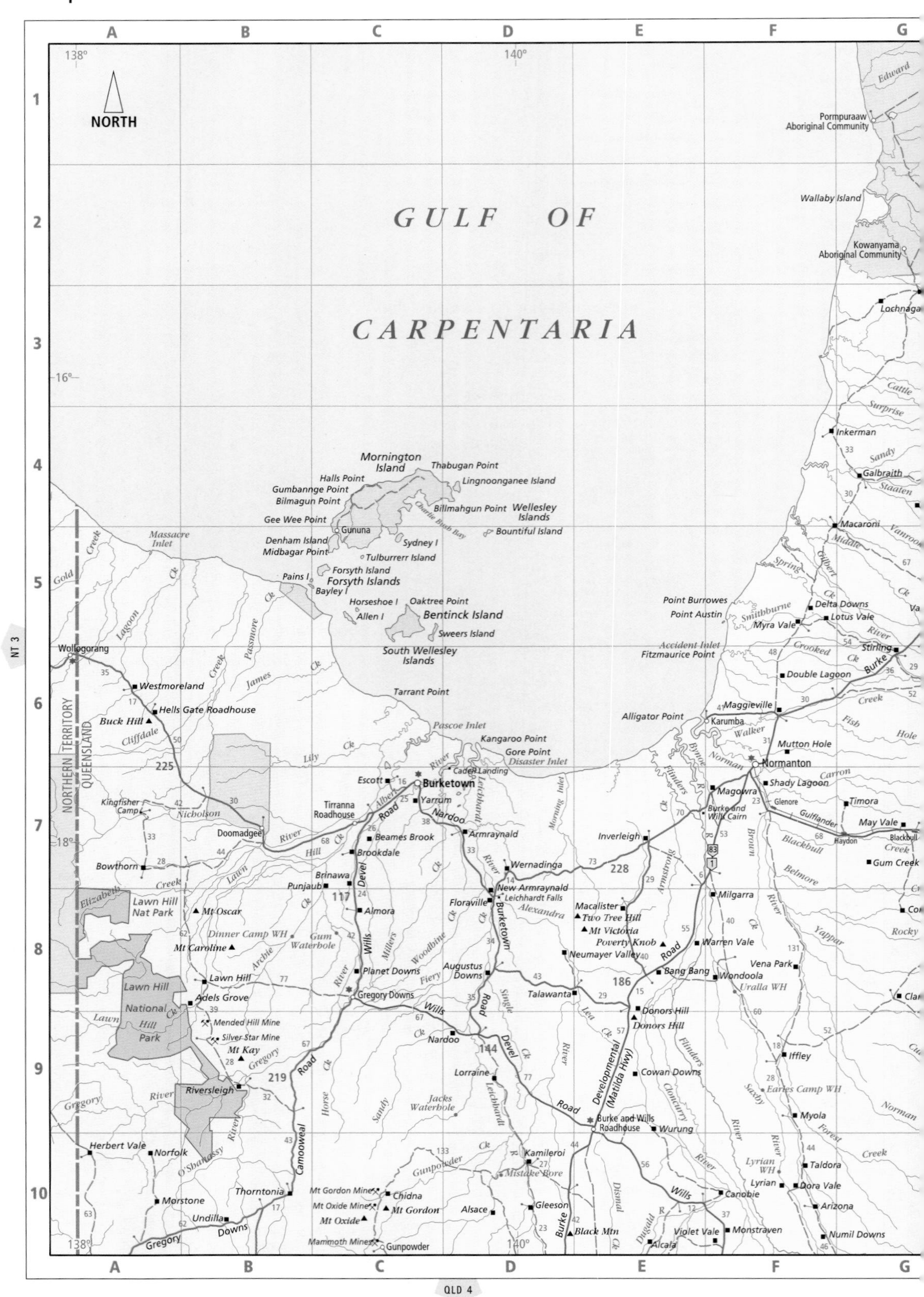

NORTH
GULF OF
CARPENTARIA
Mornington Island
Wellesley Islands
Bentinck Island
Forsyth Islands
South Wellesley Islands
Sweers Island
Burketown
Normanton
Karumba
Doomadgee
Gregory Downs
Lawn Hill National Park
Adels Grove
Riversleigh
Burke and Wills Roadhouse
Pormpuraaw Aboriginal Community
Kowanyama Aboriginal Community
NORTHERN TERRITORY
QUEENSLAND
NT 3
QLD 4

0 20 40 60 80
kilometres

QLD 1

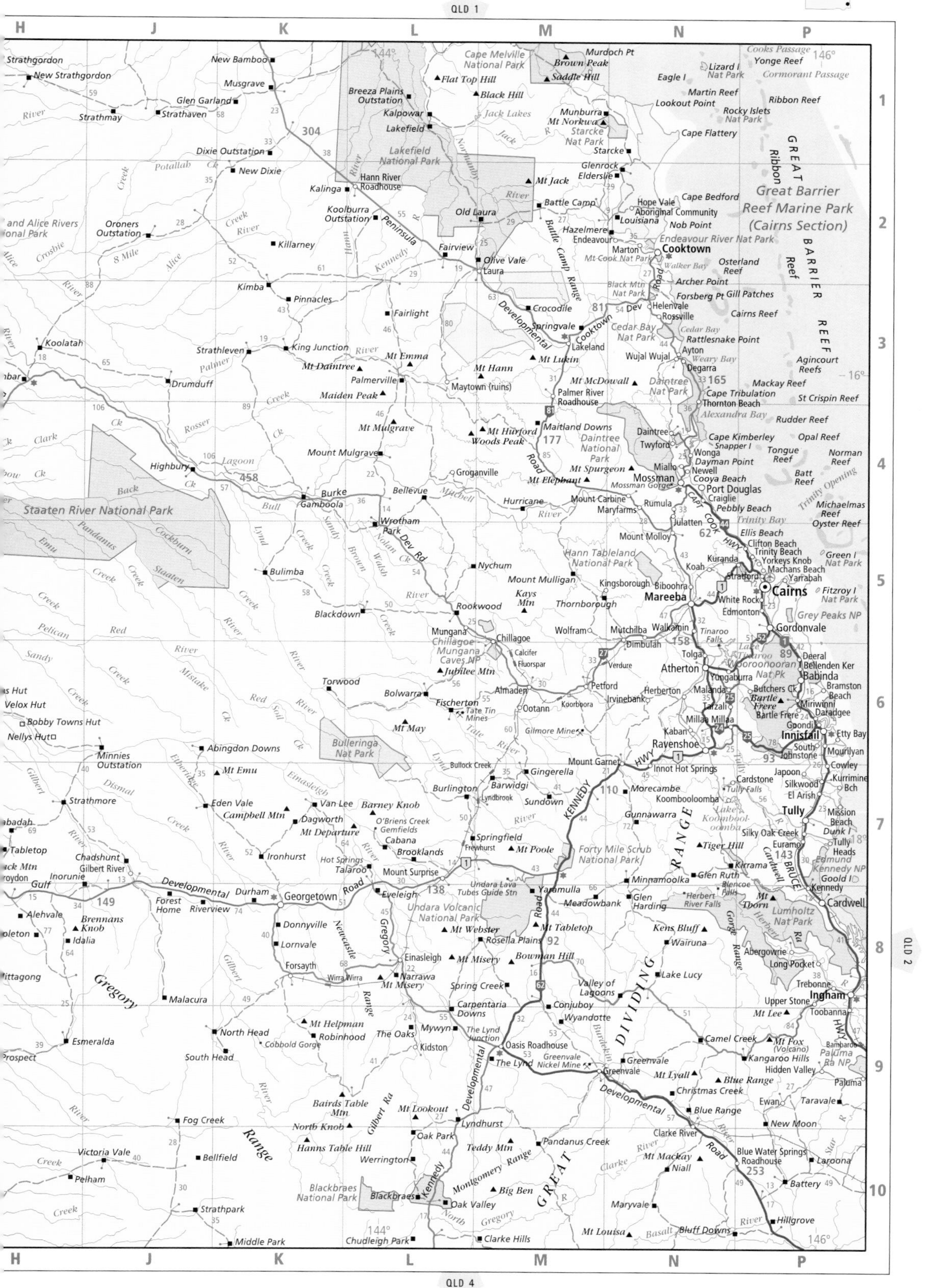

QLD 4

Map 4

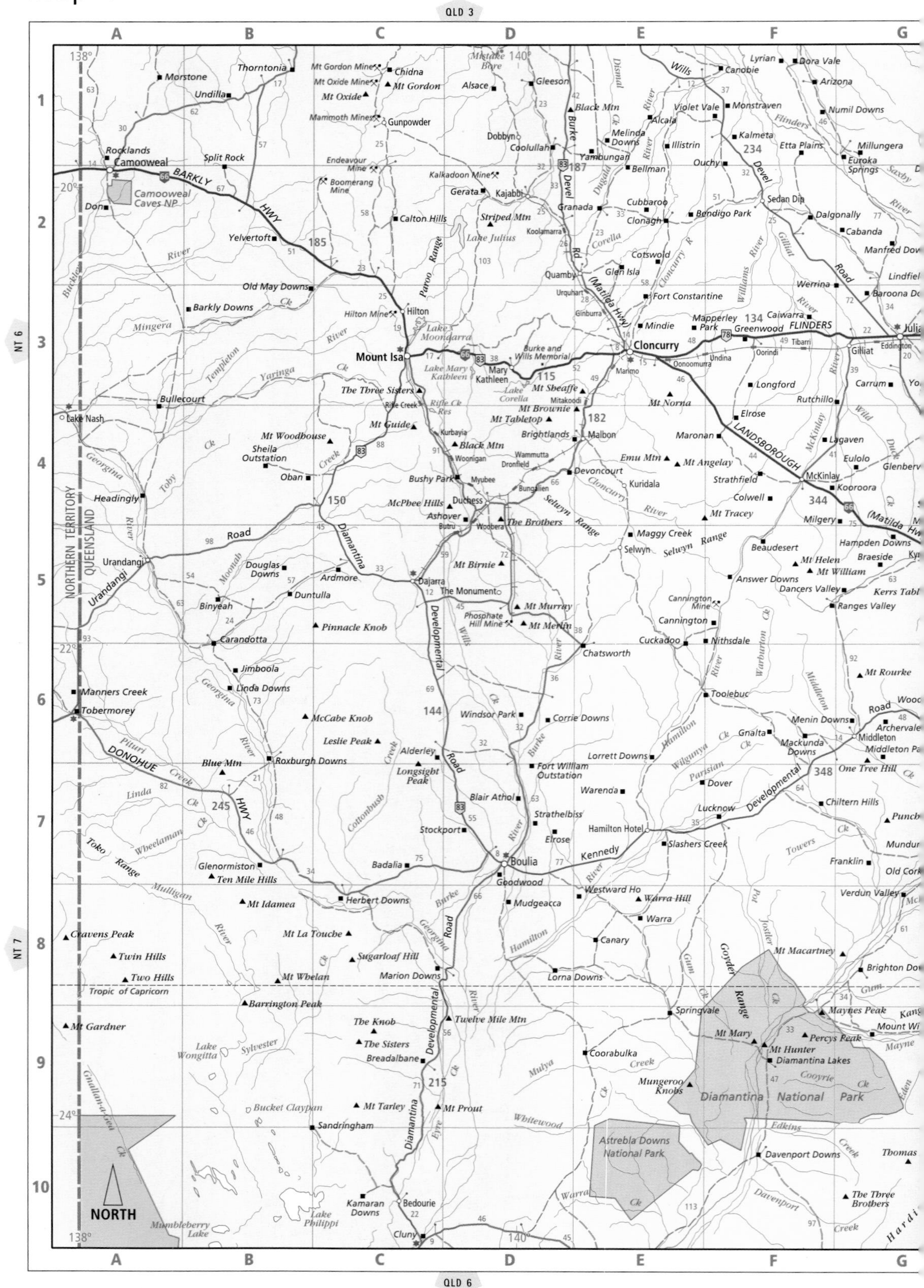
QLD 3
QLD 6
NT 6
NT 7
A
B
C
D
E
F
G
1
2
3
4
5
6
7
8
9
10
138°
140°
20°
22°
24°
Morstone
Thorntonia
Undilla
Mt Gordon Mine
Chidna
Mt Oxide Mine
Mt Gordon
Mt Oxide
Mammoth Mines
Gunpowder
Mistake Bore
Alsace
Gleeson
Black Mtn
Wills
Canobie
Lyrian
Dora Vale
Arizona
Violet Vale
Monstraven
Numil Downs
Alcala
Burke
Dismal
Flinders
Melinda Downs
Kalmeta
Dobbyn
Coolullah
Illistrin
Etta Plains
Millungera
Yambungan
Ouchy
Euroka Springs
Bellman
Rocklands
Camooweal
Split Rock
Endeavour Mine
Kalkadoon Mine
Boomerang Mine
BARKLY
HWY
Camooweal Caves NP
Don
Gerata
Kajabbi
Granada
Cubbaroo
Clonagh
Bendigo Park
Sedan Dip
Dalgonally
Cabanda
Manfred Do
Calton Hills
Striped Mtn
Koolamarra
Lake Julius
Yelvertoft
Paroo
Range
Corella
Cotswold
Glen Isla
Quamby
Urquhart
Gilliat
Lindfiel
Werrina
Baroona D
Old May Downs
Fort Constantine
Barkly Downs
Mingera
Hilton Mine
Hilton
Lake Moondarra
Ginburra
Mindie
Mapperley Park
Calwarra
Greenwood
FLINDERS
Julia
Cloncurry
Mount Isa
Burke and Wills Memorial
Tibarri
Oorindi
Eddington
Gilliat
Lake Mary Kathleen
Mary Kathleen
Undina
Oonoomurra
Marimo
Templeton
Yaringa
The Three Sisters
Mt Sheaffe
Mitakoodi
Carrum
Lake Corella
Rifle Creek
Rifle Ck Res
Mt Brownie
Mt Norna
Longford
Rutchillo
Bullecourt
Lake Nash
Mt Guide
Mt Tableltop
Elrose
LANDSBOROUGH
Kurbayia
Brightlands
Malbon
Maronan
Lagaven
Mt Woodhouse
Black Mtn
Sheila Outstation
Woonigan
Wammutta
Dronfield
Emu Mtn
Mt Angelay
Eulolo
Georgina
Toby
Oban
Bushy Park
Myubee
Devoncourt
Kuridala
Strathfield
McKinlay
Glenberv
Headingly
Bungalien
Cloncurry
Colwell
Kooroora
150
McPhee Hills
Duchess
River
Mt Tracey
344
Ashover
Selwyn
Range
Milgery
Matilda Hwy
Butru
Woobera
The Brothers
Diamantina
Maggy Creek
Beaudesert
Hampden Downs
Road
Urandangi
Douglas Downs
Selwyn
Mt Helen
Braeside
NORTHERN TERRITORY
QUEENSLAND
Mt Birnie
Mt William
Ardmore
Dajarra
Answer Downs
Dancers Valley
Kerrs Tabl
Duntulla
The Monument
Moonah
Binyeah
Phosphate Hill Mine
Mt Murray
Cannington Mine
Ranges Valley
Mt Merlin
Cannington
Pinnacle Knob
Carandotta
Chatsworth
Cuckadoo
Nithsdale
Jimboola
Mt Rourke
Manners Creek
Linda Downs
Toolebuc
Warburton
Middleton
Tobermorey
Woo
McCabe Knob
144
Windsor Park
Corrie Downs
Menin Downs
Archervale
Pituri
Leslie Peak
Gnalta
Middleton
Mackunda Downs
Middleton Pa
DONOHUE
Alderley
Lorrett Downs
Blue Mtn
Roxburgh Downs
Longsight Peak
Fort William Outstation
348
One Tree Hill
Linda
Warenda
Parsian
Dover
Cottonbush
Blair Athol
Chiltern Hills
245
HWY
Strathelbiss
Lucknow
Developmental
Punch
Stockport
Hamilton Hotel
Wheeleman
Elrose
Kennedy
Slashers Creek
Towers
Mundur
Toko
Range
Badalia
Boulia
Franklin
Old Cork
Glenormiston
Ten Mile Hills
Goodwood
Mulligan
Westward Ho
Verdun Valley
Herbert Downs
Mudgeacca
Warra Hill
Mt Idamea
Warra
Cravens Peak
Mt La Touche
Hamilton
Canary
Goyder
Mt Macartney
Twin Hills
Sugarloaf Hill
Brighton Do
Two Hills
Mt Whelan
Marion Downs
Lorna Downs
Tropic of Capricorn
Barrington Peak
Springvale
Maynes Peak
Kang
Mt Gardner
The Knob
Twelve Mile Mtn
Mount Wi
Mt Mary
Percys Peak
The Sisters
Mt Hunter
Diamantina Lakes
Mayne
Lake Wongitta
Sylvester
Breadalbane
Coorabulka
Creek
Mulya
Mungeroo Knobs
Cooyrie
Diamantina National Park
215
Bucket Claypan
Mt Tarley
Mt Prout
Whitewood
Edkins
Sandringham
Astrebla Downs National Park
Gnallan-a-gea
Davenport Downs
Thomas
Eyre
NORTH
Kamaran Downs
Bedourie
Davenport
The Three Brothers
Mumbleberry Lake
Lake Philippi
Cluny
Warra
Creek
Hardi

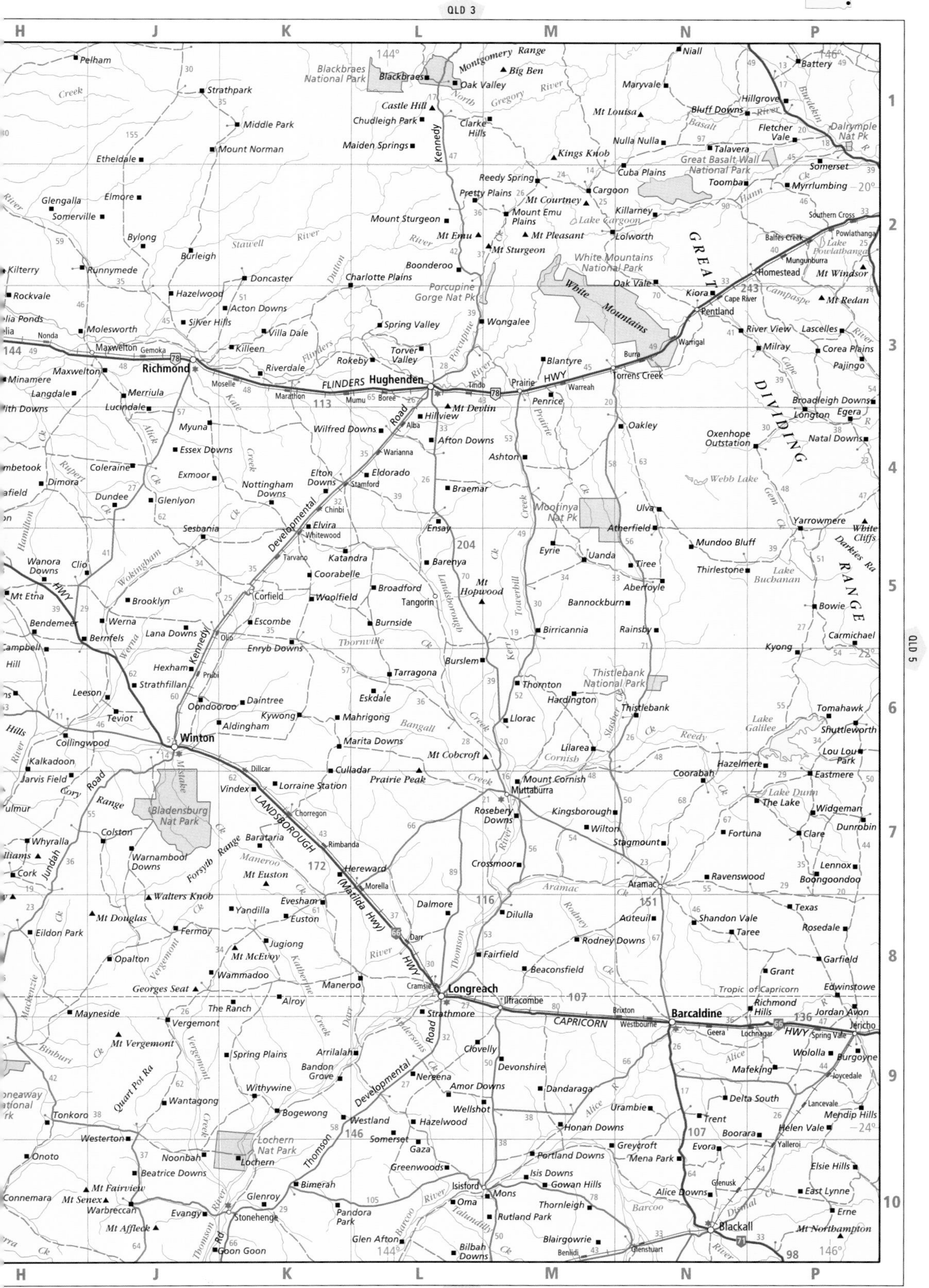
0 20 40 60 80
kilometres
QLD 3
H J K L M N P
1 2 3 4 5 6 7 8 9 10
Pelham
Strathpark
Middle Park
Mount Norman
Etheldale
Elmore
Glengalla
Somerville
Bylong
Burleigh
Kilterry
Runnymede
Doncaster
Rockvale
Hazelwood
Acton Downs
Silver Hills
Molesworth
Villa Dale
Killeen
Maxwelton
Gemoka
Nonda
Richmond
Maxwelton
Minamere
Riverdale
Moselle
Marathon
Langdale
Merriula
Lucindale
Myuna
Essex Downs
Coleraine
Exmoor
Dimora
Nottingham Downs
Dundee
Glenlyon
Sesbania
Wanora Downs
Clio
Mt Etna
Brooklyn
Corfield
Werna
Bendemeer
Bernfels
Lana Downs
Escombe
Olio
Enryb Downs
Hexham
Strathfillan
Prubi
Leeson
Teviot
Oondooroo
Daintree
Kywong
Aldingham
Collingwood
Winton
Kalkadoon
Jarvis Field
Dillcar
Vindex
Lorraine Station
Bladensburg Nat Park
Chorregon
Colston
Whyralla
Barataria
Rimbanda
Warnambool Downs
Cork
Mt Euston
Walters Knob
Yandilla
Evesham
Euston
Mt Douglas
Eildon Park
Fermoy
Jugiong
Mt McEvoy
Opalton
Wammadoo
Georges Seat
Alroy
The Ranch
Mayneside
Vergemont
Mt Vergemont
Spring Plains
Arrilalah
Bandon Grove
Withywine
Wantagong
Bogewong
Tonkoro
Westerton
Onoto
Noonbah
Lochern Nat Park
Lochern
Beatrice Downs
Mt Fairview
Connemara
Mt Senex
Warbreccan
Evangy
Mt Affleck
Stonehenge
Glenroy
Goon Goon
Blackbraes National Park
Blackbraes
Oak Valley
Montgomery Range
Big Ben
Castle Hill
Chudleigh Park
Clarke Hills
Maiden Springs
Kennedy
North Gregory River
Mount Sturgeon
Mt Emu
Mt Sturgeon
Boonderoo
Charlotte Plains
Porcupine Gorge Nat Pk
Spring Valley
Wongalee
Torver Valley
Rokeby
Hughenden
FLINDERS HWY
Mumu
Boree
Hillview
Mt Devlin
Alba
Wilfred Downs
Afton Downs
Warianna
Eldorado
Elton Downs
Stamford
Braemar
Chinbi
Elvira
Whitewood
Ensay
Tarvano
Katandra
Barenya
Coorabelle
Broadford
Woolfield
Tangorin
Mt Hopwood
Burnside
Burslem
Tarragona
Eskdale
Mahrigong
Marita Downs
Mt Cobcroft
Culladar
Prairie Peak
Hereward
Morella
(Matilda Hwy)
LANDSBOROUGH
Darr
Dalmore
Crossmoor
Dilulla
Fairfield
Beaconsfield
Maneroo
Cramsie
Longreach
Ilfracombe
Strathmore
Clovelly
Devonshire
Nereena
Amor Downs
Wellshot
Westland
Hazelwood
Somerset
Gaza
Greenwoods
Bimerah
Pandora Park
Isisford
Mons
Oma
Rutland Park
Glen Afton
Bilbah Downs
Developmental Road
Mt Courtney
Mount Emu Plains
Mt Pleasant
Reedy Spring
Pretty Plains
Kings Knob
Mt Louisa
Maryvale
Niall
Nulla Nulla
Cuba Plains
Cargoon
Lake Cargoon
Lolworth
Killarney
White Mountains National Park
Oak Vale
Blantyre
Prairie
Penrice
Warreah
Torrens Creek
Burra
Ashton
Oakley
Moorinya Nat Pk
Atherfield
Eyrie
Uanda
Tiree
Aberfoyle
Bannockburn
Birricannia
Rainsby
Thistlebank National Park
Thornton
Hardington
Thistlebank
Llorac
Lilarea
Cornish
Mount Cornish
Muttaburra
Rosebery Downs
Kingsborough
Wilton
Stagmount
Aramac
Auteuil
Rodney Downs
Dandaraga
Urambie
Honan Downs
Portland Downs
Isis Downs
Gowan Hills
Thornleigh
Blairgowrie
Benlidi
CAPRICORN HWY
Brixton
Westbourne
Greycroft
Mena Park
Alice Downs
Barcaldine
Blackall
Glenstuart
Bluff Downs
Great Basalt Wall National Park
Talavera
Toomba
Hillgrove
Fletcher Vale
Battery
Dalrymple Nat Pk
Somerset
Myrrlumbing
Southern Cross
Balfes Creek
Powlathanga
Lake Powlathanga
Mungunburra
Homestead
Mt Windsor
Kiora
Cape River
Pentland
Mt Redan
Warrigal
River View
Lascelles
Milray
Corea Plains
Pajingo
Broadleigh Downs
Longton
Egera
Oxenhope Outstation
Natal Downs
Webb Lake
Yarrowmere
White Cliffs
Mundoo Bluff
Thirlestone
Lake Buchanan
Bowie
Carmichael
Kyong
Tomahawk
Lake Galilee
Shuttleworth
Lou Lou Park
Hazelmere
Coorabah
Eastmere
Lake Dunn
The Lake
Widgeman
Fortuna
Clare
Dunrobin
Lennox
Boongoondoo
Ravenswood
Texas
Shandon Vale
Taree
Rosedale
Grant
Garfield
Tropic of Capricorn
Edwinstowe
Richmond Hills
Jordan Avon
Geera
Lochnagar
Spring Vale
Jericho
Wololla
Burgoyne
Mafeking
Joycedale
Delta South
Lancevale
Mendip Hills
Trent
Boorara
Helen Vale
Yalleroi
Evora
Elsie Hills
Glenusk
East Lynne
Erne
Mt Northampton
GREAT DIVIDING RANGE
Darkies Ra
QLD 5
QLD 6

Map 5

QLD 2

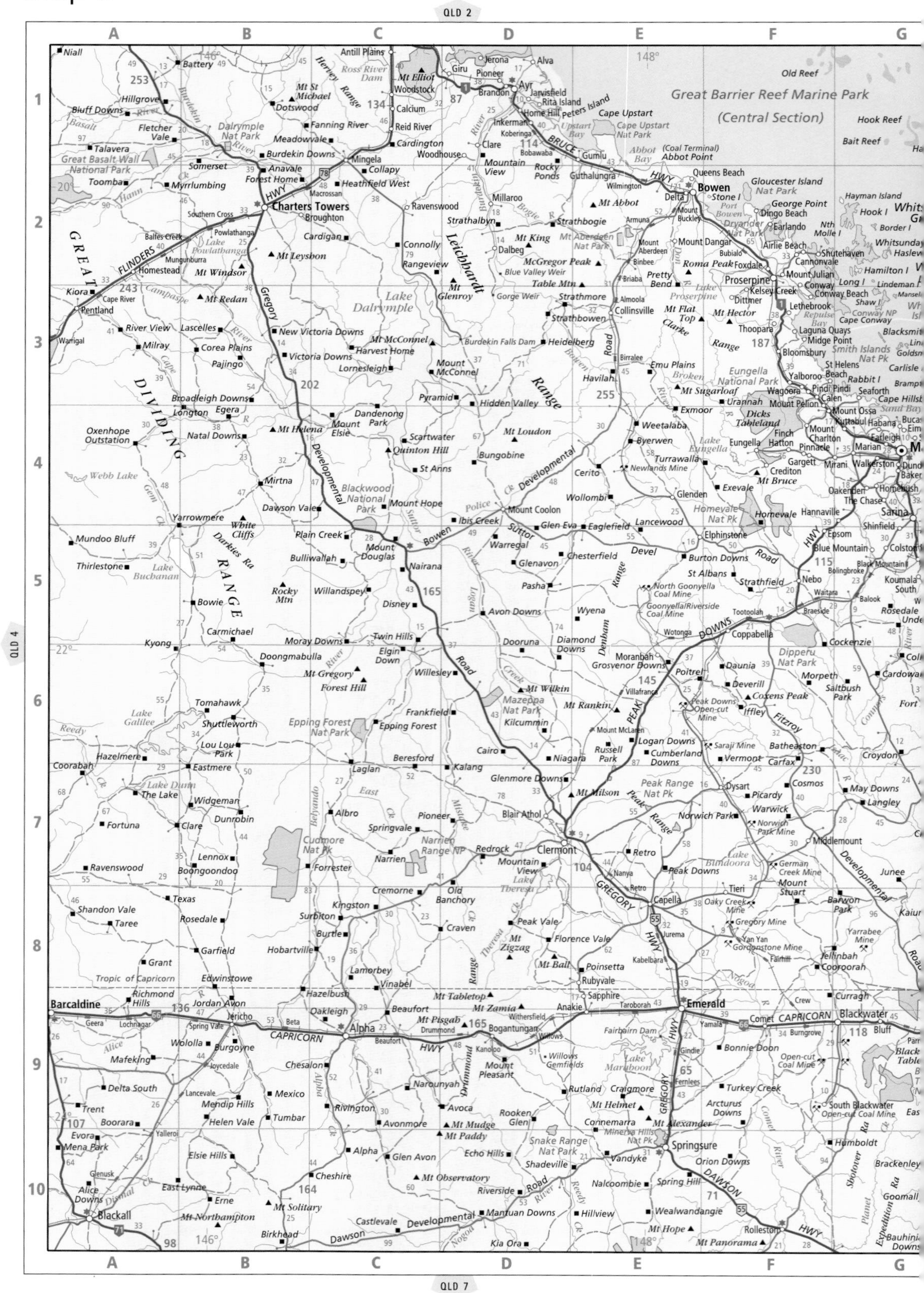

QLD 4

QLD 7

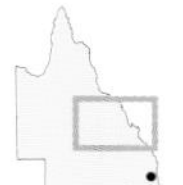

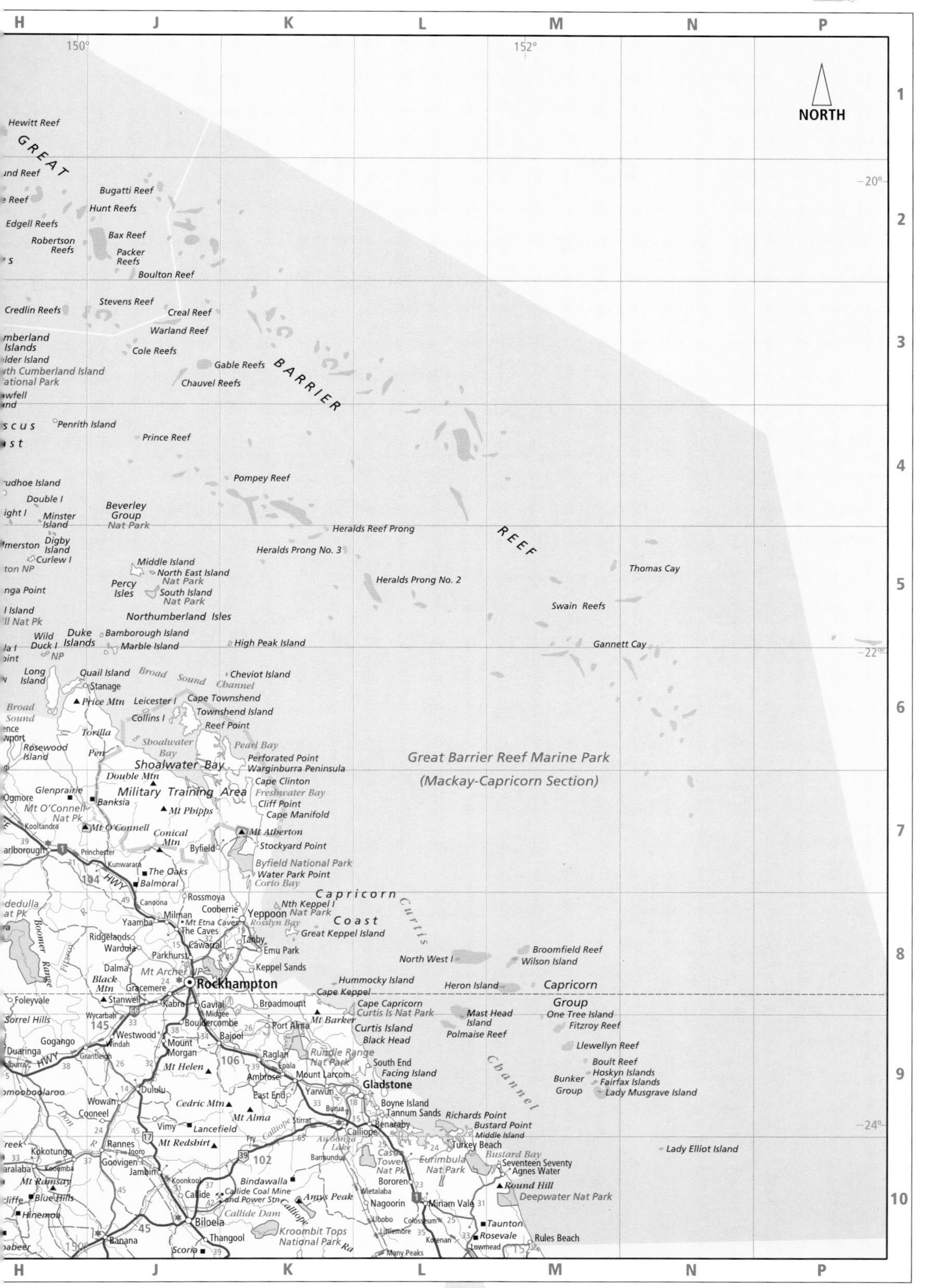

0 20 40 60 80
kilometres
NORTH
GREAT BARRIER REEF
Great Barrier Reef Marine Park
(Mackay-Capricorn Section)
Hewitt Reef
Bugatti Reef
Hunt Reefs
Edgell Reefs
Robertson Reefs
Bax Reef
Packer Reefs
Boulton Reef
Stevens Reef
Credlin Reefs
Creal Reef
Warland Reef
Cole Reefs
Gable Reefs
Chauvel Reefs
Penrith Island
Prince Reef
Pompey Reef
Beverley Group Nat Park
Heralds Reef Prong
Heralds Prong No. 3
Heralds Prong No. 2
Thomas Cay
Swain Reefs
Gannett Cay
Middle Island
North East Island Nat Park
South Island Nat Park
Percy Isles
Northumberland Isles
Bamborough Island
Marble Island
Duke Islands
High Peak Island
Cheviot Island
Broad Sound Channel
Quail Island
Stanage
Price Mtn
Leicester I
Cape Townshend
Townshend Island
Collins I
Reef Point
Shoalwater Bay
Pearl Bay
Perforated Point
Warginburra Peninsula
Cape Clinton
Freshwater Bay
Cliff Point
Cape Manifold
Military Training Area
Double Mtn
Mt Phipps
Mt Atherton
Stockyard Point
Byfield
Byfield National Park
Water Park Point
Corio Bay
Capricorn Coast
Curtis Channel
Nth Keppel I Nat Park
Yeppoon
Rosslyn Bay
Great Keppel Island
Emu Park
Keppel Sands
Broomfield Reef
Wilson Island
North West I
Heron Island
Capricorn Group
One Tree Island
Fitzroy Reef
Mast Head Island
Polmaise Reef
Llewellyn Reef
Boult Reef
Hoskyn Islands
Fairfax Islands
Bunker Group
Lady Musgrave Island
Lady Elliot Island
Hummocky Island
Cape Keppel
Cape Capricorn
Curtis Is Nat Park
Curtis Island
Black Head
Rockhampton
Gladstone
South End
Facing Island
Boyne Island
Tannum Sands
Richards Point
Bustard Point
Middle Island
Turkey Beach
Bustard Bay
Seventeen Seventy
Agnes Water
Round Hill
Deepwater Nat Park
Eurimbula Nat Park
Miriam Vale
Taunton
Rosevale
Rules Beach
Biloela
Thangool
Banana
Callide Dam
Kroombit Tops National Park
Calliope
Benaraby
Mount Larcom
Mt Alma
Mt Helen
Cedric Mtn
Mt Redshirt
Bindawalla
Callide Coal Mine and Power Stn
Amys Peak
Nagoorin
Bororen
Rundle Range Nat Park
Mt Barker
Port Alma
Raglan
Bajool
Gracemere
Mt Archer NP
Parkhurst
The Caves
Mt Etna Caves
Milman
Rossmoya
Cooberrie
Marlborough
Mt O'Connell Nat Pk
Glenprairie
Banksia
Ogmore
Rosewood Island
Conical Mtn
The Oaks
Balmoral
Westwood
Mount Morgan
Dululu
Wowan
Gogango
Duaringa
Foleyvale
Sorrel Hills
Dalma
Ridgelands
Yaamba
Kabra
Stanwell
Goovigen
Jambin
Rannes
Kokotungo
Lancefield
Vimy
Scoria

Map 6

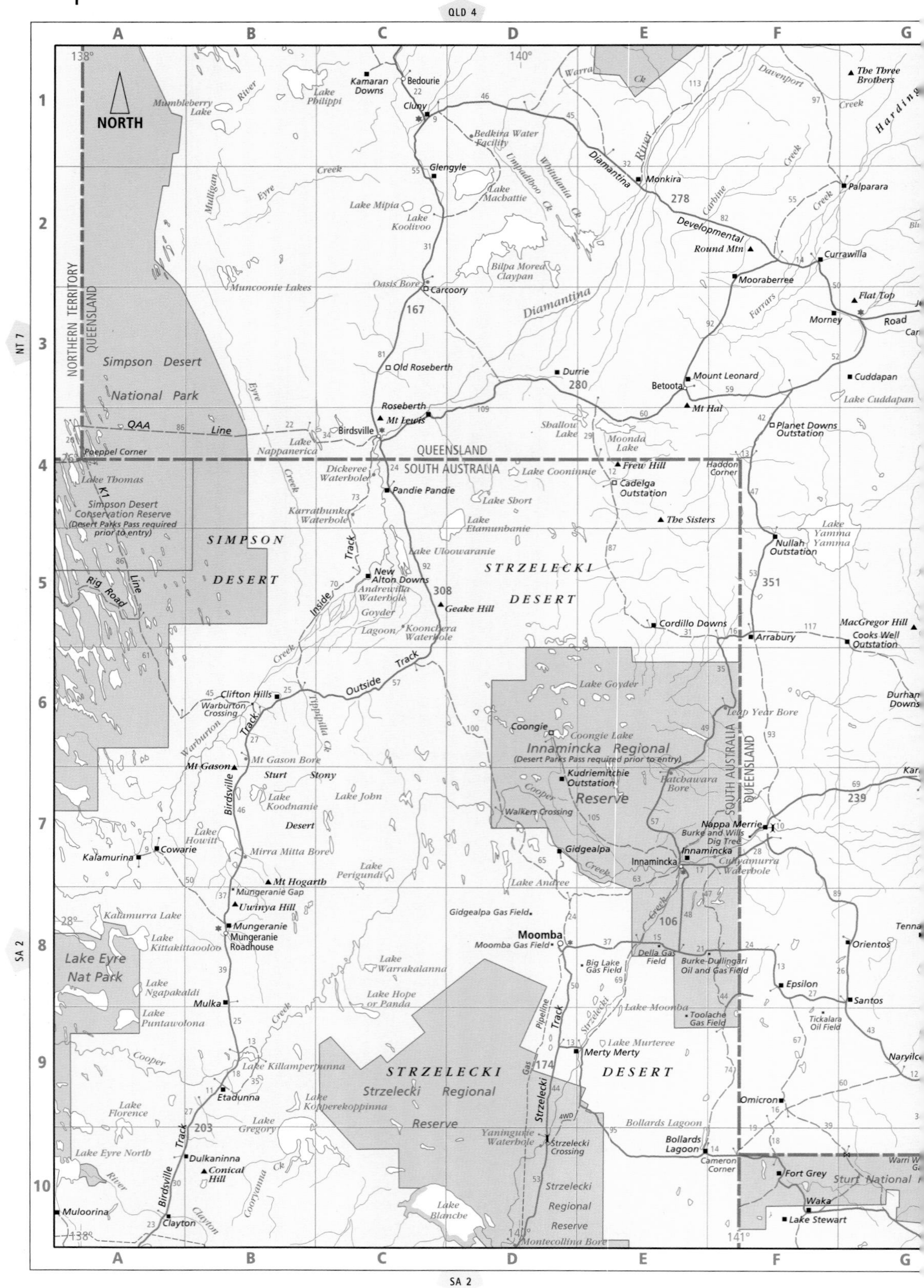
QLD 4
NT 7
SA 2
NORTH
NORTHERN TERRITORY
QUEENSLAND
SOUTH AUSTRALIA
Simpson Desert National Park
Simpson Desert Conservation Reserve
(Desert Parks Pass required prior to entry)
SIMPSON DESERT
STRZELECKI DESERT
Innamincka Regional Reserve
(Desert Parks Pass required prior to entry)
Strzelecki Regional Reserve
Lake Eyre Nat Park
Sturt National Park
Mumbleberry Lake
Lake Philippi
Kamaran Downs
Bedourie
Cluny
Bedkira Water Facility
Glengyle
Lake Machattie
Lake Mipia
Lake Koolivoo
Muncoonie Lakes
Oasis Bore
Carcoory
Bilpa Morea Claypan
Diamantina
Monkira
Developmental
Round Mtn
Mooraberree
Currawilla
Palparara
The Three Brothers
Davenport
Harding
Flat Top
Morney
Road
Old Roseberth
Durrie
Betoota
Mount Leonard
Mt Hal
Cuddapan
Lake Cuddapan
Roseberth
Mt Lewis
Birdsville
QAA Line
Poeppel Corner
Lake Nappanerica
Shallow Lake
Moonda Lake
Planet Downs Outstation
Lake Thomas
Dickeree Waterhole
Pandie Pandie
Lake Cooninnie
Frew Hill
Haddon Corner
Cadelga Outstation
Karrathunka Waterhole
Lake Short
Lake Etamunbanie
The Sisters
Lake Yamma Yamma
Nullah Outstation
Lake Uloowaranie
Rig Road
New Alton Downs
Andrewilla Waterhole
Goyder Lagoon
Koonchera Waterhole
Geake Hill
Inside Track
Outside Track
Cordillo Downs
Arrabury
MacGregor Hill
Cooks Well Outstation
Durham Downs
Clifton Hills
Warburton Crossing
Lake Goyder
Leap Year Bore
Coongie
Coongie Lake
Mt Gason
Mt Gason Bore
Sturt Stony Desert
Lake Koodnanie
Lake John
Kudriemitchie Outstation
Patchawarra Bore
Walkers Crossing
Nappa Merrie
Burke and Wills Dig Tree
Lake Howitt
Kalamurina
Cowarie
Mirra Mitta Bore
Gidgealpa
Innamincka
Cullyamurra Waterhole
Lake Perigundi
Mt Hogarth
Lake Andree
Mungeranie Gap
Uwinya Hill
Kalamurra Lake
Gidgealpa Gas Field
Mungeranie
Mungeranie Roadhouse
Lake Kittakittaooloo
Moomba
Moomba Gas Field
Della Gas Field
Burke-Dullingari Oil and Gas Field
Big Lake Gas Field
Orientos
Lake Warrakalanna
Lake Ngapakaldi
Epsilon
Santos
Mulka
Lake Hope or Panda
Lake Moomba
Toolache Gas Field
Tickalara Oil Field
Lake Puntawolona
Pipeline Track
Lake Murteree
Merty Merty
Lake Killamperpunna
Etadunna
Lake Florence
Lake Kopperekoppinna
Omicron
Lake Gregory
Bollards Lagoon
Birdsville Track
Yaningurie Waterhole
Strzelecki Crossing
Cameron Corner
Lake Eyre North
Dulkaninna
Conical Hill
Fort Grey
Waka
Lake Stewart
Lake Blanche
Muloorina
Clayton
Montecollina Bore
Strzelecki Track
Cooper Creek
Warburton
Eyre Creek
Mulligan
Farrars
Carbine
Whitulania Ck
Umpadiboo
Tippipilla Ck
Cooryanna Ck
Clayton River
138°
140°
141°
28°
A B C D E F G
1 2 3 4 5 6 7 8 9 10

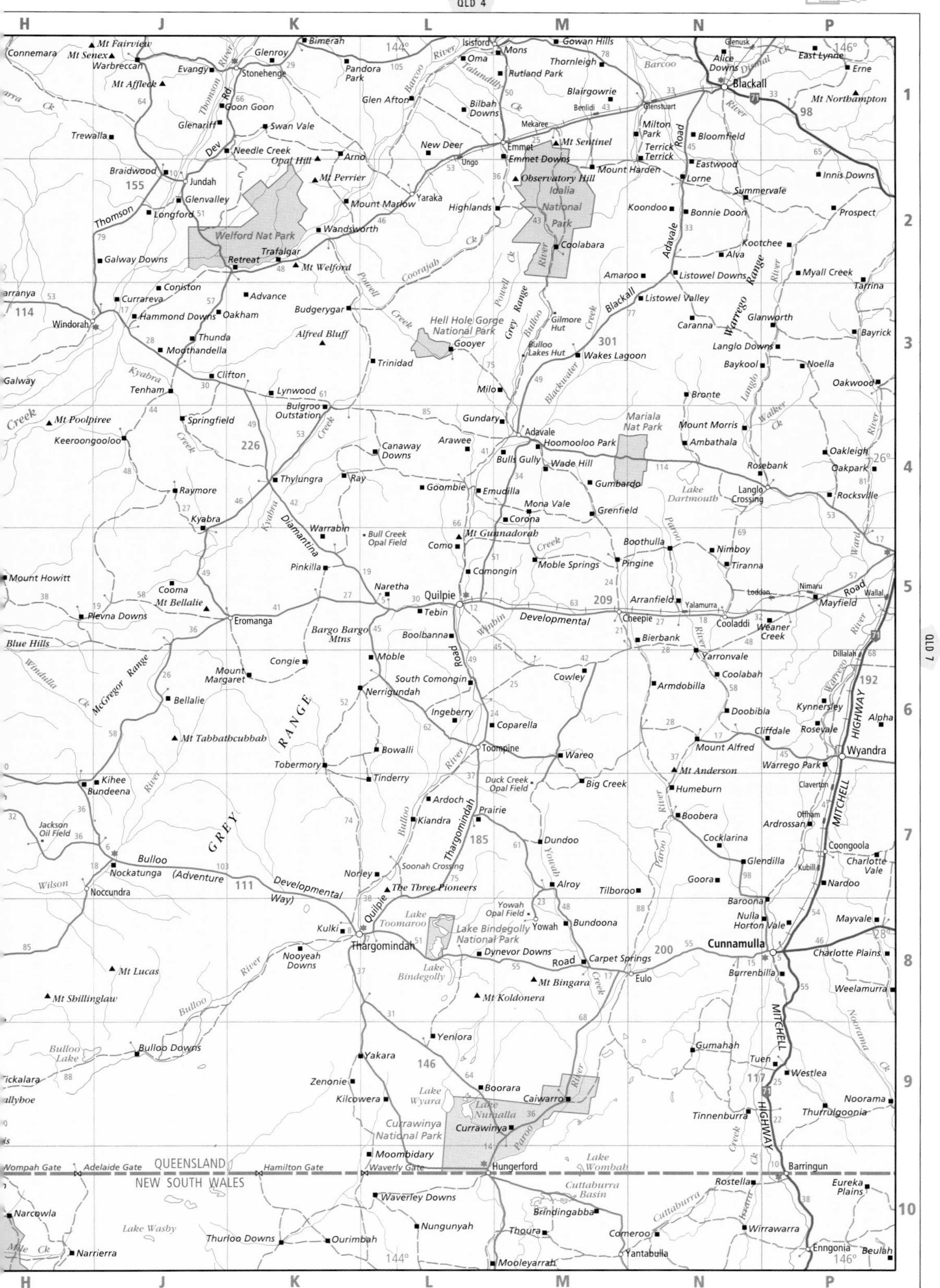
0 20 40 60 80
kilometres
QLD
QLD 7
Quilpie
Thargomindah
Cunnamulla
Windorah
Blackall
Eromanga
Wyandra
Hungerford
QUEENSLAND
NEW SOUTH WALES

Map 7

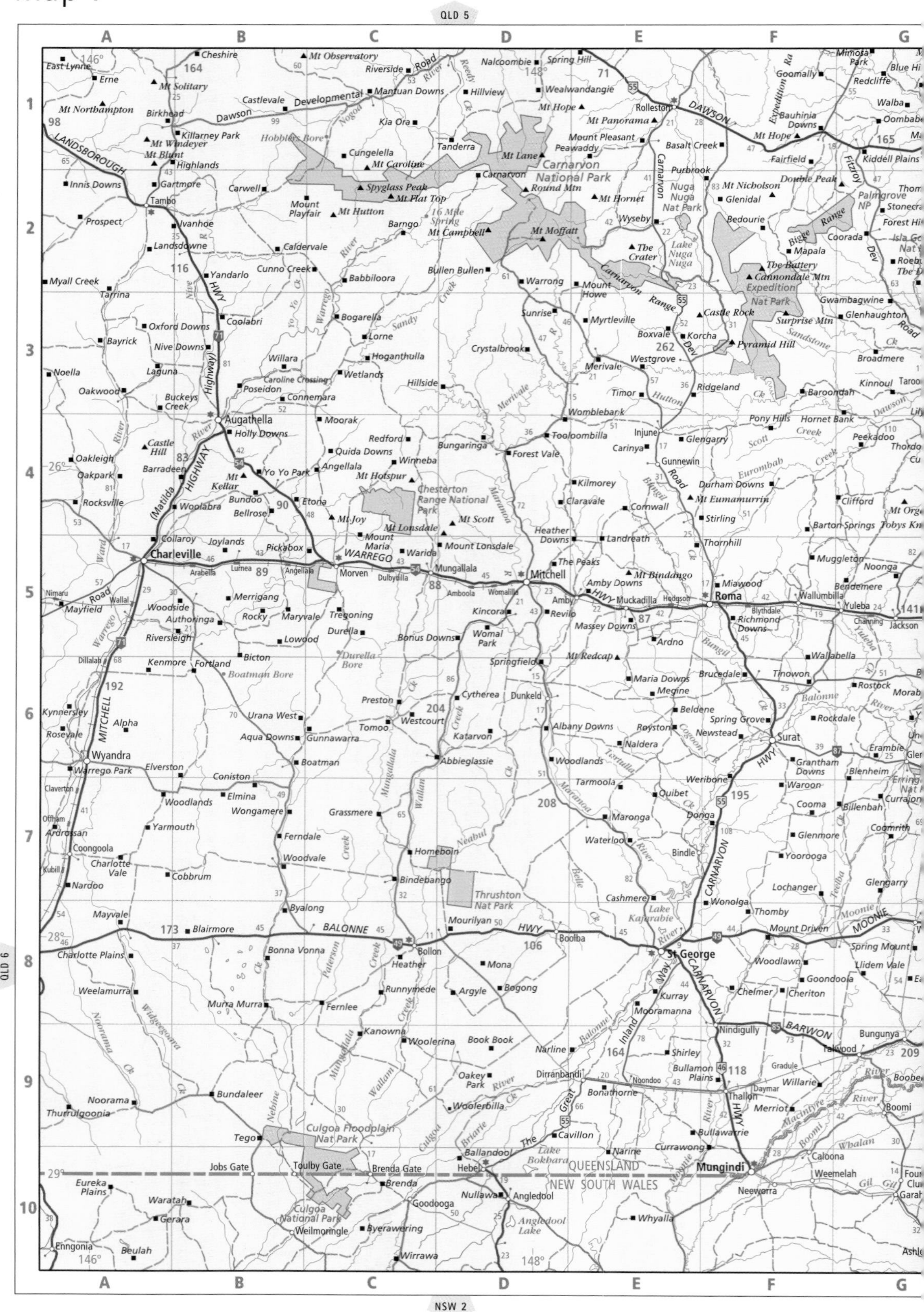
QLD 5
QLD 6
NSW 2
A
B
C
D
E
F
G
1
2
3
4
5
6
7
8
9
10
146°
148°
26°
28°
29°
Cheshire
Mt Observatory
Nalcoombie
Spring Hill
Mimosa Park
Blue Hi
East Lynne
Erne
Mt Solitary
Riverside
Road
71
Goomally
Redcliffe
Mt Northampton
Birkhead
Castlevale
Developmental
Mantuan Downs
Hillview
Wealwandangie
Rolleston
DAWSON
Walba
Oombabe
Dawson
Mt Hope
Mt Panorama
Bauhinia Downs
98
Killarney Park
Hobblers Bore
Kia Ora
Mount Pleasant
Mt Hope
165
LANDSBOROUGH
Mt Windeyer
Mt Blunt
Cungelella
Tanderra
Peawaddy
Basalt Creek
Highlands
Mt Caroline
Mt Lane
Carnarvon National Park
Fairfield
Kiddell Plains
Innis Downs
Gartmore
Carwell
Spyglass Peak
Carnarvon
Purbrook
Double Peak
Fitzroy
Tambo
Mt Flat Top
Round Mtn
Mt Nicholson
Palmgrove NP
Mount Playfair
Mt Hutton
16 Mile Spring
Mt Hornet
Nuga Nuga Nat Park
Glenidal
Stonecra
Prospect
Ivanhoe
Barngo
Mt Campbell
Mt Moffatt
Wyseby
Bedourie
Forest Hi
Range
Landsdowne
Caldervale
River
The Crater
Lake Nuga Nuga
Bigge
Coorada
Mapala
116
Cunno Creek
Bullen Bullen
The Battery
Myall Creek
Yandarlo
Babbiloora
Warrong
Mount Howe
Carnarvon Range
Cannondale Mtn
Expedition Nat Park
Tarrina
HWY
Gwambagwine
Bogarella
Sunrise
Myrtleville
Castle Rock
Surprise Mtn
Glenhaughton
Oxford Downs
Coolabri
Lorne
Boxvale
Korcha
Sandstone
Bayrick
Nive Downs
Crystalbrook
262
Pyramid Hill
Hoganthulla
Willara
Westgrove
Broadmere
Noella
Laguna
Highway
Wetlands
Merivale
Caroline Crossing
Oakwood
Poseidon
Hillside
Timor
Ridgeland
Kinnoul
Buckeys Creek
Connemara
Hutton
Baroondah
Augathella
Moorak
Womblebark
Pony Hills
Hornet Bank
Holly Downs
Redford
Tooloombilla
Injune
Glengarry
Peekadoo
Castle Hill
Bungaringa
Carinya
Scott
Creek
Quida Downs
Forest Vale
Gunnewin
Oakleigh
83
Barradeen
Winneba
Yo Yo Park
Angellala
Mt Hotspur
Eurombah
Oakpark
HIGHWAY
Mt Kellar
Chesterton Range National Park
Kilmorey
Durham Downs
Clifford
Bundoo
Etona
Claravale
Cornwall
Mt Eumamurrin
Rocksville
Woolabra
90
Bellrose
Mt Joy
Mt Lonsdale
Mt Scott
Stirling
Barton Springs
Tobys Kn
(Matilda
Mount Maria
Mount Lonsdale
Heather Downs
Landreath
Thornhill
Collaroy
Joylands
Pickabox
Warida
Muggleton
Charleville
WARREGO
The Peaks
Noonga
Arabella
Lumea
89
Angellala
Morven
Dulbydilla
Mungallala
Mitchell
Mt Bindango
Miawood
Nimaru
Wallal
Amby Downs
Bendemere
Road
Amboola
Womalilla
Amby
Muckadilla
Hodgson
Roma
Wallumbilla
Yuleba
Mayfield
Merrigang
Woodside
Rocky
Maryvale
Tregoning
88
Kincora
Revilo
Blythdale
Richmond Downs
Channing
Jackson
Authoringa
Durella
Bonus Downs
Womal Park
Massey Downs
87
Riversleigh
Lowood
Ardno
Dillalah
Bicton
Durella Bore
Springfield
Mt Redcap
Wallabella
Kenmore
Fortland
Boatman Bore
Maria Downs
Brucedale
Tinowon
Rostock
192
Cytherea
Dunkeld
Megine
Balonne
Morab
Preston
204
Beldene
Kynnersley
Urana West
Tomoo
Westcourt
Albany Downs
Royston
Spring Grove
Rockdale
Alpha
Aqua Downs
Gunnawarra
Katarvon
Newstead
Surat
Rosevale
MITCHELL
Naldera
Erambie
Wyandra
Elverston
Boatman
Abbieglassie
Woodlands
Grantham Downs
Warrego Park
Coniston
Tarmoola
Weribone
Blenheim
Claverton
Woodlands
Elmina
Quibet
Waroon
195
Offham
Wongamere
Grassmere
208
Maronga
Donga
Cooma
Billenbah
Ardrossan
Yarmouth
Mungallala
Wallan
Waterloo
Glenmore
Coomrith
Coongoola
Ferndale
Homeboin
Neabul
Bindle
Kubill
Charlotte Vale
Woodvale
Yoorooga
Cobbrum
Bindebango
Thrushton Nat Park
CARNARVON
Nardoo
Cashmere
Lochanger
Glengarry
Lake Kajarabie
Wonolga
Byalong
Thomby
Mayvale
Mourilyan
173
Blairmore
BALONNE
HWY
Mount Driven
MOONIE
106
Boolba
Charlotte Plains
Bollon
St George
Spring Mount
Bonna Vonna
Heather
Mona
Woodlawn
Lliden Vale
Weelamurra
Runnymede
Argyle
Bogong
Kurray
Goondoola
Chelmer
Cheriton
Murra Murra
Fernlee
Mooramanna
Nindigully
BARWON
Bungunya
Kanowna
Woolerina
Book Book
Narline
Inland
164
Shirley
Talwood
209
Oakey Park
Dirranbandi
Bullamon Plains
118
Gradule
Boobe
Noorama
Bundaleer
Noondoo
Bonathorne
Thallon
Daymar
Willarie
Merriot
Thurrulgoonia
Woolerbilla
Boomi
Tego
Culgoa Floodplain Nat Park
Cavillon
Bullawarrie
Ballandool
Narine
Currawong
Caloona
Jobs Gate
Toulby Gate
Brenda Gate
Hebel
Lake Bokhara
QUEENSLAND
Mungindi
Weemelah
Eureka Plains
Brenda
NEW SOUTH WALES
Neeworra
Four Clu
Garah
Waratah
Goodooga
Nullawa
Angledool
Gerara
Angledool Lake
Whyalla
Culgoa National Park
Weilmoringle
Byerawering
Enngonia
Beulah
Wirrawa
Ashle

0 20 40 60 80
kilometres

QLD 5

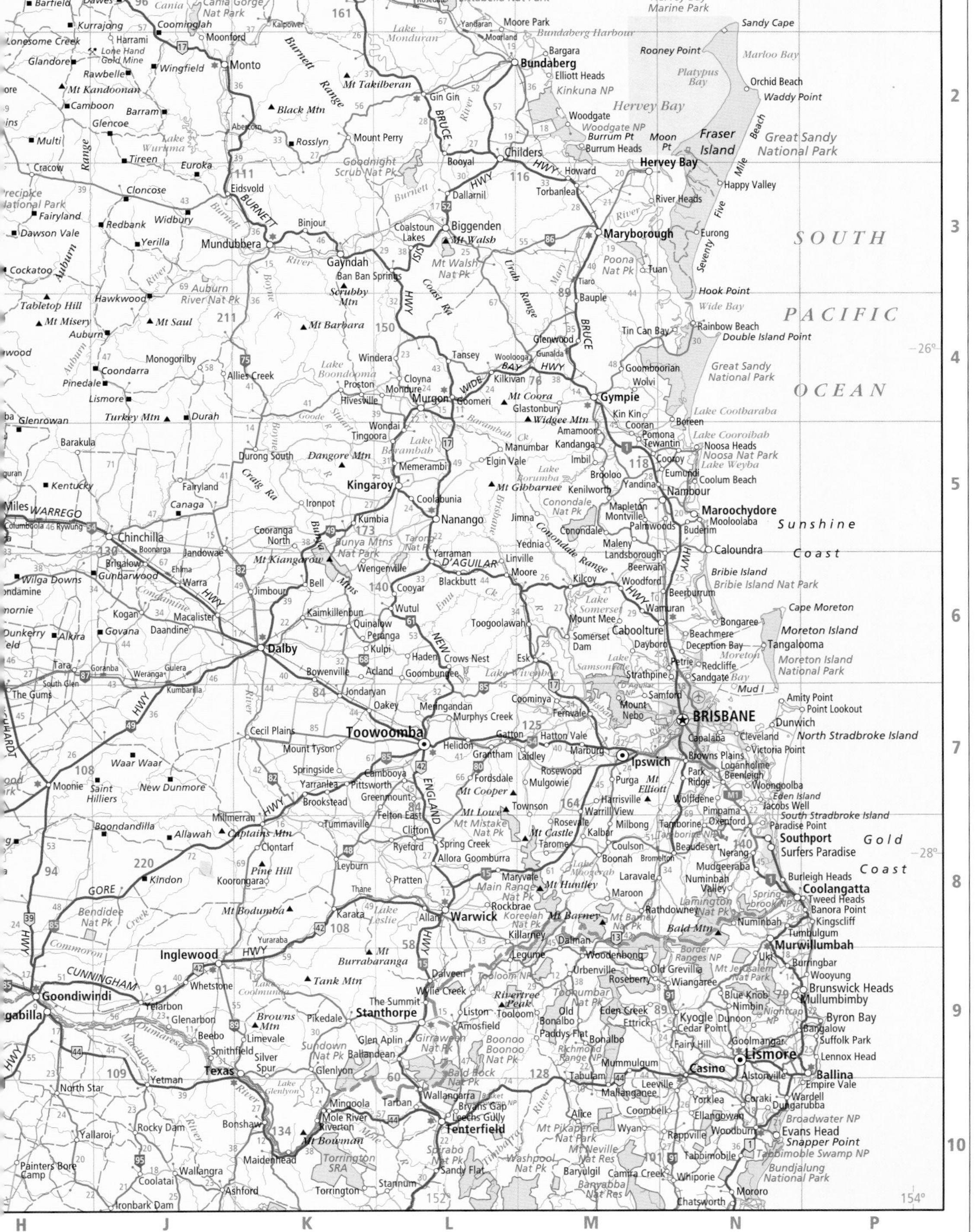

NSW 4

Map 1

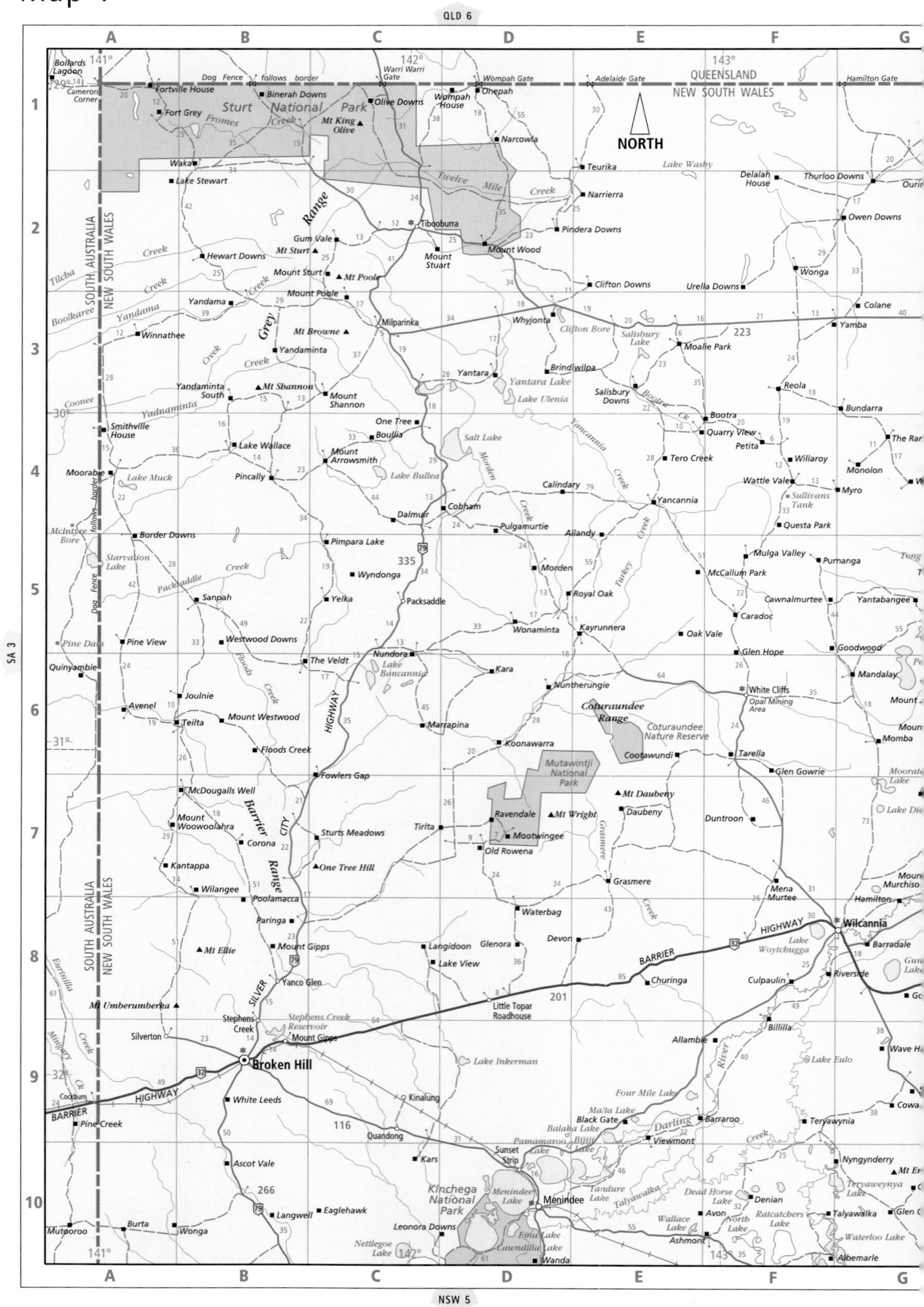
QLD 6
NSW 5
SA 3
NORTH
QUEENSLAND
NEW SOUTH WALES
SOUTH AUSTRALIA
Sturt National Park
Mutawintji National Park
Kinchega National Park
Coturaundee Nature Reserve
Coturaundee Range
Grey Range
Barrier Range
Dog Fence follows border
Bollards Lagoon
Cameron Corner
Fortville House
Fort Grey
Binerah Downs
Olive Downs
Mt King Olive
Warri Warri Gate
Wompah Gate
Wompah House
Onepah
Narcowla
Adelaide Gate
Hamilton Gate
Waka
Lake Stewart
Teurika
Lake Wasby
Delalah House
Thurloo Downs
Narrierra
Twelve Mile Creek
Tibooburra
Pindera Downs
Owen Downs
Gum Vale
Mt Sturt
Hewart Downs
Mount Stuart
Mount Wood
Mount Sturt
Mt Poole
Clifton Downs
Urella Downs
Wonga
Yandama
Mount Poole
Colane
Milparinka
Whyjonta
Clifton Bore
Salisbury Lake
Yamba
Winnathee
Mt Browne
Moalie Park
Yandaminta
Yantara
Brindiwilpa
Yantara Lake
Lake Ulenia
Yandaminta South
Mt Shannon
Mount Shannon
Salisbury Downs
Reola
Bundarra
Smithville House
One Tree
Bootra
Quarry View
Petita
The Ranch
Lake Wallace
Boullia
Salt Lake
Mount Arrowsmith
Tero Creek
Willaroy
Moorabie
Lake Muck
Pincally
Lake Bullea
Wattle Vale
Monolon
Myro
Calindary
Sullivans Tank
Yancannia
Cobham
Dalmuir
Pulgamurtie
Allandy
Questa Park
McIntyre Bore
Border Downs
Pimpara Lake
Starvation Lake
Mulga Valley
Purnanga
Morden
McCallum Park
Wyndonga
Sanpah
Yelka
Packsaddle
Royal Oak
Cawnalmurtee
Yantabangee
Caradoc
Wonaminta
Kayrunnera
Oak Vale
Pine Dam
Pine View
Westwood Downs
Goodwood
Glen Hope
Quinyambie
The Veldt
Nundora
Lake Bancannia
Kara
Mandalay
Nuntherungie
White Cliffs
Opal Mining Area
Joulnie
Avenel
Teilta
Mount Westwood
Marrapina
Momba
Floods Creek
Koonawarra
Cootawundi
Tarella
Glen Gowrie
Fowlers Gap
McDougalls Well
Mt Daubeny
Daubeny
Ravendale
Mt Wright
Duntroon
Lake Dick
Mount Woowoolahra
Tirlta
Sturts Meadows
Mootwingee
Corona
Old Rowena
Kantappa
One Tree Hill
Grasmere
Wilangee
Poolamacca
Mena Murtee
Waterbag
Paringa
Wilcannia
Hamilton
Mt Ellie
Mount Gipps
Langidoon
Glenora
Devon
Lake Woytchugga
Barradale
Lake View
Churinga
Riverside
Culpaulin
Yanco Glen
Mt Umberumberka
Little Topar Roadhouse
Stephens Creek Reservoir
Stephens Creek
Billilla
Silverton
Mount Gipps
Allambie
Broken Hill
Lake Inkerman
Lake Eulo
Wave Hill
White Leeds
Kinalung
Four Mile Lake
Cockburn
Malta Lake
Black Gate
Barraroo
Balaka Lake
Teryawynia
Pine Creek
Quandong
Pamamaroo Lake
Bijiji Lake
Viewmont
Darling River
Sunset Strip
Kars
Nyngynderry
Ascot Vale
Menindee Lake
Menindee
Tandure Lake
Talyawalka
Dead Horse Lake
Denian
Teryaweynya Lake
Eaglehawk
Langwell
Avon
Talyawalka
North Lake
Ratcatchers Lake
Mutooroo
Burta
Wonga
Leonora Downs
Wallace Lake
Nettlegoe Lake
Emu Lake
Cawndilla Lake
Ashmont
Waterloo Lake
Wanda
Albemarle
BARRIER HIGHWAY
SILVER CITY HIGHWAY

0 10 20 30 40 50
kilometres

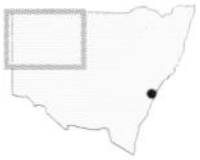

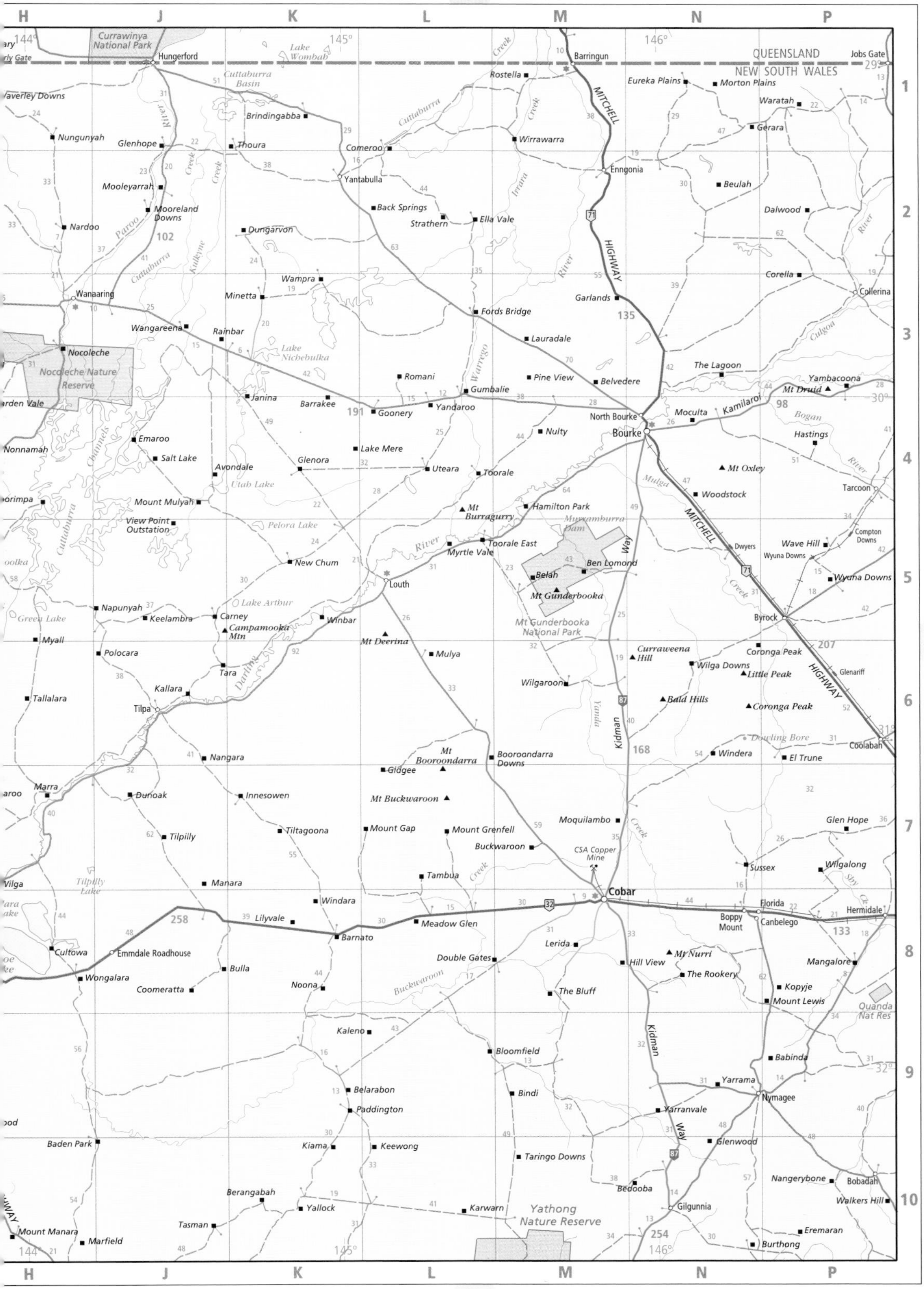

H J K L M N P

1 2 3 4 5 6 7 8 9 10

144° 145° 146° 29° 30° 31° 32°

QUEENSLAND
NEW SOUTH WALES

Currawinya National Park
Hungerford
Lake Wombah
Cuttaburra Basin
Barringun
Jobs Gate
Rostella
Eureka Plains
Morton Plains
Waverley Downs
Brindingabba
Waratah
Gerara
Nungunyah
Glenhope
Thoura
Comeroo
Wirrawarra
Yantabulla
Enngonia
Mooleyarrah
Beulah
Mooreland Downs
Back Springs
Strathern
Ella Vale
Dalwood
Nardoo
Dungarvon
Paroo River
Cuttaburra
Kulkyne Creek
Irrara Creek
Warrego River
Culgoa River
Wampra
Corella
Wanaaring
Minetta
Garlands
Collerina
Fords Bridge
Wangareena
Rainbar
Lauradale
Nocoleche
Nocoleche Nature Reserve
Lake Nichebulka
The Lagoon
Romani
Pine View
Belvedere
Yambacoona
Janina
Barrakee
Gumbalie
Mt Druid
Garden Vale
Goonery
Yandaroo
North Bourke
Moculta
Bourke
Bogan River
Emaroo
Nulty
Hastings
Nonnamah
Salt Lake
Lake Mere
Glenora
Avondale
Uteara
Toorale
Mt Oxley
Utah Lake
Woodstock
Tarcoon
Corimpa
Mount Mulyah
Mt Burragurry
Hamilton Park
Muttamburra Dam
View Point Outstation
Pelora Lake
Compton Downs
Toorale East
Wave Hill
Myrtle Vale
Dwyers
Wyuna Downs
New Chum
Ben Lomond
Belah
Mt Gunderbooka
Louth
Darling River
Mt Gunderbooka National Park
Lake Arthur
Napunyah
Carney
Keelambra
Campamooka Mtn
Winbar
Byrock
Green Lake
Myall
Mt Deerina
Currawenna Hill
Coronga Peak
Polocara
Mulya
Wilga Downs
Little Peak
Tara
Glenariff
Wilgaroon
Kallara
Bald Hills
Tallalara
Coronga Peak
Tilpa
Yanda Creek
Mulga Creek
Dowling Bore
Nangara
Mt Booroondarra
Booroondarra Downs
Windera
El Trune
Coolabah
Gidgee
Marra
Dunoak
Innesowen
Mt Buckwaroon
Moquilambo
Glen Hope
Tilpilly
Tiltagoona
Mount Gap
Mount Grenfell
Buckwaroon
CSA Copper Mine
Sussex
Wilgalong
Tambua
Wilga
Manara
Tilpilly Lake
Cobar
Windara
Florida
Hermidale
Lilyvale
Boppy Mount
Canbelego
Meadow Glen
Barnato
Lerida
Cultowa
Emmdale Roadhouse
Mt Nurri
Double Gates
Hill View
Mangalore
Wongalara
Bulla
The Rookery
Coomeratta
Noona
The Bluff
Kopyje
Mount Lewis
Buckwaroon Creek
Quanda Nat Res
Kaleno
Bloomfield
Babinda
Yarrama
Belarabon
Bindi
Nymagee
Paddington
Yarranvale
Baden Park
Kiama
Keewong
Glenwood
Taringo Downs
Nangerybone
Bobadah
Bedooba
Berangabah
Yallock
Karwarn
Yathong Nature Reserve
Gilgunnia
Walkers Hill
Tasman
Mount Manara
Marfield
Eremaran
Burthong
MITCHELL HIGHWAY
Kidman Way
Kamilaroi
71 87 32
102 135 98 191 207 168 258 133 254

NSW 2

NSW

Map 2

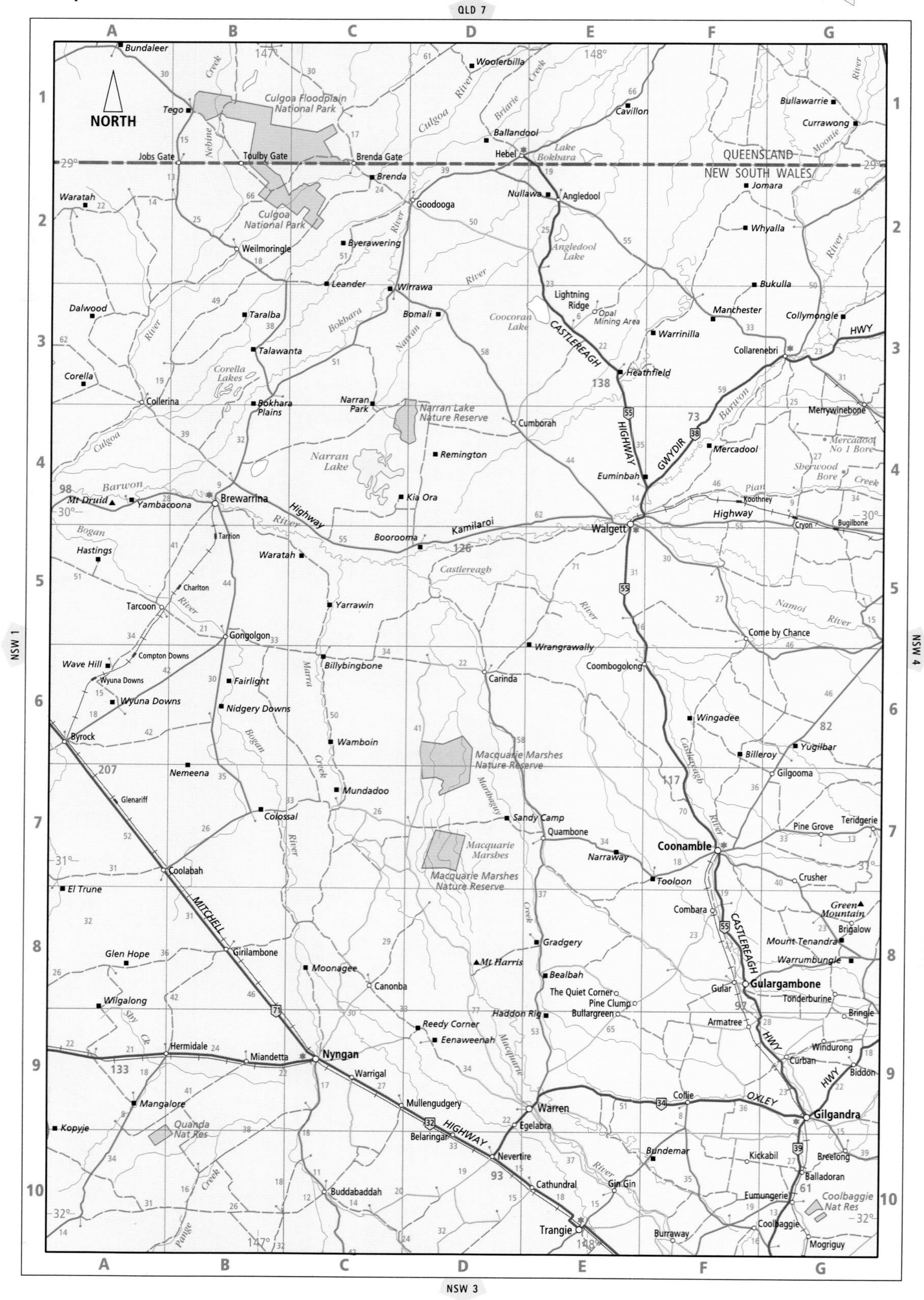

0 10 20 30 40 50
kilometres
QLD 7
NSW 1
NSW 3
NSW 4
NORTH
QUEENSLAND
NEW SOUTH WALES
Bundaleer
Woolerbilla
Culgoa Floodplain National Park
Tego
Cavillon
Bullawarrie
Currawong
Ballandool
Jobs Gate
Toulby Gate
Brenda Gate
Hebel
Lake Bokhara
Brenda
Nullawa
Angledool
Jomara
Waratah
Goodooga
Culgoa National Park
Whyalla
Byerawering
Weilmoringle
Angledool Lake
Leander
Wirrawa
Bukulla
Lightning Ridge
Opal Mining Area
Dalwood
Taralba
Bomali
Coocoran Lake
Manchester
Collymongle
HWY
Warrinilla
Talawanta
Collarenebri
Corella Lakes
Corella
Heathfield
CASTLEREAGH
HIGHWAY
Collerina
Bokhara Plains
Narran Park
Narran Lake Nature Reserve
Cumborah
Merrywinebone
Mercadool No 1 Bore
Mercadool
Remington
Narran Lake
Sherwood Bore
GWYDIR
Euminbah
Barwon
Mt Druid
Yambacoona
Brewarrina
Kia Ora
Koothney
Highway
Kamilaroi
Walgett
Cryon
Bugilbone
Tarrion
Booroorna
Hastings
Waratah
Castlereagh
Charlton
Tarcoon
Yarrawin
Namoi River
Gongolgon
Come by Chance
Compton Downs
Wrangrawally
Wave Hill
Billybingbone
Coombogolong
Wyuna Downs
Fairlight
Carinda
Nidgery Downs
Wingadee
Byrock
Wamboin
Macquarie Marshes Nature Reserve
Yugilbar
Billeroy
Nemeena
Gilgooma
Glenariff
Mundadoo
Colossal
Sandy Camp
Quambone
Pine Grove
Teridgerie
Macquarie Marshes
Narraway
Coonamble
Coolabah
Tooloon
Crusher
El Trune
Macquarie Marshes Nature Reserve
Combara
Green Mountain
Brigalow
MITCHELL
Gradgery
Mount Tenandra
Glen Hope
Girilambone
Moonagee
Mt Harris
Warrumbungle
Bealbah
Canonba
The Quiet Corner
Gular
Gulargambone
Wilgalong
Pine Clump
Tonderburine
Bullargreen
Haddon Rig
Bringle
Reedy Corner
Armatree
HWY
Eenaweenah
Windurong
Hermidale
Miandetta
Nyngan
Curban
Biddon
Warrigal
Mangalore
Mullengudgery
Collie
OXLEY
Gilgandra
Warren
Kopyje
Quanda Nat Res
Egelabra
Belaringar
HIGHWAY
Nevertire
Bundemar
Kickabil
Breelong
Balladoran
Cathundral
Gin Gin
Buddabaddah
Eumungerie
Coolbaggie Nat Res
Trangie
Burraway
Coolbaggie
Mogriguy

Map 3

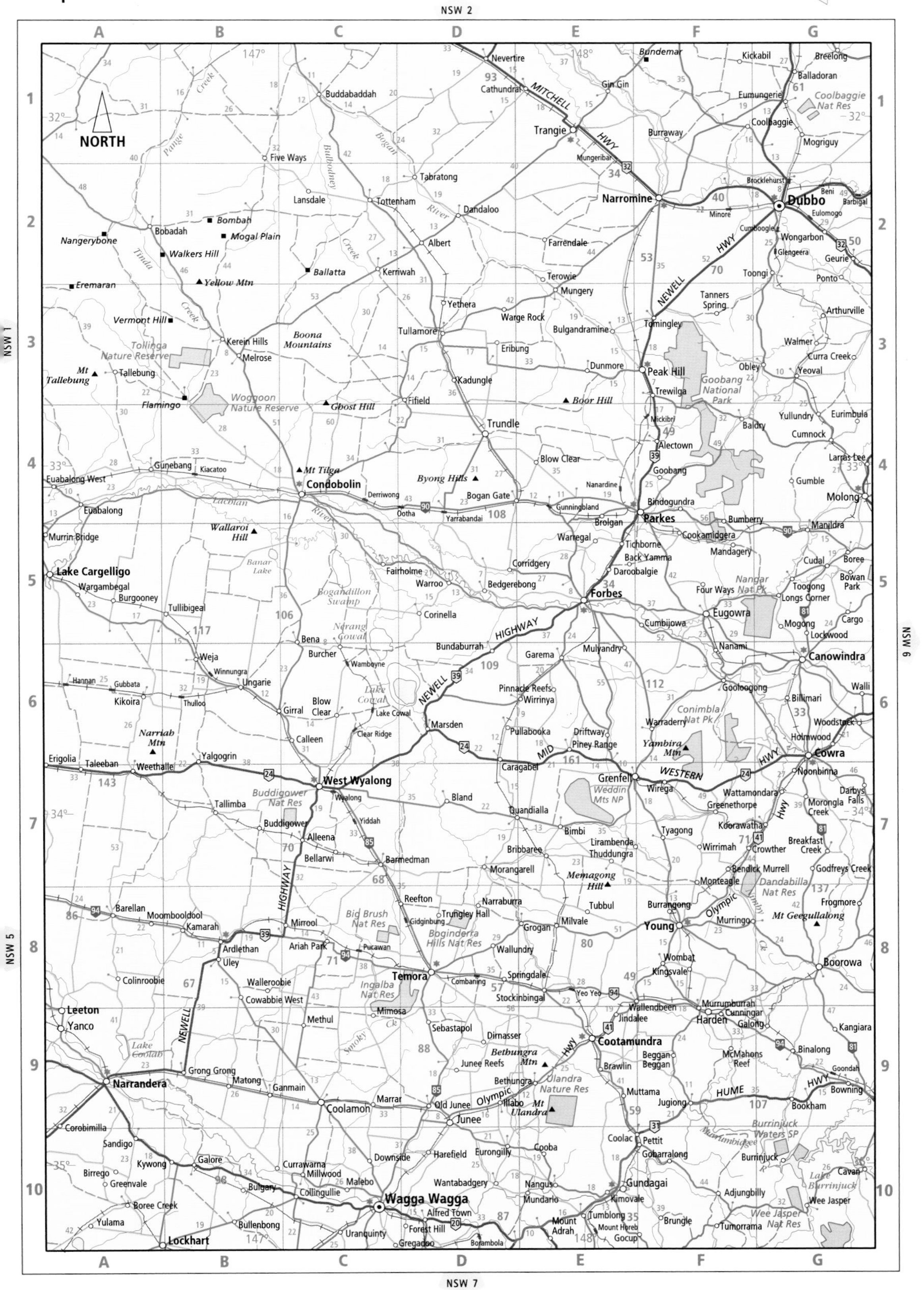
0 10 20 30 40 50
kilometres
NSW 2
NSW 7
NSW 1
NSW 5
NSW 6
NORTH
Dubbo
Narromine
Trangie
Parkes
Forbes
Condobolin
West Wyalong
Young
Cowra
Canowindra
Temora
Cootamundra
Junee
Wagga Wagga
Narrandera
Leeton
Lake Cargelligo
Gundagai
Harden
Boorowa
Grenfell
Peak Hill
Trundle
Tullamore
Molong
Lockhart
Coolamon
MITCHELL HWY
NEWELL HWY
MID WESTERN HWY
OLYMPIC HWY
HUME HWY
Goobang National Park
Weddin Mts NP
Conimbla Nat Pk
Nangar Nat Pk
Lachlan River
Bogan River
Murrumbidgee

Map 4

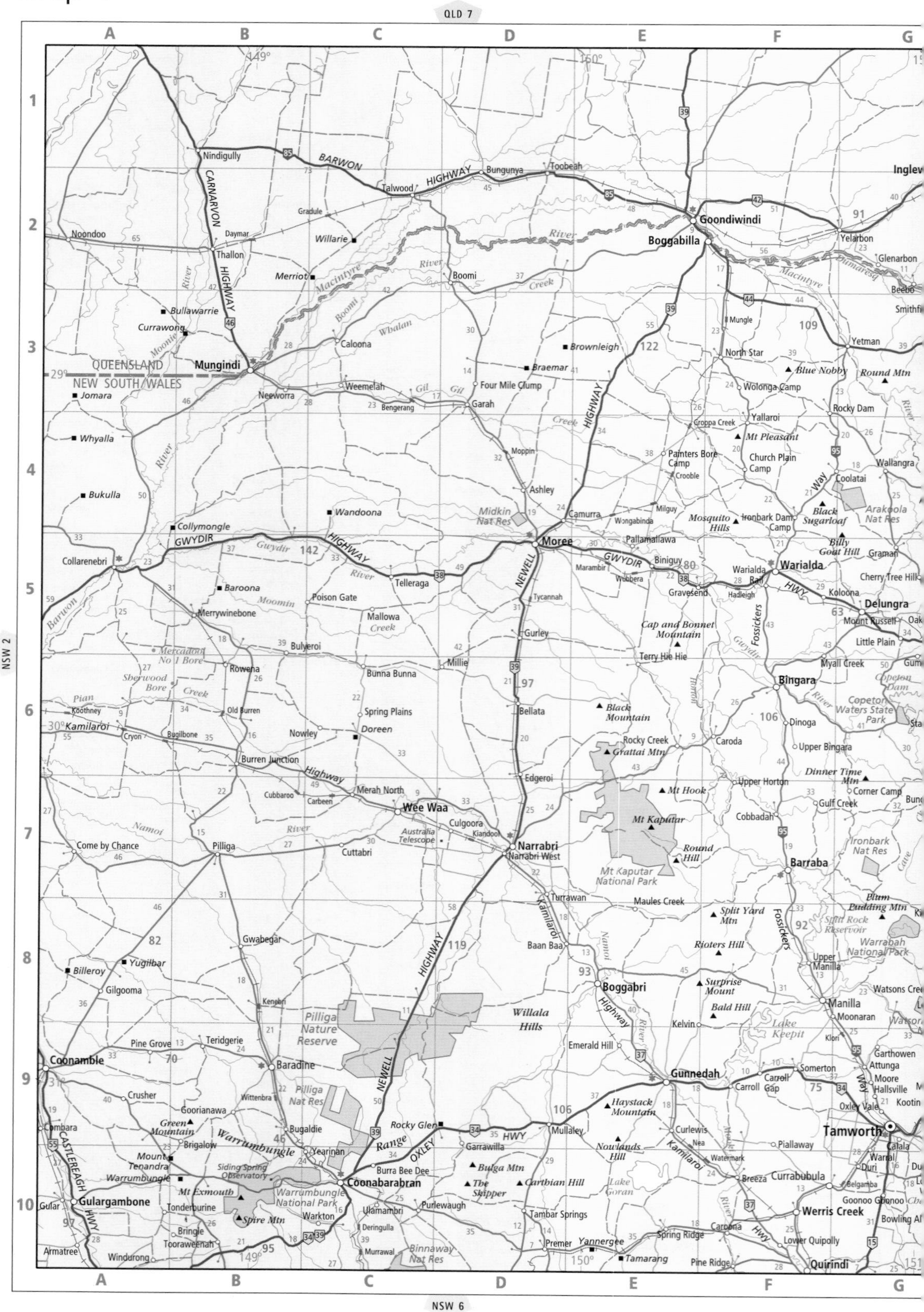
QLD 7
NSW 2
NSW 6
A
B
C
D
E
F
G
1
2
3
4
5
6
7
8
9
10
149°
150°
29°
30°
QUEENSLAND
NEW SOUTH WALES
Nindigully
CARNARVON
HIGHWAY
BARWON
HIGHWAY
Talwood
Bungunya
Toobeah
Goondiwindi
Boggabilla
Inglewood
Yelarbon
Glenarbon
Beebo
Smithfield
Gradule
Willarie
Noondoo
Daymar
Thallon
Merriot
Boomi
Macintyre
River
Dumaresq
Bullawarrie
Currawong
Moonie
Caloona
Whalan
Boomi
Mungindi
Brownleigh
Braemar
Four Mile Clump
Mungle
North Star
Blue Nobby
Round Mtn
Yetman
Jomara
Neeworra
Weemelah
Bengerang
Gil Gil
Garah
Wolonga Camp
Yallaroi
Rocky Dam
Croppa Creek
Mt Pleasant
Whyalla
River
Creek
Moppin
Painters Bore Camp
Crooble
Church Plain Camp
Wallangra
Coolatai
Bukulla
Ashley
Wandoona
Midkin Nat Res
Camurra
Wongabinda
Milguy
Mosquito Hills
Ironbark Dam Camp
Black Sugarloaf
Arakoola Nat Res
Collymongle
Moree
Pallamallawa
Billy Goat Hill
Graman
Collarenebri
GWYDIR
HIGHWAY
Gwydir
River
Telleraga
NEWELL
Marambir
Biniguy
Wubbera
Gravesend
Hadleigh
Warialda Rail
Warialda
HWY
Cherry Tree Hill
Koloona
Delungra
Barwon
Baroona
Poison Gate
Merrywinebone
Moomin
Mallowa Creek
Tycannah
Fossickers
Cap and Bonnet Mountain
Mount Russell
Oakwood
Little Plain
Bulyeroi
Gurley
Terry Hie Hie
Myall Creek
Mercadool No 1 Bore
Sherwood Bore
Rowena
Millie
Bunna Bunna
Horton
Bingara
Copeton Dam
Pian Creek
Koothney
Old Burren
Spring Plains
Bellata
Black Mountain
Copeton Waters State Park
Kamilaroi
Cryon
Bugilbone
Nowley
Doreen
Rocky Creek
Grattai Mtn
Caroda
Dinoga
Upper Bingara
Burren Junction
Highway
Edgeroi
Mt Hook
Upper Horton
Dinner Time Mtn
Corner Camp
Gulf Creek
Cubbaroo
Carbeen
Merah North
Wee Waa
Mt Kaputar
Cobbadah
Namoi
River
Culgoora
Kiandool
Australia Telescope
Come by Chance
Pilliga
Cuttabri
Narrabri
Narrabri West
Round Hill
Mt Kaputar National Park
Barraba
Ironbark Nat Res
Turrawan
Kamilaroi
Maules Creek
Plum Pudding Mtn
Split Yard Mtn
Split Rock Reservoir
Warrabah National Park
Gwabegar
HIGHWAY
Baan Baa
Rioters Hill
Upper Manilla
Billeroy
Yugilbar
Gilgooma
Boggabri
Surprise Mount
Watsons Creek
Kenebri
Pilliga Nature Reserve
Willala Hills
Bald Hill
Manilla
Moonaran
Kelvin
Lake Keepit
Klori
Pine Grove
Teridgerie
Emerald Hill
Garthowen
Attunga
Coonamble
Baradine
Gunnedah
Carroll
Carroll Gap
Somerton
Moore
Hallsville
Kootingal
Crusher
Wittenbra
Pilliga Nat Res
Haystack Mountain
Oxley Vale
Coonbara
Goorianawa
Green Mountain
Brigalow
Bugaldie
Rocky Glen
Mullaley
Curlewis
Nea
Piallaway
Tamworth
Calala
Warrumbungle
Range
OXLEY
HWY
Garrawilla
Nowlands Hill
Watermark
Warral
Duri
CASTLEREAGH
HWY
Mount Tenandra
Warrumbungle
Yearinan
Siding Spring Observatory
Burra Bee Dee
Bulga Mtn
Breeza
Currabubula
Belgamba
Mt Exmouth
Coonabarabran
The Skipper
Carthbian Hill
Lake Goran
Gular
Gulargambone
Tonderburine
Warrumbungle National Park
Ulamambri
Purlewaugh
Goonoo Goonoo
Werris Creek
Spire Mtn
Warkton
Deringulla
Tambar Springs
Bowling Alley Point
Bringle
Tooraweenah
Murrawal
Binnaway Nat Res
Spring Ridge
Carroll
Lower Quipolly
Armatree
Windurong
Premer
Yannergee
Tamarang
Pine Ridge
Quirindi

0 10 20 30 40 50
kilometres

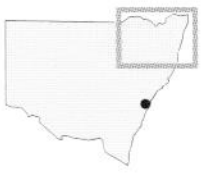

H J K L M N P

1: Laravale, Tamrookum, Numinbah Valley, Springbrook NP, Burleigh Heads, Coolangatta, Tweed Heads, Fingal Head, Banora Point, Chinderah, Kingscliff, Main Range National Park, Rockbrae, Emu Vale, Karara, Lake Leslie, Warwick, Mt Barney Nat Park, Rathdowney, Mt Barney, Koreelah Nat Pk, Limpinwood Nat Res, Lamington Nat Park, Mt Numinbah Nat Res, Numinbah, Bilambil, Chillingham, Tumbulgum, Bald Mtn, Tyalgum, Condong, Bogangar, Murwillumbah, Killarney, Dalman, Mt Lindesay, Cougal, Lindesay View, Border Ranges NP, Mt Warning Nat Pk, Uki, Pottsville Beach, Legume, Old Koreelah, Woodenbong, Mount Lion, Burringbar

2: Lake Coolmunda, Tank Mtn, Dalveen, Maryland Nat Pk, Tooloom Nat Park, Urbenville, Range, Grevillia, Old Grevillia, Roseberry, Mt Jerusalem Nat Park, Kunghur, Wooyung, Ocean Shores, Brunswick Heads, Mullumbimby, Wylie Creek, Captains Ck Nat Res, Toonumbar Nat Pk, Wiangaree, Horseshoe Creek, Blue Knob, Mt Matheson, The Summit, Rivertree Peak, Liston, Nightcap NP, Cawongla, Nimbin, Goonengerry, Stanthorpe, Tooloom, Yabbro Nat Pk, Eden Creek, Kyogle, Byron Bay, Downs Mtn, Pikedale, Amosfield, Old Bonalbo, Ettrick, Channon, The Dunoon, Rosebank, Modanville, Bangalow, Nashua, Suffolk Park, Glen Aplin, Paddys Flat, Bonalbo, Dyraaba Central, Cedar Point, Rock Valley, Goolmangar, Bexhill

3: Mt Gunyah, Sundown National Park, Ballandean, Boonoo Boonoo Nat Pk, Dividing, Richmond Range NP, Theresa Creek, Doubtful Creek, Fairy Hill, Bentley, Lismore, Lennox Head, Wollongbar, Girraween Nat Pk, Bald Rock NP, Glenlyon, Mummulgum, Woodview, Casino, Alstonville, Ballina, Silver Spur, Lake Glenlyon, Boonoo Boonoo, Sandy Hill, Bruxner, Tabulam, Hwy, Greenridge, Empire Vale, Wallangarra, Drake, Mallanganee, Hogarth Range NP, Leeville, Tuckurimba, Yorklea, Tatham, Wardell, Mole River, Mingoola, Tarban, Sunnyside, Basket Swamp NP, Mallanganee Nat Pk, Coraki, Dungarubba, Broadwater, Riverton, Bryans Gap, Leechs Gully, Alice, Busbys Flat, Coombell, Ellangowan, Bungawalbin Nat Res, 29°, Bonshaw, Tenterfield, Demon Nat Res, River, Wyan, Woodburn, Broadwater NP, Evans Head

4: Mt Bowman, Torrington SRA, Black Mtn, Great, Surface Hill, Mt Pikapene Nat Park, Rappville, Snapper Point, Maidenhead, Spirabo Nat Pk, Billyrimba, Mt Neville Nat Res, Tabbimoble, Tabbimoble Swamp NP, Bluff Rock, Pacific, Round Hill, Sandy Flat, Baryulgil, Camira Creek, Range, Bundjalung National Park, Kathida, Torrington, Burnt Down Scrub Nat Res, Whiporie, Summerland Way, Richmond, Mororo, Stannum, Bolivia, Tent Ck, Barretts Creek, Banyabba Nat Res, Chatsworth, Mulloway Point, Tent Hill, Washpool Nat Pk, Timbarra, Washpool National Park, Coaldale, The Broadwater, Iluka, Emmaville, Deepwater, Harwood, Yamba, Strathbogie

5: Butterleaf Nat Res, Gibraltar Range, Gordon Brook, Cangai, Fortis Ck Nat Pk, Lawrence, Maclean, Angourie, Wooloweyah Estuary, The Bald Knob, Dundee Rail, Dundee, Glen Elgin, Gibraltar Range NP, Gwydir, Jackadgery, Copmanhurst, Woodford Dale, Ferry, Tyndale, Yuraygir National Park, Kings Plains, Wellingrove, Bald Nob, Black Mtn, River, Koolkhan, Ulmarra, Brooms Head, Sapphire, Yarrowford, Barool Nat Pk, Nymboida National Park, Grafton, Tucabia, Sandon, Sandon Bluffs, Matheson, Hwy, South Grafton, Range, Gwydir, Swan Vale, Glen Innes, Red Range, Mann River Nature Res, Newton Boyd, Ramornie Nat Pk, OBX Creek, Pillar Valley, Minnie Water, Bare Point, Wooli

6: Stonehenge, Carters Mtn, Dalmorton, Buccarumbi, Braunstone, Coutts Crossing, Louis Point, Koukandowie Nat Res, Yuraygir National Park, Pinkett, Kangaroo Camp, Maybole, Glencoe, Guy Fawkes River Nat Pk, Chaelundi Nat Pk, Nymboida, Kungala, Halfway Creek, Mount Mitchell, Red Herring Hill, Red Rock, Corindi Beach, 30°, Single Nat Pk, Ben Lomond, Warra Nat Pk, Towallum, Glenreagh, Coast, Arrawarra, Wandsworth, Llangothlin Lake, Backwater, Chaelundi Mtn, Mt Hyland Nat Res, Clouds Creek, Byrnes Scrub Nat Res, Sherwood Nat Res, Georges Mtn, Wards Mistake, Billys Creek, Nana Glen, Woolgoolga, Tenterden, Llangothlin, Marengo Plain, Dundurrabin, Nymboi Binderary Nat Pk, Lowanna, Sandy Beach, Emerald Beach

7: Georges Mtn, Guyra, Tyringham, Paddys Plain, Coramba, Moonee Beach, Moonee Beach Nat Pk, Baldersleigh, Aberfoyle, Monkey Point, Bostobrick, Cascade, Ulong, Brooklana, Korora, Ulidarra Nat Res, Wongwibinda, Hernani, Cascade NP, Megan, Coffs Harbour, South, Booroolong Nat Res, Black Mountain, North Dorrigo, Dorrigo, Bindarri Nat Pk, Boambee, Pine Mtn, Joeys Knob, Cathedral Rock NP, Fernbrook, Dorrigo Nat Pk, Bonville, Sawtell, Mt Davidson, Ebor, Majors Point, Thora, Way, Valery, Repton, Mitchells Flat, Round Mtn, Darkwood, Bellinger River NP, Raleigh, Mylestom, Bellingen, Yarrowyck, Armidale, Waterfall, Point Lookout, Brierfield, Urunga

8: Wollomombi, Killiekrankie Mtn, Badwin Nat Res, Missabotti, Jaanngga Nat Res, Hillgrove, Jeogla, Valla Beach, New England National Park, Rocky River, Castle Doyle, Bowraville, Nambucca Heads, Uralla, Dunggir Nat Pk, Pacific, Gostwyck, Oxley Wild Rivers National Park, Five Day Creek, Burrapine, Talarm, Macksville, Enmore, Georges Creek, Hwy, Scotts Head, England, Kentucky, Borah Mtn, Comara, Bulingary, Warrell Creek, Grassy Head, Stuarts Point, Tasman, Bellbrook, Fungai, Oven Mtn, Carrai Nat Pk

9: Wollun, Trial Bay, South West Rocks, Arakoon, Baynes Mtn, Ngambaa Nat Res, Smoky Cape, Sea, Jerseyville, Walcha Road, Toorooka, Willawarrin, Clybucca, Walcha, Moona Plains, Daisy Plains, Boonanghi Nat Res, Turners Flat, Smithtown, Kinchela, 31°, Frederickton, Gladstone, Kookaburra, Korogoro Point, Ocean, Hat Head, Aberbaldie, Sherwood, Kempsey, South Kempsey, Hat Head NP, Kemps Pinnacle, Mt Banda Banda

10: Glen Morrison, Kangaroo Flat, Oxley Wild Rivers NP, Weabonga, Mt Werrikimbe, Willi Willi Nat Pk, Kumbatine Nat Pk, Kundabung, Crescent Head, Thunderbolts Way, Brackendale, Werrikimbe Nat Pk, Maria River Nat Pk, Niangala, Mt Sugarloaf, Oxley, Yarrowitch, Upper Rollands Plains, Rollands Plains, Limeburners Creek Nat Res, Point Plomer, Mummel Gulf Nat Pk, Mt Seaview, Doyles River Nat Res, Forbes River, Bellangry, Saltwater Lake, Telegraph Point, North, Ogunbil, Myrtle Scrub, Pappinbarra, Kindee, Pembrooke, Blackmans Point, Nowendoc Nat Park, Way, Riamukka, Mount Seaview, Yarras, Ellenborough, Beechwood, Wauchope, Port Macquarie, Raffles Peak, Hwy, Bagnoo, Nowendoc, Ag Rock, 152°, 153°

H J K L M N P

Map 5

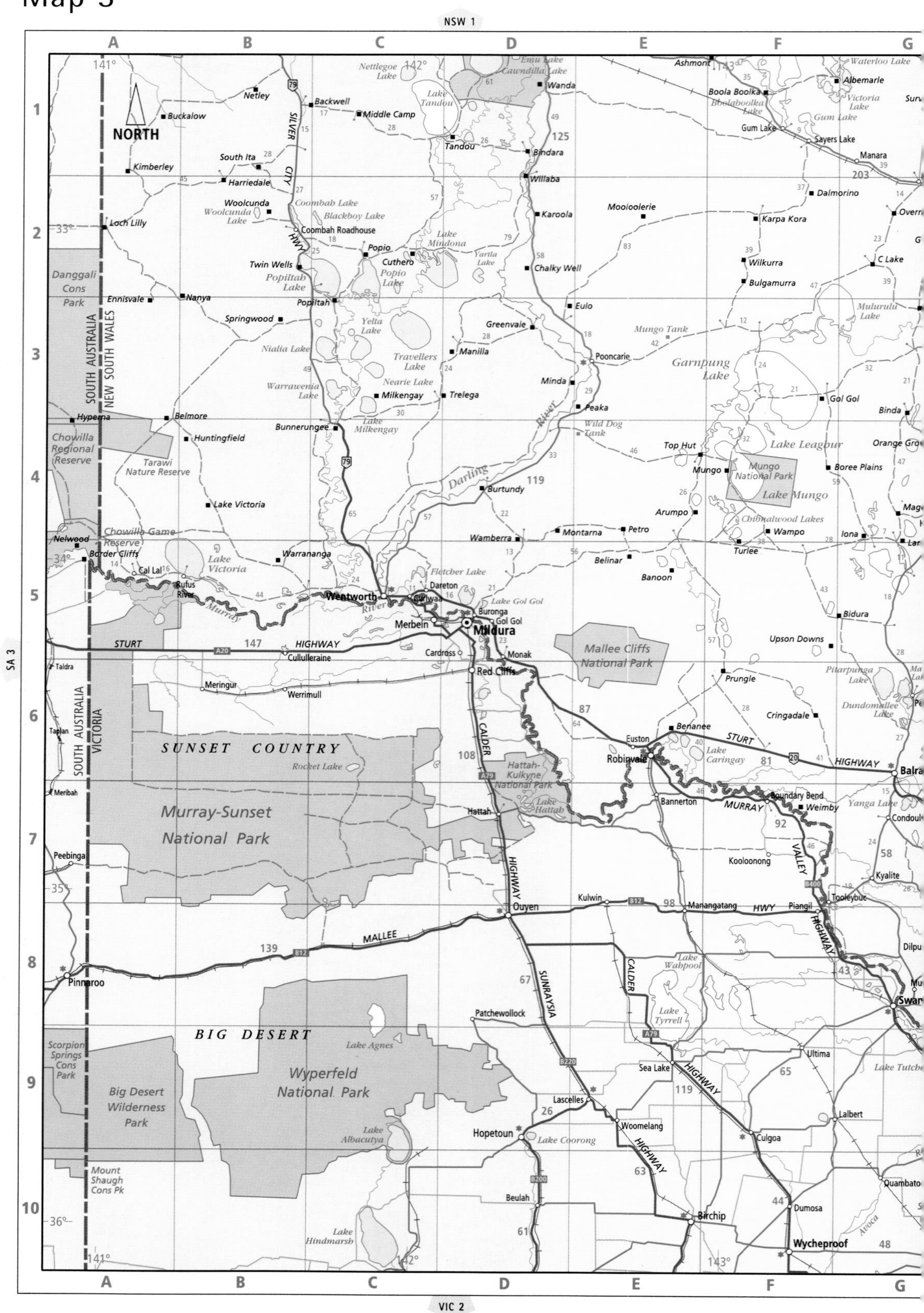
NSW 1
NORTH
SOUTH AUSTRALIA
NEW SOUTH WALES
VICTORIA
Danggali Cons Park
Chowilla Regional Reserve
Tarawi Nature Reserve
Chowilla Game Reserve
Mallee Cliffs National Park
Mungo National Park
SUNSET COUNTRY
Murray-Sunset National Park
Hattah-Kulkyne National Park
BIG DESERT
Wyperfeld National Park
Big Desert Wilderness Park
Scorpion Springs Cons Park
Mount Shaugh Cons Pk
Netley
Buckalow
Kimberley
South Ita
Harriedale
Woolcunda
Loch Lilly
Ennisvale
Nanya
Springwood
Hypurna
Belmore
Huntingfield
Lake Victoria
Nelwood
Border Cliffs
Cal Lal
Rufus River
Warrananga
Backwell
Middle Camp
Coombah Roadhouse
Twin Wells
Popiltah
Popio
Cuthero
Bunnerungee
Milkengay
Trelega
Manilla
Tandou
Wanda
Bindara
Willaba
Karoola
Chalky Well
Eulo
Greenvale
Pooncarie
Minda
Peaka
Burtundy
Wamberra
Montarna
Petro
Belinar
Banoon
Ashmont
Boola Boolka
Gum Lake
Sayers Lake
Manara
Albemarle
Dalmorino
Mooloolerie
Karpa Kora
Wilkurra
Bulgamurra
C Lake
Gol Gol
Top Hut
Mungo
Arumpo
Wampo
Turlee
Iona
Boree Plains
Bidura
Upson Downs
Prungle
Cringadale
Benanee
Euston
Robinvale
Bannerton
Boundary Bend
Weimby
Wentworth
Gurlwaa
Dareton
Buronga
Merbein
Mildura
Gol Gol
Cardross
Monak
Red Cliffs
Cullulleraine
Meringur
Werrimull
Hattah
Ouyen
Kulwin
Manangatang
Piangil
Tooleybuc
Kyalite
Kooloonong
Taldra
Taplan
Meribah
Peebinga
Pinnaroo
Patchewollock
Sea Lake
Lascelles
Woomelang
Hopetoun
Beulah
Birchip
Culgoa
Lalbert
Ultima
Dumosa
Wycheproof
Quambatook
SILVER CITY HWY
STURT HIGHWAY
CALDER HIGHWAY
MALLEE HWY
SUNRAYSIA HIGHWAY
MURRAY VALLEY HIGHWAY
Darling River
Murray River
Lake Mungo
Lake Leaghur
Garnpung Lake
Lake Tyrrell
Lake Agnes
Lake Albacutya
Lake Hindmarsh
Lake Coorong
SA 3
VIC 2

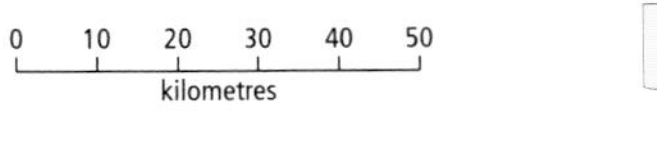
0 10 20 30 40 50
kilometres

NSW 6

NORTH
CANBERRA
Queanbeyan
Goulburn
Wollongong
Yass
Crookwell
Cooma
Bombala
Braidwood
Bungendore
Batemans Bay
Moruya
Narooma
Bega
Merimbula
Eden
Nowra
Bomaderry
Kiama
Mittagong
Bowral
Moss Vale
Ulladulla
Milton
Shellharbour
Port Kembla
Berry
Gerringong
Tathra
Bermagui
Cobargo
Mallacoota
Genoa
Cann River
Delegate
Nimmitabel
Bredbo
Michelago
Tharwa
Yass
Gunning
Collector
Tarago
Captains Flat
AUSTRALIAN CAPITAL TERRITORY
GREAT DIVIDING RANGE
HUME HWY
FEDERAL HWY
KINGS HWY
BARTON HWY
MONARO HWY
PRINCES HWY
CANN VALLEY HWY
NEW SOUTH WALES
VICTORIA
Morton National Park
Deua National Park
Wadbilliga National Park
Namadgi National Park
Murramarang Nat Park
Jervis Bay Nat Park
Ben Boyd NP
Nadgee Nature Reserve
Coopracambra National Park
Jervis Bay
Batemans Bay
Twofold Bay
Disaster Bay
Montague Island
Gabo Island
Cape Howe
Green Cape
Point Perpendicular
St Georges Head
SOUTH PACIFIC OCEAN
TASMAN SEA
H J K L M N P
1 2 3 4 5 6 7 8 9 10
149° 150° 151°
35° 36° 37°

VIC 4

Map 1

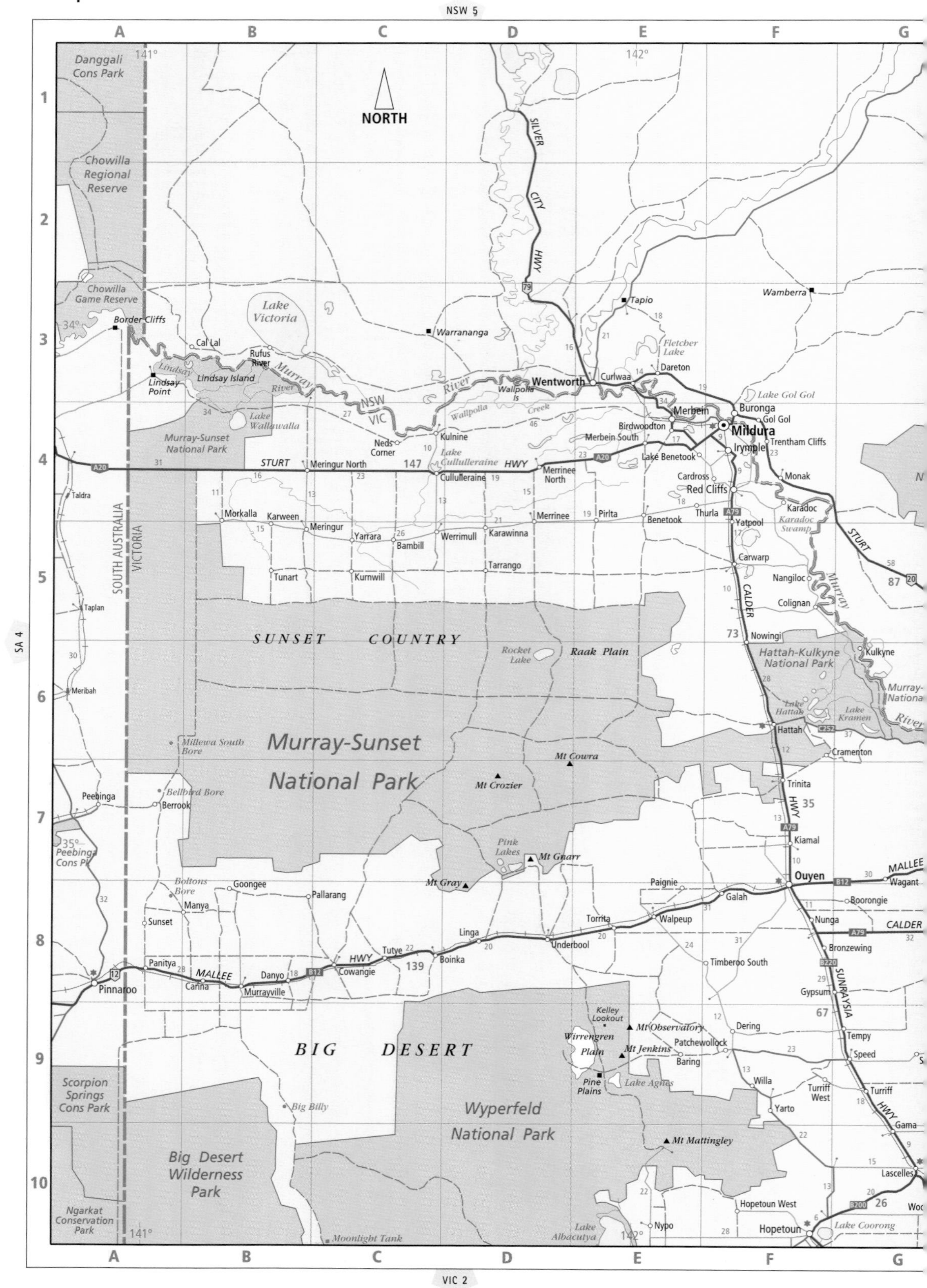
NSW 5
NORTH
Danggali Cons Park
Chowilla Regional Reserve
Chowilla Game Reserve
Border Cliffs
Lake Victoria
Cal Lal
Rufus River
Lindsay Point
Lindsay Island
Murray River
Lake Wallawalla
Murray-Sunset National Park
Warrananga
Tapio
Fletcher Lake
Dareton
Curlwaa
Wentworth
Wallpolla Is
Wallpolla Creek
Lake Gol Gol
Buronga
Gol Gol
Merbein
Birdwoodton
Merbein South
Mildura
Trentham Cliffs
Irymple
Lake Benetook
Cardross
Red Cliffs
Monak
Wamberra
SILVER CITY HWY
Neds Corner
Kulnine
Lake Cullulleraine
STURT HWY
Meringur North
Cullulleraine
Merrinee North
Taldra
Morkalla
Karween
Meringur
Yarrara
Bambill
Werrimull
Karawinna
Merrinee
Pirlta
Benetook
Thurla
Yatpool
Karadoc
Karadoc Swamp
Carwarp
Nangiloc
Colignan
Tunart
Kurnwill
Tarrango
SOUTH AUSTRALIA
VICTORIA
Taplan
SA 4
SUNSET COUNTRY
Rocket Lake
Raak Plain
CALDER HWY
Nowingi
Kulkyne
Hattah-Kulkyne National Park
Meribah
Lake Hattah
Lake Kramen
Hattah
Cramenton
Millewa South Bore
Murray-Sunset National Park
Mt Cowra
Mt Crozier
Trinita
Peebinga
Bellbird Bore
Berrook
Kiamal
Peebinga Cons Pk
Pink Lakes
Mt Gnarr
Ouyen
MALLEE
Wagant
Mt Gray
Boltons Bore
Goongee
Pallarang
Paignie
Galah
Boorongie
Manya
Sunset
Torrita
Walpeup
Nunga
CALDER
Linga
Underbool
Bronzewing
Tutye
Boinka
Timberoo South
Panitya
MALLEE HWY
Danyo
Cowangie
Pinnaroo
Carina
Murrayville
Gypsum
SUNRAYSIA HWY
Kelley Lookout
Mt Observatory
Dering
BIG DESERT
Wirrengren Plain
Mt Jenkins
Patchewollock
Baring
Tempy
Speed
Scorpion Springs Cons Park
Pine Plains
Lake Agnes
Willa
Turriff West
Turriff
Big Billy
Wyperfeld National Park
Yarto
Gama
Mt Mattingley
Big Desert Wilderness Park
Lascelles
Ngarkat Conservation Park
Hopetoun West
Nypo
Lake Albacutya
Hopetoun
Lake Coorong
Moonlight Tank
VIC 2

H J K L M N P

143° 144°

Chibnalwood Lakes
Turlee
34°
Lachlan River
Ita Lake
Prungle
Pitarpunga Lake
Lake Macommon
Ganaway Lake
Murrumbidgee
Penarie
Dundomallee Lake
Maude
Lake Benanee
River
Lake Tala
Robinvale
Lake Caringay
81
Waldaria Lake
Murrumbidgee
Balranald
HIGHWAY
131
Bannerton
Kyndalyn
MURRAY
Boundary Bend
STURT
Mangooya
Narrung
92
VALLEY
Condoulpe
Yanga Lake
Koorkab
Piambie
Condoulpe Lake
Annuello
Kenley
58
Kooloonong
Haysdale
Koimbo
Perekerten
Bolton
Kyalite
Natya
HWY
Moolpa
Kulwyne
Prooinga
Piangil North
Tooleybuc
35°
Stony Crossing
HWY 43
Manangatang
Piangil
Wood Wood
Moulamein
River
Wakool
71
Moulamein
Towan
Cocamba
Tudor
Koraleigh
Edward
Nyah
Chinkapook
Nyah West
Vinifera
Speewa
110
Daytrap
43
Beverford
Chillingollah
Pira
Tyntynder Central
River
River
Nowie North
Murray Downs
Lake Wahpool
Lake Timboram
Woorinen
Swan Hill
Lake Tyrrell
Waitchie
Channel
Tyrrell Downs
Murray
Tims
Gowanford
Lake Boga
Fish Point
103
Long Plains
Ultima
River
Ballbank
Lake Boga
Lake Tutchewop
Wakool
Goschen
Benjeroop
Sea Lake
Tresco
Winlaton
Murrabit
Lalbert Road
Kunat
Mystic Park
57
Boigbeat
Meatian
Myall
Kangaroo Lake
Lake Charm
Beauchamp
Culfearne
Lake Cullen
Lake Charm
Capels Crossing
Barham
Berriwillock
The Marsh
Koondrook
Lake Lalbert
Lalbert
Middle Lake
Westby
Bael Bael
Teal Point
NSW
VIC
Lake Bael Bael
Kerang
Culgoa
Sandhill Lake
Koroop
Gannawarra

1 2 3 4 5 6 7 8 9 10

Map 2

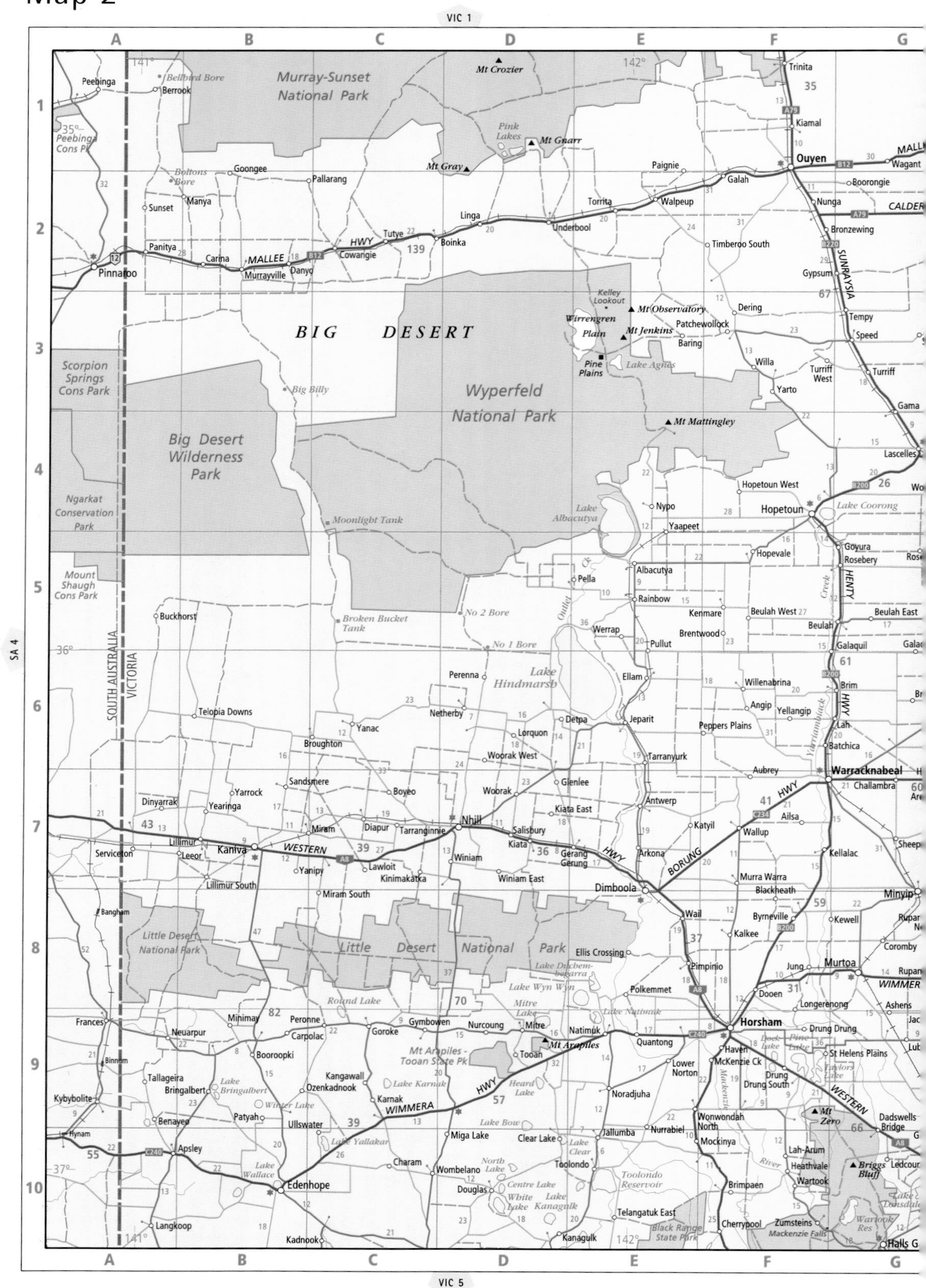
VIC 1
A
B
C
D
E
F
G
1
2
3
4
5
6
7
8
9
10
141°
142°
35°
36°
37°
Peebinga
Bellbird Bore
Berrook
Peebinga Cons Pk
Murray-Sunset National Park
Mt Crozier
Pink Lakes
Mt Gnarr
Mt Gray
Trinita
Kiamal
Ouyen
MALLEE
Wagant
Boltons Bore
Goongee
Pallarang
Manya
Sunset
Paignie
Galah
Boorongie
Nunga
CALDER
Torrita
Walpeup
Linga
Underbool
Bronzewing
Timberoo South
Panitya
Carina
MALLEE
HWY
Tutye
Boinka
Cowangie
Murrayville
Danyo
Pinnaroo
Gypsum
SUNRAYSIA
BIG DESERT
Kelley Lookout
Mt Observatory
Dering
Wirrengren Plain
Mt Jenkins
Patchewollock
Baring
Tempy
Speed
Pine Plains
Lake Agnes
Willa
Turriff West
Turriff
Yarto
Scorpion Springs Cons Park
Big Billy
Wyperfeld National Park
Gama
Mt Mattingley
Big Desert Wilderness Park
Lascelles
Ngarkat Conservation Park
Hopetoun West
Nypo
Hopetoun
Lake Coorong
Moonlight Tank
Lake Albacutya
Yaapeet
Goyura
Hopevale
Rosebery
Mount Shaugh Cons Park
Albacutya
Pella
Outlet Ck
HENTY
Creek
Rainbow
Kenmare
Beulah West
Beulah East
Buckhorst
Broken Bucket Tank
No 2 Bore
Brentwood
Beulah
Werrap
Pullut
SA 4
No 1 Bore
Galaquil
SOUTH AUSTRALIA
VICTORIA
Perenna
Lake Hindmarsh
Ellam
Willenabrina
Brim
Telopia Downs
Netherby
Detpa
Jeparit
Angip
Yellangip
Peppers Plains
Yanac
Lorquon
Yarriambiack
HWY
Lah
Broughton
Batchica
Woorak West
Tarranyurk
Aubrey
Warracknabeal
Sandsmere
Glenlee
Challambra
Yarrock
Boyeo
Woorak
Dinyarrak
Yearinga
Kiata East
Antwerp
Ailsa
HWY
Miram
Diapur
Tarranginnie
Nhill
Salisbury
Katyil
Wallup
Lillimur
Serviceton
Leeor
Kaniva
WESTERN
Kiata
Gerang Gerung
HWY
BORUNG
Arkona
Kellalac
Sheep
Yanipy
Lawloit
Winiam
Kinimakatka
Winiam East
Lillimur South
Dimboola
Murra Warra
Blackheath
Miram South
Minyip
Bangham
Wail
Byrneville
Kewell
Little Desert National Park
Little Desert National Park
Kalkee
Corombу
Ellis Crossing
Lake Duchembegarra
Pimpinio
Jung
Murtoa
Rupan
WIMMER
Lake Wyn Wyn
Polkemmet
Dooen
Round Lake
Mitre Lake
Lake Natimuk
Longerenong
Ashens
Frances
Minimay
Peronne
Gymbowen
Nurcoung
Mitre
Natimuk
Horsham
Drung Drung
Neuarpur
Carpolac
Goroke
Quantong
Mt Arapiles
Dock Lake
Pine Lake
Binnum
Booroopki
Mt Arapiles-Tooan State Pk
Tooan
Haven
McKenzie Ck
Lower Norton
St Helens Plains
Taylors Lake
Tallageira
Kangawall
Heard Lake
Drung
Bringalbert
Lake Bringalbert
Ozenkadnook
Lake Karnak
Drung South
Noradjuha
Mackenzie
Kybybolite
Karnak
WESTERN
Winter Lake
WIMMERA
HWY
Mt Zero
Dadswells Bridge
Benayeo
Patyah
Ullswater
Lake Bow
Wonwondah North
Hynam
Miga Lake
Clear Lake
Jallumba
Nurrabiel
Mockinya
Lake Yallakar
Lake Clear
Apsley
Charam
Lah-Arum
North Lake
Toolondo
Heathvale
Briggs Bluff
Ledcourt
Lake Wallace
Wombelano
River
Wartook
Edenhope
Centre Lake
Toolondo Reservoir
Brimpaen
Douglas
White Lake
Lake Kanagulk
Lake Lonsdale
Langkoop
Telangatuk East
Wartook Res
Zumsteins
Mackenzie Falls
Cherrypool
Black Range State Park
Kadnook
Kanagulk
Halls G
VIC 5

0 10 20 30 40
kilometres

NSW 7

H J K L M N P

NORTH

1 2 3 4 5 6 7 8 9 10

149° 150° 36° 37° 38°

Deua National Park
Moruya
HWY
Turlinjah
Tuross Lake
Bodalla
Narooma
Tilba Tilba
PRINCES
Cobargo
Bermagui
Biamanga Nat Park
Brogo
Mimosa Rocks National Park
Bega
Tathra
Wallagoot Lake
Bournda Nat Park
Merimbula
Ben Boyd National Park
Eden
East Boyd
Ben Boyd National Park
Narrabarba
Disaster Bay
Green Cape
Nadgee Nature Reserve
Nadgee Point
Mt Carlyle
Cape Howe
Gabo Island
Lake Barracoota
Fairhaven
Gipsy Point
Mallacoota
Mallacoota Inlet
Croajingolong National Park
Little Rame Head
Wingan Bay
Sandpatch Point
Wingan Point
Rame Head
Petrel Point
Cape Everard
Mt Everard
Croajingolong National Park
Tamboon
Tamboon Inlet
Furnell
Lake Furnell
Swan Lake
Sydenham Inlet
Bemm River
Pearl Point
East Cape
Cape Conran Coastal Park
Bellbird Creek
PRINCES
HWY
Cann River
Mt Cann
Lind Nat Park
Club Terrace
Tonghi Creek
Pyramid Hill
Noorinbee
Noorinbee North
Waldron Mtn
Mt Kaye
Weeragua
Chandlers Creek
CANN VALLEY
Coopracambra National Park
Mealing Hill
Wroxham
Wangarabell
Maramingo Hill
Genoa
Genoa Peak
Alfred Nat Park
NEW SOUTH WALES
VICTORIA
Buldah
Granite Mtn
Mt Canterbury
Mt Tennyson
Bondi Gulf Nat Pk
Errinundra National Park
Errinundra
Combienbar
Mt Ellery
Cobb Hill
Brown Mtn
Bee Tree Hill
Pike Hill
Mt Puggaree
Delegate
Delegate River
Bendoc North
Craigie
Haydens Bog
Mt Delegate
Bendoc
Bonang
Queensborough
Bombala
Delegate River
Cathcart
Ando
Nimmitabel
Coolangubra National Park
Wyndham
Tantawangalo National Park
Candelo
South East Forest National Park
Yowaka National Park
Towamba
Genoa National Park
Pericoe
Mt Imlay National Park
Mt Poole
HWY
Numbugga
Bemboka Nat Park
Wadbilliga National Park
Yowrie
GREAT DIVIDING RANGE
Numeralla
Cooma
MONARO HIGHWAY
HWY
Adaminaby
MOUNTAINS
Berridale
Snowy River
Dalgety
Mt Rix

Map 5

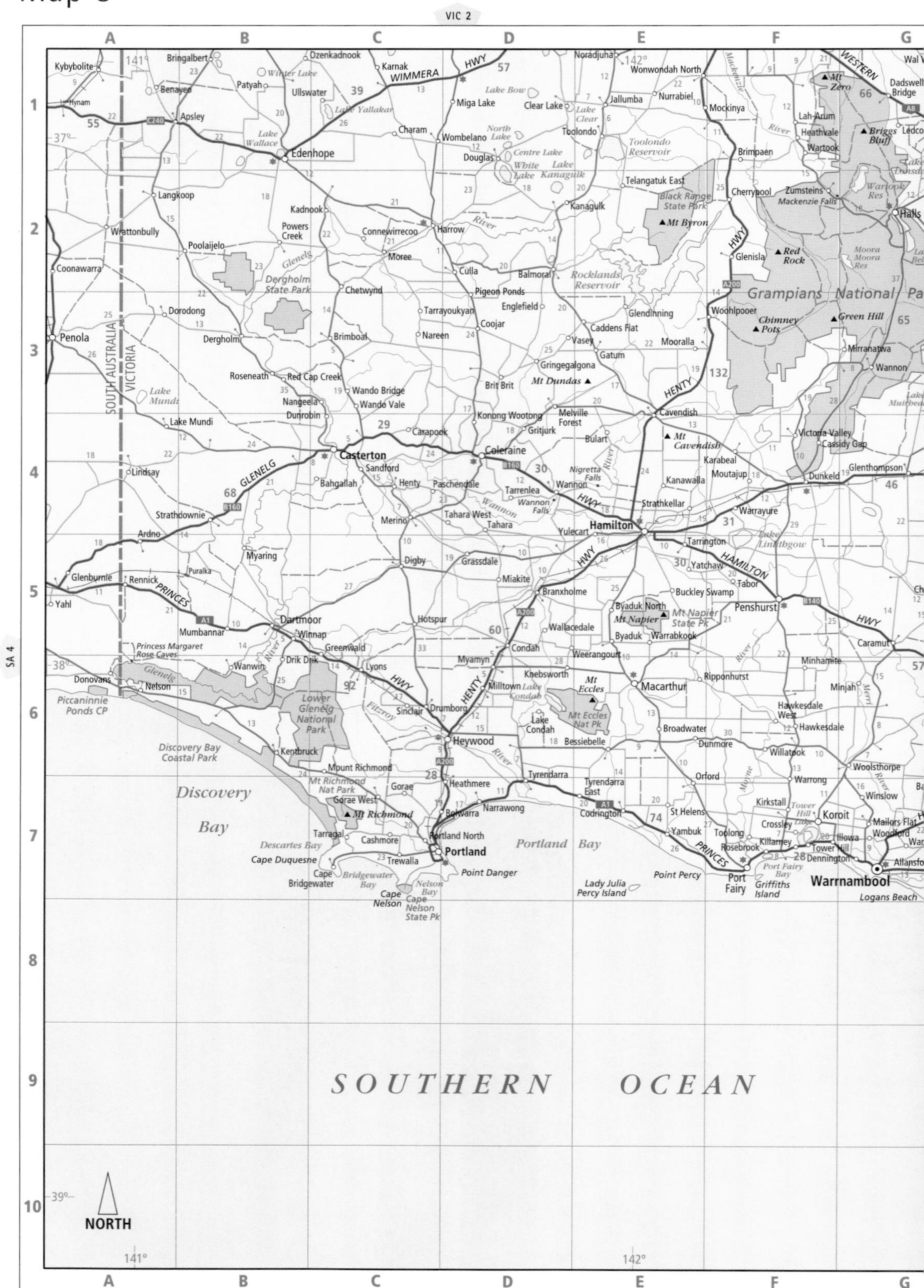
VIC 2
SA 4
A
B
C
D
E
F
G
1
2
3
4
5
6
7
8
9
10
141°
142°
37°
38°
39°
Kybybolite
Bringalbert
Ozenkadnook
Karnak
WIMMERA
HWY
57
Noradjuha
Wonwondah North
WESTERN
Wal Wal
Hynam
Benayeo
Patyah
Winter Lake
Ullswater
39
Lake Bow
Miga Lake
Clear Lake
Lake Clear
Jallumba
Nurrabiel
Mockinya
Mt Zero
66
Dadswells Bridge
55
Apsley
Lake Yallakar
Charam
Wombelano
North Lake
Toolondo
Toolondo Reservoir
Lah-Arum
Heathvale
Briggs Bluff
Lake Wallace
Edenhope
Centre Lake
Douglas
White Lake
Lake Kanagulk
Brimpaen
Wartook
Langkoop
Telangatuk East
Black Range State Park
Cherrypool
Zumsteins
Mackenzie Falls
Wartook Res
Kadnook
Kanagulk
Halls Gap
Wrattonbully
Powers Creek
Connewirrecoo
Harrow
River
Mt Byron
Poolaijelo
Moree
Glenisla
Red Rock
Moora Moora Res
Coonawarra
Dergholm State Park
Culla
Balmoral
Rocklands Reservoir
Chetwynd
Pigeon Ponds
Grampians National Park
Dorodong
Tarrayoukyan
Englefield
Glendinning
Woohlpooer
Chimney Pots
Green Hill
65
Penola
Dergholm
Brimboal
Nareen
Coojar
Caddens Flat
Vasey
Mooralla
Gatum
Mirranatwa
SOUTH AUSTRALIA
VICTORIA
Gringegalgona
Roseneath
Red Cap Creek
132
Wannon
Lake Mundi
Wando Bridge
Brit Brit
Mt Dundas
HENTY
Nangeela
Wando Vale
Dunrobin
Konong Wootong
Melville Forest
Cavendish
Lake Mundi
29
Carapook
Gritjurk
Mt Cavendish
Victoria Valley
Cassidy Gap
Bulart
Casterton
Coleraine
Karabeal
Lindsay
GLENELG
Sandford
30
Nigretta Falls
Moutajup
Dunkeld
Glenthompson
Bahgallah
Henty
Paschendale
Kanawalla
46
68
Tarrenlea
Wannon
Wannon Falls
HWY
Strathdownie
Strathkellar
Warrayure
Merino
Tahara West
Tahara
Hamilton
Ardno
Yulecart
31
Lake Linlithgow
Tarrington
Myaring
Digby
Grassdale
30
Yatchaw
HAMILTON
Glenburnie
Rennick
Puralka
Miakite
Tabor
PRINCES
Branxholme
Buckley Swamp
Yahl
Byaduk North
Mt Napier
Mt Napier State Pk
Penshurst
Dartmoor
Hotspur
Mumbannar
Winnap
60
Wallacedale
Byaduk
Warrabkook
Caramut
Princess Margaret Rose Caves
Greenwald
Condah
Weerangourt
Minhamite
Wanwin
Drik Drik
Myamyn
Knebsworth
Donovans
Nelson
Lyons
Milltown
Lake Condah
Mt Eccles
Macarthur
Ripponhurst
Minjah
57
Piccaninnie Ponds CP
Lower Glenelg National Park
Sinclair
Drumborg
Mt Eccles Nat Pk
Hawkesdale West
Hawkesdale
Fitzroy
Heywood
Bessiebelle
Broadwater
Discovery Bay Coastal Park
Kentbruck
Dunmore
Willatook
Woolsthorpe
Mount Richmond
Tyrendarra
Orford
Warrong
Mt Richmond Nat Park
Gorae
Heathmere
Tyrendarra East
Discovery Bay
Gorae West
Mt Richmond
Narrawong
Kirkstall
Winslow
Bolwarra
Codrington
74
St Helens
Tower Hill Lake
Koroit
Tarragal
Portland North
Yambuk
Toolong
Crossley
Mailors Flat
Woodford
Cashmore
Portland Bay
Rosebrook
Killarney
Illowa
Tower Hill
Descartes Bay
Portland
Dennington
Cape Duquesne
Trewalla
Allansford
Point Danger
Port Fairy Bay
Cape Bridgewater
Bridgewater Bay
Nelson Bay
Lady Julia Percy Island
Point Percy
Port Fairy
Griffiths Island
Warrnambool
Cape Nelson
Cape Nelson State Pk
Logans Beach
SOUTHERN OCEAN
NORTH

0 10 20 30 40
kilometres

VIC 2

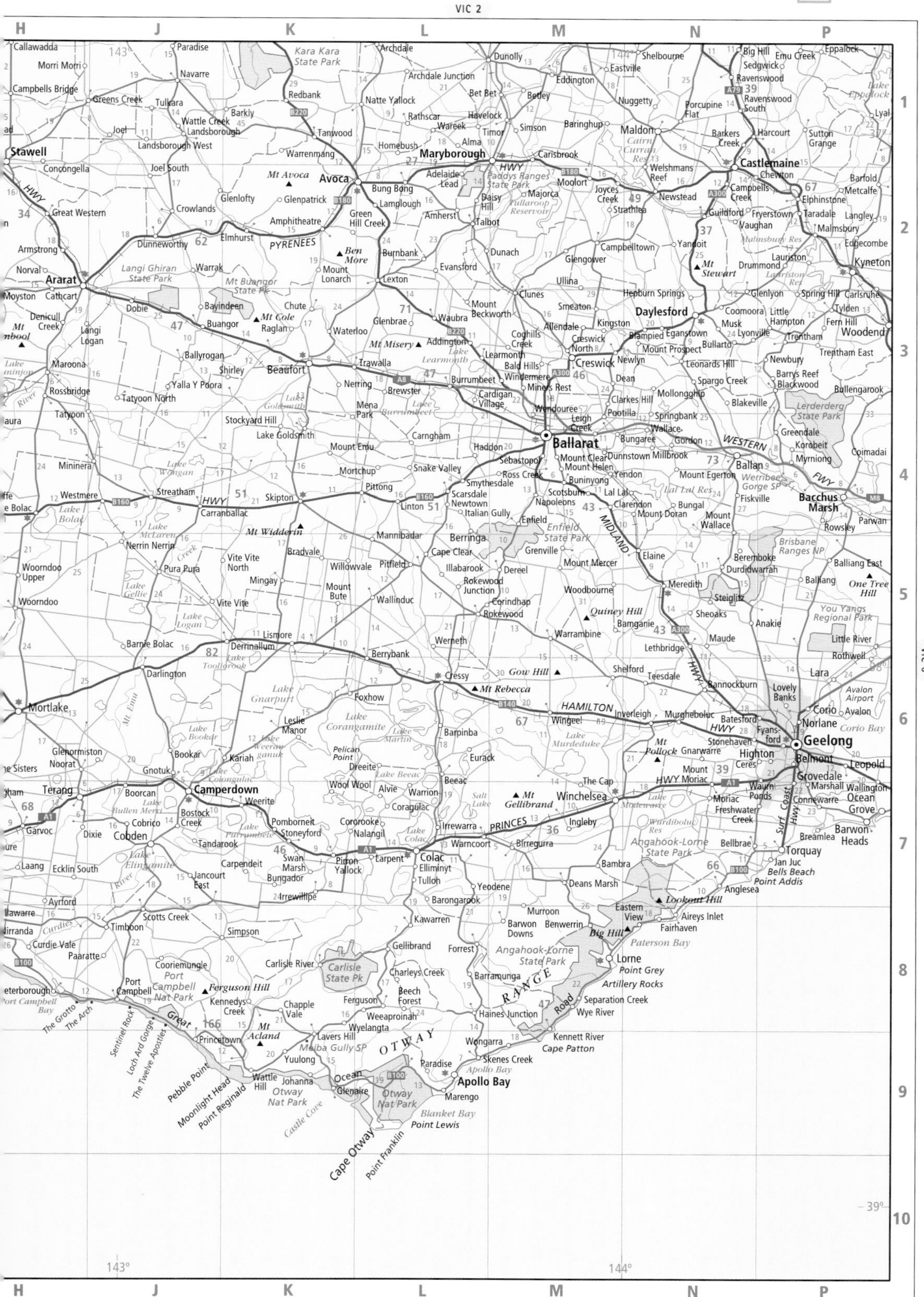

VIC 6

Map 6

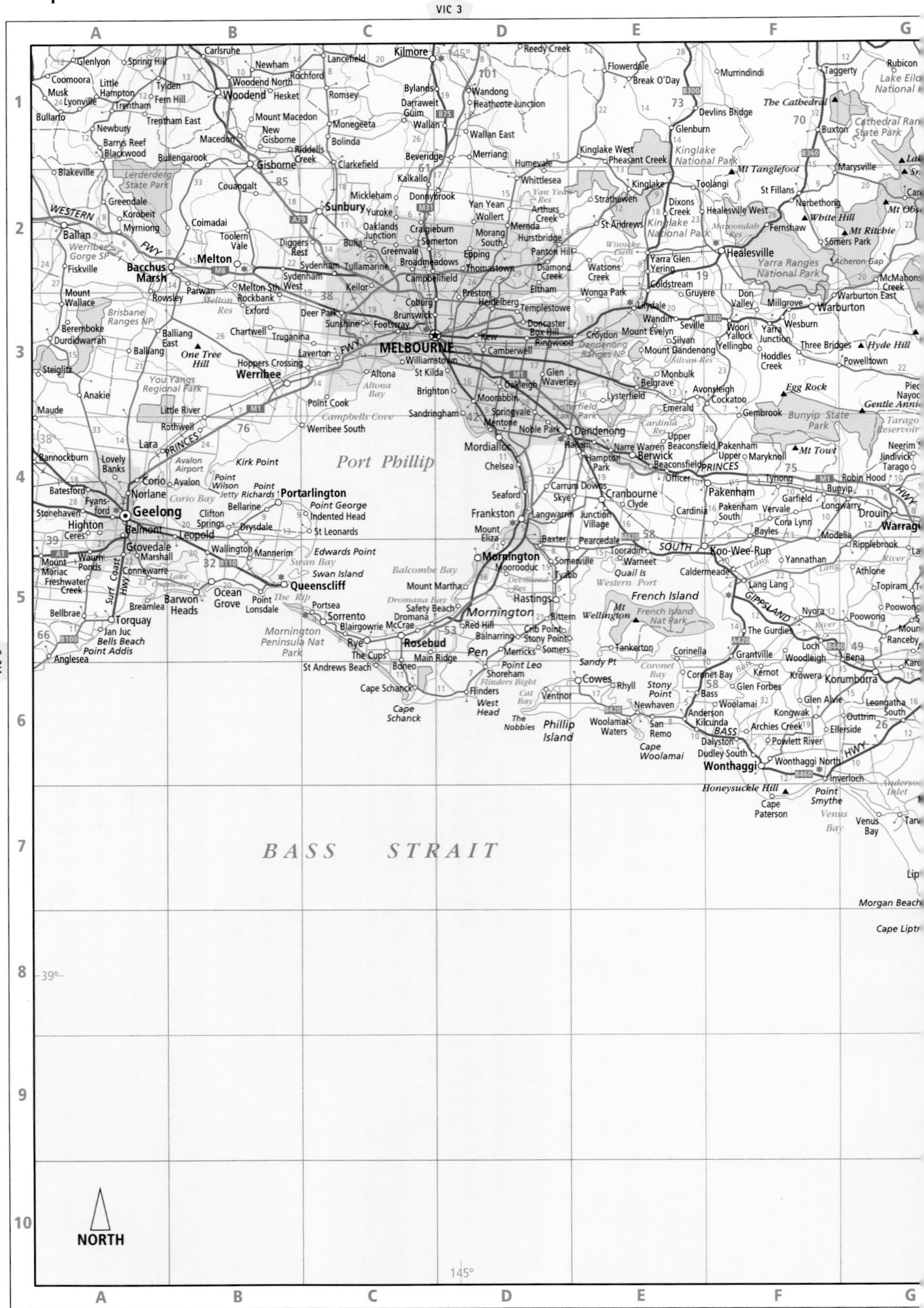
VIC 3
VIC 5
A
B
C
D
E
F
G
1
2
3
4
5
6
7
8
9
10
NORTH
145°
38°
39°
Carlsruhe
Glenlyon
Spring Hill
Coomoora
Little Hampton
Tylden
Newham
Woodend North
Rochford
Lancefield
Kilmore
Reedy Creek
Flowerdale
Break O'Day
Murrindindi
Taggerty
Rubicon
Musk
Lyonville
Trentham
Fern Hill
Woodend
Hesket
Romsey
Bylands
Wandong
Heathcote Junction
Darraweit Guim
Wallan
Bullarto
Trentham East
Mount Macedon
Monegeeta
Kinglake West
Pheasant Creek
Kinglake National Park
Devlins Bridge
Glenburn
The Cathedral
Cathedral Range State Park
Buxton
Marysville
Newbury
Barrys Reef
Blackwood
Macedon
New Gisborne
Bolinda
Wallan East
Beveridge
Merriang
Humevale
Whittlesea
Blakeville
Bullengarook
Gisborne
Riddells Creek
Clarkefield
Kalkallo
Lerderderg State Park
Couangalt
Mickleham
Donnybrook
Yan Yean
Yan Yean Res
Strathewen
Kinglake
Toolangi
Mt Tanglefoot
St Fillans
Narbethong
White Hill
Mt Ritchie
Greendale
Korobeit
Myrniong
Coimadai
Sunbury
Yuroke
Oaklands Junction
Craigieburn
Wollert
Mernda
Arthurs Creek
St Andrews
Dixons Creek
Healesville West
Fernshaw
Somers Park
Maroondah Res
Ballan
Werribee Gorge SP
Fiskville
Bacchus Marsh
Melton
Toolern Vale
Diggers Rest
Bulla
Greenvale
Somerton
Morang South
Hurstbridge
Panton Hill
Winneke Dam
Watsons Creek
Yarra Glen
Yering
Healesville
Yarra Ranges National Park
Acheron Gap
McMahons Creek
Warburton East
Warburton
Mount Wallace
Rowsley
Parwan
Melton Sth
Rockbank
Melton Res
Exford
Sydenham
Sydenham West
Tullamarine
Broadmeadows
Epping
Thomastown
Diamond Creek
Eltham
Campbellfield
Keilor
Coburg
Preston
Heidelberg
Templestowe
Wonga Park
Coldstream
Gruyere
Don Valley
Millgrove
Brisbane Ranges NP
Deer Park
Brunswick
Lilydale
Wandin
Seville
Woori Yallock
Yarra Junction
Wesburn
Beremboke
Durdidwarrah
Balliang East
Chartwell
Truganina
Sunshine
Footscray
Doncaster
Box Hill
Croydon
Mount Evelyn
Silvan
Yellingbo
Balliang
One Tree Hill
Laverton
MELBOURNE
Kew
Camberwell
Ringwood
Dandenong Ranges NP
Mount Dandenong
Silvan Res
Hoddles Creek
Three Bridges
Hyde Hill
Powelltown
Steiglitz
Hoppers Crossing
Werribee
Williamstown
St Kilda
Altona
Altona Bay
Brighton
Oakleigh
Glen Waverley
Monbulk
Belgrave
Avonsleigh
Cockatoo
Egg Rock
Anakie
You Yangs Regional Park
Lysterfield
Emerald
Gembrook
Bunyip State Park
Gentle Annie
Maude
Little River
Point Cook
Campbells Cove
Sandringham
Moorabbin
Springvale
Mentone
Lysterfield Lake Park
Cardinia Res
Werribee South
Rothwell
Lara
PRINCES
Noble Park
Dandenong
Upper Beaconsfield
Pakenham Upper
Maryknoll
Mt Towt
Neerim
Jindivick
Tarago
Bannockburn
Lovely Banks
Avalon Airport
Kirk Point
Port Phillip
Mordialloc
Hallam
Narre Warren
Berwick
Hampton Park
Beaconsfield
Chelsea
Officer
Tynong
Robin Hood
Corio
Avalon
Point Wilson
Point Richards
Batesford
Norlane
Corio Bay
Jetty
Portarlington
Seaford
Carrum Downs
Skye
Cranbourne
Clyde
Pakenham
Garfield
Bunyip
Stonehaven
Fyansford
Geelong
Bellarine
Point George
Indented Head
Frankston
Langwarrin
Junction Village
Cardinia
Pakenham South
Vervale
Longwarry
Drouin
Highton
Ceres
Belmont
Leopold
Clifton Springs
Drysdale
St Leonards
Mount Eliza
Cora Lynn
Bayles
Modella
Ripplebrook
Grovedale
Marshall
Wallington
Mannerim
Edwards Point
Baxter
Pearcedale
Tooradin
Warneet
Koo-Wee-Rup
Yannathan
Mount Moriac
Waurn Ponds
Freshwater Creek
Connewarre
Lake Connewarre
Swan Bay
Swan Island
Balcombe Bay
Mornington
Somerville
Mooroodue
Tyabb
Quail Is
Western Port
Caldermeade
Athlone
Surf Coast Hwy
Barwon Heads
Ocean Grove
Queenscliff
Point Lonsdale
The Rip
Mount Martha
Hastings
French Island
Lang Lang
Topiram
Bellbrae
Breamlea
Portsea
Sorrento
Dromana Bay
Safety Beach
Dromana
Mornington
Bittern
Mt Wellington
French Island Nat Park
GIPPSLAND
Nyora
Poowong
Torquay
Jan Juc
Bells Beach
Point Addis
Anglesea
Mornington Peninsula Nat Park
Blairgowrie
McCrae
Rye
Rosebud
Red Hill
Balnarring
Crib Point
Stony Point
Somers
Pen
The Gurdies
Tankerton
Corinella
Grantville
Lock
Ranceby
Woodleigh
Bena
The Cups
Main Ridge
Merricks
Sandy Pt
Coronet Bay
Kernot
Korumburra
St Andrews Beach
Boneo
Point Leo
Shoreham
Flinders Bight
Cowes
Rhyll
Stony Point
Bass
Glen Forbes
Krowera
Cape Schanck
Flinders
West Head
Cat Bay
Ventnor
Newhaven
Woolamai
Glen Alvie
Leongatha South
Anderson
Kilcunda
Kongwak
Outtrim
The Nobbies
Phillip Island
Woolamai Waters
San Remo
Cape Woolamai
Dalyston
Archies Creek
Ellerside
Powlett River
Dudley South
Wonthaggi
Wonthaggi North
Inverloch
Anderson Inlet
Honeysuckle Hill
Cape Paterson
Point Smythe
Venus Bay
BASS STRAIT
Morgan Beach
Cape Liptrap
WESTERN FWY
PRINCES FWY
SOUTH
BASS HWY

0 10 20 30 40
kilometres

H J K L M N P

1

Jamieson
Jamieson
Goulburn
Mt Sunday
Alpine National Park
Mt McAdam
Mt Cynthia
Treasure
Mt Birregun
Mt Ewen
Mt Delusion
Brookville
Swifts Creek
Doctors Flat
Ensay North
Ensay
Howittville
Wongungarra
Ten Mile
Mt Terrible
Mt Reynard
Enoch Point
Knockwood
Mt Arbuckle
Mt Dawson
Dingo Knob
Mt Steve
Seldom Seen
Dawson City
Mt Skene
Crooked River
Nicholson
Dogtown
Stirling
Gaffneys Creek
Macalister River
A1 Mine Settlement
Mt Lookout
East Pinnacle
Dargo
Tambo Crossing
Tambo River
Mt Shillinglaw
Glencairn
Castle Hill
Waterford
Morris Peak
Forktown
Reward
Red Hill
Bruni Knob
Lamb Hill
Mt Sugarloaf

2

Matlock
Woods Point
Echo Point
Freestone Creek
Castleburn
Tabberabbera
Mt Hoad
Pheasant Hill
Clair
Fiddlers Green
Mt Ronald
Deptford
The Oaks
Matlock
Mt Hump
Mt Blomford
Cobbannah
Bullumwaal
Licola
Avon Wilderness Park
Hut
The Green Hill
Davey Knob
Mitchell River Nat Park
Mt Little Dick
Mt Gregory
Aberfeldy
Mt Useful
Big Hill
Mt Angus
Clifton Creek
Bruthen
Basalt Hill
Lake Thompson
Wright Hill
Mt Ray
Wiseleigh
Morgan
Mount Taylor
Mossiface
Myrrhee
Mt Whitelaw
Sullivans
Glenaladale
Iguana Creek
Sarsfield
Rocky Knob
Culloden
Woodglen
Walpa
Lindenow
Wy Yung
Tambo Upper
Tanjil Bren
Mt Baw Baw
Beardmore
Avon
The Fingerboards
Lucknow
Nicholson

3

Mt Margaret
Valencia Creek
Stockdale
Bairnsdale
Baw Baw Alpine Village
Murderers Hill
Glenmaggie
Glenmaggie Reservoir
Maffra West Upper
Briagolong
Lindenow South
HWY
Swan Beach
Creek
Fernbank
Jones Bay
Metung
Fumina
Baw Baw National Park
Coongulla
Boisdale
Bushy Park
Eagle Point
Lake King
Paynesville
Newry
Munro
Delvine
PRINCES
Forge Creek
Raymond I
Tyers Junction
Walhalla
Seaton
Pt Best
Rawson
Point Wilson
Fumina South
Thomson
Cowwarr Weir
Heyfield
Maffra
Tinamba
Stratford
Bengworden
Goon Nure
Erica
Riverslea
Meerlieu
The Lakes NP
Hill End
Moondarra
Mt Lookout
Cowwarr
River
Airly
River
Pelican Point
Denison
Bundalaguah
Perry Bridge
Moondarra State Pk
Clydebank
Lake Victoria
Grove
Blue Rock Lake
Winnindoo
Nambrok
Myrtlebank

4

Moondarra Reservoir
Toongabbie
Nambrok West
Cobains
Lake Wellington
Holland Landing
Loch Sport
Tyers Park
Glengarry
Kilmany
Fulham
RAAF Base East Sale
Sale
Tanjil South
Lake Narracan
Yallourn North
Wurruk
The Heart
Seacombe
Beach
Tyers
Kilmany South
River
Longford
Gippsland Lakes Coastal Park
Moe
La Trobe
Dutson
Reeve
Lake Coleman
Traralgon
Rosedale
Newborough
Flynn
Deadman Hill
Paradise Beach
Trafalgar
Holey Plains State Park
Golden Beach
Coalville
Morwell
HYLAND
Flynns Creek
Merriman
HWY
Narracan
Traralgon South
Willung
Delray Beach
Hazelwood Cooling Pond
Hiamdale
Stradbroke West
Creek
Flamingo Beach

5

Thorpdale
Gormandale
Glomar Beach
Childers
HWY
Churchill
Stradbroke
Yinnar
Koornalla
Willung South
Toms Cap
Mile
Allambee South
Carrajung
Ck
Boolarra
Carrajung South
Giffard West
The Honeysuckles
Morwell Nat Park
Seaspray
Mirboo North
Budgeree
Blackwarry
Giffard
Boolarra South
Balook
Tarra-Bulga Nat Park
HWY
GIPPSLAND
Mardan
Wonwron
Darriman
Mirboo
Mirboo East
Tarra Valley
Macks Creek
Jack Smith Lake
Hiawatha
Ninety
Dumbalk North
Tarwin East
Ryton
Staceys Bridge
Devon
Woodside

6

Turtons Creek
Greenmount
SOUTH
Dollar
Wonyip
Woodside Beach
Binginwarri
Yarram
Hunterson
Mount Best
Alberton West
Hazel Park
Woorarra
Alberton
McLoughlins Beach
Tarraville
St. Margaret Island
Foster
Toora
Hedley
Manns Beach
Bennison
Agnes
Welshpool
Port Albert
Port Franklin
Shallow Inlet
Hoddle
Barry Beach
Port Welshpool
Sunday Island
Kate Kearney Entrance
Clonmel Island

7

Corner Inlet
Snake Island
Port Albert Entrance
North
Yanakie
Entrance Point
Townsend Point
Duck Point
Mt Hunter
Lighthouse Pt
Chinaman Knob
Three Mile Point
Wilsons Promontory
Monkey Pt
Cotters Beach
Wilsons Promontory Nat Pk
Five Mile Beach

8

Tongue Point
Whisky Bay
Sealers Cove
Leonard Point
Refuge Cove
Tidal River
Mt Oberon
Cape Wellington
Oberon Bay
Great Glennie Island
Mt Norgate
Waterloo Bay
Mt Boulder
South West Point
Anser Island
South Point
South East Point

9

Rodondo Island
Hogan Island

10

Kent Group
Erith Island
Dover Island
Deal Island
Curtis Island

147°
38°
39°

H J K L M N P

VIC 4

VIC

Map 1

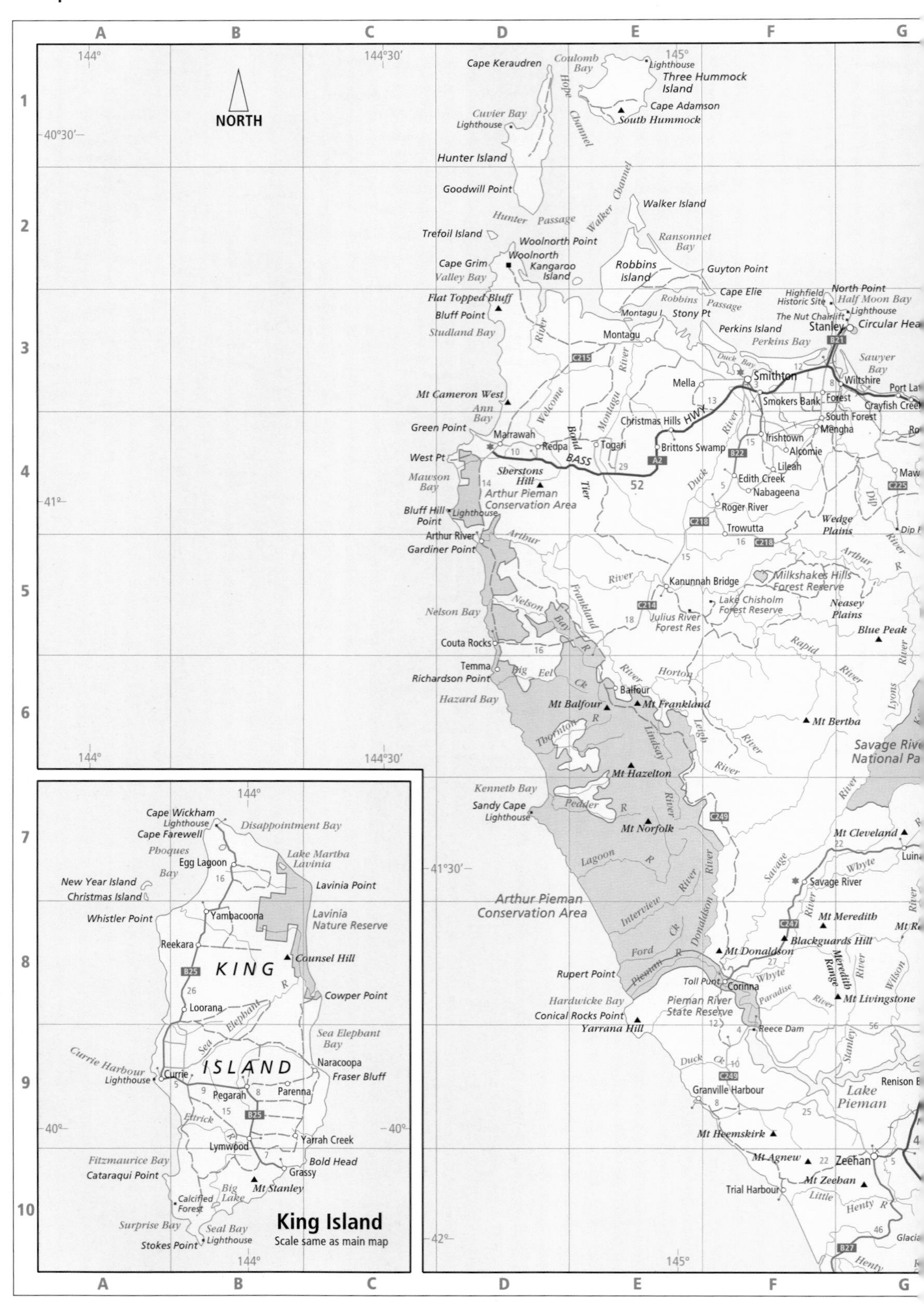

NORTH
Cape Keraudren
Coulomb Bay
Lighthouse
Three Hummock Island
Cape Adamson
South Hummock
Hope Channel
Cuvier Bay
Lighthouse
Hunter Island
Goodwill Point
Walker Channel
Walker Island
Hunter Passage
Trefoil Island
Woolnorth Point
Ransonnet Bay
Cape Grim
Woolnorth
Kangaroo Island
Robbins Island
Guyton Point
Valley Bay
Flat Topped Bluff
Bluff Point
Robbins Passage
Cape Elie
Montagu
Stony Pt
Highfield Historic Site
North Point
Half Moon Bay
The Nut Chairlift
Lighthouse
Studland Bay
Perkins Island
Stanley
Circular Head
Perkins Bay
Duck Bay
Sawyer Bay
Smithton
Wiltshire
Mella
Mt Cameron West
Smokers Bank
Forest
Crayfish Creek
Ann Bay
Christmas Hills
HWY
South Forest
Green Point
Marrawah
Redpa
Togari
Irishtown
Mengha
Brittons Swamp
Alcomie
West Pt
BASS
Lileah
Mawson Bay
Sherstons Hill
Edith Creek
Nabageena
Arthur Pieman Conservation Area
Bluff Hill Point
Lighthouse
Roger River
Wedge Plains
Arthur River
Trowutta
Gardiner Point
Milkshakes Hills Forest Reserve
Kanunnah Bridge
Lake Chisholm Forest Reserve
Neasey Plains
Nelson Bay
Julius River Forest Res
Blue Peak
Couta Rocks
Temma
Richardson Point
Hazard Bay
Balfour
Mt Balfour
Mt Frankland
Mt Bertha
Savage River National Park
Mt Hazelton
Kenneth Bay
Sandy Cape
Lighthouse
Mt Norfolk
Mt Cleveland
Savage River
Arthur Pieman Conservation Area
Mt Meredith
Blackguards Hill
Mt Donaldson
Rupert Point
Toll Punt
Corinna
Mt Livingstone
Hardwicke Bay
Pieman River State Reserve
Conical Rocks Point
Yarrana Hill
Reece Dam
Granville Harbour
Lake Pieman
Mt Heemskirk
Mt Agnew
Zeehan
Mt Zeehan
Trial Harbour
Cape Wickham
Lighthouse
Cape Farewell
Disappointment Bay
Phoques Bay
Egg Lagoon
Lake Martha Lavinia
New Year Island
Christmas Island
Lavinia Point
Whistler Point
Yambacoona
Lavinia Nature Reserve
Reekara
Counsel Hill
KING
Loorana
Cowper Point
Sea Elephant Bay
Currie Harbour
Lighthouse
Currie
ISLAND
Naracoopa
Fraser Bluff
Pegarah
Parenna
Yarrah Creek
Lymwood
Fitzmaurice Bay
Bold Head
Cataraqui Point
Grassy
Mt Stanley
Calcified Forest
Surprise Bay
Seal Bay
Lighthouse
Stokes Point
King Island
Scale same as main map

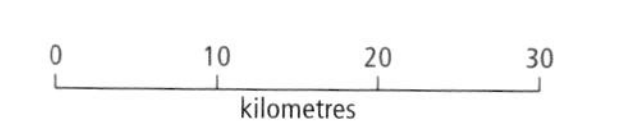
0
10
20
30
kilometres

TAS
TAS 2

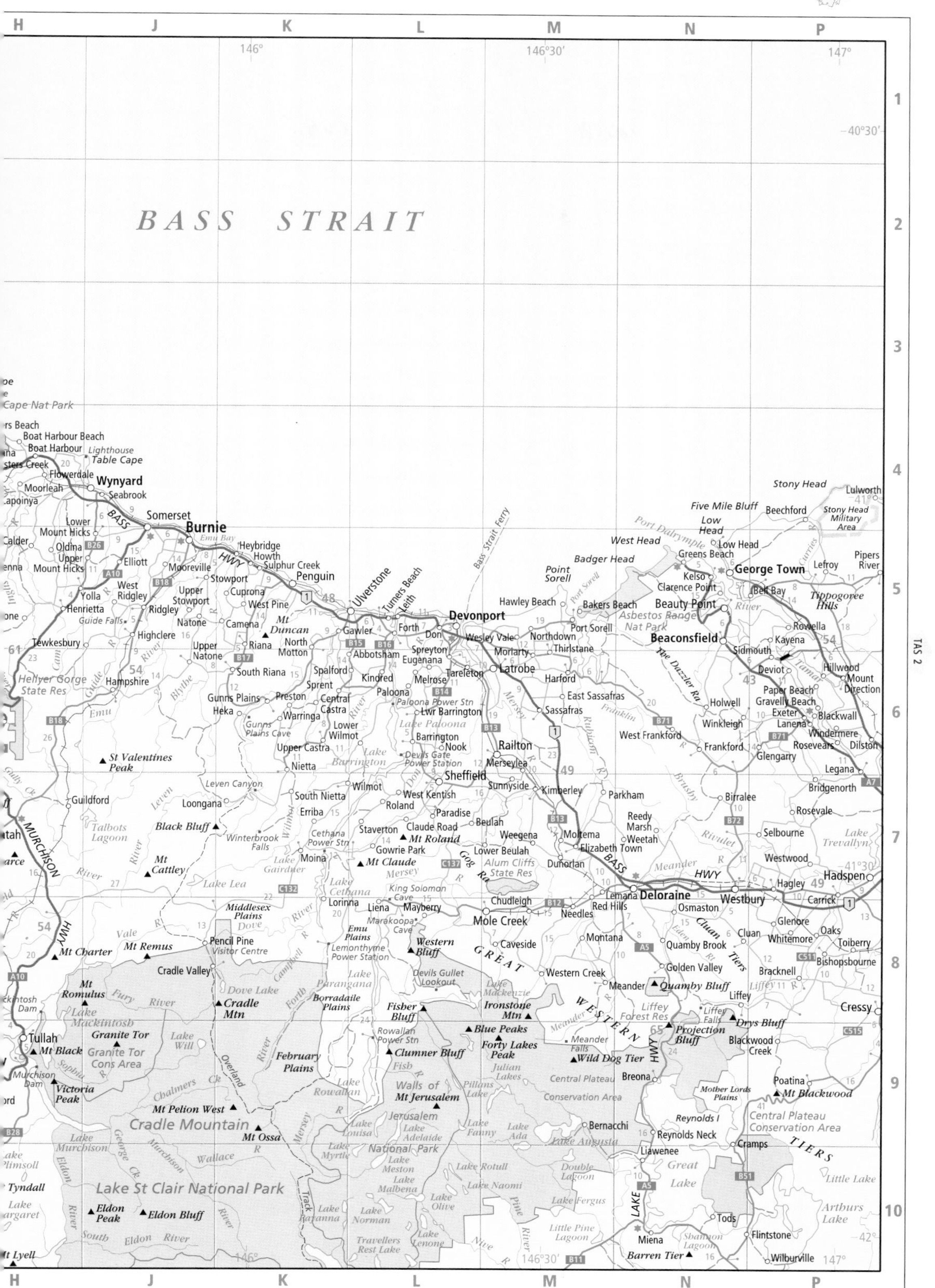
H
J
K
L
M
N
P
146°
146°30′
147°
40°30′
41°
41°30′
42°
1
2
3
4
5
6
7
8
9
10
BASS STRAIT
Cape Nat Park
Boat Harbour Beach
Boat Harbour
Lighthouse
Table Cape
Flowerdale
Wynyard
Moorleah
Seabrook
Somerset
Burnie
Emu Bay
Lower
Mount Hicks
Oldina
Upper
Mount Hicks
Elliott
Calder
Heybridge
Howth
Sulphur Creek
Penguin
Mooreville
Stowport
Cuprona
Upper
Stowport
West Pine
West
Ridgley
Yolla
Henrietta
Ridgley
Guide Falls
Natone
Camena
Mt
Duncan
Riana
Highclere
Tewkesbury
Upper
Natone
North
Motton
South Riana
Hampshire
Hellyer Gorge
State Res
Gunns Plains
Heka
Preston
Gunns
Plains Cave
Warringa
Central
Castra
Lower
Wilmot
Upper Castra
Nietta
Spalford
Sprent
Kindred
Paloona
Ulverstone
Turners Beach
Leith
Gawler
Forth
Don
Abbotsham
Spreyton
Eugenana
Melrose
Devonport
Wesley Vale
Moriarty
Latrobe
Tarleton
Paloona Power Stn
Lwr Barrington
Lake Paloona
Barrington
Nook
Devils Gate
Power Station
Lake
Barrington
Sheffield
Railton
Merseylea
Sunnyside
Kimberley
St Valentines
Peak
Leven Canyon
Loongana
Guildford
Wilmot
South Nietta
Erriba
West Kentish
Roland
Paradise
Claude Road
Beulah
Staverton
Mt Roland
Gowrie Park
Cethana
Power Stn
Weegena
Lower Beulah
Alum Cliffs
State Res
Moina
Mt Claude
Mersey
Black Bluff
Winterbrook
Falls
Talbots
Lagoon
Lake
Gairdner
Mt
Cattley
Lake Lea
Lake
Cethana
King Solomon
Cave
Lorinna
Liena
Mayberry
Marakoopa
Cave
Chudleigh
Mole Creek
Caveside
Middlesex
Plains
Dove
Emu
Plains
Lemonthyme
Power Station
Western
Bluff
Pencil Pine
Visitor Centre
Mt Charter
Mt Remus
Cradle Valley
Devils Gullet
Lookout
Lake
Parangana
Lake
Mackenzie
Mt
Romulus
Fury
River
Dove Lake
Cradle
Mtn
Borradaile
Plains
Fisher
Bluff
Ironstone
Mtn
Lake
Mackintosh
Mackintosh
Dam
Tullah
Mt Black
Granite Tor
Granite Tor
Cons Area
Lake
Will
Overland
February
Plains
Rowallan
Power Stn
Clumner Bluff
Blue Peaks
Forty Lakes
Peak
Julian
Lakes
Fish
Murchison
Dam
Victoria
Peak
Chalmers
Lake
Rowallan
Walls of
Mt Jerusalem
Pillans
Lake
Jerusalem
Mt Pelion West
Cradle Mountain
Mt Ossa
Lake
Murchison
Lake
Louisa
Lake
Adelaide
Lake
Fanny
Lake
Ada
Wallace
Lake
Myrtle
National Park
Lake
Meston
Lake Rotull
Lake Naomi
Lake Augusta
Double
Lagoon
Lake
Malbena
Lake St Clair National Park
Tyndall
Lake
Margaret
Lake
Plimsoll
Eldon
Peak
Eldon Bluff
Lake
Rayanna
Lake
Norman
Lake
Olive
Lake Fergus
Travellers
Rest Lake
Lake
Lenone
Little Pine
Lagoon
South
Eldon
River
Nive
Mt Lyell
Track
Pine
River
MURCHISON
HWY
BASS
HWY
GREAT
WESTERN
TIERS
LAKE
Hawley Beach
Point
Sorell
Port Sorell
Northdown
Thirlstane
Harford
East Sassafras
Sassafras
Bakers Beach
Asbestos Range
Nat Park
Badger Head
West Head
Port Dalrymple
Five Mile Bluff
Low
Head
Low Head
Greens Beach
Kelso
Clarence Point
Beauty Point
George Town
Beaconsfield
The Dazzler Ra
Stony Head
Beechford
Stony Head
Military
Area
Lulworth
Lefroy
Pipers
River
Bell Bay
Tippogoree
Hills
Rowella
Kayena
Sidmouth
Deviot
Hillwood
Mount
Direction
Paper Beach
Gravelly Beach
Exeter
Blackwall
Lanena
Windermere
Rosevears
Dilston
Legana
Glengarry
Holwell
Winkleigh
Frankford
West Frankford
Rubicon
Franklin
Brushy
Bridgenorth
Birralee
Rosevale
Parkham
Reedy
Marsh
Weetah
Selbourne
Lake
Trevallyn
Moltema
Elizabeth Town
Dunorlan
Westwood
Hadspen
Meander
Hagley
Lemana
Deloraine
Westbury
Carrick
Red Hills
Needles
Osmaston
Cluan
Tiers
Glenore
Whitemore
Oaks
Toiberry
Bishopsbourne
Montana
Quamby Brook
Golden Valley
Bracknell
Western Creek
Meander
Quamby Bluff
Liffey
Liffey
Forest Res
Liffey
Falls
Cressy
Drys Bluff
Projection
Bluff
Meander
Falls
Wild Dog Tier
Blackwood
Creek
Central Plateau
Conservation Area
Breona
Poatina
Mother Lords
Plains
Mt Blackwood
Reynolds I
Reynolds Neck
Bernacchi
Central Plateau
Conservation Area
Cramps
TIERS
Liawenee
Great
Lake
Little Lake
Arthurs
Lake
Tods
Flintstone
Miena
Shannon
Lagoon
Barren Tier
Wilburville
Bass Strait Ferry
A10
A5
A7
B11
B12
B13
B14
B15
B16
B17
B18
B26
B28
B51
B71
B72
C132
C137
C511
C515

Map 2

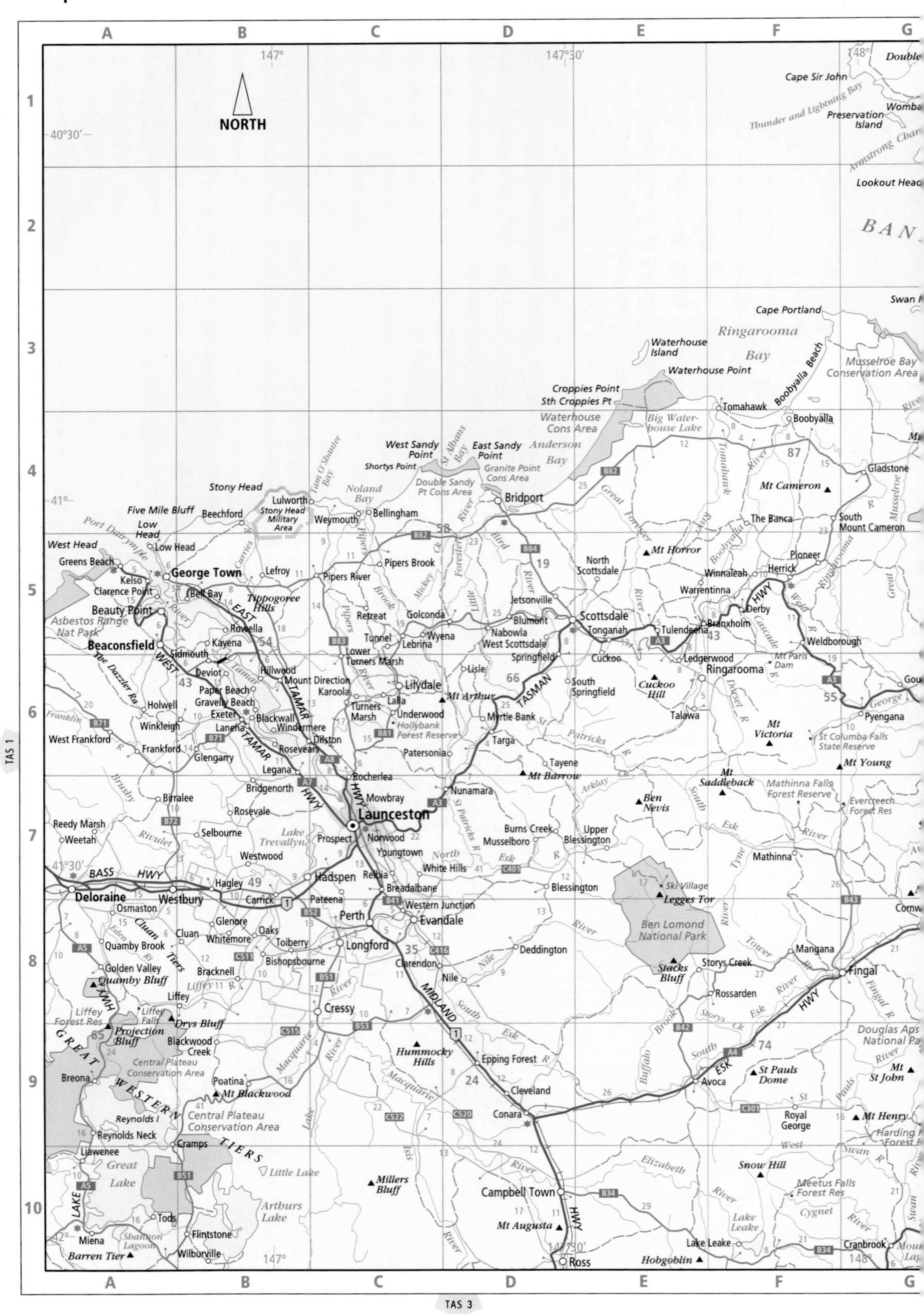

NORTH
147°
147°30'
148°
40°30'
41°
41°30'
42°
Cape Sir John
Thunder and Lightning Bay
Preservation Island
Armstrong Channel
Lookout Head
Cape Portland
Ringarooma Bay
Waterhouse Island
Waterhouse Point
Boobyalla Beach
Musselroe Bay Conservation Area
Croppies Point
Sth Croppies Pt
Waterhouse Cons Area
Big Waterhouse Lake
Tomahawk
Boobyalla
West Sandy Point
Shortys Point
East Sandy Point
Anderson Bay
Granite Point Cons Area
Double Sandy Pt Cons Area
Noland Bay
Tam O'Shanter Bay
St Albans Bay
Stony Head
Lulworth
Stony Head Military Area
Weymouth
Bellingham
Bridport
Gladstone
Mt Cameron
South Mount Cameron
The Banca
Five Mile Bluff
Beechford
Low Head
Port Dalrymple
West Head
Greens Beach
Kelso
Clarence Point
George Town
Lefroy
Pipers River
Pipers Brook
North Scottsdale
Mt Horror
Pioneer
Herrick
Winnaleah
Warrentinna
Derby
Branxholm
Weldborough
Beauty Point
Asbestos Range Nat Park
Bell Bay
Tippogoree Hills
Retreat
Golconda
Jetsonville
Blumont
Scottsdale
Tonganah
Tulendeena
Beaconsfield
Rowella
Kayena
Sidmouth
Tunnel
Wyena
Lebrina
Nabowla
West Scottsdale
Springfield
Cuckoo
Ledgerwood
Ringarooma
Mt Paris Dam
The Dazzler Ra
Deviot
Hillwood
Lower Turners Marsh
Lisle
Mount Direction
Karoola
Lilydale
Mt Arthur
South Springfield
Cuckoo Hill
Talawa
Pyengana
Paper Beach
Gravelly Beach
Holwell
Exeter
Blackwall
Windermere
Turners Marsh
Lalla
Underwood
Hollybank Forest Reserve
Myrtle Bank
Targa
Mt Victoria
St Columba Falls State Reserve
Franklin
West Frankford
Winkleigh
Frankford
Lanena
Glengarry
Dilston
Rosevears
Patersonia
Tayene
Mt Barrow
Mt Young
Legana
Rocherlea
Bridgenorth
Nunamara
Ben Nevis
Mt Saddleback
Mathinna Falls Forest Reserve
Evercreech Forest Res
Birralee
Mowbray
Rosevale
Launceston
Reedy Marsh
Weetah
Selbourne
Lake Trevallyn
Prospect
Norwood
Burns Creek
Musselboro
Upper Blessington
Mathinna
Westwood
Youngtown
Hadspen
Relbia
White Hills
Blessington
Ski Village
Legges Tor
Deloraine
Westbury
Hagley
Carrick
Breadalbane
Osmaston
Pateena
Perth
Western Junction
Evandale
Cluan Tiers
Glenore
Cluan
Oaks
Whitemore
Toiberry
Longford
Ben Lomond National Park
Quamby Brook
Deddington
Mangana
Golden Valley
Quamby Bluff
Bracknell
Bishopsbourne
Clarendon
Nile
Storys Creek
Stacks Bluff
Fingal
Liffey
Cressy
Rossarden
Liffey Forest Res
Liffey Falls
Drys Bluff
Projection Bluff
Blackwood Creek
Central Plateau Conservation Area
Hummocky Hills
Epping Forest
Douglas Apsley National Park
St Pauls Dome
Mt St John
Breona
Poatina
Mt Blackwood
Cleveland
Avoca
Great Western Tiers
Reynolds I
Reynolds Neck
Conara
Royal George
Mt Henry
Harding Falls Forest Res
Liawenee
Cramps
Little Lake
Snow Hill
Great Lake
Millers Bluff
Arthurs Lake
Campbell Town
Meetus Falls Forest Res
Tods
Mt Augusta
Lake Leake
Miena
Shannon Lagoon
Flintstone
Cranbrook
Barren Tier
Wilburville
Ross
Hobgoblin
BASS HWY
EAST TAMAR HWY
WEST TAMAR HWY
TASMAN HWY
MIDLAND HWY
ESK HWY
LAKE HWY
B82
B84
A3
A7
A8
B71
B72
B81
B83
B41
B52
B51
B53
C515
C511
C520
C522
C401
C416
B42
A4
C301
B43
B34
A5
TAS 1
TAS 3

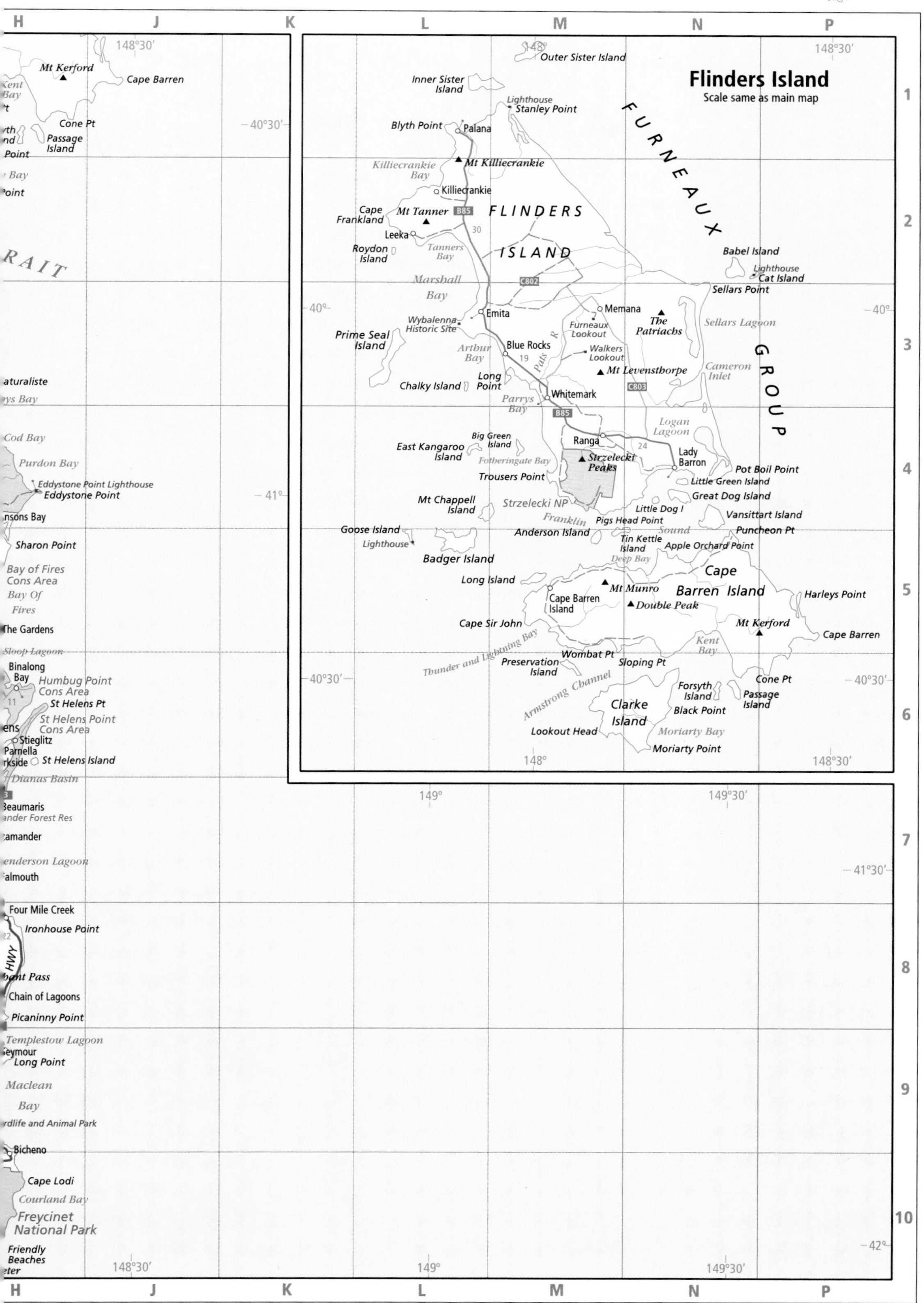

0 10 20 30
kilometres
Flinders Island
Scale same as main map
FURNEAUX GROUP
FLINDERS ISLAND
Outer Sister Island
Inner Sister Island
Lighthouse
Stanley Point
Blyth Point
Palana
Mt Killiecrankie
Killiecrankie Bay
Killiecrankie
Cape Frankland
Mt Tanner
Leeka
Roydon Island
Tanners Bay
Marshall Bay
Babel Island
Lighthouse
Cat Island
Sellars Point
Memana
The Patriarchs
Sellars Lagoon
Furneaux Lookout
Emita
Wybalenna Historic Site
Prime Seal Island
Arthur Bay
Blue Rocks
Pats R
Walkers Lookout
Mt Leventhorpe
Cameron Inlet
Long Point
Chalky Island
Whitemark
Parrys Bay
Logan Lagoon
Big Green Island
East Kangaroo Island
Ranga
Strzelecki Peaks
Lady Barron
Fotheringate Bay
Trousers Point
Pot Boil Point
Little Green Island
Great Dog Island
Mt Chappell Island
Strzelecki NP
Little Dog I
Vansittart Island
Franklin Sound
Pigs Head Point
Goose Island
Lighthouse
Anderson Island
Puncheon Pt
Tin Kettle Island
Apple Orchard Point
Badger Island
Deep Bay
Cape Barren Island
Long Island
Mt Munro
Cape Barren Island
Harleys Point
Double Peak
Cape Sir John
Mt Kerford
Cape Barren
Thunder and Lightning Bay
Wombat Pt
Kent Bay
Preservation Island
Sloping Pt
Cone Pt
Armstrong Channel
Forsyth Island
Passage Island
Clarke Island
Black Point
Lookout Head
Moriarty Bay
Moriarty Point
B85
C802
C803
Mt Kerford
Cape Barren
Cone Pt
Passage Island
Eddystone Point Lighthouse
Eddystone Point
Sharon Point
Bay of Fires Cons Area
Bay Of Fires
The Gardens
Sloop Lagoon
Binalong Bay
Humbug Point Cons Area
St Helens Pt
St Helens Point Cons Area
Stieglitz
Parnella
St Helens Island
Dianas Basin
Beaumaris
Falmouth
Four Mile Creek
Ironhouse Point
Chain of Lagoons
Picaninny Point
Templestow Lagoon
Long Point
Maclean Bay
Bicheno
Cape Lodi
Courland Bay
Freycinet National Park
Friendly Beaches
148°30′
149°
149°30′
40°30′
41°
41°30′
42°
TAS

Map 3

TAS 1
A
B
C
D
E
F
G
1
2
3
4
5
6
7
8
9
10
42°
42°30′
43°
43°30′
145°30′
146°
146°30′
Eldon Bluff
Cradle Mountain
Lake St Clair NP
Henty Glacial Moraine
Henty Dunes
Queenstown
Gormanston
Mt Lyell
Lake Burbury
Mt Owen
Lynchford
Strahan
Regatta Point
Swan Basin Picnic Ground
Macquarie Heads
Cape Sorell Lighthouse
Ocean Beach
John Butters PS
Crotty Dam
Teepookana Forest Res
Darwin Dam
Mt Sorell
Mt Darwin
Sophia Pt
Liberty Pt
Table Head
Sloop Point
Macquarie Harbour
Gorge Point
Gould Pt
Sarah Island Historic Site
Rum Pt
Kelly Basin
Heritage Landing
Birthday Bay
Gulley Point
Varna Bay
Hibbs Bay
Point Hibbs
Spero Bay
Endeavour Bay
Victoria Pass
LYELL HWY
Pyramid Mtn
Mt Olympus
Lake St Clair
Mt Rufus
Visitor Centre
Derwent Bridge
Mt Alma
Franklin River Nature Trail
Mt King William I
Mt King William II
Mt King William III
Frenchmans Cap
Franklin-Gordon
Wild Rivers National Park
Lake Rufus
Lake Richmond
Travellers Rest Lake
Lake Lenone
Clarence Lagoon
Pine Tier Lagoon
Bronte Park
Lake Big Jim
London Lakes
Lake Samuel
Laughing Jack Lagoon
Lake King William
Bronte Lagoon
Bradys Lake
Dee Lagoon
Butlers Gorge Power Station
Lake Binney
Tarraleah Power Station
Tarraleah
Wayatinah
Wayatinah Lagoon
Wayatinah Power Station
Lake Catagunya
Catagunya Power Station
Lake Repulse
Repulse Power Station
Misery Plateau
Wylds Craig
Mt McCall
Cracroft Hills
Western Plains
Goodwins Peak
Elliot Ra
Mt Humboldt
Prince of Wales Range
Denison Range
Lake Curly
The Pleiades
D'Aguilar Range
Mt Lee
Southwest
Conservation
Area
Moores Valley
Mt Lewis
Charles Range
High Rocky Point
Mt Osmund
Hamilton Range
Nicholls Ra
Princess Range
Gordon Dam
Strathgordon
Teds Beach
Serpentine Dam
Mt Sprent
Lake Gordon
Clear Hill
Tiger Ra
Mount Field Nat Park
Mt Field West
Lake Fenton
Lake Belton
Tim Shea
Mt Mueller
Ibsens Peak
Frodshams Pass
Creepy Crawly Walk
Mount Wedge Forest Res
Mt Bowes
Starfish Hill
McPartlan Pass
The Coronets
Double Peak
Frankland Range
Lake Pedder
Mt Solitary
Scotts Peak
Scotts Peak Dam
Edgar Dam
Mt Giblin
Mt Eliza
Mt Anne
Lake Judd
Mt Weld
Gallagher Plateau
Low Rocky Point
Elliott Bay
Lawson Range
Rookery Plain
Propsting Range
Piners Peak
Folded Range
White Monolith Range
Nye Bay
Elliot Point
Mulcahy Bay
Brier Holme Head
De Witt Range
Mt Hean
Davey Gorge
Mt Hesperus
Arthur Range
Mt Orion
West Portal
The Razorback
Mt Picton
Sth Picton Range
Lost World Plateau
Settlement Point
Svenor Point
Wreck Bay
Southwest
National Park
Mt Norold
Ripple Mtn
Federation Peak
Cracroft Gorge
Lake Geeves
White Horse Plains
James Kelly Basin
Davey Head
North Head
Point St Vincent
Port Davey
Erskine Ra
Rugby Ra
Mt Rugby
Rowitta Plains
Mt Pollux
Spiro Range
Mt Bobs
Bobs Knobs
Bathurst Harbour
Hilliard Head
Stephens Bay
Mutton Bird Island
Melaleuca Ranger Station & Bird Observation
South West Cape Range
Melaleuca Range
Mt Counsel
Ray Range
Mt Louisa
Mt Victoria Cross
Precipitous Bluff
New River Lagoon
Window Pane Bay
Mt Melaleuca
Doorstop Bay
Cox Bight
Red Point Hills
Ironbound Range
Mt Karamu
Cox Bluff
South West Cape
Telopea Point
Red Point
Louisa Bay
Louisa Island
Havelock Bluff
Prion Bay
Wilson Bight
New Harbour
Ile du Golfe
Point Cecil
Point Vivian
Surprise Bay
Shoemaker Point
SOUTHERN
OCEAN
NORTH
Maatsuyker Group
De Witt Island
Flat Witch Island
Walker Island
Maatsuyker I

0 10 20 30
kilometres

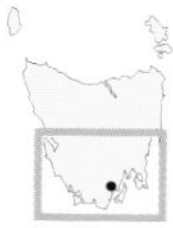

H J K L M N P

Flintstone, 147°, Great Lake, 147°30′, Lake Leake, Lake Leake, 148°, Moulting Lagoon, Freycinet Nat Park, Friendly Beaches, 42°

Wilburville, Ross, Hobgoblin, Mt Franklin, Wyefield Rt, Lost Falls Forest Res, Cranbrook, Mt Peter, Mt Paul, 1

Steppes, Woods Lake, Lake Sorell, Lagoon of Islands, LAKE, Alma Pass, Interlaken, Tunbridge, O'Connor Rt, Nine Mile Beach, Hepburn Point, Coles Bay, Lighthouse, Cape Tourville, Coles Bay, Sleepy Bay, Swansea, Meredith River, Great, Mt Dove, Wineglass Bay, Fleurieu Pt, Cape Forestier

Woodbury, Macquarie River, Kittys Rt, Old Mans Head, Antill Ponds, Lake Crescent, Spiky Bridge, Promise Bay, Oyster, Mayfield Bay Cons Area, Faddens Tier, Tooms Lake, Buxton River, Mt Graham, Mt Freycinet, 2

Table Mtn, Vincent Hill, York Plains, Weatherhead Point, Freycinet Pen, Mayfield Bay, Buxton Pt, Bay, Bryans Beach, Baldy Bluff, Cape Degerando, Woods Quoin, Oatlands, Callington Mill Historic Site, Pawtella, Lemont, Little Swanport, Schouten Passage, Schouten Island, Lake Dulverton, Andover, Little Swanport, Seaford Point, Rooster Point, Cape Faure, Cape Sonnerat

Nicholas Sugarloaf, Thorpe Water Mill, Northumbria Hill, Parattah, Pt Bailly, Freycinet National Park, Bothwell, Green Hill, Jericho, Pike Hill, Little Swanport River, Little Swanport Hill, Boltons Beach Cons Area, Spring Hill, Stonor, Mount Seymour, Ravensdale Rt, Clyde, Mt Reid, Whitefoord, Buckland Military Training Area, 3

Lake Tiberias, Baden, Tunnack, Grindstone Point, Black Tier, Melton Mowbray, Rhyndaston, Woodsdale, Bluestone Tier, Mt Murray, Coal River, Eldon, HWY, Triabunna, Cape Bougainville, 42°30′

Hollow Tree, Kempton, Colebrook, Levendale, Mt Hobbs, Louisville, Okehampton Bay, Hamilton, MIDLAND, Quoin Mtn, Craigbourne Dam, Prosser, Stony Rt, Sand Rt, Back River, Orford, Prosser Bay, Lighthouse, Mt Spode, Pelham, Dysart, Spring Beach, Cape Boullanger, Passage

Eldersfie, Mangalore Tier, Jordan, Native Hut Rt, Brown Mtn, Thumbs Picnic Area, Johnsons Pt, Darlington, Maria Island National Park, 4

Bagdad, Lowdina, Buckland, Return Pt, Maria Island, Mt Maria, Broadmarsh, Mangalore, Tasman, Runnymede, Rheban, Booming Bay, Gretna, Campania, Mt Morrison, Prossers Sugarloaf, Pt Lesueur, Mistaken Cape, Glenora, Rosegarland, Pontville, Currajong Rt, Shoal Bay, Riedle Bay

Macquarie Plains, Mt Dromedary, Brighton, Tea Tree, Sandspit River Forest Res, Mercury Passage, Oyster Bay, Bushy Park, Black Hills, Dromedary, Bridgewater, Richmond, Nugent, Sandspit, Cape Maurouard, Plenty, Hayes, Magra, Granton, Pawleena, Cape Bernier, Cape Peron, Salmon Ponds, Moogara, Old Beach, Grasstree Hill, Orielton, Kellevie, Feilton, New Norfolk, Boyer, Claremont, Sorell, Wattle Hill, Marion, 5

Glenfern, Malbina, Molesworth, Otago, Risdon Vale, Midway Point, Pitt Water, Forcett, ARTHUR, Bream Creek, Mount Lloyd, Lachlan, Glenlusk, Glenorchy, Cambridge, Seven Mile Beach Protected Area, Lewisham, Copping, Bay, Cape Paul Lamanon, Collinsvale, Mt Rumney, Dodges Ferry, North Bay, Collins Cap, Lookout, Seven Mile Beach, Carlton River, Carlton, Dunalley, Cape Frederick Hendrick, Trestle Mtn, Lookout, Mt Wellington, HOBART, Rokeby, Primrose Sands, Blue Hill, Frederick Henry Bay, Dunalley Bay, Mt Forestier, High Yellow Bluff

Fern Tree, Ridgeway, Lauderdale, Green Head, Lime Bay Nat Res, Forestier, Mt Misery, Crabtree, Mountain River, Neika, Taroona, Ralphs Bay, Sandford, Sloping I, Smooth I, Murdunna, Cape Surville, Huonvale, Lucaston, Grove, HWY, Leslie Vale, Shot Tower, Cremorne, Chronicle Pt, Peninsula, Judbury, Lower Longley, Longley, Kingston, Cape Deslacs, Coal Mines Historic Site, 6

Ranelagh, Sandfly, Blackmans Bay, Opossum Bay, Clifton Beach, Norfolk Bay, Eaglehawk Neck, Tessellated Pavement, 43°, Glen Huon, Huonville, Kaoota, Howden, South Arm, Saltwater River, Pirates Bay, Tasman Blowhole, Tasman Arch, Devils Kitchen, Waterfall Bay, Divide, Pelverata, Margate, Derwent, Iron Pot Lighthouse, Betsey Island, Premaydena, Tasmanian Devil Park, Taranna, Pelverata Falls, Electrona, Nth West Bay, Tinderbox, Franklin, Snug Falls, Snug, Dennes Point, Outer North Head, Koonya, HUON, Woodstock, Coningham, Kilora, One Tree Point, Tasman, Peninsula, O'Hara Bluff, South Franklin, Cradoc, Oyster Cove, Kettering, Barnes Bay, Wedge Bay, Nubeena, Tasman Trail

Port Huon, Glaziers Bay, Ferry, The Yellow Bluff, White Beach, Fortescue Bay, Geeveston, Wattle Grove, Cygnet, Nicholls Rivulet, Trumpeter Bay, Two Island Bay, Port Arthur, Convict Ruins, Cape Huay, 7

Petcheys Bay, Woodbridge, Birchs Bay, STORM, Highcroft, Palmers Lookout, Munro Bight, Cairns Bay, Lymington, Gardners Bay, Variety Bay, Curio Bay, Remarkable Cave, Tasman National Park, Waterloo, Great Bay, North Bruny Island, BAY, Tasman National Park, Maingon Bay, Cape Pillar, Surges Bay, Middleton, Glendevie, Police Point, Garden Island Creek, Simpsons Pt, Cape Queen Elizabeth, Raoul Bay, Tasman I Lighthouse, Esperance, Hideaway Bay, Gordon, Isthmus Bay, Channel, Cape Raoul, Surveyors Bay, Verona Sands, Simpsons Bay, Dover, Huon I, Adventure Bay, Maggot Pt, Esperance Pt, Port Esperance, D'Entrecasteaux

Raminea, Strathblane, Alonnah, Fluted Cape, 8

Ventenat Point, South, Adventure Bay, Capt Cook's Landing Place, Lunawanna, Bligh Museum, Partridge Island, Great Taylors Bay, Bruny Island, Cape Connella, Thermal Pool, Hopwood Point, Bay of Islands, Lune River, Southport, Mangana Bluff, South Bruny National Park, Ida Bay, South Bruny Nat Park, Southport Lagoon, Historic Lighthouse, Cloudy Bay, Mt Bruny, Boreel Head, Cape Bruny

TASMAN SEA, 43°30′, 9

Eliza Point, West Cloudy Head, East Cloudy Head, Tasman Head, The Friars, Recherche Bay, Catamaran, Whale Sculpture, Cockle Creek

Whale Head

10

147°, 147°30′, 148°

H J K L M N P

TAS

Map 1

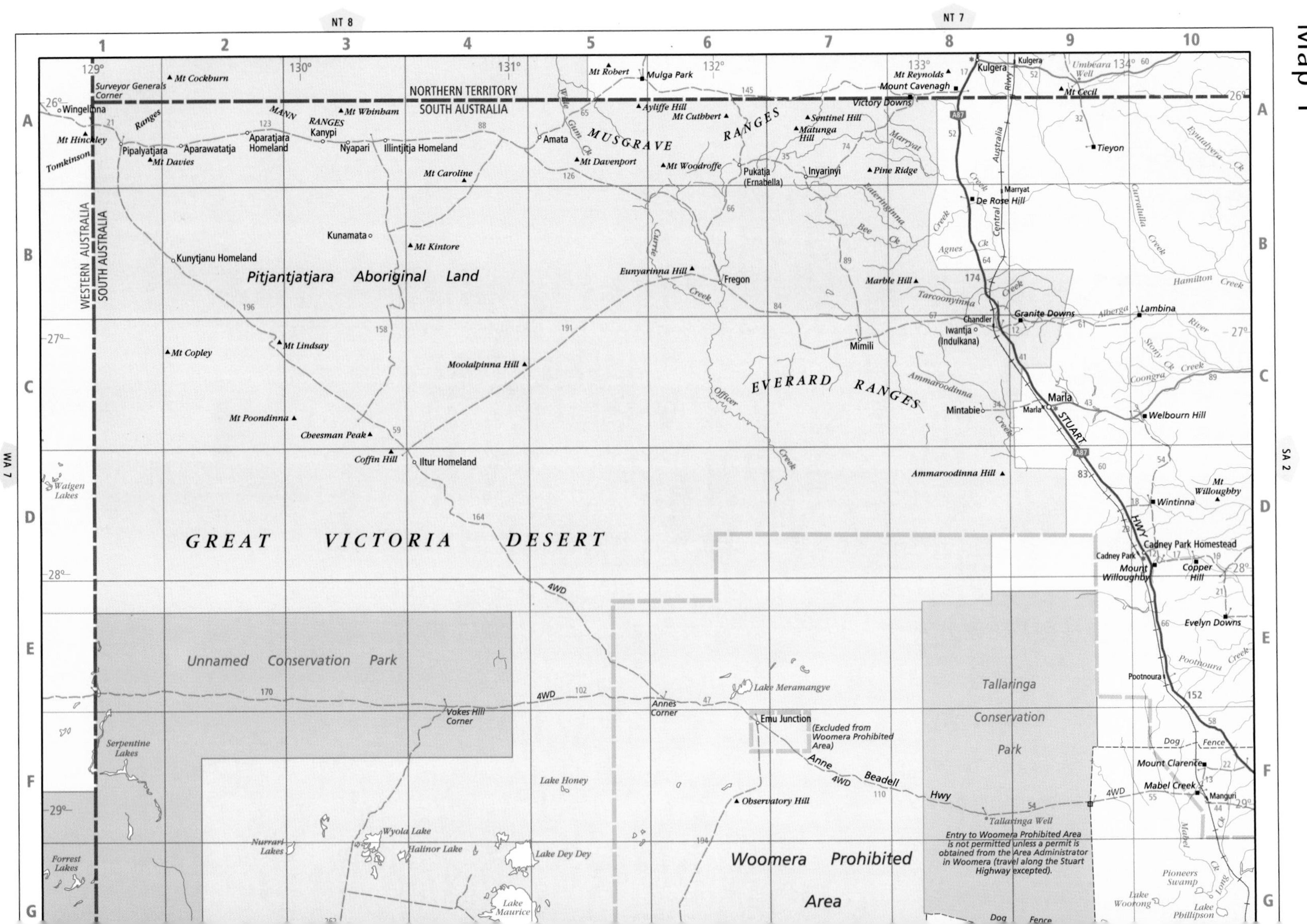

NT 8
NT 7
SA 2
WA 7
NORTHERN TERRITORY
SOUTH AUSTRALIA
WESTERN AUSTRALIA
Surveyor Generals Corner
Wingellina
Pipalyatjara
Aparawatatja
Aparatjara Homeland
Kanypi
Nyapari
Illintjitja Homeland
Amata
Mulga Park
Pukatja (Ernabella)
Inyarinyi
Fregon
Mimili
Kulgera
Mount Cavenagh
Victory Downs
De Rose Hill
Marryat
Granite Downs
Chandler
Iwantja (Indulkana)
Mintabie
Marla
Lambina
Welbourn Hill
Wintinna
Cadney Park Homestead
Cadney Park
Copper Hill
Mount Willoughby
Evelyn Downs
Pootnoura
Mount Clarence
Mabel Creek
Manguri
Tieyon
Kunamata
Kunytjanu Homeland
Iltur Homeland
Emu Junction
Annes Corner
Vokes Hill Corner
MUSGRAVE RANGES
MANN RANGES
EVERARD RANGES
Pitjantjatjara Aboriginal Land
GREAT VICTORIA DESERT
Tallaringa Conservation Park
Unnamed Conservation Park
Woomera Prohibited Area
(Excluded from Woomera Prohibited Area)
Entry to Woomera Prohibited Area is not permitted unless a permit is obtained from the Area Administrator in Woomera (travel along the Stuart Highway excepted).
STUART HWY
Anne Beadell Hwy
Lake Meramangye
Lake Honey
Lake Dey Dey
Lake Maurice
Wyola Lake
Halinor Lake
Serpentine Lakes
Forrest Lakes
Waigen Lakes
Nurrari Lakes
Pioneers Swamp
Lake Woorong
Lake Phillipson
Officer Creek
Currie Creek
Agnes Creek
Marryat Creek
Alberga River
Hamilton Creek
Mt Cockburn
Mt Davies
Mt Caroline
Mt Kintore
Mt Lindsay
Mt Copley
Mt Poondinna
Cheesman Peak
Coffin Hill
Moolalpinna Hill
Eunyarinna Hill
Marble Hill
Ammaroodinna Hill
Observatory Hill
Mt Willoughby
Mt Woodroffe
Mt Davenport
Mt Cuthbert
Mt Robert
Mt Reynolds
Mt Cecil
Pine Ridge
Sentinel Hill
Matunga Hill
Ayliffe Hill
Mt Whinham
Mt Hinckley
Tallaringa Well

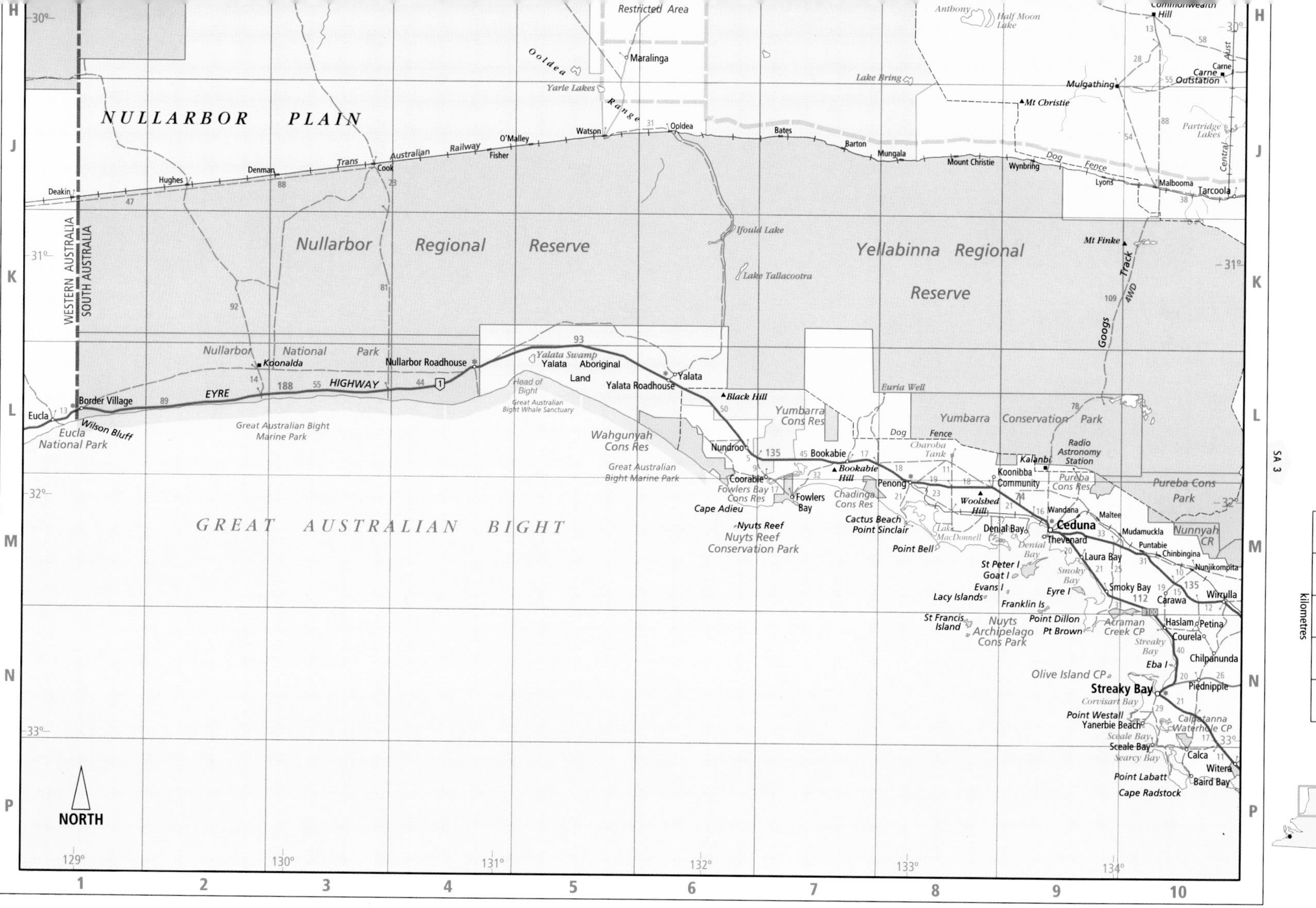

NULLARBOR PLAIN
Nullarbor Regional Reserve
Yellabinna Regional Reserve
Nullarbor National Park
GREAT AUSTRALIAN BIGHT
EYRE HIGHWAY
Trans Australian Railway
Dog Fence
Restricted Area
Maralinga
Ooldea Range
Ooldea
Yarle Lakes
Lake Bring
Anthony
Half Moon Lake
Commonwealth Hill
Mulgathing
Carne Outstation
Mt Christie
Partridge Lakes
Central Aust
Deakin
Hughes
Denman
Cook
Fisher
O'Malley
Watson
Bates
Barton
Mungala
Mount Christie
Wynbring
Lyons
Malbooma
Tarcoola
WESTERN AUSTRALIA
SOUTH AUSTRALIA
Ifould Lake
Lake Tallacootra
Mt Finke
Googs Track 4WD
Koonalda
Nullarbor Roadhouse
Yalata Swamp
Yalata Aboriginal Land
Yalata
Yalata Roadhouse
Black Hill
Euria Well
Yumbarra Cons Res
Yumbarra Conservation Park
Radio Astronomy Station
Pureba Cons Park
Pureba Cons Res
Nunnyah CR
Border Village
Eucla
Wilson Bluff
Eucla National Park
Great Australian Bight Marine Park
Head of Bight
Great Australian Bight Whale Sanctuary
Wahgunyah Cons Res
Nundroo
Coorabie
Fowlers Bay Cons Res
Fowlers Bay
Cape Adieu
Nyuts Reef
Nuyts Reef Conservation Park
Bookabie
Bookabie Hill
Chadinga Cons Res
Charoba Tank
Penong
Cactus Beach
Point Sinclair
Point Bell
Woolsbed Hill
Lake MacDonnell
Koonibba Community
Kalanbi
Denial Bay
Wandana
Ceduna
Thevenard
Maltee
Mudamuckla
Puntabie
Chinbingina
Nunjikompita
Laura Bay
Smoky Bay
Carawa
Wirrulla
St Peter I
Goat I
Evans I
Lacy Islands
Eyre I
Franklin Is
St Francis Island
Nuyts Archipelago Cons Park
Point Dillon
Pt Brown
Acraman Creek CP
Haslam
Petina
Courela
Chilpanunda
Eba I
Olive Island CP
Streaky Bay
Piednippie
Corvisart Bay
Point Westall
Yanerbie Beach
Calpatanna Waterhole CP
Sceale Bay
Searcy Bay
Calca
Witera
Point Labatt
Baird Bay
Cape Radstock
NORTH
0 20 40 60 80 100
kilometres
WA 9
SA 3
SA

Map 2

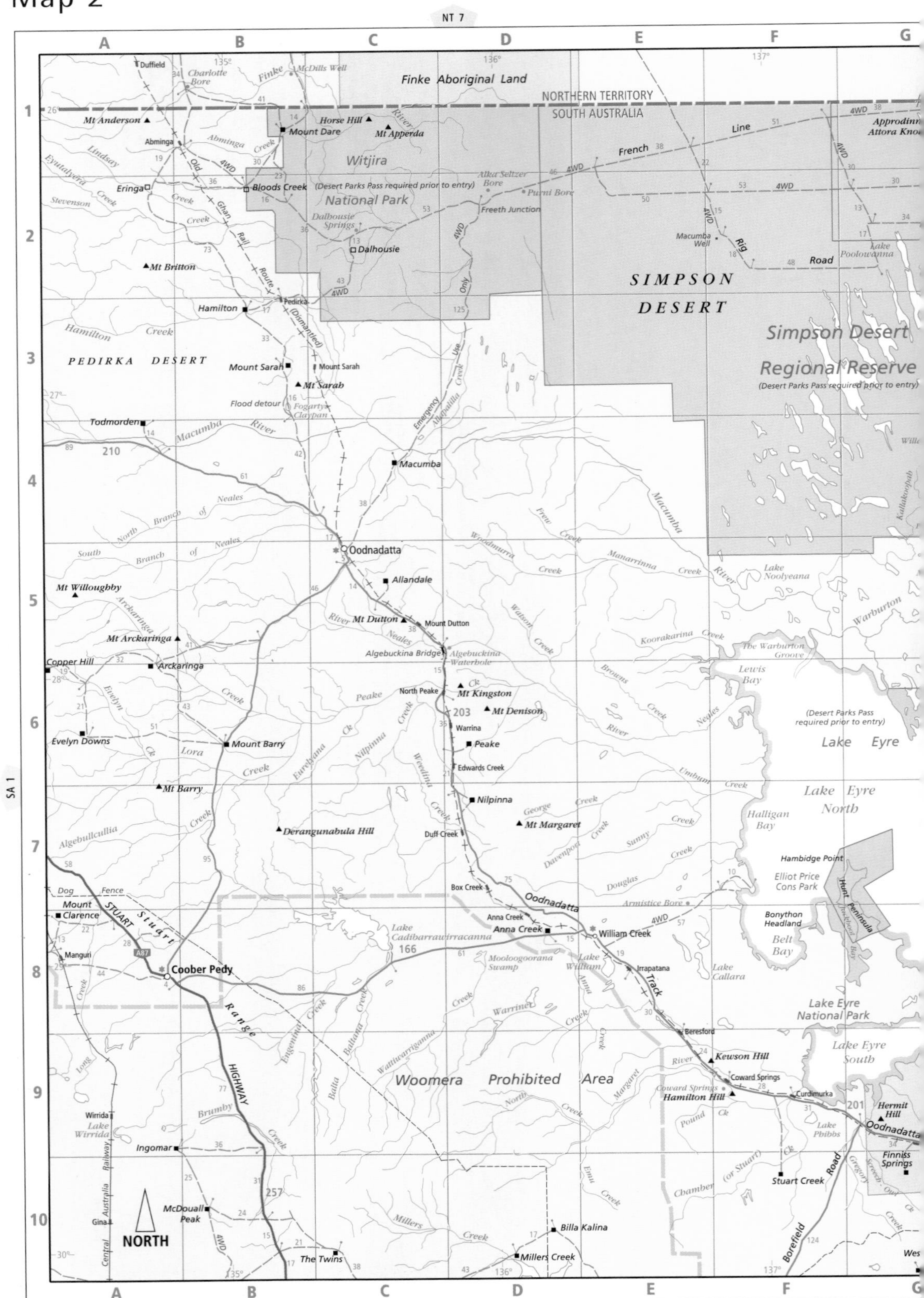

NT 7
Finke Aboriginal Land
NORTHERN TERRITORY
SOUTH AUSTRALIA
Duffield
Charlotte Bore
McDills Well
Mt Anderson
Horse Hill
Mount Dare
Mt Apperda
Abminga
Witjira
National Park
(Desert Parks Pass required prior to entry)
Eringa
Bloods Creek
Alka Seltzer Bore
Purni Bore
Freeth Junction
Dalhousie Springs
Dalhousie
French Line
Macumba Well
Rig Road
Lake Poolowanna
Approdinna Attora Knoll
Mt Britton
Hamilton
Pedirka
SIMPSON DESERT
Simpson Desert Regional Reserve
(Desert Parks Pass required prior to entry)
PEDIRKA DESERT
Mount Sarah
Mt Sarah
Flood detour
Fogarty's Claypan
Todmorden
Macumba River
Macumba
Oodnadatta
Allandale
Mt Willoughby
Mt Dutton
Mount Dutton
Mt Arckaringa
Arckaringa
Algebuckina Bridge
Algebuckina Waterhole
Copper Hill
North Peake
Mt Kingston
Mt Denison
Warrina
Evelyn Downs
Mount Barry
Peake
Edwards Creek
Mt Barry
Nilpinna
Mt Margaret
Derangunabula Hill
Duff Creek
Lake Noolyeana
The Warburton Groove
Lewis Bay
(Desert Parks Pass required prior to entry)
Lake Eyre
Lake Eyre North
Halligan Bay
Hambidge Point
Elliot Price Cons Park
Hunt Peninsula
Bonython Headland
Belt Bay
Box Creek
Oodnadatta Track
Armistice Bore
Dog Fence
Mount Clarence
STUART HIGHWAY
Stuart Range
Anna Creek
William Creek
Lake Cadibarrawirracanna
Manguri
Coober Pedy
Mooloogoorana Swamp
Lake William
Irrapatana
Lake Callara
Lake Eyre National Park
Lake Eyre South
Beresford
Kewson Hill
Coward Springs
Woomera Prohibited Area
Hamilton Hill
Curdimurka
Hermit Hill
Wirrida
Lake Wirrida
Lake Phibbs
Finniss Springs
Ingomar
Stuart Creek
Borefield Road
Central Australia Railway
McDouall Peak
Gina
Billa Kalina
NORTH
The Twins
Millers Creek
SA 1
SA 3

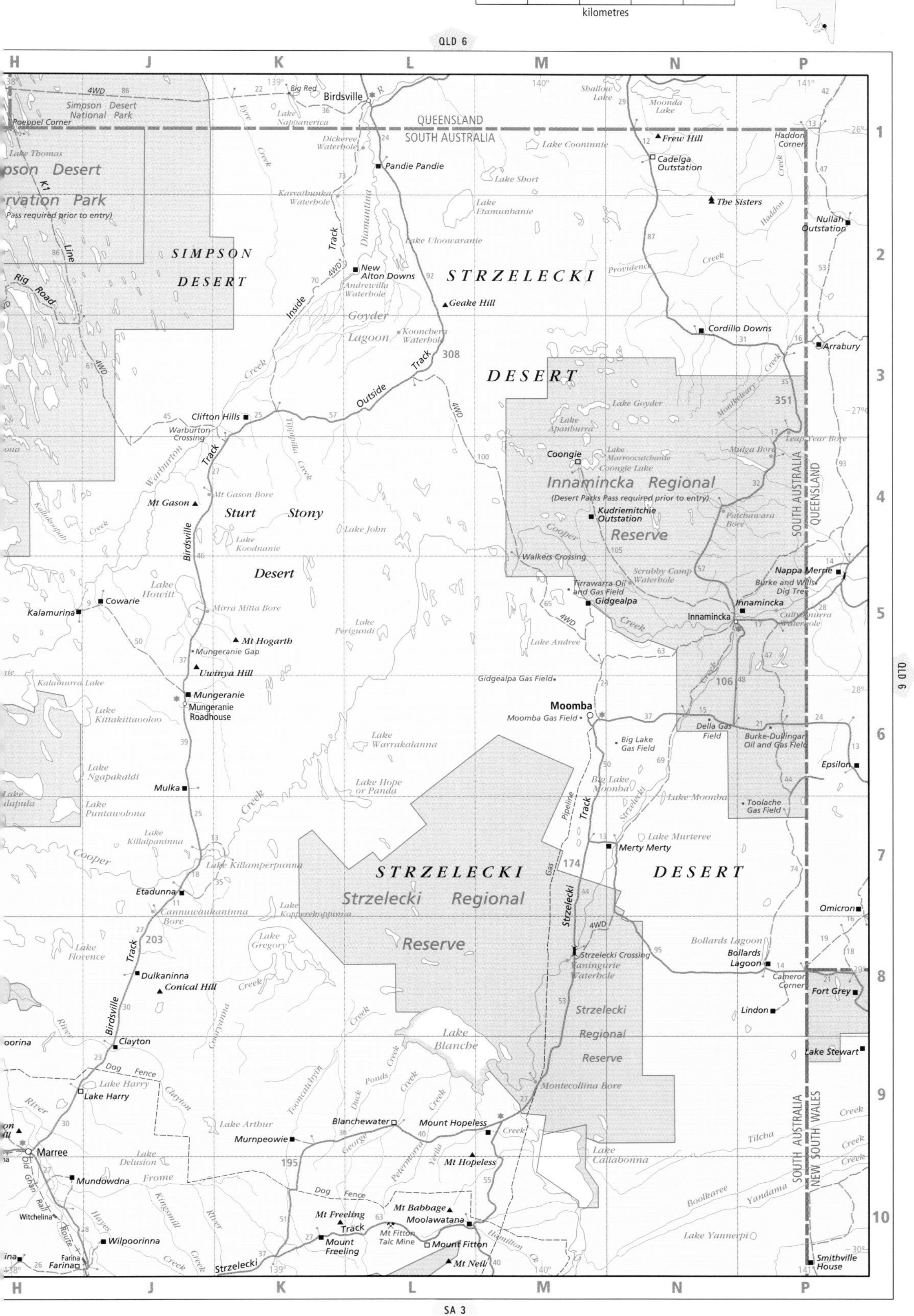
0 20 40 60 80 100
kilometres
QLD 6
H J K L M N P
Birdsville
Big Red
Simpson Desert National Park
Poeppel Corner
QUEENSLAND
SOUTH AUSTRALIA
Lake Nappanerica
Dickeree Waterhole
Pandie Pandie
Karrathunka Waterhole
Lake Short
Lake Cooninnie
Frew Hill
Cadelga Outstation
The Sisters
Haddon Corner
Nullah Outstation
Lake Etamunbanie
Lake Uloowaranie
Diamantina
Inside Track
Outside Track
New Alton Downs
Andrewilla Waterhole
Goyder Lagoon
Koonchera Waterhole
Geake Hill
SIMPSON DESERT
STRZELECKI DESERT
Providence
Creek
Cordillo Downs
Arrabury
Rig Road
K1 Line
4WD
Clifton Hills
Warburton Crossing
Warburton
Lake Goyder
Lake Apanburra
Coongie
Lake Marroocutchanie
Coongie Lake
Innamincka Regional Reserve
(Desert Parks Pass required prior to entry)
Kudriemitchie Outstation
Montebeary Creek
Mulga Bore
Leap Year Bore
Patchawara Bore
Mt Gason
Mt Gason Bore
Sturt Stony Desert
Lake John
Lake Koodnanie
Birdsville Track
Walkers Crossing
Cooper Creek
Scrubby Camp Waterhole
Nappa Merrie
Burke and Wills Dig Tree
Innamincka
Cullyamurra Waterhole
Kalamurina
Cowarie
Lake Howitt
Mirra Mitta Bore
Tirrawarra Oil and Gas Field
Gidgealpa
Lake Perigundi
Mt Hogarth
Mungeranie Gap
Uwinya Hill
Lake Andree
Gidgealpa Gas Field
Kalamurra Lake
Mungeranie
Mungeranie Roadhouse
Moomba
Moomba Gas Field
Della Gas Field
Burke-Dullingari Oil and Gas Field
Epsilon
Lake Kittakittaooloo
Lake Warrakalanna
Big Lake Gas Field
Lake Ngapakaldi
Lake Hope or Panda
Big Lake Moomba
Lake Moomba
Toolache Gas Field
Mulka
Lake Puntawolona
Lake Killalpaninna
Lake Murteree
Merty Merty
Lake Killamperpunna
STRZELECKI Strzelecki Regional Reserve
DESERT
Etadunna
Cannuwaukaninna Bore
Lake Kopperekoppinna
Gas Pipeline Track
Strzelecki Track
Omicron
Lake Florence
Lake Gregory
Bollards Lagoon
Strzelecki Crossing
Yaningurie Waterhole
Cameron Corner
Fort Grey
Dulkaninna
Conical Hill
Lindon
Strzelecki Regional Reserve
Clayton
Lake Blanche
Lake Stewart
Dog Fence
Lake Harry
Montecollina Bore
Blanchewater
Mount Hopeless
Lake Arthur
Murnpeowie
Marree
Lake Callabonna
Tilcha
Mt Hopeless
Lake Delusion
Frome
Mundowdna
Oodnadatta Track
Witchelina
Mt Freeling
Mt Babbage
Moolawatana
Bookaree
Yandama
Lake Yanner pi
Wilpoorinna
Farina
Mount Freeling
Mt Fitton Talc Mine
Mount Fitton
Hamilton Ck
Mt Neill
Strzelecki
Smithville House
SOUTH AUSTRALIA
QUEENSLAND
NEW SOUTH WALES
SA
SA 3

Map 3

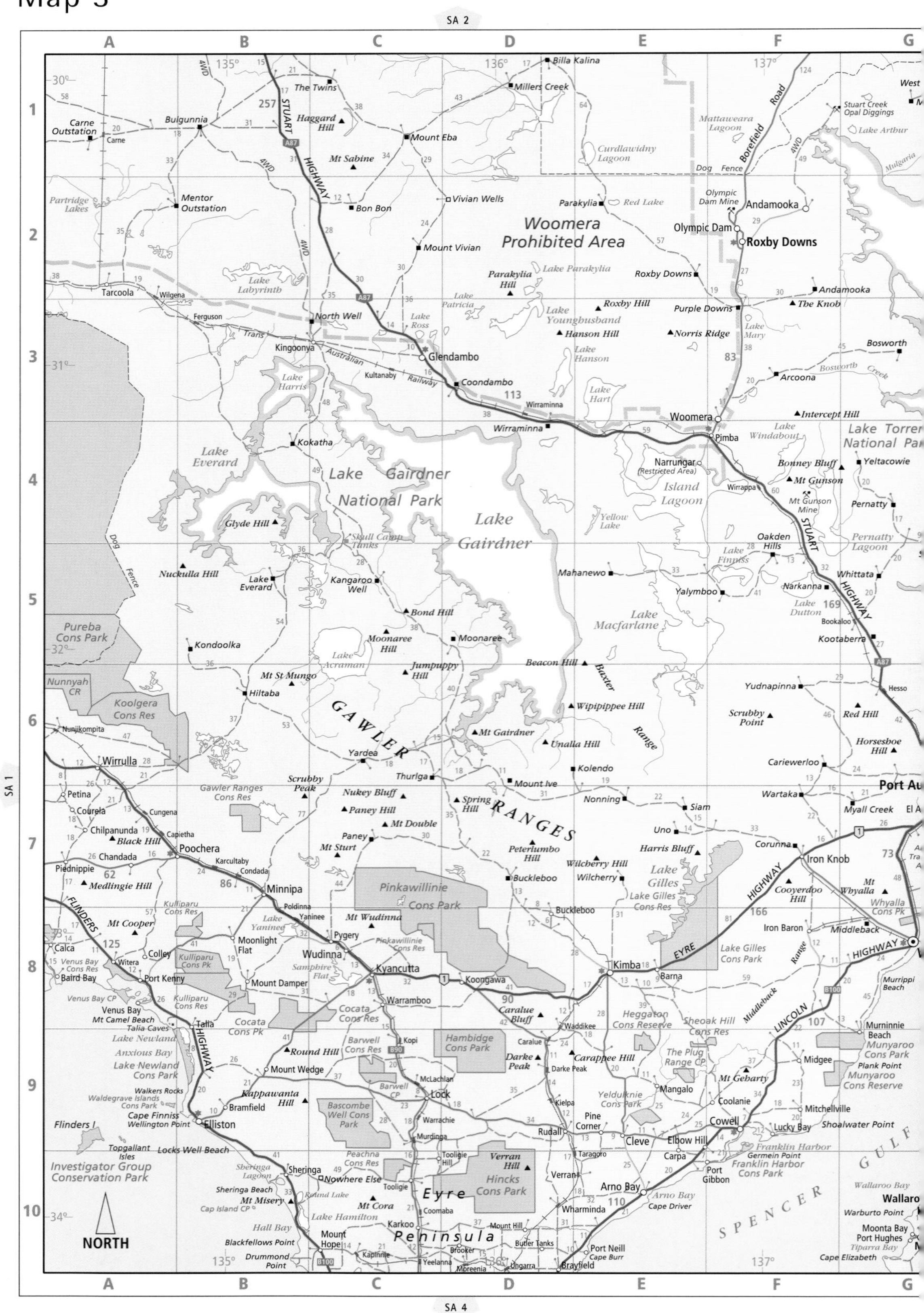
SA 2
A
B
C
D
E
F
G
1
2
3
4
5
6
7
8
9
10
SA 1
SA 4
135°
136°
137°
30°
31°
32°
34°
Billa Kalina
The Twins
Millers Creek
Stuart Creek Opal Diggings
Lake Arthur
Carne Outstation
Carne
Bulgunnia
Haggard Hill
Mount Eba
Curdlawidny Lagoon
Mattaweara Lagoon
Borefield Road
Mt Sabine
Dog Fence
Mentor Outstation
Partridge Lakes
Bon Bon
Vivian Wells
Parakylia
Red Lake
Olympic Dam Mine
Andamooka
Olympic Dam
Roxby Downs
Woomera Prohibited Area
Mount Vivian
Parakylia Hill
Lake Parakylia
Lake Labyrinth
Tarcoola
Wilgena
Ferguson
Trans
Australian
Railway
Kingoonya
North Well
Lake Patricia
Lake Ross
Lake Youngbusband
Roxby Hill
Hanson Hill
Purple Downs
The Knob
Norris Ridge
Lake Mary
Glendambo
Lake Hanson
Bosworth
Bosworth Creek
Arcoona
Kultanaby
Coondambo
Lake Harris
Lake Hart
Wirraminna
Woomera
Intercept Hill
Pimba
Lake Windabout
Lake Torrens National Park
Kokatha
Lake Everard
Narrungar (Restricted Area)
Bonney Bluff
Yeltacowie
Lake Gairdner National Park
Island Lagoon
Mt Gunson
Wirrappa
Mt Gunson Mine
Pernatty
Glyde Hill
Lake Gairdner
Yellow Lake
Skull Camp Tanks
Pernatty Lagoon
Oakden Hills
Lake Finniss
Dog Fence
Nuckulla Hill
Lake Everard
Kangaroo Well
Mahanewo
Whittata
Narkanna
Yalymboo
Lake Dutton
Bookaloo
Bond Hill
Lake Macfarlane
Pureba Cons Park
Moonaree Hill
Moonaree
Kootaberra
Kondoolka
Lake Acraman
Jumpuppy Hill
Beacon Hill
Baxter Range
Mt St Mungo
Yudnapinna
Hesso
Nunnyah CR
Hiltaba
Koolgera Cons Res
Gawler Ranges
Wipipippee Hill
Scrubby Point
Red Hill
Nunjikompita
Mt Gairdner
Unalla Hill
Horseshoe Hill
Wirrulla
Yardea
Carieweerloo
Kolendo
Thurlga
Mount Ive
Port Augusta
Petina
Scrubby Peak
Gawler Ranges Cons Res
Nukey Bluff
Spring Hill
Nonning
Wartaka
Siam
Coorabie
Cungena
Paney Hill
Myall Creek
Chilpanunda
Capietha
Mt Double
Uno
Black Hill
Paney
Corunna
Poochera
Mt Sturt
Peterlumbo Hill
Harris Bluff
Chandada
Karcultaby
Condada
Wilcherry Hill
Iron Knob
Piednippie
Minnipa
Wilcherry
Lake Gilles
Mt Whyalla
Medlingie Hill
Pinkawillinie Cons Park
Buckleboo
Lake Gilles Cons Res
Cooyerdoo Hill
Whyalla Cons Pk
Flinders Highway
Kulliparu Cons Res
Poldinna
Yaninee
Lake Yaninee
Mt Wudinna
Buckleboo
Mt Cooper
Pygery
Iron Baron
Middleback
Calca
Moonlight Flat
Pinkawillinie Cons Res
Lake Gilles Cons Park
Colley
Wudinna
Kulliparu Cons Pk
Venus Bay Cons Res
Witera
Kyancutta
Kimba
Eyre Highway
Baird Bay
Samphire Flat
Koongawa
Barna
Port Kenny
Mount Damper
Murrippi Beach
Venus Bay CP
Kulliparu Cons Res
Warramboo
Venus Bay
Mt Camel Beach
Caralue Bluff
Heggaton Cons Reserve
Middleback Range
Lincoln Highway
Talia
Cocata Cons Res
Talia Caves
Cocata Cons Pk
Waddikee
Sheoak Hill Cons Res
Murninnie Beach
Lake Newland
Barwell Cons Res
Kopi
Hambidge Cons Park
Caralue
Munyaroo Cons Park
Anxious Bay
Round Hill
Darke Peak
Carappee Hill
The Plug Range CP
Midgee
Lake Newland Cons Park
Mount Wedge
Plank Point
Munyaroo Cons Reserve
Walkers Rocks
McLachlan
Barwell CP
Yeldulknie Cons Park
Mt Gebarty
Waldegrave Islands Cons Park
Kappawanta Hill
Lock
Mangalo
Flinders I
Bramfield
Bascombe Well Cons Park
Kielpa
Coolanie
Mitchellville
Cape Finniss
Wellington Point
Elliston
Warrachie
Pine Corner
Cowell
Lucky Bay
Shoalwater Point
Topgallant Isles
Locks Well Beach
Murdinga
Rudall
Cleve
Elbow Hill
Franklin Harbor
Investigator Group Conservation Park
Sheringa Lagoon
Sheringa
Peachna Cons Res
Toolgie Hill
Verran Hill
Taragoro
Carpa
Germein Point
Franklin Harbor Cons Park
Nowhere Else
Hincks Cons Park
Verran
Port Gibbon
Spencer Gulf
Wallaroo Bay
Sheringa Beach
Round Lake
Toolgie
Eyre Peninsula
Arno Bay
Wallaroo
Cap Island CP
Mt Misery
Mt Cora
Coomaba
Arno Bay
Cape Driver
Warburto Point
Lake Hamilton
Wharminda
Hall Bay
Karkoo
Mount Hill
Moonta Bay
Blackfellows Point
Mount Hope
Butler Tanks
Port Hughes
Tiparra Bay
Drummond Point
Kapinnie
Brooker
Port Neill
Cape Burr
Cape Elizabeth
Yeelanna
Ungarra
Moreenia
Brayfield
NORTH
Stuart Highway
A87
B100
B90

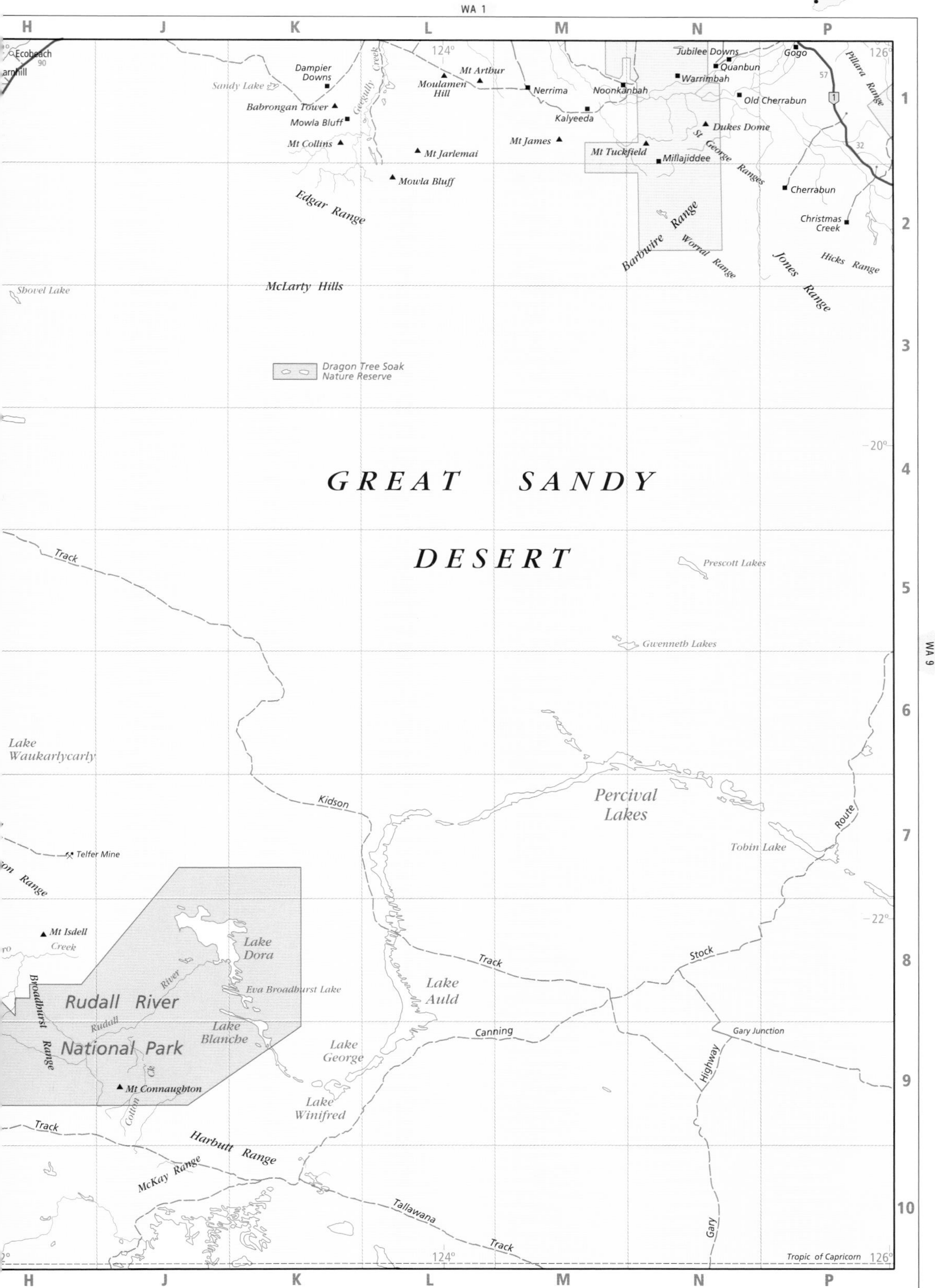
0 20 40 60 80 100
kilometres
GREAT SANDY DESERT
Ecobeach
Dampier Downs
Sandy Lake
Babrongan Tower
Mowla Bluff
Mt Collins
Moulamen Hill
Mt Arthur
Nerrima
Noonkanbah
Kalyeeda
Mt James
Mt Jarlemai
Mowla Bluff
Mt Tuckfield
Millajiddee
Jubilee Downs
Quanbun
Warrimbah
Gogo
Old Cherrabun
Dukes Dome
St George Ranges
Cherrabun
Christmas Creek
Pillara Range
Edgar Range
Barbwire Range
Worral Range
Jones Range
Hicks Range
Shovel Lake
McLarty Hills
Dragon Tree Soak Nature Reserve
Prescott Lakes
Gwenneth Lakes
Lake Waukarlycarly
Kidson
Track
Percival Lakes
Tobin Lake
Route
Telfer Mine
Mt Isdell
Creek
Lake Dora
Eva Broadhurst Lake
Broadhurst Range
Rudall River National Park
Lake Blanche
Mt Connaughton
Lake Auld
Lake George
Lake Winifred
Stock
Canning
Gary Junction
Highway
Harbutt Range
McKay Range
Tallawana
Track
Gary
Tropic of Capricorn
124°
126°
20°
22°
H J K L M N P
1 2 3 4 5 6 7 8 9 10

WA 9

Map 4

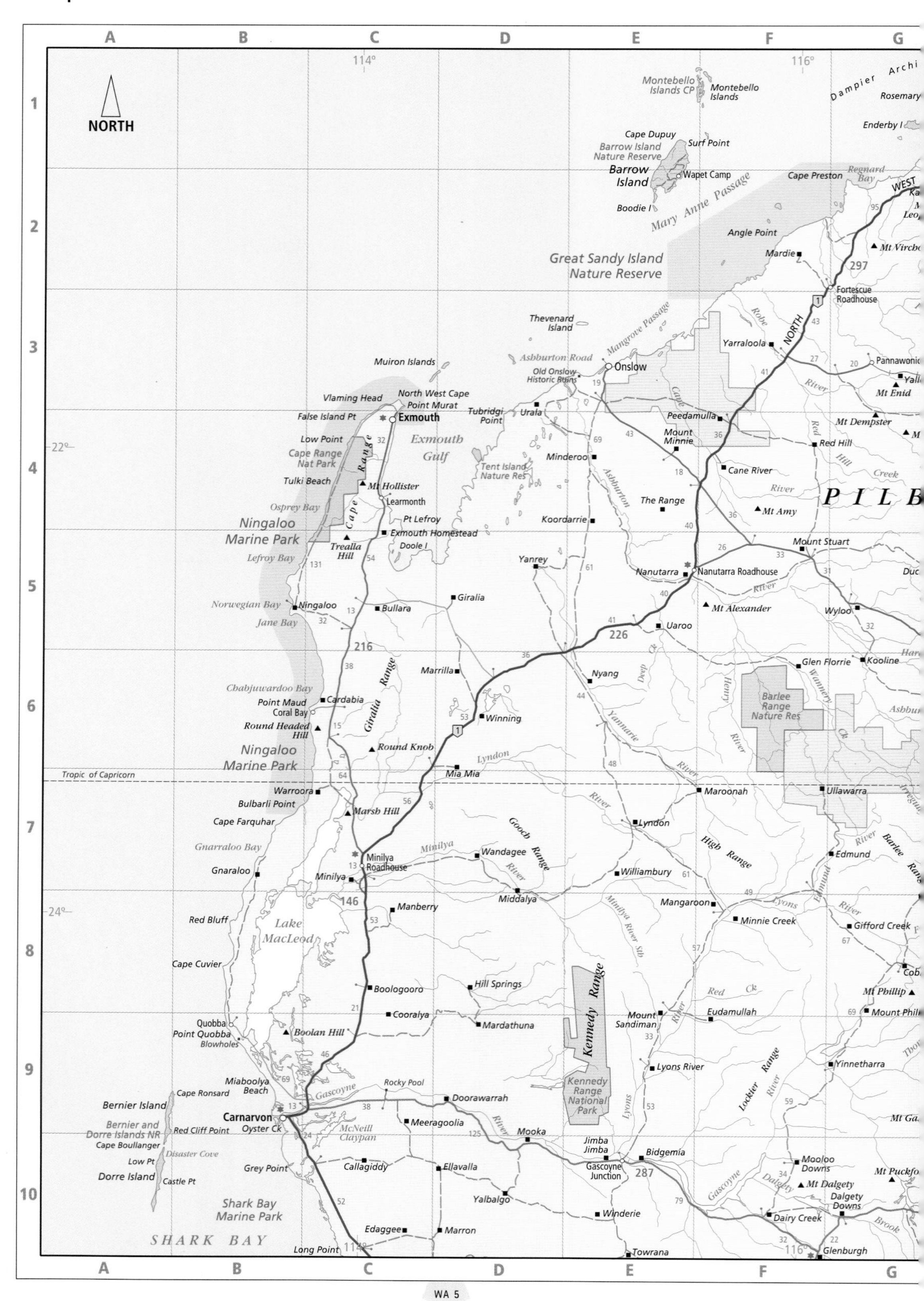

NORTH
Montebello Islands CP
Montebello Islands
Dampier Archi
Rosemary
Enderby I
Cape Dupuy
Surf Point
Barrow Island Nature Reserve
Barrow Island
Wapet Camp
Cape Preston
Regnard Bay
Boodie I
Mary Anne Passage
Angle Point
Mardie
Mt Virchow
Great Sandy Island Nature Reserve
Fortescue Roadhouse
Thevenard Island
Mangrove Passage
Yarraloola
Muiron Islands
Ashburton Road
Onslow
Pannawonica
Old Onslow Historic Ruins
Mt Enid
Vlaming Head
North West Cape
Point Murat
Tubridgi Point
Urala
Peedamulla
Mt Dempster
False Island Pt
Exmouth
Low Point
Cape Range Nat Park
Exmouth Gulf
Minderoo
Mount Minnie
Red Hill
Tent Island Nature Res
Cane River
Tulki Beach
Mt Hollister
Learmonth
Osprey Bay
The Range
Mt Amy
PILB
Ningaloo Marine Park
Pt Lefroy
Exmouth Homestead
Koordarrie
Trealla Hill
Doole I
Mount Stuart
Lefroy Bay
Yanrey
Nanutarra
Nanutarra Roadhouse
Norwegian Bay
Ningaloo
Giralia
Bullara
Mt Alexander
Wyloo
Jane Bay
Uaroo
Marrilla
Nyang
Glen Florrie
Kooline
Chabjuwardoo Bay
Point Maud
Coral Bay
Cardabia
Giralia Range
Barlee Range Nature Res
Round Headed Hill
Winning
Round Knob
Mia Mia
Tropic of Capricorn
Warroora
Maroonah
Ullawarra
Bulbarli Point
Marsh Hill
Cape Farquhar
Gooch Range
Lyndon
Gnarraloo Bay
Minilya Roadhouse
Wandagee
High Range
Edmund
Gnaraloo
Minilya
Williambury
Middalya
Red Bluff
Manberry
Mangaroon
Minnie Creek
Gifford Creek
Lake MacLeod
Cape Cuvier
Kennedy Range
Boologooro
Hill Springs
Mt Phillip
Mount Sandiman
Eudamullah
Mount Phillip
Quobba
Point Quobba
Blowholes
Cooralya
Mardathuna
Boolan Hill
Lyons River
Lockier Range
Yinnetharra
Miaboolya Beach
Rocky Pool
Bernier Island
Cape Ronsard
Doorawarrah
Kennedy Range National Park
Bernier and Dorre Islands NR
Carnarvon
Oyster Ck
Meeragoolia
Red Cliff Point
McNeill Claypan
Mooka
Cape Boullanger
Disaster Cove
Jimba Jimba
Bidgemia
Low Pt
Grey Point
Callagiddy
Ellavalla
Gascoyne Junction
Mooloo Downs
Mt Puckford
Dorre Island
Castle Pt
Yalbalgo
Mt Dalgety
Dalgety Downs
Shark Bay Marine Park
Winderie
Dairy Creek
SHARK BAY
Edaggee
Marron
Long Point
Towrana
Glenburgh

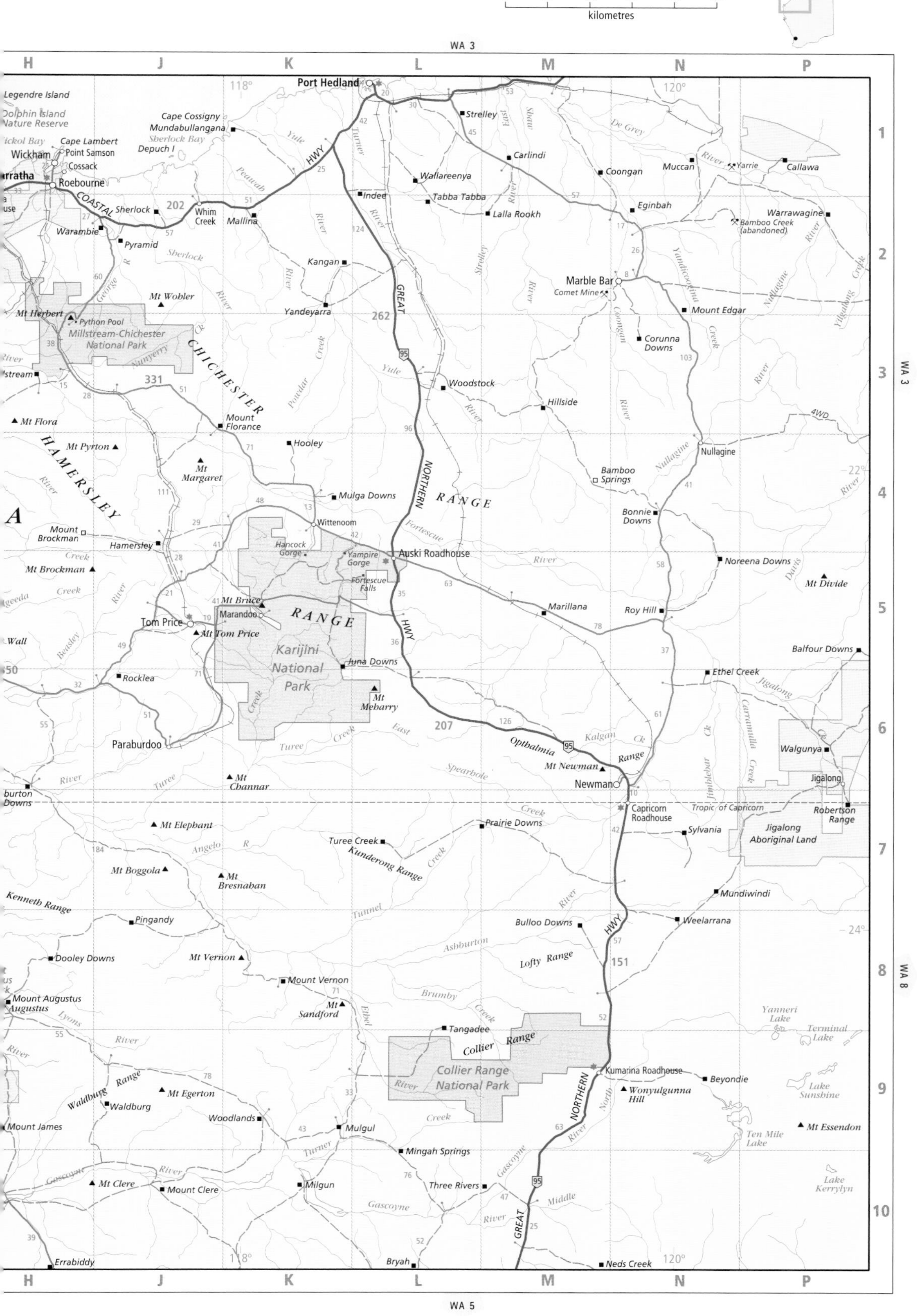

0 20 40 60 80 100
kilometres
WA 3
WA 5
WA 8
WA
Port Hedland
Strelley
Cape Cossigny
Mundabullangana
Sherlock Bay
Depuch I
Legendre Island
Dolphin Island Nature Reserve
Cape Lambert
Point Samson
Wickham
Cossack
Roebourne
COASTAL HWY
Sherlock
Whim Creek
Mallina
Warambie
Pyramid
Carlindi
Coongan
Muccan
Yarrie
Callawa
Wallareenya
Indee
Tabba Tabba
Lalla Rookh
Egingbah
Warrawagine
Bamboo Creek (abandoned)
Kangan
Marble Bar
Comet Mine
Mount Edgar
Yandeyarra
Mt Wohler
Mt Herbert
Python Pool
Millstream-Chichester National Park
CHICHESTER
Corunna Downs
GREAT NORTHERN HWY
Woodstock
Hillside
Mount Florance
Mt Flora
HAMERSLEY
Mt Pyrton
Mt Margaret
Hooley
Nullagine
Bamboo Springs
Mulga Downs
RANGE
Bonnie Downs
Mount Brockman
Hamersley
Wittenoom
Hancock Gorge
Yampire Gorge
Fortescue Falls
Auski Roadhouse
Noreena Downs
Mt Brockman
Mt Bruce
Marandoo
Mt Divide
Tom Price
Mt Tom Price
Karijini National Park
Marillana
Roy Hill
Balfour Downs
Juna Downs
Ethel Creek
Rocklea
Mt Meharry
Paraburdoo
Ophthalmia Range
Mt Newman
Newman
Walgunya
Jigalong
Mt Channar
Capricorn Roadhouse
Tropic of Capricorn
Robertson Range
Prairie Downs
Sylvania
Jigalong Aboriginal Land
Mt Elephant
Turee Creek
Kunderong Range
Mt Boggola
Mt Bresnahan
Mundiwindi
Kenneth Range
Pingandy
Bulloo Downs
Weelarrana
Lofty Range
Dooley Downs
Mt Vernon
Mount Vernon
Mount Augustus
Mt Sandford
Yanneri Lake
Terminal Lake
Tangadee
Collier Range
Collier Range National Park
Kumarina Roadhouse
Beyondie
Wonyulgunna Hill
Lake Sunshine
Waldburg Range
Mt Egerton
Waldburg
Woodlands
Mulgul
Mount James
Ten Mile Lake
Mt Essendon
Mingah Springs
Mt Clere
Mount Clere
Milgun
Three Rivers
Lake Kerrylyn
Errabiddy
Bryah
Neds Creek
H J K L M N P
1 2 3 4 5 6 7 8 9 10

Map 5

WA 4
A
B
C
D
E
F
G
1
2
3
4
5
6
7
8
9
10
114°
26°
28°
30°
Shark Bay
Marine Park
SHARK BAY
Cape Inscription
Cape Levillain
Dirk Hartog Island
Long Point
Cape Peron North
Herald Bight
Herald Bluff
Francois Peron Nat Park
Cape Lesueur
Peron Homestead (Historic Site)
Monkey Mia
Quoin Head
Denham Sound
Denham
Faure Island
Dubaut Point
Petit Pt
Gladstone
Cape Bellefin
L'Haridon Bight
Hamelin Pool Marine Nature Reserve
Westernmost point of Australian mainland
Steep Point
Useless Loop (No access)
Goulet Bluff
Mt Direction
Nanga Bay
Cararang Pen
Garden Pt
Zuytdorp Point
Carrarang
Henri Freycinet Harbour
Hamelin
Overlander Roadhouse
Tamala
Coburn
Zuytdorp Cliffs
Billabong Roadhouse
Zuytdorp Nature Reserve
Toolonga Nature Reserve
Nerren Nerren
Edaggee
Marron
Wahroonga
Wooramel
Wooramel Roadhouse
Carlaweelban Hill
Yaringa
Carbla
Meedo
Woodleigh
Winderie
Towrana
Pimbee
Carey Downs
Gilroyd
Callytharra Springs
Yalardy
Talisker
Wooramel River
Dairy Creek
Dalgety Downs
Glenburgh
Erong Springs
Yalbra
Coordewandy
Innouendy
Daurie Creek
Byro
Breberle Lake
Curbur
Manfred
Mount Narryer
Muggon
Murchison Roadhouse
Meeberrie
Murchison
Wooleen
Roderick
Twin Peaks
Murgoo
Sanford
New Forest
Yallalong
Billabalong
NORTH WEST COASTAL HWY
Kalbarri National Park
Murchison House
Gantheaume Bay
Kalbarri
Red Bluff
Shell House
Bluff Point
Eagle Gorge
Natural Bridge
Hawks Head Lookout
Eurardy
Coolcalalaya
Mary Springs
Yandi
Galena
Wagoe Beach
Kulla Kulla Hill
Ajana
Mallee
Woolgorong
Pinegrove
Bullardoo
Wandina
Narloo
Yuin
Tardie
Tallering Peak
Marlana
Pindaring Rocks
Gabyon
Urawa Nat Res
Tallering
Half Way Bay
Shoal Point
Hutt Lagoon
Binnu
Wandana Nature Res
Gregory
Broken Anchor Bay
North Island
Whaleboat Cove
Horrocks
Bowes Hill
Northampton
Yuna
East Yuna Nature Res
Naraling
Mullewa
Pindar
Wurarga
Houtman Abrolhos
Geelvink Channel
Wallabi Group
Nabawa
Nanson
Greenough
Coronation Beach
Drummond Cove
Champion Bay
Geraldton
Point Moore
Moonyoonooka
Barnong
Easter Group
Mangrove Group
Pelsaert Group
Cape Burney
Burma Road NR
Sullivan
Tardun
Canna
Gutha
Mellenbye
Walkaway
Flat Rocks
BRAND HWY
Yarragadee
Pintharuka
Kadji Kadji
Seven Mile Beach
Irwin
Mingenew
Nullewa Lake
Morawa
Strawberry Hill
Dongara
Port Denison
Billeranga Hills
Koolanooka
Weelhamby Lake
Bowgada
White Point
Yardanogo Nature Res
Arrino
Perenjori
INDIAN OCEAN
Cliff Head
Three Springs
Freshwater Point
Wotto Nat Res
Carnamah
Bunjil
Illawong
Beekeepers Nature Res
Yarra Yarra Lakes
Winchester
Woodada Hill
Eneabba
Latham
Coolimba
Tathra Nat Pk
Capamauro Nature Res
Coorow
Maya
Leeman
South Eneabba NR
Lake Logue NR
Alexander Morrison NP
Pinjarrega Nat Res
Green Head
Marchagee
Wubin
Lesueur Nat Pk
Coomallo Nat Res
Pinjarrega Lake
Salt Lakes
North Head
Drovers Cave NP
Watheroo Nat Park
Watheroo
Jurien Bay
Jurien
Badgingarra
Dalwallinu
NORTH
WA 6

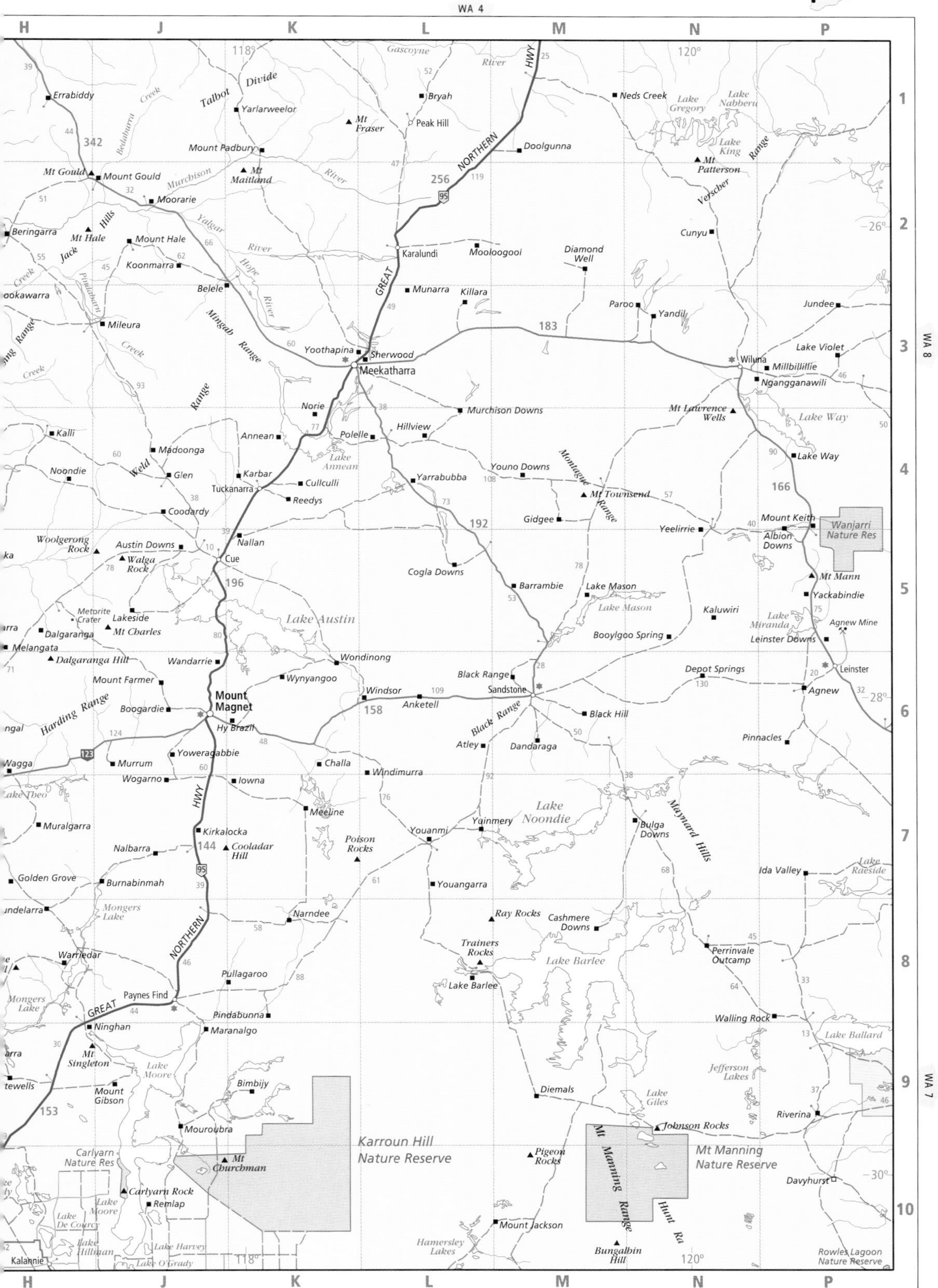
0 20 40 60 80 100
kilometres
Errabiddy
Talbot Divide
Yarlarweelor
Mount Padbury
Mt Gould
Mount Gould
Murchison River
Mt Maitland
Moorarie
Beringarra
Mt Hale
Jack Hills
Mount Hale
Koonmarra
Belele
Mileura
Mingah Range
Weld Range
Kalli
Madoonga
Noondie
Glen
Coodardy
Woolgerong Rock
Austin Downs
Walga Rock
Cue
Nallan
Tuckanarra
Karbar
Cullculli
Reedys
Annean
Lake Annean
Norie
Polelle
Hillview
Meekatharra
Yoothapina
Sherwood
Munarra
Karalundi
Mooloogool
Killara
Bryah
Peak Hill
Mt Fraser
Doolgunna
GREAT NORTHERN HWY
Neds Creek
Lake Gregory
Lake Nabberu
Lake King
Mt Patterson
Verscher Range
Cunyu
Diamond Well
Paroo
Yandil
Jundee
Lake Violet
Wiluna
Millbillillie
Ngangganawili
Murchison Downs
Mt Lawrence Wells
Lake Way
Youno Downs
Montague Range
Mt Townsend
Yarrabubba
Gidgee
Yeelirrie
Mount Keith
Albion Downs
Wanjarri Nature Res
Cogla Downs
Barrambie
Lake Mason
Mt Mann
Yackabindie
Kaluwiri
Lake Miranda
Agnew Mine
Leinster Downs
Booylgoo Spring
Leinster
Depot Springs
Agnew
Black Range
Sandstone
Black Hill
Pinnacles
Dandaraga
Atley
Lake Austin
Metorite Crater
Lakeside
Mt Charles
Dalgaranga
Melangata
Dalgaranga Hill
Wandarrie
Wondinong
Wynyangoo
Windsor
Anketell
Mount Farmer
Harding Range
Boogardie
Mount Magnet
Hy Brazil
Yoweragabbie
Murrum
Wogarno
Iowna
Challa
Windimurra
Lake Noondie
Maynard Hills
Bulga Downs
Yuinmery
Youanmi
Meeline
Poison Rocks
Youangarra
Muralgarra
Kirkalocka
Cooladar Hill
Nalbarra
Golden Grove
Burnabinmah
Ida Valley
Lake Raeside
Mongers Lake
Narndee
Ray Rocks
Cashmere Downs
Trainers Rocks
Lake Barlee
Perrinvale Outcamp
Warriedar
Pullagaroo
Paynes Find
Pindabunna
Ninghan
Maranalgo
Walling Rock
Lake Ballard
Mt Singleton
Lake Moore
Mount Gibson
Bimbijy
Diemals
Jefferson Lakes
Lake Giles
Riverina
Johnson Rocks
Mouroubra
Karroun Hill Nature Reserve
Carlyarn Nature Res
Mt Churchman
Pigeon Rocks
Mt Manning Range
Mt Manning Nature Reserve
Hunt Ra
Davyhurst
Carlyarn Rock
Remlap
Lake De Courcy
Lake Hillman
Lake Harvey
Lake O'Grady
Kalannie
Mount Jackson
Hamersley Lakes
Bungalbin Hill
Rowles Lagoon Nature Reserve
Gascoyne River
Bedaburra Creek
Yalgar River
Hope River
Pindabarn Creek
WA 8
WA 7
WA

Map 6

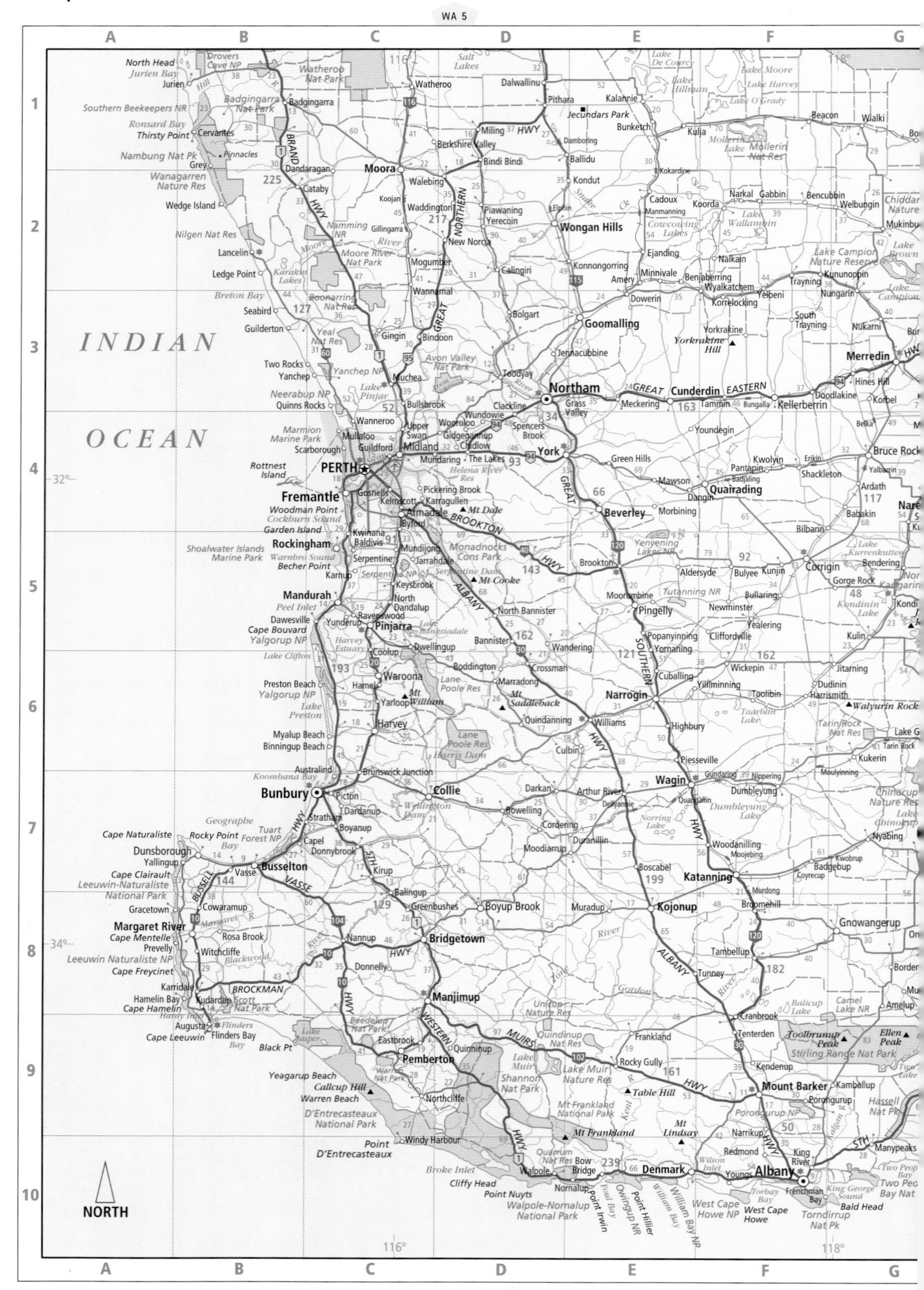
WA 5
A
B
C
D
E
F
G
1
2
3
4
5
6
7
8
9
10
INDIAN
OCEAN
NORTH
32°
34°
116°
118°
North Head
Jurien Bay
Jurien
Drovers Cave NP
Watheroo Nat Park
Watheroo
Salt Lakes
Dalwallinu
Pithara
Kalannie
Lake De Courcy
Lake Hillman
Lake Moore
Lake Harvey
Lake O'Grady
Southern Beekeepers NR
Badgingarra Nat Park
Badgingarra
Jecundars Park
Bunketch
Kulja
Beacon
Wialki
Ronsard Bay
Thirsty Point
Cervantes
Miling
Berkshire Valley
Damboring
Lake Mollerin
Mollerin Nat Res
Nambung Nat Pk
Pinnacles
Grey
Dandaragan
Moora
Bindi Bindi
Ballidu
Kokardine
Wanagarren Nature Res
Cataby
Walebing
Kondut
Wedge Island
Koojan
Waddington
Piawaning
Yerecoin
Cadoux
Manmanning
Koorda
Narkal
Gabbin
Bencubbin
Welbungin
Chiddarcooping Nature Res
Mukinbudin
Nilgen Nat Res
Namming NR
Gillingarra
Wongan Hills
Lake Wallambin
Cowcowing Lakes
Lancelin
Moore River Nat Park
New Norcia
Ejanding
Nalkain
Lake Campion Nature Reserve
Lake Brown
Ledge Point
Karakin Lakes
Mogumber
Calingiri
Konnongorring
Minnivale
Benjaberring
Wyalkatchem
Kununoppin
Trayning
Amery
Yelbeni
Nungarin
Breton Bay
Boonanarring Nat Res
Wannamal
Dowerin
Korrelocking
Seabird
Bolgart
Goomalling
South Trayning
Nukarni
Guilderton
Yeal Nat Res
Gingin
Bindoon
Yorkrakine
Yorkrakine Hill
Avon Valley Nat Park
Jennacubbine
Merredin
Two Rocks
Yanchep
Yanchep NP
Muchea
Toodyay
Northam
Hines Hill
Lake Pinjar
Bullsbrook
GREAT EASTERN HWY
Cunderdin
Doodlakine
Neerabup NP
Quinns Rocks
Clackline
Grass Valley
Meckering
Tammin
Bungalla
Kellerberrin
Korbel
Wanneroo
Upper Swan
Wooroloo
Wundowie
Spencers Brook
Youndegin
Marmion Marine Park
Mullaloo
Midland
Gidgegannup
Chidlow
Scarborough
Guildford
York
Rottnest Island
PERTH
Mundaring
The Lakes
Helena River Res
Green Hills
Kwolyin
Erikin
Bruce Rock
Pantapin
Badjaling
Shackleton
Yalbarrin
Fremantle
Gosnells
Pickering Brook
Mawson
Dangin
Quairading
Ardath
Woodman Point
Cockburn Sound
Kelmscott
Karragullen
Armadale
Mt Dale
Beverley
Morbining
Babakin
Narembeen
Garden Island
Byford
BROOKTON HWY
Kwinana
Baldivis
Shoalwater Islands Marine Park
Rockingham
Mundijong
Monadnocks Cons Park
Yenyening Lakes NR
Bilbarin
Lake Kurrenkutten
Warnbro Sound
Becher Point
Serpentine
Jarrahdale
Serpentine Dam
Brookton
Aldersyde
Bulyee
Kunjin
Corrigin
Bendering
Karnup
Serpentine NP
Mt Cooke
Gorge Rock
Keysbrook
Mandurah
North Dandalup
Moorumbine
Tutanning NR
Bullaring
Kondinin
Kondinin Lake
Peel Inlet
North Bannister
Pingelly
Newminster
Dawesville
Ravenswood
Cape Bouvard
Yunderup
Pinjarra
Lake Banksiadale
Yalgorup NP
Harvey Estuary
Bannister
Wandering
Popanyinning
Yornaning
Cuballing
Cliffordville
Yealering
Kulin
Lake Clifton
Coolup
Dwellingup
Crossman
Wickepin
Jitarning
Boddington
Lane Poole Res
Preston Beach
Hamel
Waroona
Marradong
Yillminning
Dudinin
Narrogin
Toolibin
Harrismith
Mt William
Mt Saddleback
Yarloop
Lake Preston
Quindanning
Williams
Taarblin Lake
Walyurin Rock
Harvey
Tarin Rock Nat Res
Highbury
Lake Grace
Myalup Beach
Binningup Beach
Harris Dam
Culbin
Piesseville
Kukerin
Australind
Brunswick Junction
Koombana Bay
Darkan
Arthur River
Wagin
Gundaring
Nippering
Moulyinning
Bunbury
Picton
Collie
Dellyannie
Quangallin
Dumbleyung
Chinocup Nature Res
Geographe Bay
Dardanup
Wellington Dam
Bowelling
Norring Lake
Dumbleyung Lake
Lake Chinocup
Tuart Forest NP
Stratham
Boyanup
Cordering
Duranillin
Cape Naturaliste
Rocky Point
Capel
Moodiarrup
Woodanilling
Nyabing
Dunsborough
Donnybrook
Moojebing
Kwobrup
Yallingup
Busselton
Vasse
Kirup
Boscabel
Badgebup
Coyrecup
Cape Clairault
Leeuwin-Naturaliste National Park
Katanning
Gracetown
Cowaramup
Balingup
Greenbushes
Boyup Brook
Muradup
Kojonup
Murdong
Broomehill
Margaret River
Gnowangerup
Cape Mentelle
Rosa Brook
Nannup
Bridgetown
Prevelly
Witchcliffe
Leeuwin Naturaliste NP
Tambellup
Cape Freycinet
Donnelly
Tunney
Border
Karridale
BROCKMAN HWY
Manjimup
Hamelin Bay
Kudardup
Scott Nat Park
Cape Hamelin
Hardy Inlet
Augusta
Flinders
Unicup Nature Res
Balicup Lake
Camel Lake NR
Amelup
Cranbrook
Cape Leeuwin
Flinders Bay
Beedelup Nat Park
Lake Jasper
Eastbrook
Quinninup
Quindinup Nat Res
Frankland
Tenterden
Toolbrunup Peak
Ellen Peak
Stirling Range Nat Park
Black Pt
Pemberton
Lake Muir
Rocky Gully
Kendenup
Yeagarup Beach
Warren Nat Park
Lake Muir Nature Res
Shannon Nat Park
Mount Barker
Kamballup
Callcup Hill
Table Hill
Warren Beach
Northcliffe
Porongurup
Porongurup NP
Hassell Nat Pk
D'Entrecasteaux National Park
Mt Frankland National Park
Mt Frankland
Mt Lindsay
Narrikup
Point D'Entrecasteaux
Windy Harbour
Quarram Nat Res
Bow Bridge
Redmond
King River
Manypeaks
Broke Inlet
Walpole
Denmark
Wilson Inlet
Youngs
Albany
Two Peoples Bay
Two Peoples Bay Nat Res
Cliffy Head
Nornalup
Frenchman Bay
King George Sound
Point Nuyts
Walpole-Nornalup National Park
Point Irwin
Point Hillier
Owingup NR
William Bay
William Bay NP
West Cape Howe NP
West Cape Howe
Torbay
Torndirrup Nat Pk
Bald Head

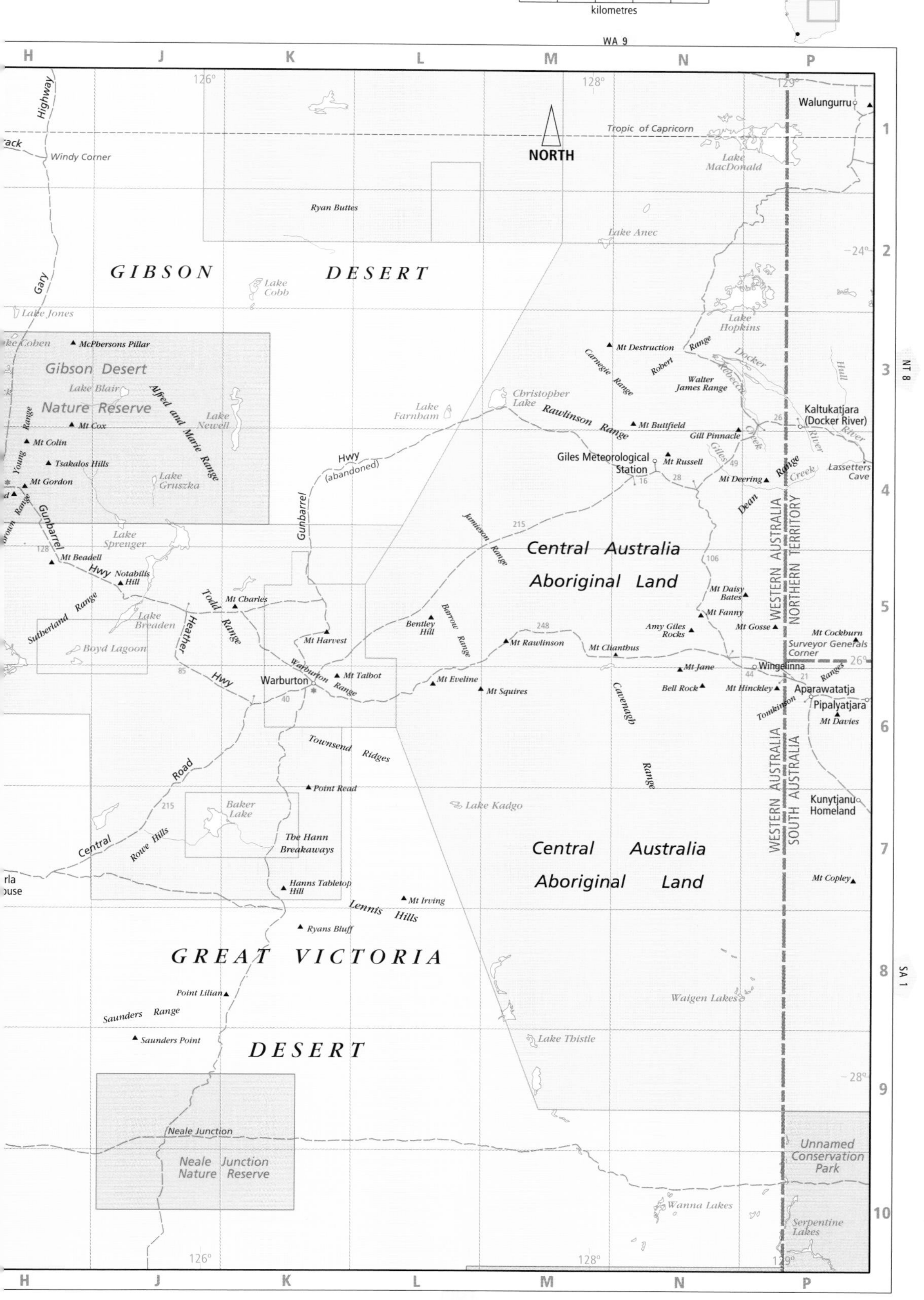

0 20 40 60 80 100
kilometres
NORTH
Tropic of Capricorn
GIBSON DESERT
Gibson Desert Nature Reserve
Central Australia Aboriginal Land
GREAT VICTORIA DESERT
Neale Junction Nature Reserve
Unnamed Conservation Park
Warburton
Giles Meteorological Station
Walungurru
Kaltukatjara (Docker River)
Wingelinna
Aparawatatja
Pipalyatjara
Kunytjanu Homeland
Surveyor Generals Corner
Lassetters Cave
Windy Corner
Neale Junction
Lake MacDonald
Lake Hopkins
Lake Anec
Lake Cobb
Lake Jones
Lake Blair
Lake Newell
Lake Gruszka
Lake Sprenger
Lake Breaden
Boyd Lagoon
Baker Lake
Lake Kadgo
Lake Thistle
Waigen Lakes
Wanna Lakes
Serpentine Lakes
Christopher Lake
Lake Farnham
Ryan Buttes
McPhersons Pillar
Mt Cox
Mt Colin
Tsakalos Hills
Mt Gordon
Mt Beadell
Notabilis Hill
Mt Charles
Mt Harvest
Mt Talbot
Mt Eveline
Mt Squires
Mt Rawlinson
Bentley Hill
Mt Destruction
Mt Buttfield
Mt Russell
Gill Pinnacle
Mt Deering
Mt Daisy Bates
Mt Fanny
Mt Gosse
Amy Giles Rocks
Mt Cockburn
Mt Clianthus
Mt Jane
Bell Rock
Mt Hinckley
Mt Davies
Mt Copley
Point Read
The Hann Breakaways
Hanns Tabletop Hill
Mt Irving
Ryans Bluff
Lennis Hills
Point Lilian
Saunders Range
Saunders Point
Townsend Ridges
Rowe Hills
Alfred and Marie Range
Young Range
Sutherland Range
Todd Range
Warburton Range
Barrow Range
Jamieson Range
Rawlinson Range
Carnegie Range
Robert Range
Walter James Range
Dean Range
Cavenagh Range
Tomkinson Ranges
Petermann Ranges
Docker River
Rebecca Creek
Giles Creek
Hull River
Gary Highway
Gunbarrel Hwy
Gunbarrel Hwy (abandoned)
Heather Hwy
Central Road
WESTERN AUSTRALIA
NORTHERN TERRITORY
SOUTH AUSTRALIA
H J K L M N P
1 2 3 4 5 6 7 8 9 10
126° 128° 129° 24° 26° 28°
NT 8
SA 1
WA

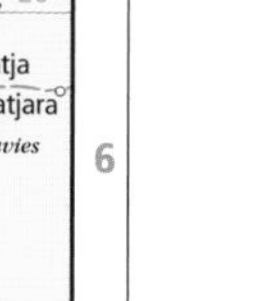

Map 9

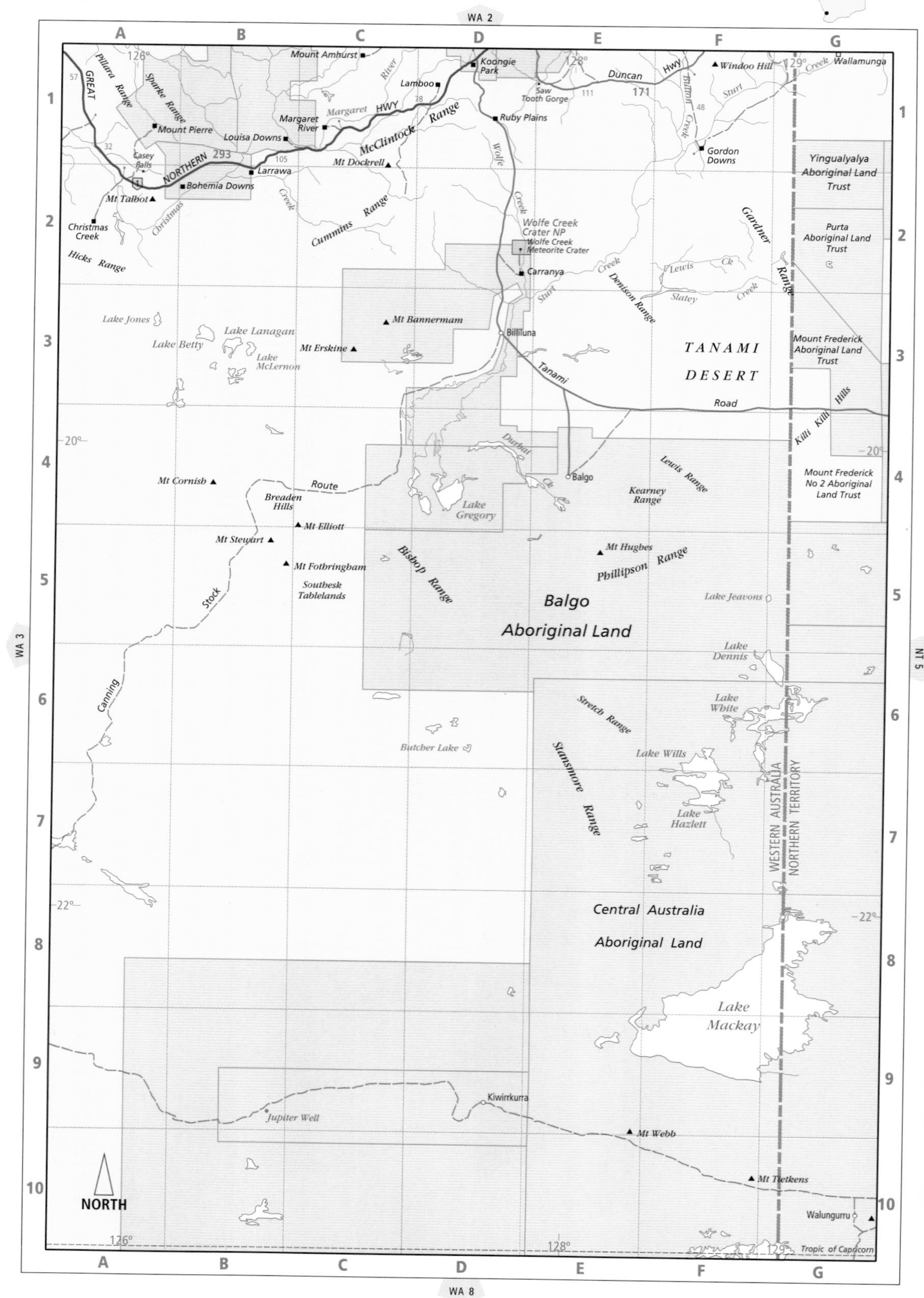

0 20 40 60 80 100
kilometres
WA 2
WA 3
WA 8
NT 5
Mount Amhurst
Koongie Park
Lamboo
Saw Tooth Gorge
Duncan Hwy 171
Windoo Hill
Wallamunga
Pillara Range
Sparke Range
GREAT NORTHERN 293
Mount Pierre
Margaret River
Margaret HWY
McClintock Range
Ruby Plains
Louisa Downs
Casey Falls
Larrawa
Bohemia Downs
Mt Dockrell
Gordon Downs
Yingualyalya Aboriginal Land Trust
Mt Talbot
Christmas Creek
Cummins Range
Wolfe Creek Crater NP
Wolfe Creek Meteorite Crater
Gardner Range
Purta Aboriginal Land Trust
Hicks Range
Carranya
Lewis Ck
Denison Range
Slatey Creek
Sturt Creek
Lake Jones
Lake Lanagan
Mt Bannermam
Billiluna
Lake Betty
Lake McLernon
Mt Erskine
TANAMI DESERT
Mount Frederick Aboriginal Land Trust
Tanami Road
Killi Killi Hills
20°
Durbat Ck
Mt Cornish
Route
Breaden Hills
Balgo
Lewis Range
Kearney Range
Mount Frederick No 2 Aboriginal Land Trust
Lake Gregory
Mt Elliott
Mt Stewart
Mt Hughes
Mt Fotbringbam
Bishop Range
Phillipson Range
Southesk Tablelands
Stock
Balgo Aboriginal Land
Lake Jeavons
Lake Dennis
Canning
Stretch Range
Lake White
Butcher Lake
Lake Wills
Stansmore Range
Lake Hazlett
WESTERN AUSTRALIA
NORTHERN TERRITORY
22°
Central Australia Aboriginal Land
Lake Mackay
Kiwirrkurra
Jupiter Well
Mt Webb
Mt Tietkens
NORTH
Walungurru
126°
128°
129°
Tropic of Capricorn

Map 1

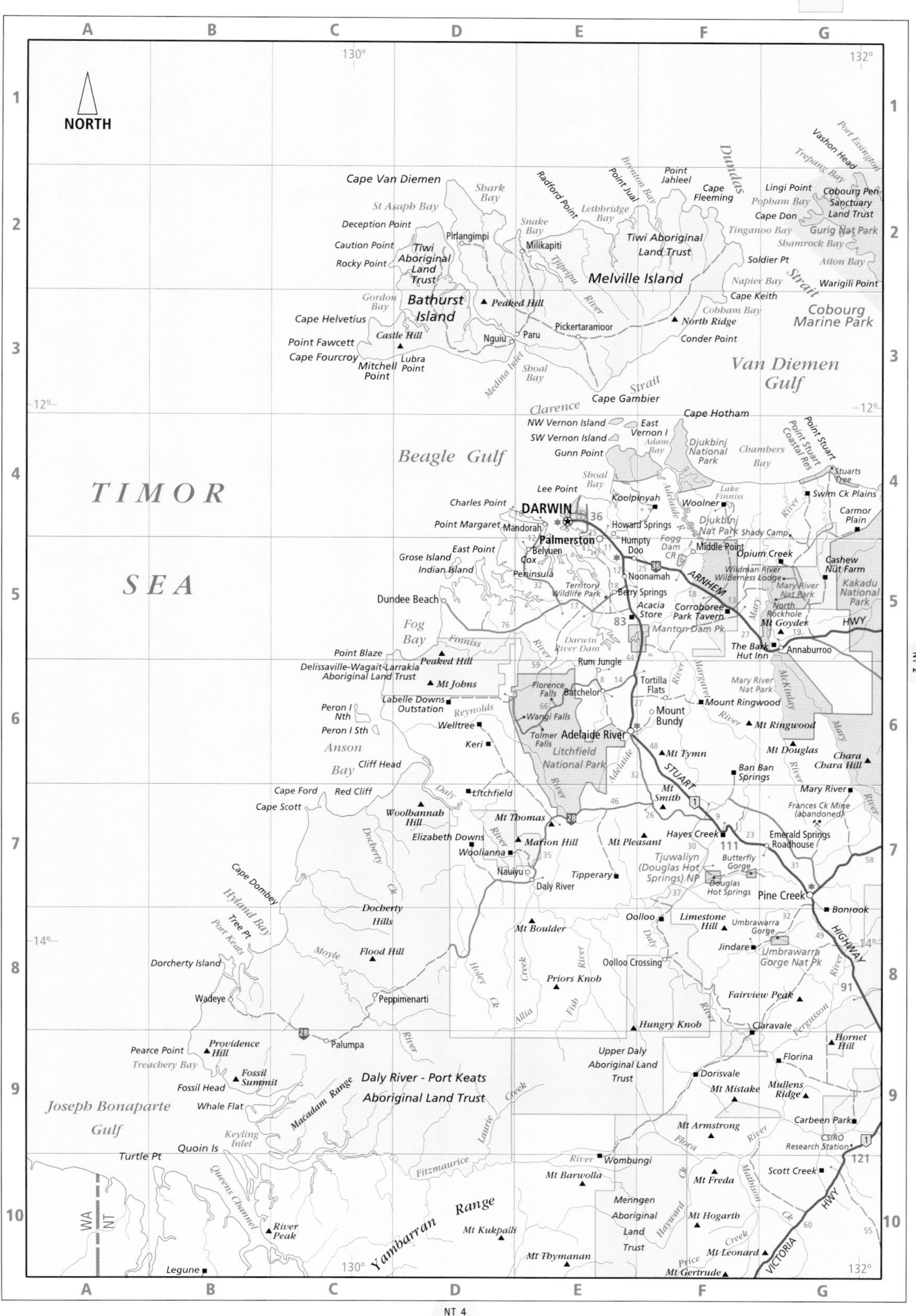
0 20 40 60 80
kilometres
NORTH
TIMOR
SEA
Beagle Gulf
Van Diemen Gulf
Joseph Bonaparte Gulf
Melville Island
Bathurst Island
Tiwi Aboriginal Land Trust
Cobourg Marine Park
Clarence Strait
Dundas Strait
DARWIN
Palmerston
Howard Springs
Humpty Doo
Noonamah
Berry Springs
Acacia Store
Batchelor
Adelaide River
Litchfield National Park
Daly River - Port Keats Aboriginal Land Trust
Upper Daly Aboriginal Land Trust
Menngen Aboriginal Land Trust
Pine Creek
Wadeye
Peppimenarti
Palumpa
Nauiyu
Daly River
Dundee Beach
Mandorah
Belyuen
Cox Peninsula
Cape Van Diemen
Cape Hotham
Cape Gambier
Djukbinj National Park
Kakadu National Park
Umbrawarra Gorge Nat Pk
Tjuwaliyn (Douglas Hot Springs) NP
Mary River Nat Park
Yambarran Range
Macadam Range
STUART HIGHWAY
ARNHEM HWY
VICTORIA HWY
WA
NT
130°
132°
12°
14°
NT 2

Map 2

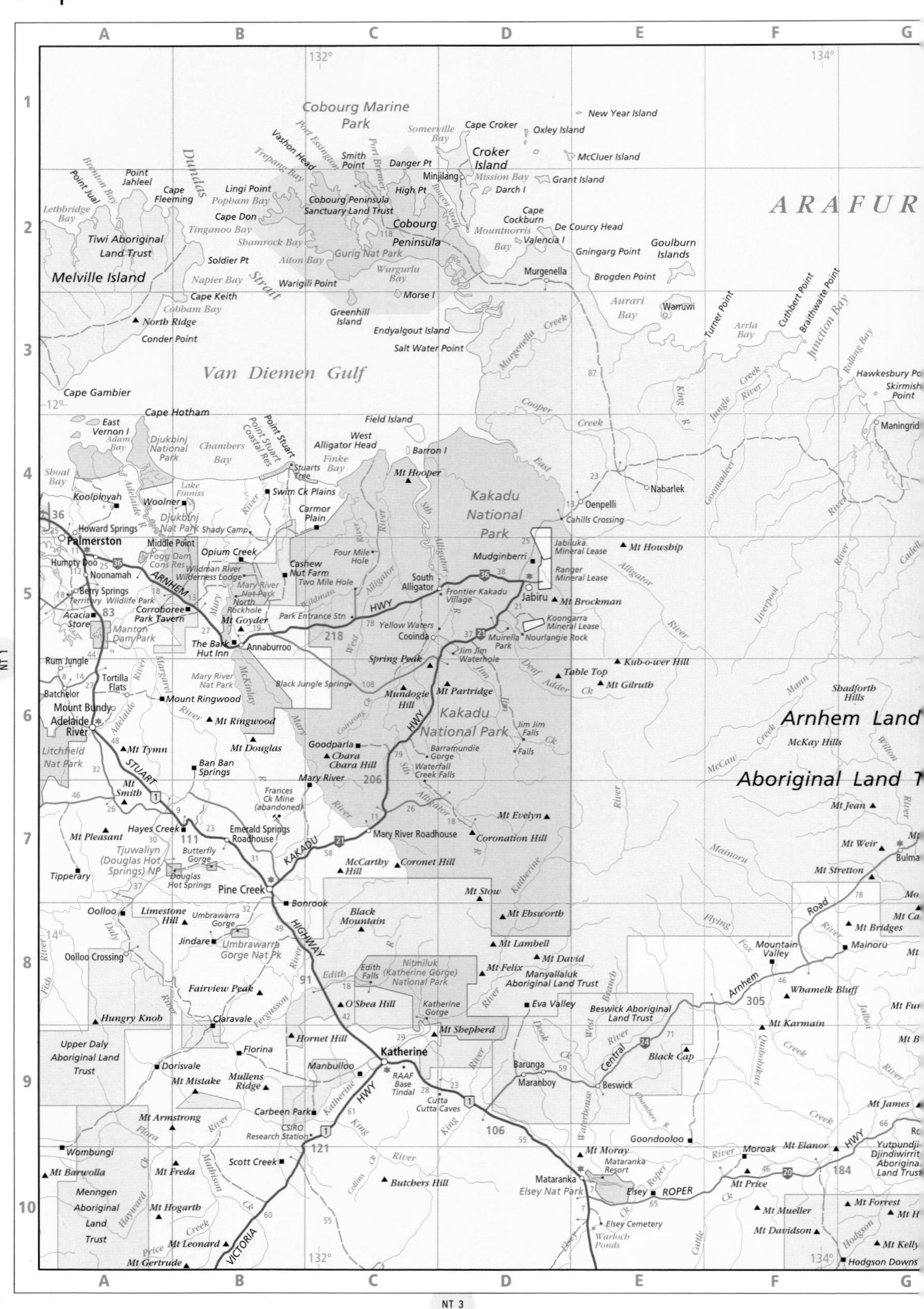

A B C D E F G
1 2 3 4 5 6 7 8 9 10
132° 134° 12° 14°
Cobourg Marine Park
New Year Island
Cape Croker
Oxley Island
Somerville Bay
Port Essington
Port Bremer
Vashon Head
Trepang Bay
Smith Point
Danger Pt
Croker Island
McCluer Island
Minjilang
Mission Bay
Grant Island
Darch I
Brenton Bay
Point Jahleel
Point Jual
Dundas
Cape Fleeming
Lingi Point
Popham Bay
High Pt
Bowen Strait
Cobourg Peninsula Sanctuary Land Trust
Lethbridge Bay
Cape Don
Tinganoo Bay
Cobourg Peninsula
Cape Cockburn
Mountnorris Bay
De Courcy Head
Valencia I
ARAFUR
Tiwi Aboriginal Land Trust
Shamrock Bay
Gurig Nat Park
Gningarg Point
Goulburn Islands
Soldier Pt
Aiton Bay
Wurgurlu Bay
Murgenella
Melville Island
Napier Bay
Strait
Warigili Point
Brogden Point
Cape Keith
Morse I
Cobham Bay
Aurari Bay
Warruwi
Turner Point
Cuthbert Point
Braithwaite Point
Junction Bay
North Ridge
Greenhill Island
Endyalgout Island
Arrla Bay
Conder Point
Salt Water Point
Murgenella Creek
Rolling Bay
Van Diemen Gulf
Hawkesbury Po
Skirmish Point
Cape Gambier
King R
Jungle Creek
River
Cooper Creek
Cape Hotham
Field Island
East Vernon I
Adam Bay
Djukbinj National Park
Chambers Bay
Point Stuart
Point Stuart Coastal Res
West Alligator Head
Finke Bay
Barron I
Maningrid
Shoal Bay
Stuarts Tree
Mt Hooper
East
Goomadeer
Koolpinyah
Adelaide R
Lake Finniss
Swim Ck Plains
Kakadu National Park
Nabarlek
Woolner
Djukbinj Nat Park
Carmor Plain
Oenpelli
Cahills Crossing
Howard Springs
Shady Camp
Palmerston
Middle Point
Jabiluka Mineral Lease
Mt Howship
Humpty Doo
Fogg Dam Cons Res
Opium Creek
Four Mile Hole
Mudginberri
Noonamah
Wildman River Wilderness Lodge
Cashew Nut Farm
Two Mile Hole
South Alligator
Ranger Mineral Lease
ARNHEM
Berry Springs
Territory Wildlife Park
Mary River Nat Park
North Rockhole
Frontier Kakadu Village
Jabiru
Mt Brockman
Liverpool
Acacia Store
Corroboree Park Tavern
Mt Goyder
Park Entrance Stn
HWY
Yellow Waters
Koongarra Mineral Lease
Manton Dam Park
The Bark Hut Inn
Annaburroo
Cooinda
Muirella Park
Nourlangie Rock
NT 1
Rum Jungle
Jim Jim Waterhole
Spring Peak
Kub-o-wer Hill
Tortilla Flats
Mary River Nat Park
McKinlay
Black Jungle Spring
Table Top
Deaf Adder Ck
Mt Gilruth
Batchelor
Mount Ringwood
Mundogie Hill
Mt Partridge
Shadforth Hills
Mount Bundy
Mt Ringwood
Kakadu National Park
Arnhem Land
Adelaide River
Jim Jim Falls
McKay Hills
Litchfield Nat Park
Mt Tymn
Mt Douglas
Goodparla
Chara Chara Hill
Barramundie Gorge
Twin Falls
Ban Ban Springs
Waterfall Creek Falls
STUART
Mary River
Aboriginal Land T
Mt Smith
Frances Ck Mine (abandoned)
Mt Jean
Mt Evelyn
Mt Pleasant
Hayes Creek
Emerald Springs Roadhouse
Mary River Roadhouse
Coronation Hill
Tjuwaliyn (Douglas Hot Springs) NP
Butterfly Gorge
KAKADU
Mt Weir
Bulman
McCarthy Hill
Coronet Hill
Mainoru
Mt Stretton
Tipperary
Douglas Hot Springs
Pine Creek
Mt Stow
Katherine
Bonrook
Oolloo
Limestone Hill
Umbrawarra Gorge
Black Mountain
Mt Ebsworth
Flying Fox
Road
Mt Bridges
Jindare
Umbrawarra Gorge Nat Pk
Mt Lambell
Mainoru
Oolloo Crossing
HIGHWAY
Mt David
Mountain Valley
Nitmiluk (Katherine Gorge) National Park
Edith Falls
Mt Felix
Manyallaluk Aboriginal Land Trust
Fairview Peak
Whamelk Bluff
Arnhem
O'Shea Hill
Eva Valley
Beswick Aboriginal Land Trust
Mt Fu
Hungry Knob
Claravale
Katherine Gorge
Mt Karmain
Fergusson
Mt Shepherd
Upper Daly Aboriginal Land Trust
Hornet Hill
Florina
Dook Ck
West Branch
Quinbakbuni
Mt B
Dorisvale
Manbulloo
Black Cap
Central
Barunga
Maranboy
Beswick
Mt Mistake
Mullens Ridge
RAAF Base Tindal
Cutta Cutta Caves
Chambers R
Mt James
Carbeen Park
Mt Armstrong
Waterhouse
CSIRO Research Station
King R
Goondooloo
Wombungi
Moroak
Mt Elanor
Yutpundji-Djindiwirrit Aboriginal Land Trust
Mt Moray
Mataranka Resort
Mt Barwolla
Mt Freda
Scott Creek
Butchers Hill
Mataranka
Elsey Nat Park
Elsey
ROPER
Mt Price
Menngen Aboriginal Land Trust
Mt Hogarth
Mt Forrest
Mt Mueller
Elsey Cemetery
Mt Davidson
Warloch Ponds
Mt Leonard
VICTORIA
Mt Kelly
Mt Gertrude
Hodgson Downs
Cattle Ck
Hodgson
NT 3

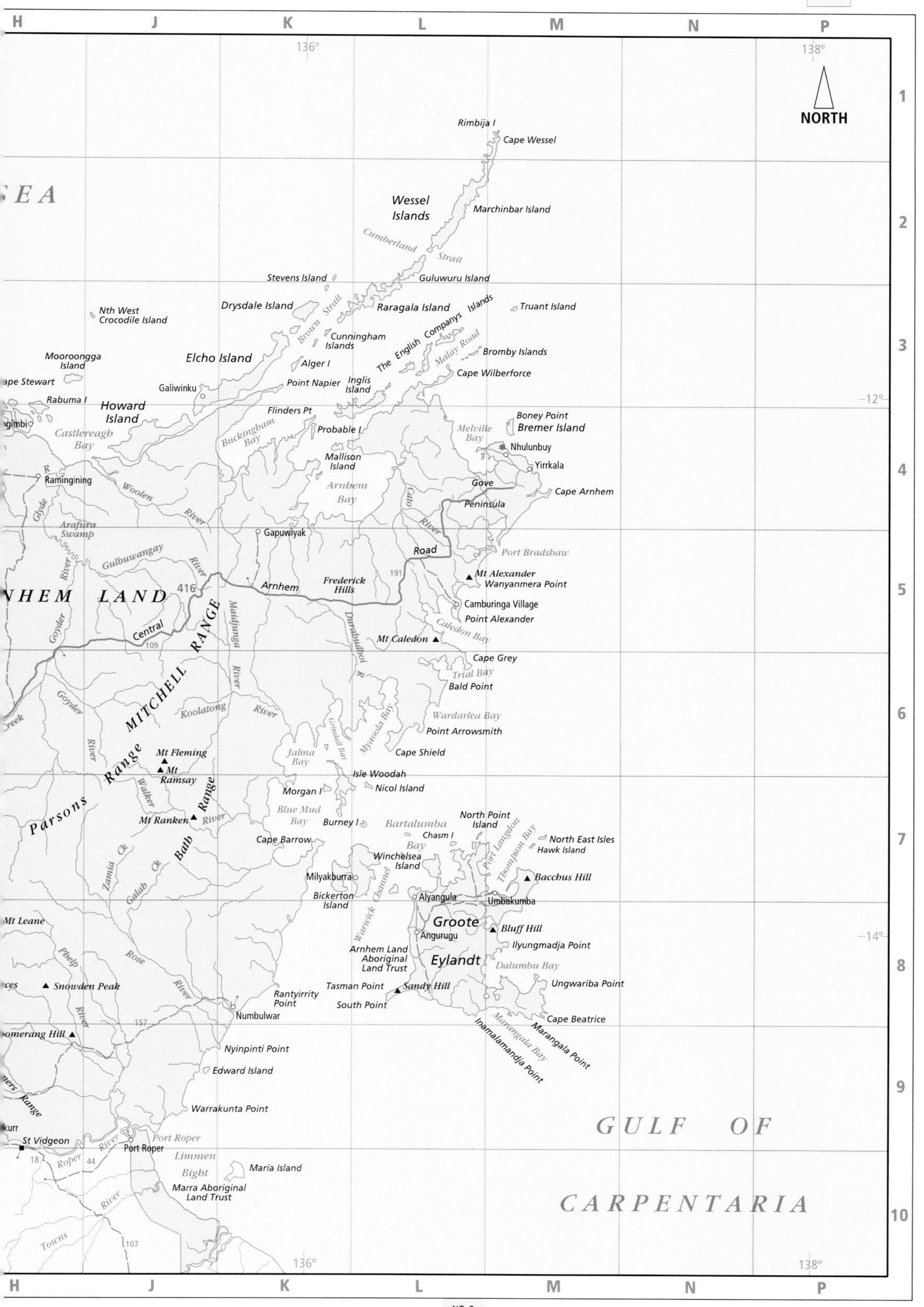
0 20 40 60 80
kilometres
NORTH
H J K L M N P
1 2 3 4 5 6 7 8 9 10
136°
138°
-12°
-14°
SEA
Rimbija I
Cape Wessel
Wessel Islands
Marchinbar Island
Cumberland Strait
Stevens Island
Guluwuru Island
Nth West Crocodile Island
Drysdale Island
Brown Strait
Raragala Island
The English Companys Islands
Truant Island
Cunningham Islands
Malay Road
Bromby Islands
Mooroongga Island
Elcho Island
Alger I
Inglis Island
Cape Wilberforce
Cape Stewart
Galiwinku
Point Napier
Rabuma I
Howard Island
Flinders Pt
Boney Point
Bremer Island
Castlereagh Bay
Buckingham Bay
Probable I
Melville Bay
Nhulunbuy
Mallison Island
Yirrkala
Ramingining
Woolen River
Arnhem Bay
Gove Peninsula
Cape Arnhem
Glyde River
Arafura Swamp
Cato River
Gapuwiyak
Road
Port Bradshaw
Gulbuwangay
River
Mt Alexander
Wanyanmera Point
ARNHEM LAND
416
Arnhem
Frederick Hills
191
Camburinga Village
Point Alexander
Central
MITCHELL RANGE
Maidjunga River
Durabudboi R
Caledon Bay
Mt Caledon
Goyder
109
Cape Grey
Trial Bay
Bald Point
Creek
Goyder River
Koolatong River
Wardarlea Bay
Point Arrowsmith
Grindall Bay
Myaoola Bay
Jalma Bay
Cape Shield
Mt Fleming
Mt Ramsay
Parsons Range
Walker River
Isle Woodah
Nicol Island
Morgan I
Bath Range
Mt Ranken
Blue Mud Bay
Burney I
Bartalumba Bay
North Point Island
Chasm I
Port Langdon
Thompson Bay
North East Isles
Hawk Island
Cape Barrow
Winchelsea Island
Zamia Ck
Galab Ck
Milyakburra
Warwick Channel
Bacchus Hill
Bickerton Island
Alyangula
Umbakumba
Mt Leane
Groote Eylandt
Bluff Hill
Angurugu
Ilyungmadja Point
Phelp River
Rose River
Arnhem Land Aboriginal Land Trust
Dalumbu Bay
Snowden Peak
Tasman Point
Sandy Hill
Ungwariba Point
Rantyirrity Point
South Point
Numbulwar
157
Cape Beatrice
Boomerang Hill
Inamalamandja Point
Marangala Bay
Marangala Point
Nyinpinti Point
Edward Island
Range
Warrakunta Point
GULF OF CARPENTARIA
St Vidgeon
Port Roper
River
Roper
18
44
Limmen Bight
Maria Island
Marra Aboriginal Land Trust
River
Towns
107
NT

Map 3

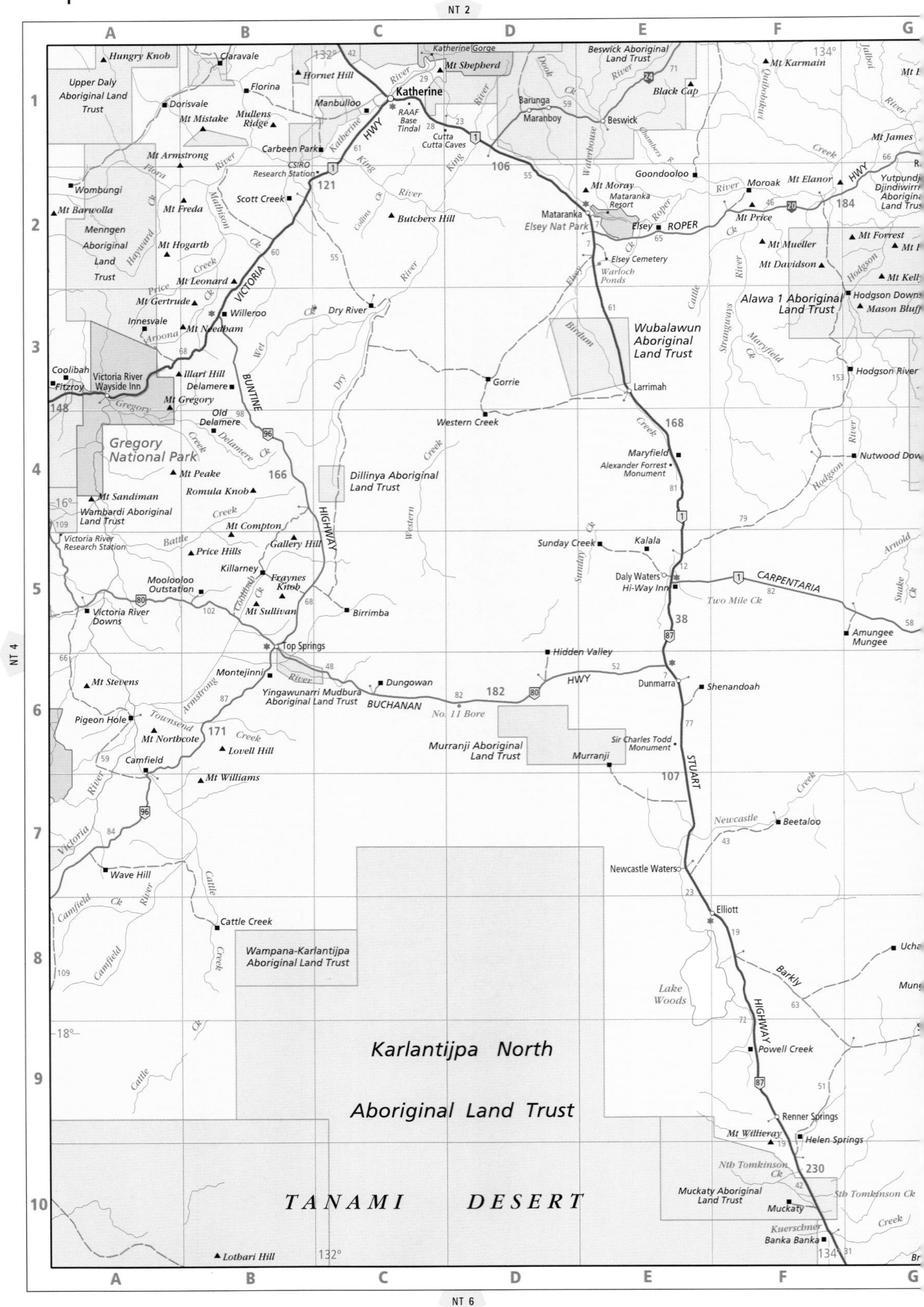
NT 2
NT 4
NT 6
A
B
C
D
E
F
G
1
2
3
4
5
6
7
8
9
10
Hungry Knob
Claravale
Hornet Hill
Katherine Gorge
Mt Shepherd
Beswick Aboriginal Land Trust
Mt Karmain
Upper Daly Aboriginal Land Trust
Florina
Katherine
Black Cap
Dorisvale
Mt Mistake
Mullens Ridge
Manbulloo
RAAF Base Tindal
Barunga
Maranboy
Beswick
Cutta Cutta Caves
Mt James
Mt Armstrong
Carbeen Park
CSIRO Research Station
106
Goondooloo
Moroak
Mt Elanor
HWY
Yutpundji Djindiwirri Aboriginal Land Trust
Wombungi
Mt Moray
Mataranka Resort
Mt Barwolla
Mt Freda
Scott Creek
121
Mataranka
Elsey Nat Park
Elsey
ROPER
Mt Price
184
Menngen Aboriginal Land Trust
Butchers Hill
Mt Hogarth
Mt Mueller
Mt Forrest
Elsey Cemetery
Warloch Ponds
Mt Davidson
Mt Kelly
Mt Leonard
VICTORIA
Hodgson Downs
Mt Gertrude
Willeroo
Dry River
Alawa 1 Aboriginal Land Trust
Mason Bluff
Innesvale
Mt Needham
Wubalawun Aboriginal Land Trust
Coolibah
Fitzroy
Victoria River Wayside Inn
Illari Hill
Delamere
BUNTINE
Gorrie
Hodgson River
148
Mt Gregory
Larrimah
Old Delamere
Western Creek
168
Gregory National Park
Maryfield
Alexander Forrest Monument
Mt Peake
166
Dillinya Aboriginal Land Trust
Nutwood Downs
Romula Knob
16°
Mt Sandiman
Wambardi Aboriginal Land Trust
HIGHWAY
Victoria River Research Station
Mt Compton
Gallery Hill
Sunday Creek
Kalala
Price Hills
Killarney
Fraynes Knob
Daly Waters
Hi-Way Inn
CARPENTARIA
Mooloooloo Outstation
Victoria River Downs
Mt Sullivan
Birrimba
Two Mile Ck
38
Amungee Mungee
Top Springs
Hidden Valley
Mt Stevens
Montejinni
Yingawunarri Mudbura Aboriginal Land Trust
Dungowan
182
HWY
Dunmarra
Shenandoah
BUCHANAN
No. 11 Bore
Pigeon Hole
Mt Northcote
171
Lovell Hill
Murranji Aboriginal Land Trust
Sir Charles Todd Monument
Murranji
Camfield
Mt Williams
107
STUART
Beetaloo
Newcastle
Wave Hill
Newcastle Waters
Elliott
Cattle Creek
Wampana-Karlantijpa Aboriginal Land Trust
Barkly
Lake Woods
HIGHWAY
18°
Karlantijpa North Aboriginal Land Trust
Powell Creek
Renner Springs
Mt Willieray
Helen Springs
Nth Tomkinson Ck
230
Muckaty Aboriginal Land Trust
Muckaty
Sth Tomkinson Ck
TANAMI DESERT
Kuerschner
Banka Banka
Lotbari Hill
132°
134°

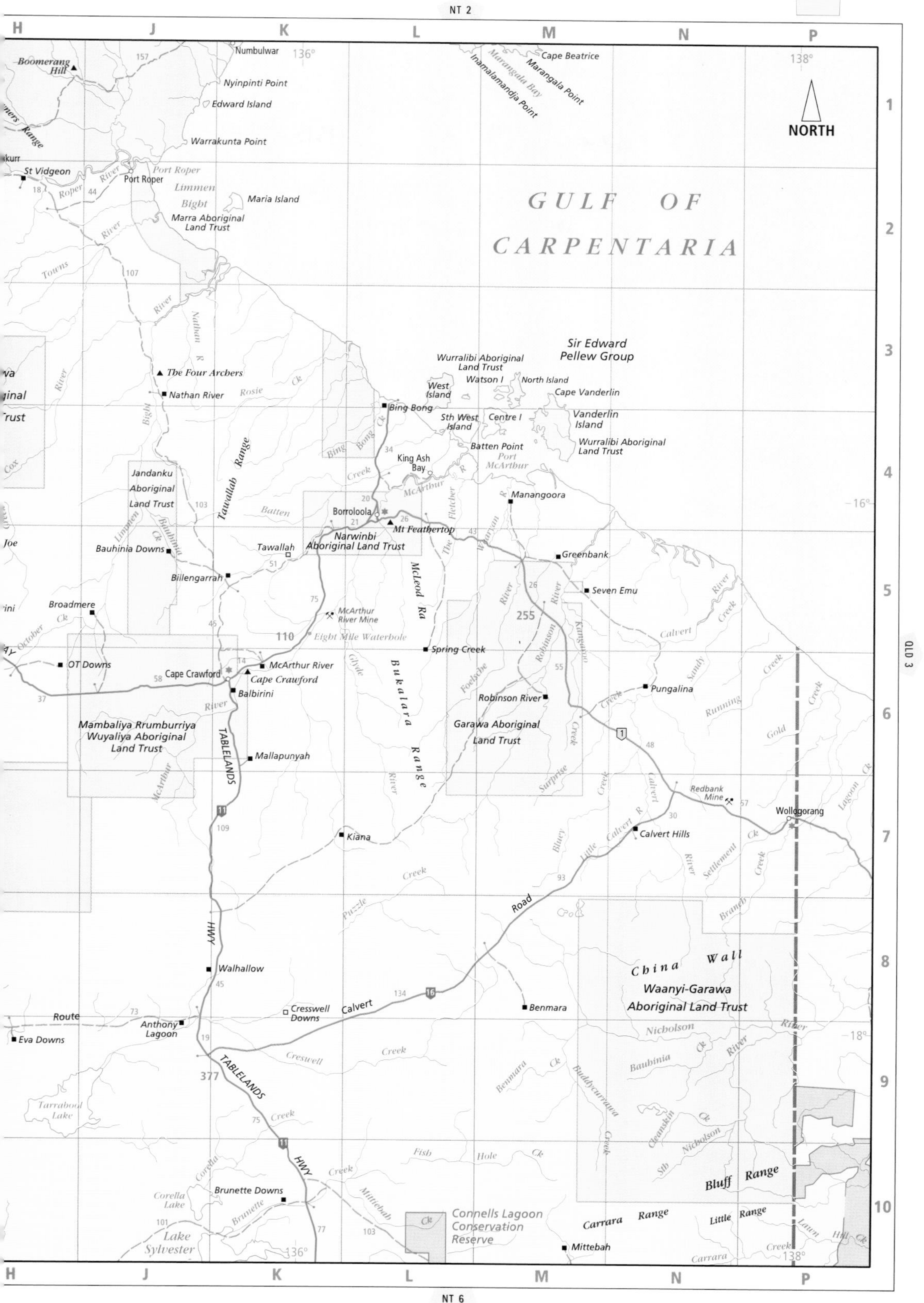

0 20 40 60 80
kilometres
NT 2
NORTH
GULF OF CARPENTARIA
Numbulwar
Boomerang Hill
Nyinpinti Point
Edward Island
Warrakunta Point
St Vidgeon
Port Roper
Roper River
Limmen Bight
Maria Island
Marra Aboriginal Land Trust
Cape Beatrice
Marangala Point
Inamalamandja Point
Sir Edward Pellew Group
Wurralibi Aboriginal Land Trust
Watson I
North Island
West Island
Cape Vanderlin
Vanderlin Island
Sth West Island
Centre I
Batten Point
Port McArthur
Wurralibi Aboriginal Land Trust
Bing Bong
King Ash Bay
The Four Archers
Nathan River
Jandanku Aboriginal Land Trust
Tawallah Range
Borroloola
Mt Feathertop
Narwinbi Aboriginal Land Trust
Manangoora
Greenbank
Seven Emu
Bauhinia Downs
Tawallah
Billengarrah
McLeod Ra
Broadmere
McArthur River Mine
Eight Mile Waterhole
Spring Creek
OT Downs
Cape Crawford
McArthur River
Balbirini
Bukalara Range
Robinson River
Pungalina
Mambaliya Rrumburriya Wuyaliya Aboriginal Land Trust
Garawa Aboriginal Land Trust
Mallapunyah
TABLELANDS
Redbank Mine
Wollogorang
Kiana
Calvert Hills
Road
China Wall
Waanyi-Garawa Aboriginal Land Trust
Walhallow
Benmara
Cresswell Downs
Calvert
Route
Anthony Lagoon
Eva Downs
Nicholson River
TABLELANDS HWY
Tarrabool Lake
Brunette Downs
Corella Lake
Lake Sylvester
Connells Lagoon Conservation Reserve
Carrara Range
Little Range
Bluff Range
Mittebah
NT 6
QLD 3
NT

Map 4

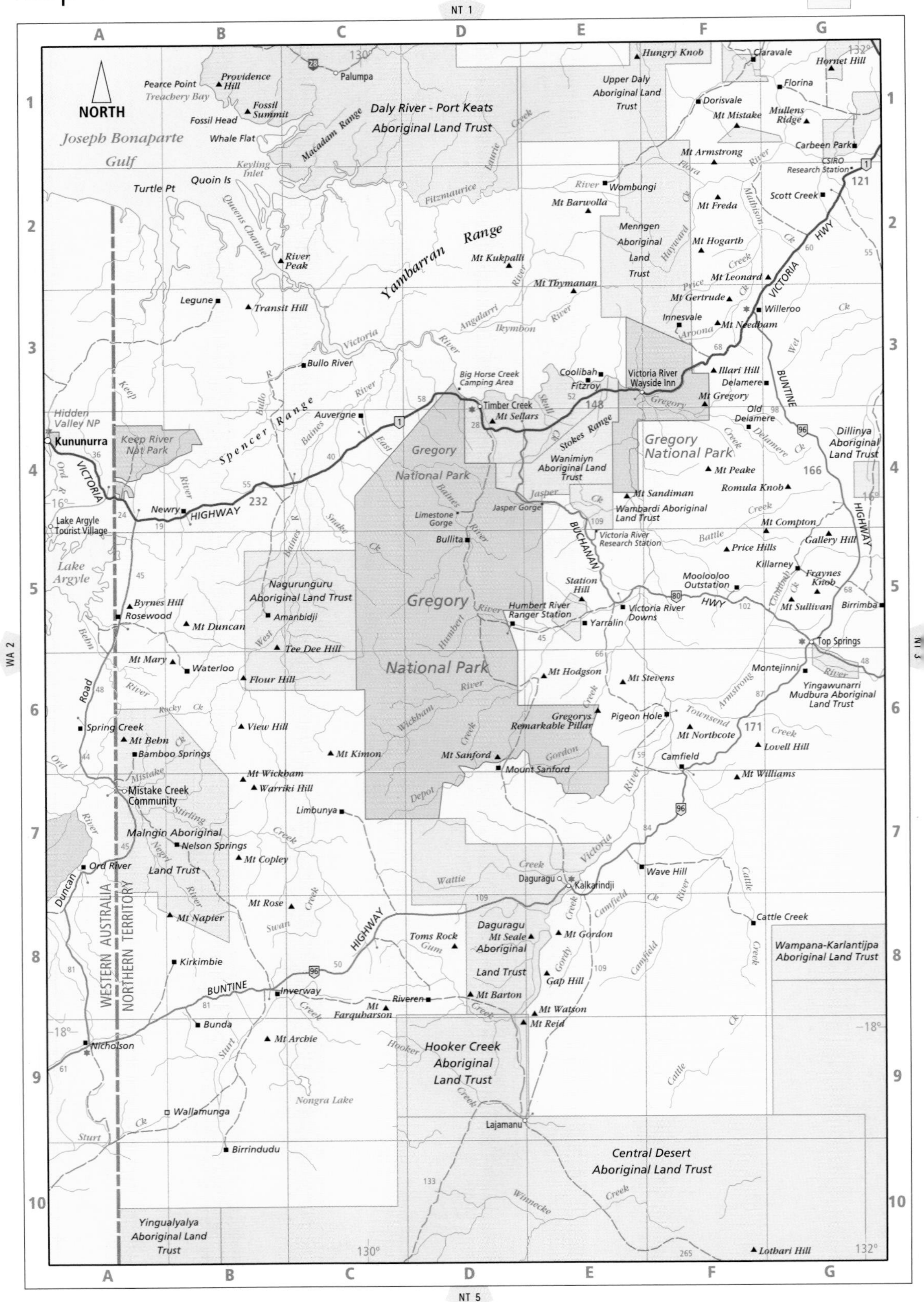
0 20 40 60 80
kilometres
NT 1
NT 5
WA 2
NT 3
NORTH
Joseph Bonaparte Gulf
Pearce Point
Treachery Bay
Providence Hill
Fossil Summit
Fossil Head
Whale Flat
Palumpa
Macadam Range
Daly River - Port Keats Aboriginal Land Trust
Keyling Inlet
Quoin Is
Turtle Pt
Queens Channel
Fitzmaurice
Laurie Creek
Hungry Knob
Upper Daly Aboriginal Land Trust
Claravale
Hornet Hill
Florina
Dorisvale
Mt Mistake
Mullens Ridge
Carbeen Park
Mt Armstrong
CSIRO Research Station
Scott Creek
Wombungi
Mt Barwolla
Mt Freda
Menngen Aboriginal Land Trust
Mt Hogarth
Yambarran Range
Mt Kukpalli
Mt Thymanan
River Peak
Legune
Transit Hill
Mt Leonard
Mt Gertrude
Willeroo
Innesvale
Mt Needbam
VICTORIA HWY
Angalarri
Ikymbon
Victoria River
Bullo River
Illari Hill
Delamere
Coolibah
Fitzroy
Victoria River Wayside Inn
Big Horse Creek Camping Area
Timber Creek
Mt Sellars
Mt Gregory
Old Delamere
Spencer Range
Auvergne
Hidden Valley NP
Kununurra
Keep River Nat Park
Gregory National Park
Stokes Range
Wanimiyn Aboriginal Land Trust
Dillinya Aboriginal Land Trust
Mt Peake
Romula Knob
Mt Sandiman
Wambardi Aboriginal Land Trust
Jasper Gorge
Limestone Gorge
Bullita
Newry
HIGHWAY
Lake Argyle Tourist Village
Lake Argyle
Mt Compton
Gallery Hill
Victoria River Research Station
Price Hills
Killarney
Fraynes Knob
BUCHANAN
Nagurunguru Aboriginal Land Trust
Amanbidji
Byrnes Hill
Rosewood
Mt Duncan
Station Hill
Moolooloo Outstation
Humbert River Ranger Station
Yarralin
Victoria River Downs
Mt Sullivan
Birrimba
Top Springs
Tee Dee Hill
Mt Mary
Waterloo
Flour Hill
Mt Hodgson
Mt Stevens
Montejinni
Yingawunarri Mudbura Aboriginal Land Trust
Spring Creek
Mt Behn
Bamboo Springs
View Hill
Mt Kimon
Gregorys Remarkable Pillar
Pigeon Hole
Mt Northcote
Lovell Hill
Mt Sanford
Mount Sanford
Camfield
Mt Williams
Mt Wickham
Warriki Hill
Mistake Creek Community
Limbunya
Malngin Aboriginal Land Trust
Nelson Springs
Mt Copley
Ord River
Wave Hill
Daguragu
Kalkarindji
WESTERN AUSTRALIA
NORTHERN TERRITORY
Mt Rose
Mt Napier
Dagurugu Aboriginal Land Trust
Mt Seale
Mt Gordon
Cattle Creek
Toms Rock
Wampana-Karlantijpa Aboriginal Land Trust
Kirkimbie
Gap Hill
BUNTINE
Inverway
Riveren
Mt Farquharson
Mt Barton
Mt Watson
Mt Reid
Bunda
Nicholson
Mt Archie
Hooker Creek Aboriginal Land Trust
Nongra Lake
Wallamunga
Lajamanu
Birrindudu
Central Desert Aboriginal Land Trust
Yingualyalya Aboriginal Land Trust
Lotbari Hill
Duncan Road

NT 6

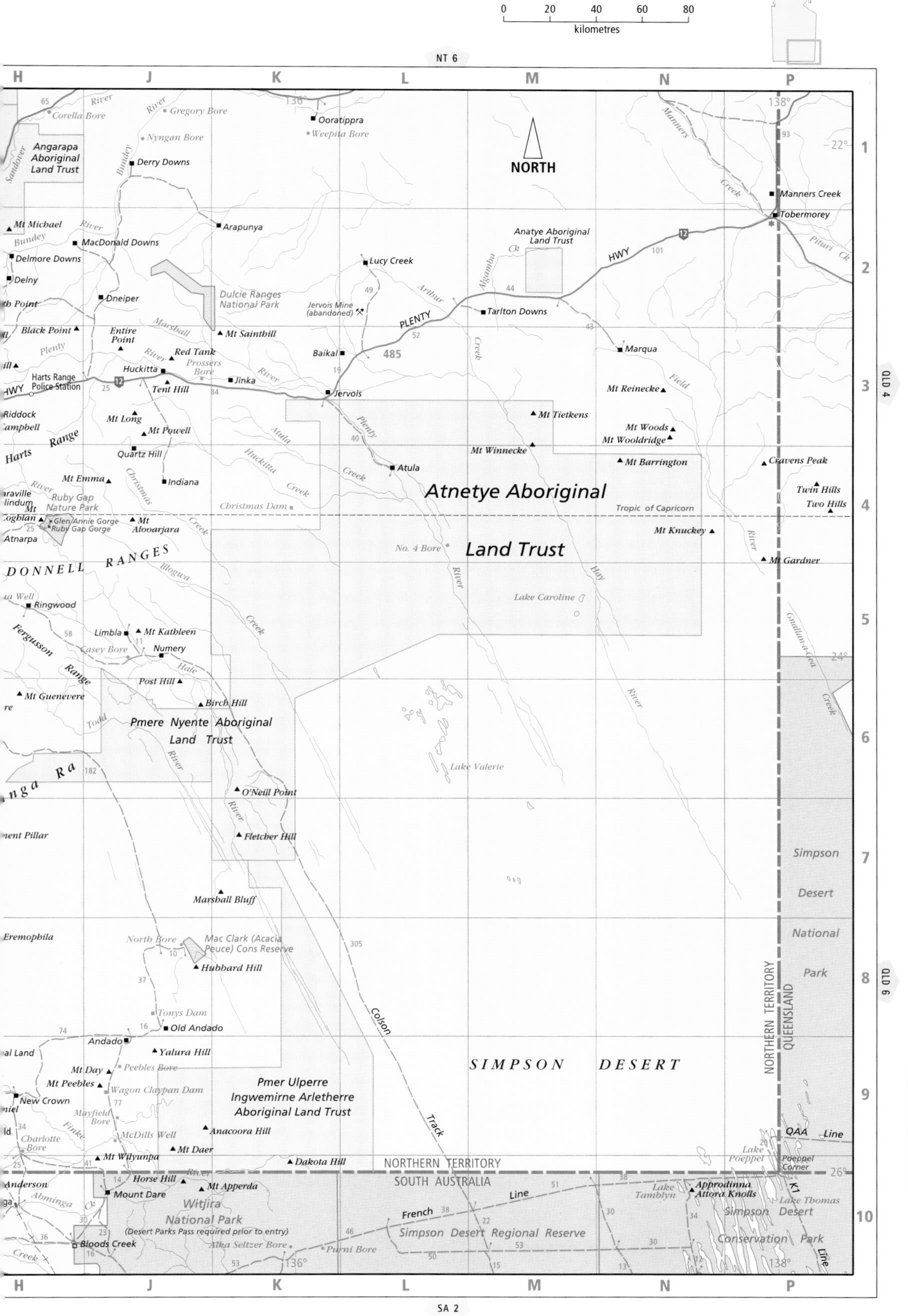

QLD 4
QLD 6
SA 2

Map 8

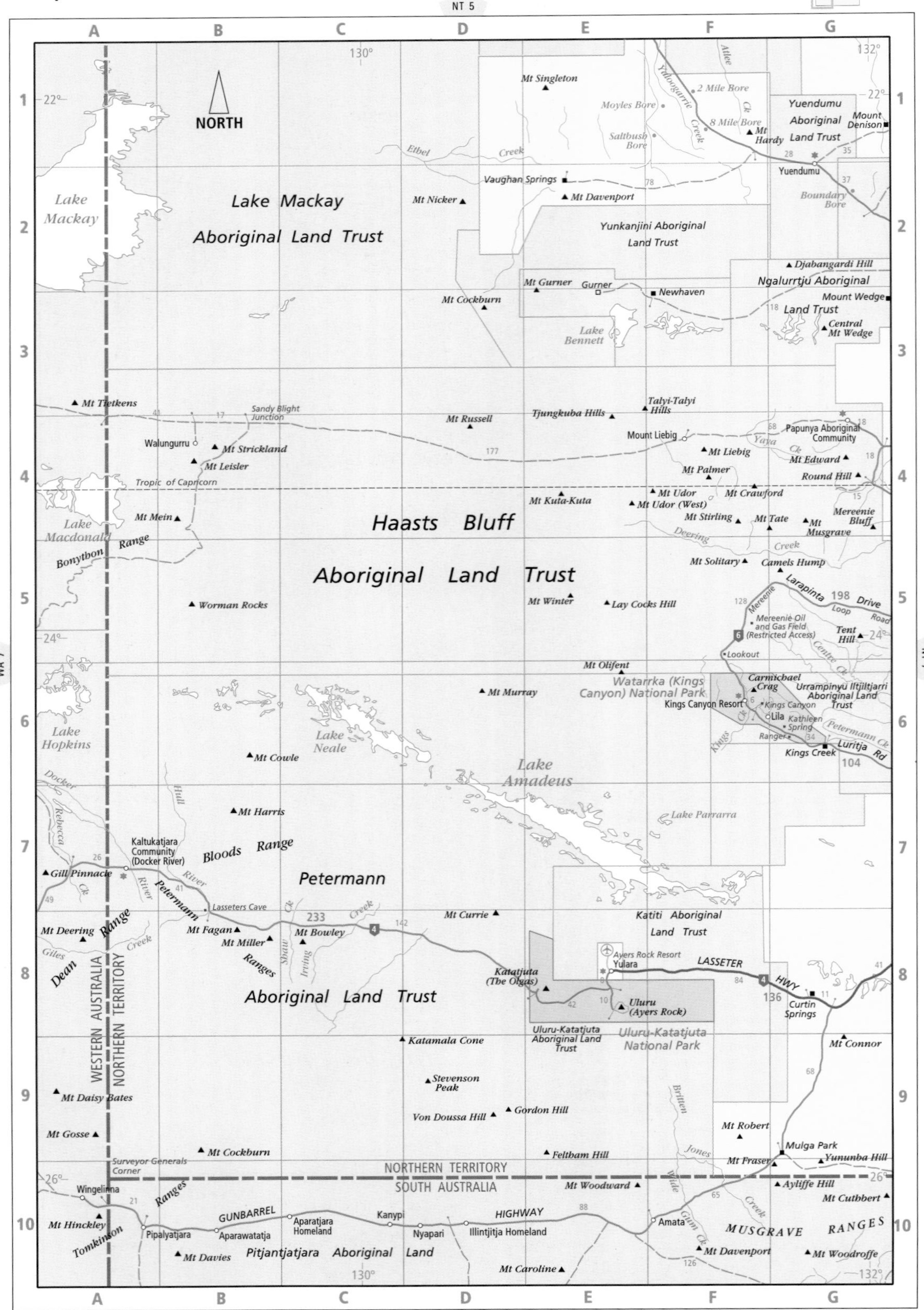
0 20 40 60 80
kilometres
NT 5
NORTH
Lake Mackay Aboriginal Land Trust
Lake Mackay
Mt Singleton
Moyles Bore
2 Mile Bore
8 Mile Bore
Saltbush Bore
Mt Hardy
Yuendumu Aboriginal Land Trust
Mount Denison
Yuendumu
Boundary Bore
Vaughan Springs
Mt Davenport
Mt Nicker
Yunkanjini Aboriginal Land Trust
Djabangardi Hill
Ngalurrtju Aboriginal Land Trust
Mt Gurner
Gurner
Newhaven
Mount Wedge
Mt Cockburn
Lake Bennett
Central Mt Wedge
Mt Tietkens
Sandy Blight Junction
Mt Russell
Tjungkuba Hills
Talyi-Talyi Hills
Walungurru
Mt Strickland
Mt Leisler
Mount Liebig
Papunya Aboriginal Community
Mt Liebig
Mt Edward
Mt Palmer
Round Hill
Tropic of Capricorn
Mt Kuta-Kuta
Mt Udor
Mt Udor (West)
Mt Crawford
Mt Mein
Lake Macdonald
Bonytbon Range
Haasts Bluff Aboriginal Land Trust
Mt Stirling
Mt Tate
Mt Musgrave
Mereenie Bluff
Mt Solitary
Camels Hump
Worman Rocks
Mt Winter
Lay Cocks Hill
Larapinta Drive
Mereenie Loop Road
Mereenie Oil and Gas Field (Restricted Access)
Tent Hill
Lookout
Mt Olifent
WA 7
NT 7
Mt Murray
Watarrka (Kings Canyon) National Park
Carmichael Crag
Urrampinyu Iltjiltjarri Aboriginal Land Trust
Kings Canyon Resort
Kings Canyon
Lila
Kathleen Spring
Ranger
Kings Creek
Luritja Rd
Lake Hopkins
Lake Neale
Mt Cowle
Lake Amadeus
Lake Parrarra
Mt Harris
Kaltukatjara Community (Docker River)
Bloods Range
Petermann
Gill Pinnacle
Lasseters Cave
Mt Deering
Mt Fagan
Mt Miller
Mt Bowley
Mt Currie
Katiti Aboriginal Land Trust
Dean Range
Petermann Ranges
Aboriginal Land Trust
Ayers Rock Resort
Yulara
LASSETER HWY
Katatjuta (The Olgas)
Uluru (Ayers Rock)
Curtin Springs
Uluru-Katatjuta Aboriginal Land Trust
Uluru-Katatjuta National Park
WESTERN AUSTRALIA
NORTHERN TERRITORY
Katamala Cone
Mt Connor
Stevenson Peak
Mt Daisy Bates
Von Doussa Hill
Gordon Hill
Mt Gosse
Mt Robert
Mt Cockburn
Feltham Hill
Mulga Park
Mt Fraser
Yunumba Hill
Surveyor Generals Corner
NORTHERN TERRITORY
SOUTH AUSTRALIA
Wingelinna
Mt Woodward
Ayliffe Hill
Mt Cuthbert
Tomkinson Ranges
GUNBARREL HIGHWAY
Mt Hinckley
Pipalyatjara
Aparawatatja
Aparatjara Homeland
Kanypi
Nyapari
Illintjitja Homeland
Amata
MUSGRAVE RANGES
Mt Davies
Pitjantjatjara Aboriginal Land
Mt Davenport
Mt Woodroffe
Mt Caroline
SA 1

Index to Events

Index to Places

Text entries for places are shown in **bold**. Map references appear in the form of map title and grid reference, eg. WA 6 F2.

Abbreviations

CA	Conservation Area
CP	Conservation Park
NP	National Park
NR	Nature Reserve

Acknowledgements

The Publisher would like to thank all the event organisers who submitted images for this book. The Publisher believes that permission for use of all images has been obtained from the copyright owners, however, if any errors or omissions have occurred Global Book Publishing would be pleased to hear from copyright owners.

Cover, main image: Carols by Candlelight at the Sidney Myer Music Bowl, Victorian Arts Centre. Photographer: Greg Bartley. Image courtesy of Victorian Arts Centre
Cover, inset: Image courtesy of Northern Territory Tourist Commission
p. 1: Image courtesy of Tourism New South Wales
p. 2: Image courtesy of Tourism Victoria
p. 3: Image courtesy of Tourism Victoria
pp. 8–9, bottom: Image courtesy of Tourism Victoria
pp. 14–15, top: Image courtesy of Tourism Victoria
p. 15, middle: Image courtesy of Steve Fynmore
p. 18, middle: Image courtesy of Limestone Coast Tourism
p. 18, bottom: Image courtesy of Limestone Coast Tourism
p. 20: Image courtesy of Tourism Victoria
p. 22, top: Image courtesy of Brisbane Marketing
p. 22, bottom: Image courtesy of Golden Grove Estate
p. 23, top: Image courtesy of G. Evatt
p. 23, bottom: Image courtesy of Goulburn District Tourism
p. 24, bottom: Image courtesy of Tourism New South Wales
pp. 24–25, bottom: Image courtesy of Tourism Victoria
p. 33, middle: Image courtesy of Tourism Queensland Image Library
p. 39, bottom: Image courtesy of Tourism Victoria
p. 40, bottom: Image courtesy of Tourism Victoria
p. 49, middle: Image courtesy of Northern Territory Tourist Commission
pp. 50–51, bottom: Image courtesy of Royal Agricultural Society of NSW
p. 52, bottom: Image courtesy of Tourism Victoria
pp. 58–59, top: Image courtesy of Tourism New South Wales
p. 61, top: Image courtesy of Tourism Victoria
p. 63, top: Image courtesy of National Trust of Australia (Tasmania)
p. 68, top: Image courtesy of Tourism Queensland Image Library
p. 69, top: Image courtesy of Tourism Queensland Image Library
p. 70, top: Image courtesy of A. Zotos
p. 71, top: Image courtesy of Tourism New South Wales
p. 79, middle: Image courtesy of Tourism Queensland Image Library
p. 80, top: Image courtesy of Manly Council
p. 80, middle: Image courtesy of Mike Faulkner
p. 81, middle: Image courtesy of Tourism New South Wales
p. 87, top: Image courtesy of Tourism New South Wales
p. 89, top: Image courtesy of Tourism Queensland Image Library
p. 89, middle: Image courtesy of Tourism Queensland Image Library
p. 94, middle: Image courtesy of Northern Territory Tourist Commission
pp. 94–95, bottom: Image courtesy of Northern Territory Tourist Commission
p. 100, middle: Image courtesy of Richard Layt
p. 103, middle right: Image courtesy of Royal Agricultural & Horticultural Society of South Australia Incorporated
p. 105, bottom: Image courtesy of Northern Territory Tourist Commission
p. 108, top: Image courtesy of Tourism Queensland Image Library
p. 109, top: Image courtesy of Tourism Queensland Image Library
p. 113, top: Image courtesy of Tourism New South Wales
pp. 116–117, bottom: Image courtesy of Tourism Victoria
p. 132, bottom: Image courtesy of Sanctuary Cove
p. 133, top: Image courtesy of Manly Council
p. 139, top: Image courtesy of Tourism Victoria
p. 142, middle: Image courtesy of Tourism Victoria
p. 148, top: Image courtesy of Mary M. Smith
pp. 148–149, bottom: Image courtesy of Annie Keating
p. 151, bottom: Image courtesy of Tourism Victoria
p. 155, bottom: Image courtesy of Scott Mitchell, The Alpine Angler
p. 156, middle left: Image courtesy of Tourism New South Wales
p. 161, bottom: Image courtesy of Tourism Victoria
p. 162, bottom: Image courtesy of Tony Dewan
p. 163, bottom: Image courtesy of Tony Dewan
p. 167, top: Image courtesy of Rhonda Stubbs
p. 169, bottom: Image courtesy of Barry Allwright
p. 170: Image courtesy of Tourism New South Wales
p. 173, middle: Image courtesy of Nick Wilson
p. 173, bottom: Image courtesy of Tourism New South Wales
p. 174, top: Image courtesy of Tourism Victoria
p. 175, middle: Image courtesy of Ballarat Begonia Festival
p. 177, middle: Image courtesy of Iain Lang
p. 177, bottom: Image courtesy of Nick Osborne

C R E A T

SPAWN®: CREATION
ISBN 1 85286 828 7

Published by Titan Books Ltd
42 - 44 Dolben St
London SE1 0UP
In association with Image Comics™

This book collects issues 1–5 of the Image Comics' series *Spawn.* Originally collected in the USA as *Spawn Volume 1.*

British Library Cataloguing-In-Publication data. A catalogue record for this book is available from the British Library.

First edition: February 1997
10 9 8 7 6 5 4 3 2 1

Printed in Italy.

CREATION

SPAWN®

TODD McFARLANE

TITAN BOOKS
in association with IMAGE COMICS™

INTRODUCTION

Before you begin exploring the world of Spawn, I'd like to take this opportunity to introduce you to both the character of Spawn, and explain why he exists in the first place. There is not one central event that brought Spawn into being, but rather several factors which culminated in its publication. After years of working for both Marvel and DC Comics drawing such characters as the Hulk, Spider-Man and Batman, I became disenchanted with the entire comic book industry due to their lack of respect towards the creative forces behind such characters.

Thus, in 1992, I, along with five other artists, broke away from the traditional companies and formed Image Comics: a company where artists could create and maintain control over their characters. We, at Image Comics, set out to make positive changes in a stagnant industry, and this step resulted in my most difficult task: producing an original character from scratch. Contrary to some opinions, I did not create Spawn overnight. Almost fifteen years ago, before I broke into the comic book industry, I possessed a portfolio of characters I had dreamed up: one was Spawn. Being one of my favourites, I dusted off my old drawings, used them as a guide, and brought Spawn to life both physically and emotionally by incorporating my life encounters into his development.

Myriad experiences and surrounding circumstances contribute to Spawn's personality, making him, in my opinion, a unique character in the comic book industry. Without revealing too much of the plot, Spawn is the story of a man, Al Simmons, who died in the line of duty working for the US Government as an assassin. Being devoted to his wife, Wanda, Al sold his soul to Malebolgia, the

leader of the forces of evil, in exchange for a second chance back on Earth. Malebolgia chose Al to become a spawn, an event which only occurs every four hundred years, because the essence of his psyche possessed the necessary elements required by a warrior for the forces of darkness. Al understands evil's purpose, and after working for the government, he knows how to take orders, making him an ideal candidate for a spawn. But, corrupt actions do not inescapably make one bad. Evil, like good, is not measured by one's deeds, but by the internal make-up of each individual. Like most, Al possesses both qualities. Al made the deal with Malebolgia only because of his intense love for his wife. Having his life cut short he wanted one last chance to be with her, and would do anything to make that possible, including selling his soul. Unfortunately, Al did not realise he would be returned to Earth five years into the future, only to find his wife remarried and with a family. Having had the motive for his return to Earth stripped away, Spawn must now attempt to reassemble his life while forging for a meaningful purpose to go on. Also, he quickly found there's

Right: *One of Todd McFarlane's earliest portfolio sketches of Spawn,* Circa *1982*

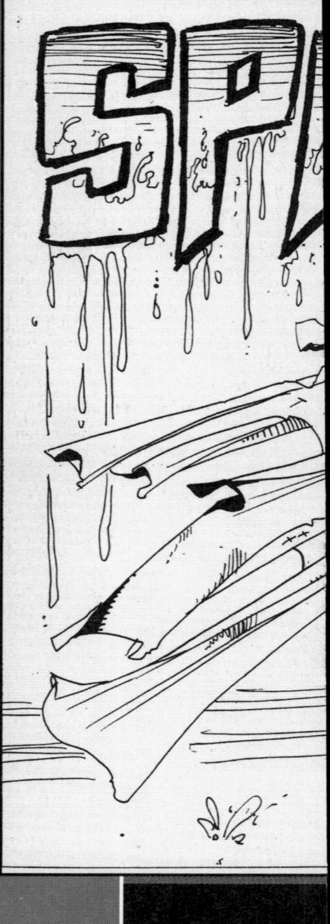

more to being a spawn than he could imagine, putting both the reader and Spawn in the same predicament. You, the readers, grasp more about Spawn as he learns more about himself. Even though Al is no longer human, he still thinks on a human level. This creates difficulties as he becomes involved in a larger battle waged at a more complex level. Out of this strife, he comes to grips with both humanity and himself.

As you begin your journey through Spawn's world, I hope you enjoy the ride. You'll find that sometimes it may get a bit heavy and at other times a bit too light, but it will always be an exciting journey. As each issue unfolds, you will discover new strands in my ongoing attempt to weave a complex tapestry. I hope the story of Al Simmons, on some levels, has an eternal quality and that it can be assimilated by any culture. Spawn's struggle with the universal theme of good versus evil is not specific to any one society or time period. Try not to get bogged down with the American details for they are secondary to the overall theme and character development woven throughout Spawn. Welcome to the beginning.

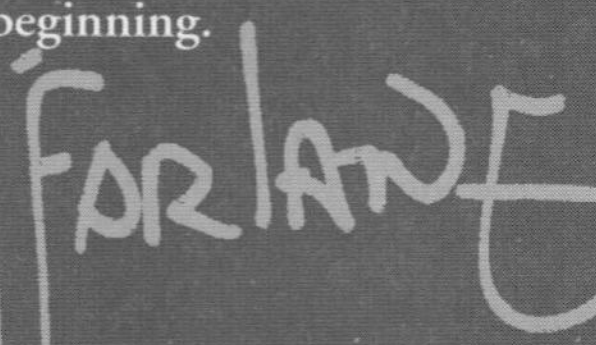

97

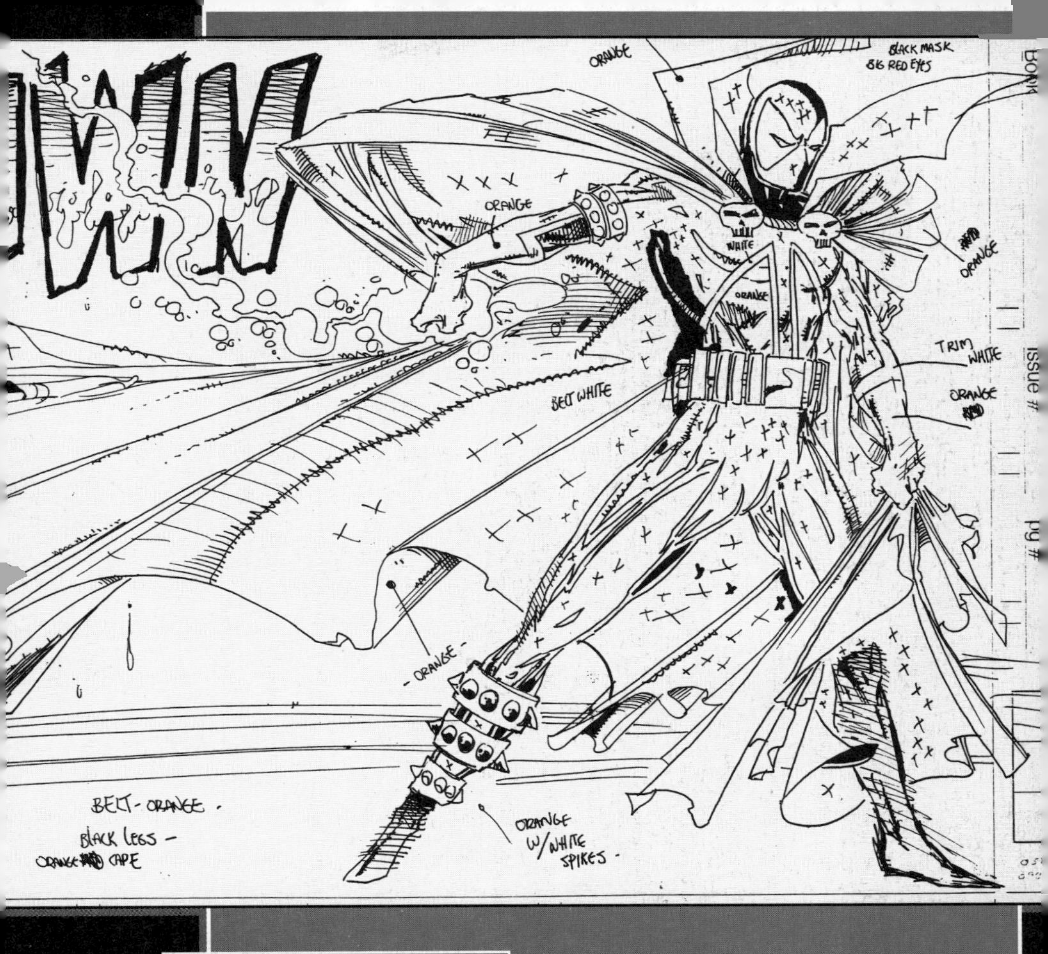

TODD McFARLANE is one of the most influential comic artists of the '90s, having inspired a fan following second to none and pushed back the boundaries of both art and story. After long and highly acclaimed runs on both *The Incredible Hulk* and *The Amazing Spider-Man*, McFarlane spearheaded Marvel's most successful ever launch. The first issue of the new *Spider-Man* comic sold in excess of three million copies and springboarded McFarlane's move into self-publishing. With fellow artists Jim Lee, Rob Liefeld, and Marc Silvestri, McFarlane formed Image Comics, launching his own creator-owned title *Spawn* to huge acclaim. Fifty plus issues (and many spin-off series, including *Angela*, *Violator* and *The Curse of Spawn*) later, *Spawn* is still consistently the top seller on the Diamond Distributors top 100.

1

QUESTIONS

I DON'T BELONG.
NOT HERE. NOT NOW.
I HAVE TO GET BACK THERE.
THE BET WAS RIGGED, HE MADE ME BELIEVE.
NOW THERE'S DARKNESS IN MY SOUL.
I WANT TO DIE...
...AGAIN.

BUT I CHOSE TO COME BACK.
WHY?

SIMMONS AT ARLINGTON CEMETARY IN
INIA. SIMMONS IS BEST KNOWN FOR HIS
RAGEOUS INVOLVEMENT IN SAVING THE
SIDENT FROM AN ASSASSINATION ATTEMPT.

MONS ROSE THROUGH THE RANKS OF THE
INE CORPS FOLLOWING HIS SERVICE OVERSEAS.
MEMORY WAS HONORED BY BOTH THE PRESI-
AND VICE PRESIDENT, AS WELL AS HUNDREDS OF
CERS FROM ALL THE ARMED SERVICES.

HIS WIFE, **WANDA BLAKE,** REMAINED QUIET FOR
THE DURATION OF THE FUNERAL, BUT SEEMED TO
NEED HELP NEAR THE END OF THE PROCEEDINGS

FRIENDS AND FAMILY HAVE ALL BEEN SUPPORT
AND WILL START A NEW SCHOLARSHIP FUND I
HIS NAME THAT WILL BENEFIT THE UNITED NE
COLLEGE FUND.

1987

COLONEL SIMMONS, WHO DISAPPEARED
M PUBLIC VIEW SHORTLY AFTER THE HINCKLEY
DENT, WAS BELIEVED TO HAVE BEEN INVOLVED
NUMEROUS COVERT GOVERNMENT TASK FORCES.

RMED SOURCES SAY THAT HIS PRESENCE IN
WANA AT THE SAME TIME AS YOUNGBLOOD
NTS WAS NO COINCIDENCE.

KLY, THIS STINKS OF A GOVERNMENT
ER-UP. SO WHAT ELSE IS NEW?

THOUGH I'M SURE LT. COL. SIMMONS WAS A
OF COURAGE AND INTEGRITY, IT'S THE GOVER
MENT'S **BOYS' CLUB ATTITUDE** THAT APPALLS

INFORMATION IS GIVEN OUT AT THEIR DISCRETI
AN ALMOST HOLLYWOOD-TYPE FASHION, AN
ALL KNOW HOW MOVIE MAKERS **NEVER** STRE
THE TRUTH

THE LOVELY WANDA BLAKE WAS ABSO**LUTE**LY
NE IN A DISARMINGLY SIMPLE JET BLACK
VANNI ORIGINAL. AND **SAY,** WHO WAS THAT
, DARK AND HANDSOME **PRINCE** ON HER ARM
HE CEREMONY?

, A LITTLE BIRD TOLD ME THAT **MARTIN**
XANDER WAS WANDA'S CLOSEST FRIEND
K IN HIGH SCHOOL. **HE** INTRODUCED HER TO
IMMONS AT THE REPUBLICAN CONVENTION
984.

WELL, WHERE THIS POTENTIAL AFFAIR IS LEADING
REMAINS TO BE SEEN. **WE'LL** BE KEEPING AN EYE
AS FOR **YOU, MIS**TER MARTIN ALEXANDER, SHA
SHAME ON YOU! LET THE POOR WOMAN **GRIEV**
BESIDES, SHE'LL HAVE A TOUGH TIME FINDING A
REPLACEMENT FOR A HUSBAND VOTED ONE OF
TEN SEXIEST MEN" TWO YEARS AGO. EVEN THOU
THE GOVERNMENT TRIED TO **HIDE** THIS SWEET
MORSEL FROM ALL OF US, **THIS** CHARISMATIC
GENTLEMAN COULDN'T BE KEPT OUT OF SIGHT.

I REMEMBER THERE WAS SOMEONE.
SOMEONE TO LOVE.

SOMEONE TO HATE.

AND I WAS SOMETHING.

SOMETHING SPECIAL.

AND PROUD OF IT. FOR A TIME.

THEN THEY TURNED ON ME.

HE TURNED ON ME.

I REMEMBER...

...DYING.

AND HER. OH, GOD, SHE'S SO BEAUTIFUL.

I NEEDED.

HE GAVE.

I HAD TO.

ALL I COULD THINK OF
WAS HER.

SO I PROMISED,

AND HE ACCEPTED.

ALL BECAUSE OF HER.

DAMN HIS LIES.
HE ACCEPTED THE DEAL... ON HIS TERMS. HIS RULES. HIS WAY.
AND SOMEWHERE IN TIME HE BUST A GUT LAUGHING.
9:9:9:9

9:9:9:9
YEAH, HE GAVE ME POWER, BUT HE ROBBED ME OF MY MEMORIES.
IF I CAN JUST FIND HER, THEN I'LL KNOW WHAT THIS IS ABOUT. BUT... I CAN'T EVEN REMEMBER WHO SHE IS.
NONE OF THIS MAKES ANY SENSE. A HANDFUL OF IMAGES DARTING IN MY MIND. THAT'S IT?! THAT'S ALL I HAVE OF MY LIFE?!
I FEEL I CAN DO ANYTHING... ANYTHING AT ALL WITH MY POWER. BUT WHY CAN'T I REMEMBER?
SHE'LL KNOW WHO I AM.

I'M GOING TO FIND HER, ALRIGHT.

...I'M GOING TO FIND HIM. THE ONE WHO FRAMED ME.
AND WHEN I HAVE SOME ANSWERS...

"OKAY, TWITCH. LET'S TRY THIS ONE MORE TIME."
YOU'RE TELLING ME THAT SOMEBODY THREW CARLO GIAMOTTI FROM A WINDOW--
THROUGH A WINDOW, SIR.
--THROUGH A WINDOW, ON THE THIRTY-FOURTH FLOOR--
FORTY-FOURTH, SIR.
AND HE WASN'T KILLED BY THE FALL?
NO, SIR. IT WAS HIS HEART.
HEART FAILURE?
Umm-- YOU MIGHT SAY THAT, SIR. IT WAS REMOVED.
REMOVED?
YES, SIR. IT WAS STUFFED IN HIS MOUTH.
TWITCH.
YES, SIR?
WE GOT THREE DEAD HIT MEN IN THE LAST FORTY-EIGHT HOURS AND YOU'RE TRYIN' TO BE A COMEDIAN. I DON'T NEED THAT
NO, SIR.
I AIN'T COMPLAININ', MIND YOU. SOMEBODY'S SAVIN' ME A LOT OF WORK. I FIGURE WE GOT OURSELVES EITHER A GRADE-A WACKO OR THE BEST DAMN VOLUNTEER COP IN NEW YORK CITY.
YES, SIR.
PROBABLY BOTH.
IT'S A HELLUVA TOWN, TWITCH.
YES, SIR.

NO! NO! PLEASE DON'T!
SHADDUP, BITCH.
BOYS, LOOKS LIKE SHE'S GOT ENOUGH FOR ALL OF US.
FORTUNATELY, I GET FIRST DIBS.
BACK OFF, GUYS.
I GOT ME AN IDEA.
LET'S SEE HOW LOUD THE TRAMP CAN SCREAM AFTER I CUT OUT HER TONGUE.
WAIT A SEC...
...I WANT A CLOSER LOOK WHILE THE BODY'S STILL WARM.

GET OUT.
NOW!
OR YOU'RE ALL DEAD.
WHAT THE HELL?
HEY SHANK, LOOKS LIKE ONE O' THEM YOUNG-BLOODS!
WHO CARES? CHECK THIS OUT, GUYS--

I'M GONNA CARVE ME A SUPER--
--HKKKHH!
BAD IDEA.

NOW, WHO'S NEXT?
YOU CRAZY M.F., NOBODY JERKS WITH ME.
FAT BOY.
YOU'RE WAY OUT OF YOUR LEAGUE.
BOOM

THEY'RE GONE. YOU NEEDN'T BE AFRAID.
PLEASE... DON'T-- I'LL... I'LL DO WHAT YOU WANT.
"UH!!"
NO.
NOT AGAIN.
NOOOOO

ONCE AGAIN YOUR MIND EXPLODES WITH A SEARING PAIN. A FLOODGATE OF MEMORIES BURSTS WIDE.
YET IT IS HER FACE THAT KEEPS HAUNTING YOU.
ALWAYS HER FACE.
WHO IS SHE?
THEN THINGS BEGIN TO CRYSTALIZE.
YOU REMEMBER YOUR FUNERAL. BEGGING AND PLEADING FOR SOMEONE TO RELEASE YOU FROM THE DARK-NESS. YOU'RE NOT DEAD. YOU CAN'T BE.
THEN YOU FEEL HER PRESENCE. WARM. CARING. SOOTHING. BUT SOMEWHERE DEEP INSIDE SHE FEELS EMPTY NOW.
SHE HAS NO REASON. NO MEANING NO SOUL.

BUT YOUR SOUL LIVES.
WHILE HERS IS DYING.
HH-HUHHH HHUHHHH ...
HEY-- COME ON. IT'S OKAY. YOU'RE ALRIGHT. IT'S ALL OVER NOW.

POLICE ARE INVESTIGATING THE FOURTH GANGLAND HOMICIDE IN TWO DAYS. THE MURDER OF ***CARLO GIAMOTTI*** MAKES THE SEVENTH GANGLAND MURDER THIS YEAR, BUT CHIEF OF POLICE TIM BANKS DENIES ANY TRUTH TO THE RUMOR OF A POSSIBLE "MOB WAR."

INSIDE SOURCES HAVE ALSO REPORTED THAT THE THREE MOST RECENT DEATHS WERE UNLIKE ANY THEY HAD SEEN BEFORE. IT WAS QUOTED, *"EVEN THE BAD GUYS DON'T SINK THIS LOW."* THE MYSTERY OF THESE DEATHS SEEMS TO HAVE...

1992

THIS MIGHT BE JUST WHAT THIS CITY NEEDS. WITH PEOPLE LIKE ***JAKE MORELLI,*** DISGUISED AS A WELL-DRESSED BUSINESSMAN, IT'S NO WONDER THE POLICE WON'T MAKE ANY ARRESTS. POLICE CHIEF BANKS SAYS HE'LL SEND OUT AN INVESTIGATIVE UNIT TO FLUSH OUT SOME ANSWERS. ***WHAT'S TO INVESTIGATE?*** JUST BECAUSE SOMETHING SMELLS ***NOW*** DOESN'T MEAN IT WASN'T GARBAGE ***BEFORE.***

I FOR ONE HOPE THE POLICE DON'T ***FIND*** ANY ANSWERS. OR WORSE YET, TRY AND ***STOP*** THIS LATEST RASH OF PUBLIC EXECUTIONS. IF IT'S GOOD GUYS KILLING BAD OR ***BAD*** GUYS KILLING BAD-- ***WHO CARES?*** GIVE ME A CALL IF YOU CITIZENS NEED ANY HELP.

...I'LL NEVER UNDERSTAND ***HOW*** THOSE TWO HAVE MANAGED TO STAY TOGETHER ALL THESE YEARS. ***SOME***ONE MUST BE ***TOR***TURING ME.

AND ***FINALLY,*** WORD OUT OF NEW YORK IS THAT THERE'S A NEW ***MYSTERY MAN*** IN THE BIG APPLE. ONLY A HANDFUL OF REPORTS SO FAR, BUT FROM WHAT I CAN ***TELL,*** OUR BIG BRUISER HAS A FETISH FOR ***ZORRO.***

I MEAN, LET'S GET ***SERIOUS.*** A ***CAPE!*** WIT THE ***YOUNGBLOOD*** FASHIONS BEING ALL THE RAGE, ***WHY*** ON ***EARTH*** WOULD ***ANY***ONE TRY TO BRING BACK SUCH A ***GAUCHE*** AND TOTALLY ***USE***LESS AC***CES***SORY?

NOW THOSE ***SPIKES*** AND ***CHAINS*** HE HAS, ***THOSE*** ARE SIMPLY ***DAR***LING. A PERFECTLY ***RIVETING*** STATEMENT.

SO BEAUTIFUL. BUT WHO IS SHE? WHY DO I KEEP--
GOD. NO.
SHE'S MY WIFE.
I HAVE A WIFE.
BUT I CAN'T REMEMBER ANYTHING ELSE. I DON'T KNOW WHAT HER NAME IS OR THE COLOR OF HER EYES. BUT WE WERE HUSBAND AND WIFE. THAT'S WHY SHE WAS GRIEVING AT THE FUNERAL. IT WAS HER THAT MADE ME WANT TO COME BACK.
I LET MY MERCENARY INSTINCTS TAKE OVER TOO QUICKLY. GOT TOO CAUGHT UP IN THIS DAMN COSTUME. I'M NO HERO.
IT'S JUST THAT EVERYTHING IS SO DIFFERENT. WHAT HAPPENED TO THE LAST FIVE YEARS? I'M STRANDED HERE NOT KNOWING WHAT'S GOING ON.
I KNOW I'M ALIVE BUT I CAN'T FEEL IT.
ONLY THING I FEEL IS THIS DAMN COSTUME. GOT TO GET IT OFF-- GET AWAY FROM IT.

MY FACE--
FELT LIKE--
JESUS!!
WHAT AM I?

WHAT AM I?
I DUNNO, TWITCH...
IF IT REALLY IS SOME GOVERNMENT HERO GONE WACKO, THEM WASHINGTON STIFFS AIN'T GONNA LET US GET CLOSE. THEM TIGHT ASSES. BUT IF THIS GUY DECIDES HE WANTS TO START SNUFFING OUT "JOE AVERAGE," THEN WE GOT OURSELVES A SERIOUS PROBLEM.
AND THE DAMAGE THIS GUY HAS DONE TO THOSE THREE BODIES IS FRIGGIN' UNREAL. WONDER HOW MUCH POWER THIS GUY HAS IN HIM?

9:9:9:5

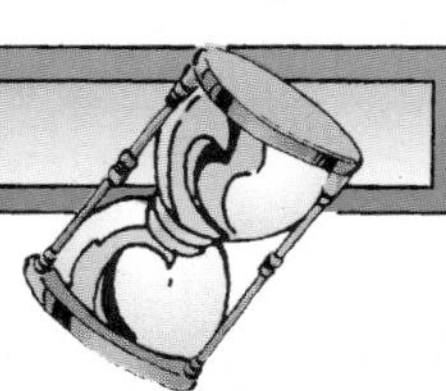

"LIKE I SAID, IT'S A HELLUVA TOWN."
"YES SIR. BY THE WAY, I HEAR YOU HAD ONLY THIRTEEN DOUGHNUTS TODAY. DIDN'T KNOW YOU WERE DIETING."
"SHUDDUP, TWITCH. I'M NOT IN A MOOD FOR YOUR JOKES."
"YES SIR."
HAHA AHAH HAHA HAH HAHA AH HAHA
SOMEWHERE
HAH
IN
HAHA AH
TIME
HAHA AHAH HAHA
HAHAHAHAHAHA... Simmons... if you think you've got problems now...
...I promise, your troubles have just begun. HAHAHAHAHAHA
NEXT ISSUE: the VIOLATOR!

SPAWN
image
2
JUNE
$1.95
$2.35
Canada
McFARLANE 92
SIMMONS

-- AND THEN I'LL TELL HIM-- IF HE BEGS ME REALLY, **REALLY,** NICE LIKE, I MIGHT ONLY AMPUTATE ***ONE*** LEG.
BUT!
IF HE PUTS UP A ***FIGHT...***
... I'M GONNA HAFTA RIP HIS ***INNARDS*** OUT, MAKE FILLETS OUTTA HIS ***LUNGS,*** MAKE A ***MILK SHAKE*** OUTTA HIS **HEART,** AND SOFT-BOIL HIS ***EYEBALLS,*** 'CAUSE...
...I'M THE VIOLATOR!
meow.
IMPRESSIVE. I KNOW.

BUT, WHEN YOU'RE STRIKING FEAR INTO THE HEARTS OF OTHERS, A LITTLE BRAVADO GOES A LONG WAY.
BESIDES, IT SEEMS TO WORK IN COMICS.
ANYWAYS, IT'LL FINALLY COME DOWN TO THAT BIG, LONG, DRAWN-OUT BATTLE.
BUT!
JUST WHEN I'M ABOUT TO PULL HIS SPINE THROUGH HIS NOSE--
--I'LL STOP!
--TELL 'IM I COULD KILL 'IM SIXTY-FIVE DIFFERENT WAYS... BUT I'M NOT ALLOWED TO...!
HE'LL START TO BEG ME. AND I'LL SPIT IN HIS FACE. THEN HE'LL CRY. AT WHICH TIME I'LL KICK HIS TEETH IN!
AND WHEN HE THINKS IT CAN'T GET ANY WORSE... I'LL PULVERIZE IM' INTO A LITTLE ITTY BITTY CUBE AND SUCK 'IM LIKE A LIFESAVER!
HAHAHAHAHAHAA
I GOTTA TELL YA, Mr. PUSSY, I'M HAVING FAR TOO MUCH FUN.
THE BOSS WILL BE TOTALLY IMPRESSED.
HELL! I'M TOTALLY IMPRESSED!
OH, I LOVE BEING ME!!
AND I'D HATE TO BE HIM TONIGHT!

"I'D HATE TO BE
SPAWN!"
MY WIFE.
I'VE GOT TO FIND HER... LET HER KNOW I'M BACK, I'M ALIVE. PEOPLE THINK I DIED FIVE YEARS AGO. WHAT'S SHE GOING TO THINK?
NOT GOING TO MATTER MUCH IF I CAN'T FIND HER.
DON'T KNOW WHERE WE LIVED. OR WHERE WE WORKED.
THIS WHOLE THING IS COMPLETELY NUTS. I'M FLOATING IN LIMBO ONE SECOND, THEN, BANG!-- HERE I AM. ALIVE! OR SO IT SEEMS. BUT OTHER THAN HER, ALL I REMEMBER IS MAKING A DEAL...
...ONE THAT INCLUDED MY SOUL.

DON'T KNOW HOW IT WAS DONE. AT LEAST I KNOW WHY. IT WAS FOR HER.
GOD, I WISH I COULD REMEMBER HER NAME.
FOR TWO DAYS I'VE BEEN TRYING TO MAKE SOME SENSE OF THIS. NO NAME. NO MONEY. NO HOME.
SO I HID...
...HOPING THIS WAS ALL JUST A DREAM. IT'S NOT.
WHATEVER DEAL WAS MADE, I GOT SCREWED!
HE'S PLAYING WITH MY MEMORIES, GIVING ME BITS AND PIECES AT HIS LEISURE. IT'S ALL SOME SICK GAME TO HIM. AND I FELL RIGHT INTO HIS TRAP.
HE GAVE ME POWER. LIFE. BUT IT COST ME MY SOUL, MY IDENTITY. THE SCUM EVEN STOLE MY FACE.
I DON'T EVEN THINK I'M HUMAN ANYMORE.
SO WHY WOULD MY WIFE WANT ME AGAIN?

CAN'T WORRY ABOUT THAT NOW. I NEED HER! THAT'S WHAT MATTERS.
IT'S ALL I HAVE.
THIS COSTUME FEELS MORE COMFORTABLE THAN MY REAL SKIN. WHAT'S LEFT OF IT.
THIS NEW LOOK SEEMED TO WORK AGAINST THOSE RAPISTS THE OTHER NIGHT, THOUGH.
I LET MY INSTINCTS CARRY ME THROUGH THAT. WONDER IF THAT LADY'S ALRIGHT? I JUST ABOUT SCARED HER TO DEATH, 'TIL I FREAKED!
THE MEMORIES KEEP HITTING ME LIKE A FREIGHT TRAIN. THAT COULD BE TROUBLE.
IF THAT HAPPENS WHEN I'M...
uh?
MAYBE THIS CHURCH IS A CLUE. IT'S THE SECOND TIME I'VE BEEN DRAWN TO THIS PLACE.
WHAT'S THAT GUY DOING, WAVING? RATHER ODD LITTLE MAN. NOW WHAT?
HE'S DISAPPEARED INTO THE SHADOWS. STRANGE.

LATER, AT THE DAWNCORP BUILDING...
IT WAS BUILT IN RECORD TIME, AND EVEN CAME IN UNDER BUDGET, WHILE BEING FITTED WITH THE LATEST TECHNOLOGY... ESPECIALLY ITS SECURITY SYSTEM. "UNBEATABLE," THEY SAID. "IMPENETRABLE."
NOW, NEW YORK CITY'S ORGANIZED CRIME COULD BE SAFE.

OR SO THEY THINK.
GOD ALMIGHTY! WHAT ARE YOU?!!
NO! NO! STAY BACK! I'LL KILL YOU!
BLAM BLAM BLAM
SWEET MOTHER OF MERCY.

GNNAAAAAAAAAA
HOLD ON, BOSS! I'M COMING!

WAM WAM
OPEN UP! BOSS, OPEN THE DOOR!

YOUR BOSS IS UNAVAILABLE.
BUT HE DID SAY HE WANTED YOU...
UMMPH!
...TO JOIN HIM TONIGHT.

NITE-NITE, BOYS.

WELL, WELL, WELL. IT BREAKS MY HEART TO REPORT ANOTHER COUPLE OF MAFIA KILLINGS. IT LOOKS LIKE OUR BOY THE "HEART SURGEON" IS AT IT AGAIN. THOUGH THE POLICE HAVEN'T CONFIRMED ANY CONNECTION TO THE ***OTHER*** DEATHS, ONLY THOSE OF US WHO ARE BRAIN-DEAD CAN'T FIGURE ***THIS*** ONE OUT.

THE POLICE ALSO REPORT THAT THEY'VE DOUBLED THE TASK FORCE INVESTIGATING THESE VEG-O-MATIC KILLINGS. MY ONLY QUESTION: ***WHY?!!*** LAST TIME I CHECKED, ***ALL*** SIX OF THEM WERE 'LEG-BREAKERS.

WHAT'S TO INVESTIGATE? AM I THE ONLY ONE ASKING THIS QUESTION?

I'VE GOT A BETTER IDEA-- LET ME HELP DIG THE GRAVES.

AS I'VE *STATED* BEFORE, RUMORS ARE THE UGLY SIDE OF SHOW BIZ.

THE YOUNGBLOODS, CHANGING THEIR COSTUMES FOR ONE UNIFIED LOOK? ***C'MON,*** IT'S THE MYRIAD COLORS AND ENSEMBLES THAT ***TOOK*** THEM TO THE TOP. ***WHY*** IN HEAVEN'S NAME WOULD THEY WANT TO ALIENATE THEIR FANS ***NOW?***

SEX APPEAL HAS ***AL***WAYS BEEN A BIG PRIORITY TO THE MARKETING GENIUSES BEHIND OUR HEROES IN TIGHTS. 'BLOOD MERCHANDISE IS OVER THE $2.2 ***BIL***LION MARK AL***READY.*** I JUST ***KNEW*** THERE'D BE A DAY THEY'D TOPPLE THOSE PIZZA-EATING TURTLES.

AND ***SPEAKING*** OF GREEN GUYS, CHICAGO IS REPORTING THE APPEARANCE OF A ***DRAGON,*** FIN AND ***ALL***. NOW WOULDN'T ***THAT*** MAKE A GREAT TICKLER.

... SOURCES ALSO INDICATE THAT SINCE TONIGHT'S MURDERS, OVER A DOZEN OF NEW YORK'S MOST POWERFUL MEN HAVE ASKED FOR POLICE PROTECTION. ALL OF THESE MEN HAVE 'ALLEGED' CONNECTIONS TO CRIMINAL AFFAIRS.

ON A MORE POSITIVE NOTE, ***WANDA BLAKE,*** WIDOW OF ***LT. COL. AL SIMMONS,*** HELPED OPEN ANOTHER CARE CLINIC FOR DISABLED CHILDREN.

MONEY GENERATED BY HER LATE HUSBAND'S MEMORIAL FUND HELPED FINISH THE CENTER, WHICH HAD BEEN ON HOLD. THE CURRENT RECESSION IS BLAMED.

THIS IS THE THIRD SUCH PROJECT THAT Ms. BLAKE HAS BEEN INVOLVED WITH.

I'M HOPING THESE NEW POWERS CAN HELP ME FIND MY WIFE.
WHY'D I EVEN GET THESE POWERS? ALL I WANTED WAS TO SEE HER.
TO HOLD MY WIFE.
HA! JOKE'S ON ME. WHY WOULD SHE WANT TO HOLD ME WHEN I LOOK LIKE A ROTTING CORPSE?
DON'T EVEN KNOW IF I'M ALIVE, MUCH LESS A MAN.
THINGS MADE MORE SENSE WHEN I WAS DEAD.
DAMN HIM.

FUNNY--
--GUESS I BEAT HIM TO IT.
WELL, LET'S SEE EXACTLY WHAT THESE FRIGGIN' POWERS CAN DO. SEE IF THEY CAN MAKE ME WHOLE AGAIN.
9:9:9:5
MAN! WHAT A JOLT!
FEEL GOOD THOUGH. STRONG. ALMOST AFRAID TO LOOK, BUT...

OH
MY
GOD.
NO!!
JEEZ, NO.
COME ON!!
WORK!!
NOT AGAIN.
THIS CAN'T BE.
I'M A BLACK MAN!

WORLD'S GONE CRAZY, TWITCH.
CHIEF'S BEEN ON MY BUTT ALL NIGHT. FIGURES WE AIN'T MOVING FAST ENOUGH.
HOW'S HE EXPECT US TO DO FIVE REPORTS TONIGHT.
SIX, SIR.
STUPID REPORTERS GOT EVERYONE IN A PANIC. SURE AIN'T MAKIN' MY JOB EASIER.
NO ONE SAID THEY WOULD, SIR.

JUST ONCE I'D LIKE TO SPEND A QUIET NIGHT AT THE OFFICE. NO REPORTS. NO PHONES RINGING. NO WORRIES. NO NOTHIN'.
THEN YOU'D BE DEAD.
DON'T I WISH.
Los Angeles Times
HEART ATTACKS

WHAT KIND OF JOLLIES DO THEY GET OUTTA DESCRIBING HOW DEEP THE HEART HAS BEEN SHOVED DOWN A GUY'S THROAT.
DON'T NOBODY WANNA HEAR ABOUT DOC GOODEN'S SHOULDER ANY-MORE.
PLUS, WE STILL GOT THAT PROBLEM OF SOME COSTUME FREAK HIDING IN ALLEYWAYS.
CAN YOU IMAGINE. A HERO THAT AIN'T RICH. WHAT'S THE WORLD COMING TO.
DUNNO, SIR.

WELL, ME NEITHER. EXCEPT WE GET PAID TO FIND ANSWERS...THAT MEANS NOT SLEEPING OR EATING FOR THREE OR FOUR DAYS. WHO ARE WE TO QUESTION, RIGHT?
BY THE WAY, SIR.
YEAH?
HOW IS GOODEN'S SHOULDER THESE DAYS?
TWITCH.
YES, SIR.
SHUDDUP!

RELAX, GINO.
YOU'RE BAD, AND I ADMIRE THAT.
UNFORTUNATELY, I NEED YOU TO HELP ME.
HERE'S THE DEAL. YOU LEND ME A SMALL PIECE OF YOUR ANATOMY, AND I LET YOUR SOUL GET TORTURED FOREVER.
SO... GUESS WHAT'S NEXT?
JESUS!
JESUS!
JESUS!
JESUS!
JESUS!
BAD GUESS!

I WON'T STAY LIKE THIS. NOT WHITE.
SOMEONE'S PLAYING A BAD JOKE. SCREWING WITH MY MIND.
WHY?!
DAMN YOU!
WHAT DID I DO TO DESERVE THIS?! I JUST WANTED TO SEE MY WIFE! NOW SHE WON'T EVEN KNOW WHO I AM! IF THIS IS SOME KIND OF WAR...
...THEN COME GET ME!
GOD.
AM I GOING CRAZY ?!
I JUST WANT TO BE ME. BUT THESE FRIGGIN' POWERS WON'T WORK.
CAN'T MAKE ME WHOLE.
WHY?
SEE IF YOU CAN KILL ME AGAIN!
SUDDENLY, YOUR MIND EXPLODES. THEN, AS IF ON CUE...

ANOTHER FLASHBACK. ANOTHER CLUE.
JASON WYNN. HE WAS YOUR BOSS... THE ONE THE PRESIDENT SAID WOULD TAKE CARE OF YOU. BE YOUR MENTOR.
HE TAUGHT YOU, ALRIGHT. TAUGHT YOU HOW TO FIGHT. HOW TO KILL. HOW TO OBEY.
FOR A TIME YOU WERE LIKE BROTHERS. BUT ALL SIBLINGS EVEN-TUALLY LOCK HORNS.
THE FIGHTS BECAME MORE FREQUENT--THE INTENSITY MUCH HIGHER. YOU SMELLED COVER-UP TOO MANY TIMES.
LIBERTIES WERE BEING TAKEN, RULES BROKEN, ALL IN THE NAME OF DEMOCRACY. FREEDOM. BUT THE PRICE PAID WAS OBSCENE: INNOCENT PEOPLE WHOSE CHOICES WERE TAKEN AWAY...
...WHOSE OPTIONS HAD BEEN TAKEN FROM THEM.
AMERICA HAD BECOME A BULLY, OR SO YOUR CLOUDED MIND WAS CONVINCED. ONLY ONE THOUGHT MADE YOU ANGRIER:
...THAT HE DIDN'T CARE.

EVEN WORSE, HE SEEMED TO REVEL IN THE PAIN HE CAUSED OTHERS. AS THE DAYS WENT BY, YOU COULD SEE IT IN HIS EYES.
JASON HAD BECOME TRULY EVIL.
CAIN AND ABEL HAD NOTHING ON YOU TWO.

9:4:3:2

No! No!
AAAAAAA
WHAT'D'YA DO TO HIM?! STAY AWAY FROM ME-- I SAID--
NOOOOO!
AAAAAA!
YES.
GLOP
GLOP
THIS IS GETTING BORING.

help.
HEY! MISTER! YOU NEED HELP?
UH?!
C'MON, BUD. SHAKE IT OFF!
YA KNOW, I COULDN'T TELL IF YOU WERE JUST TANKED OR WHAT... NOT THAT IT MATTERS, I ENJOY A NIP EVERY NOW AN' THEN, TOO. BUT THAT MOANING OF YOURS DIDN'T SOUND LIKE THE ENJOYABLE KIND.
WHO... WHO ARE YOU?!
NOT THAT I'M COMPLAINING, MIND YOU. WHO'S THINKING OF SLEEP AT TWO IN THE MORNING ANYWAYS?
NOT ME. I'M WIRED!!
I'M OKAY NOW. JUST A BIT DIZZY.
HOW'D MY MASK GET BACK ON?
DON'T WORRY. I PUT IT BACK ON WHILE YOU WERE IN LA-LA LAND. HECK OF AN ACNE PROBLEM YOU GOT THERE.
YOU MUST HAVE TO SCRAPE THE PUSS OFF THE MIRROR WHEN YOU'RE DONE.
I KNOW YOU.
Oh-oh.
I SAW YOU FROM THE TOP OF THE CHURCH... YOU WAVED AT ME! DO YOU KNOW WHO I AM?
YEAH. YEAH. YEAH. YOU'RE THE SPAWN. SO WHAT'S THE BIG DEAL?
THE SPAWN?
YEAH. YOU KNOW. NOT LIKE SALMON OR NOTHIN', BUT LIKE A HELLSPAWN GET IT?

I DO GET IT. SO HOW DO YOU KNOW ABOUT ME?
GOD...
DO YOU KNOW WHERE MY WIFE IS?!
NEVER SEEN THE CHICK!
AND STOP USING THAT G-WORD. HURTS MY EARS.
SINCE MY COVER'S BEEN BLOWN, LET ME TELL YOU WHY I'M HERE.
WHETHER YOU BELIEVE IT OR NOT, I COULD BEAT YOU SILLY WITH ONE HAND BEHIND MY BACK, OR I COULD RIP THE TOENAILS FROM YOUR FEET AND SEVER THE TENDONS IN YOUR CALVES.
AND ANOTHER THING, MR. BIG SHOT, I COULD RIP YOUR SPINE OUT AND USE IT LIKE A WHIP! -AND I COULD SNAP YOUR BONES LIKE THE BRITTLE CHUNKS THAT THEY ARE! -AND I COULD TEAR YOUR HEAD OFF AND USE IT FOR A BASKETBALL! -AND I COULD CUT YOU UP INTO BITE-SIZE PIECES AND MAIL YOU ACROSS FIFTY ZIP CODES!
ARE YA SCARED YET?

- AND ANOTHER THING! IF I'M IN A REALLY PISSY MOOD I MIGHT JUST... JUST...
OH-OH.
Um.
COULD YOU EXCUSE ME A MOMENT?
hee hee
ZIP!
NOW WHERE WAS I...
OH YEAH!
... AND I COULD MAKE JELLY MOLDS OUTTA YOUR INTESTINES, SMEAR COOL WHIP ON TOP AND EAT THE WHOLE THING WITHOUT PUKING!!
- AND I COULD...
LISTEN, BUDDY, I DON'T HAVE TIME FOR THIS.
OR YOU.
AWWW!
C'MON, MISTER...

...HAVE A HEART!
NEXT ISSUE:
SPAWN VS. the TRUE VIOLATOR!

3

Q U E S T I O N S

Part Three

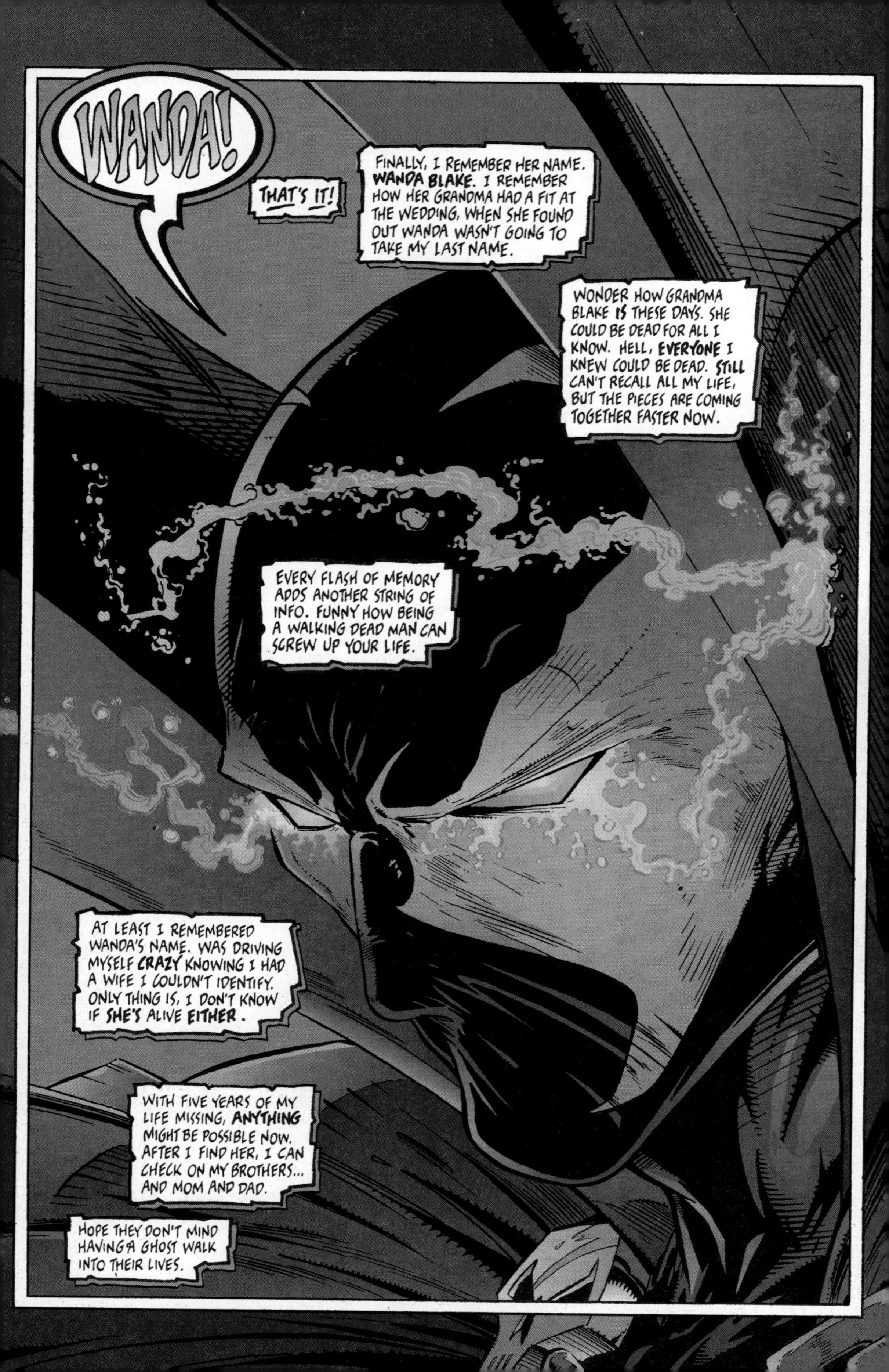
WANDA!
THAT'S IT!
FINALLY, I REMEMBER HER NAME. WANDA BLAKE. I REMEMBER HOW HER GRANDMA HAD A FIT AT THE WEDDING, WHEN SHE FOUND OUT WANDA WASN'T GOING TO TAKE MY LAST NAME.
WONDER HOW GRANDMA BLAKE IS THESE DAYS. SHE COULD BE DEAD FOR ALL I KNOW. HELL, EVERYONE I KNEW COULD BE DEAD. STILL CAN'T RECALL ALL MY LIFE, BUT THE PIECES ARE COMING TOGETHER FASTER NOW.
EVERY FLASH OF MEMORY ADDS ANOTHER STRING OF INFO. FUNNY HOW BEING A WALKING DEAD MAN CAN SCREW UP YOUR LIFE.
AT LEAST I REMEMBERED WANDA'S NAME. WAS DRIVING MYSELF CRAZY KNOWING I HAD A WIFE I COULDN'T IDENTIFY. ONLY THING IS, I DON'T KNOW IF SHE'S ALIVE EITHER.
WITH FIVE YEARS OF MY LIFE MISSING, ANYTHING MIGHT BE POSSIBLE NOW. AFTER I FIND HER, I CAN CHECK ON MY BROTHERS... AND MOM AND DAD.
HOPE THEY DON'T MIND HAVING A GHOST WALK INTO THEIR LIVES.

I MISS EVERYONE. EVEN THOSE I CAN'T REMEMBER. HARD TO BELIEVE I'VE BEEN AWAY ONLY A FEW DAYS. IT SEEMS LIKE A LIFETIME AGO.
I DON'T KNOW IF I EVEN HAVE A LIFE ANYMORE. THAT'S THE SCARIEST PART.
SOME ANSWERS SEEM SO DAMN DIFFICULT.
LIKE, THAT LITTLE FAT GUY LAST NIGHT-- WHAT WAS THAT ALL ABOUT? AND WHAT WAS THE PURPOSE OF THAT FACE PAINT OF HIS? I WAS SO SURE HE HAD SOME KNOWLEDGE OF ME.
AN OBNOXIOUS PAIN IN THE ASS IS WHAT HE WAS. STILL, THERE WAS SOMETHING FAMILIAR ABOUT HIM. Ah WELL, HE'S THE LEAST OF MY PROBLEMS.
WHAT I NEED TO DO IS GET THE FILE ON WANDA. SEE WHERE SHE LIVES. START FROM THERE. AND I KNOW JUST WHERE THE BOYS AT THE AGENCY KEEP THAT INFORMATION. AMUSING, HOW I USED TO BITCH AT THEM FOR INVADING PEOPLES' PRIVACY... THEY MIGHT HAVE THE MISSING CLUES I'M LOOKING FOR.
GETTING INTO THE BUILDING WILL BE A CINCH WITH THESE POWERS. I'M ALMOST LIKE A FRIGGIN' YOUNGBLOOD. WONDER IF THEY'RE STILL AROUND. THERE'S PROBABLY A HUNDRED OF 'EM, KNOWING THOSE GOVERNMENT STIFFS. "EXPLOIT AND OVERKILL," THE MOTTO OF ANY GOVERNMENT SYSTEM.
WE'VE GOT A FEW SCORES TO SETTLE, UNCLE SAM AND I. LIKE, NUMBER ONE...
...HOW DID I DIE. THAT ONE STILL HASN'T COME BACK TO ME. I'LL PUT THAT ONE ON THE BACK-BURNER...
...FOR NOW.
HAVE TO FIGURE THIS CRAP OUT ONE BIT AT A TIME. FIRST, I HAVE TO SEE WANDA... SHE'S THE ONLY REASON I'M EVEN BACK.

THEN, I'M GOING TO FIND HIM. THE SCUMBAG WHO'S MESSING WITH MY SO-CALLED LIFE.
FOR SOMEONE WHO DIDN'T BELIEVE IN RELIGION, I SURE GOT THROWN INTO A BIBLICAL NIGHTMARE.
DEMONS. SOULS. DEALS. LIES. THAT'S WHAT'S IN THE GREAT BEYOND, NOT SOME CUTE OLD MAN IN A BEARD.
THE TV EVANGELISTS WOULD HAVE HEART ATTACKS IF THEY KNEW WHAT LAY IN WAIT FOR THEM. GUESS THEY'LL BE GETTING THEIR JUST DUES, SAME AS I DID.
NOW THAT'D BE WORTH SEEING.
I HOPE THERE IS ANOTHER OPTION AT DEATH, THOUGH, BECAUSE GRANDMA BLAKE DOESN'T DESERVE WHAT I'VE GOT. HELL, NO ONE DESERVES WHAT I'VE GOT.
IT WAS A HELLUVA DEAL I MADE. "LET ME SEE MY WIFE AND YOU CAN HAVE MY SOUL." SOUNDED SIMPLE. I NEVER FACTORED IN THAT HE'D STRIP AWAY EVERYTHING I HAD. MY FACE. MY SKIN. AND HE SEEMS TO BE TOYING WITH MY MEMORIES. GIVING ME SELECTIVE RECALL. WELL, YOUR TIME WILL COME, DEVIL.
YOU'D BETTER BE PREPARED.

SOME-WHERE IN TIME...

HA HA HA HA HA

Oh, my. Simmons, you poor, pathetic FOOL!

Threaten away, you little **maggot**. It'll do you no good, 'cause you've been locked into a deal I can't lose.

HA HA HA HA HA HA HA HA HA HA HA HA HA HA HA HA HA HA HA HA HA HA HA HA HA HA HA HA HA HA HA HA

I've dealt with your kind a million times. Always begging for more. Always needing something. Well, now you have something...

...something BIG and MEAN and UGLY!!

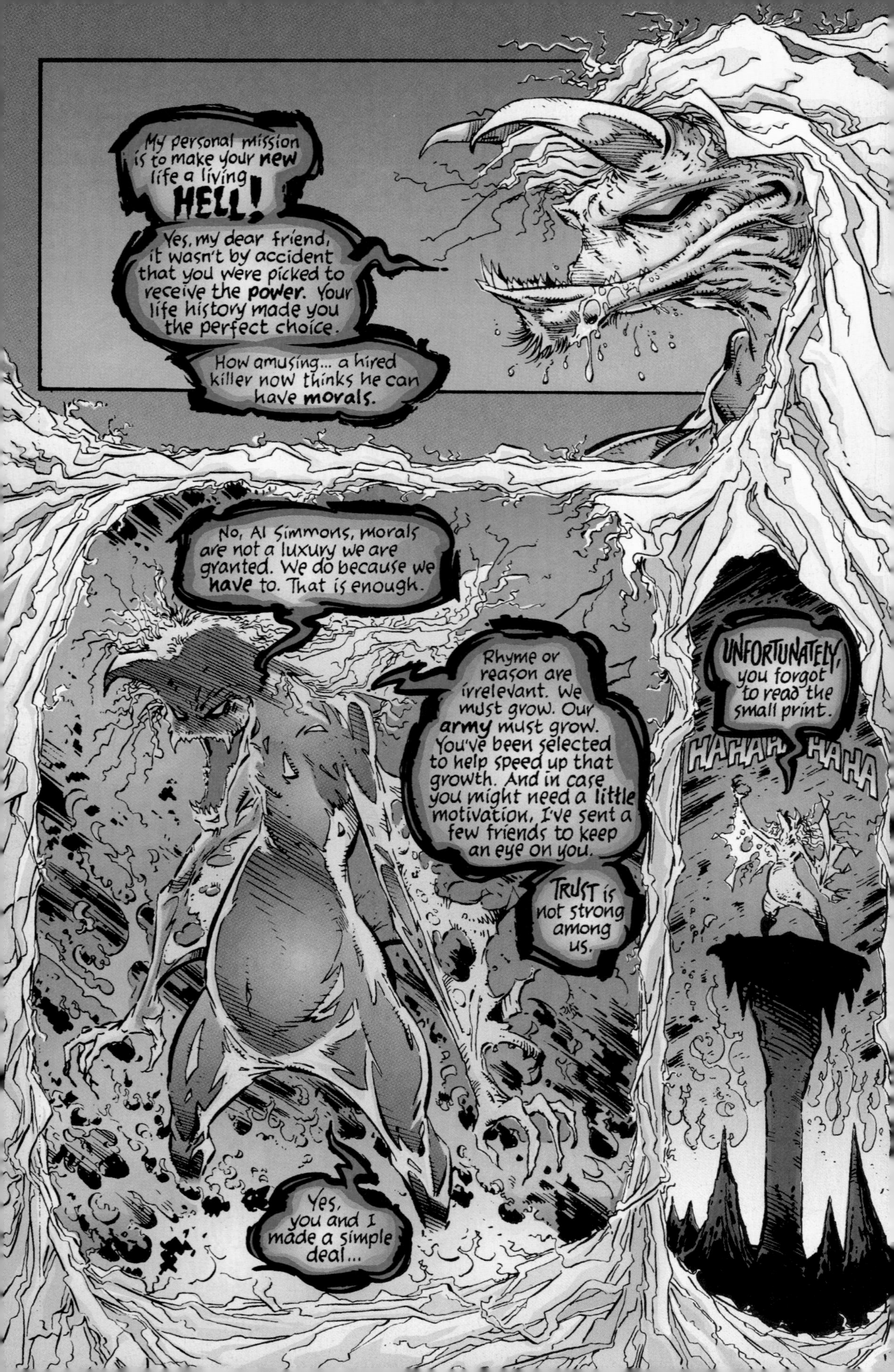
My personal mission is to make your new life a living HELL!
Yes, my dear friend, it wasn't by accident that you were picked to receive the power. Your life history made you the perfect choice.
How amusing... a hired killer now thinks he can have morals.
No, Al Simmons, morals are not a luxury we are granted. We do because we have to. That is enough.
Rhyme or reason are irrelevant. We must grow. Our army must grow. You've been selected to help speed up that growth. And in case you might need a little motivation, I've sent a few friends to keep an eye on you.
TRUST is not strong among us.
Yes, you and I made a simple deal...
UNFORTUNATELY, you forgot to read the small print.
HAHAHA HAHA

CRIPES!! TWITCH, WHAT'S THE CHIEF THINKING OF?!
HE'S BURYING US UNDER THESE STUPID REPORTS! WHY'S HE KEEPING US OFF THE STREET? AFRAID WE MIGHT ACTUALLY GET SOME RESULTS?!!
HIM AND HIS DAMN TASK FORCE.
THEY AIN'T DONE SNOT!
I'M STUCK IN THE OFFICE, WITH THIS FRIGGIN' CHAIR FEELING MORE AND MORE LIKE A PIMPLE ON MY BUTT!
PLUS, I GOTTA LOOK AT YOUR UGLY MUG, TWITCH.
THANK YOU, SIR. I'LL TAKE THAT AS A COMPLIMENT.
BUT! ...
NO PUN INTENDED...
...THAT STILL ISN'T SOLVING ANY OF OUR PROBLEMS.
YEAH, YEAH, I KNOW. WE GOT A PILE OF DEAD MAFIA WISE GUYS... MINUS THEIR HEARTS! AND EVEN THOUGH I AIN'T LOSING MUCH SLEEP OVER THEM, SOMEONE SICK IS RESPONSIBLE.
I DON'T CARE IF CRIME IS DOWN...
...WE WERE HIRED TO UPHOLD THE LAW. I'LL BE DAMNED IF I'M GONNA LET SOME PENCIL-NECK POLITICIAN-WANNABE SLOW ME DOWN.
'UH, SIR...
"... I DO SO ENJOY BEING WITH YOU IN YOUR FESTIVE MOODS."
DEE-LOOP-DEE-LOO! DEE-LOOP-DEE-LIE!
I KNOW A HERO... WHO'S GOING TO DIE!!
HEE HEE
I'M A POET AND I DON'T EVEN KNOW IT.
BETTER YET...
... I'M THE VIOLATOR!
AND IF I DON'T KILL YOU TODAY... I'LL TRY-IT-LATER!
dang, I'm good.

THE C.I.A.-- NEW YORK HEADQUARTERS...
GOT MY WIFE'S FILE. THIS SHOULD GIVE ME SOME ANSWERS.
JUST NEED TO TAKE CARE OF ONE SMALL DETAIL.
IT'S ALMOST MIDNIGHT, LINDA, WHY DON'T WE CALL IT A NIGHT.
PERHAPS I CAN BUY YOU A DRINK?
Uh... NO THANK YOU, MR. MILLER, MY HUSBAND IS WAITING FOR ME.
AND HOW IS THE NEW HUBBY, ANYWAYS. SURELY HE WON'T MIND IF YOU'RE NOT HOME RIGHT ON TIME.
ACTUALLY, SIR, HE... uh... NEEDS ME TO HELP COOK DINNER.
AT THIS LATE HOUR? NOT MUCH OF A MAN IF HE JUST SITS AROUND WAITING FOR YOU TO COOK.
SPEAKING OF COOKING, WHY WASTE THOSE BEAUTIFUL LIPS ON FOOD, WHEN I CAN THINK OF A NUMBER OF THINGS I'D MUCH RATHER SEE THEM DO.
Hmmmm.
PLEASE, MR. MILLER, I CAN'T--!
OH YES YOU CAN. BUT NOT TONIGHT, I GUESS.
OKAY, GATHER YOUR STUFF. I'LL SEE YOU IN THE MORNING. AND WEAR THAT CUTE LITTLE BLUE OUTFIT I LIKE SO MUCH.
HEY!!
WHO'S BEEN SCREWING WITH MY FILES?
C
FILE

GHK!
YOU LISTEN! AND YOU LISTEN GOOD!
WORD IS THAT SINCE YOUR DIVORCE YOU HAVEN'T PAID A PENNY IN ALIMONY OR CHILD SUPPORT.
I HIGHLY RECOMMEND THAT YOU CORRECT THIS OVERSIGHT QUICKLY...
...BECAUSE IF I HAVE TO COME BACK AGAIN, SHE'LL GET THE MONEY FROM YOUR LIFE INSURANCE POLICY.
DO WE UNDERSTAND EACH OTHER ?
SURE.
GOOD.
THERE ARE SOME OF US WHO WOULD GIVE OUR LIVES TO HAVE A WIFE OR FAMILY.

Oh, yeah.
If you ever touch your secretary again, you'll never use those hands again.
THUD

They always said you were scum, Billy.
UNH?!
How do you know my name?
WHERE ARE YOU, DAMMIT?!!
WHO ARE YOU?!

Pray you never learn.

YES!
THAT'S IT! Become evil! Vicious! Violent!!
HaHaHaHaHa

SHE STARTED A SCHOLAR-SHIP IN MY NAME, TO HELP THE UNDER-PRIVILEGED.

SHE ALWAYS DID HAVE A BIG HEART. BUT WHERE IS SHE LIVING?
QUEENS?
WHY WOULD SHE MOVE THERE WHEN HER PARENTS LIVED ON STATEN ISLAND? MUST BE A REASON WHY...
WHAT'S THIS?!
NO!

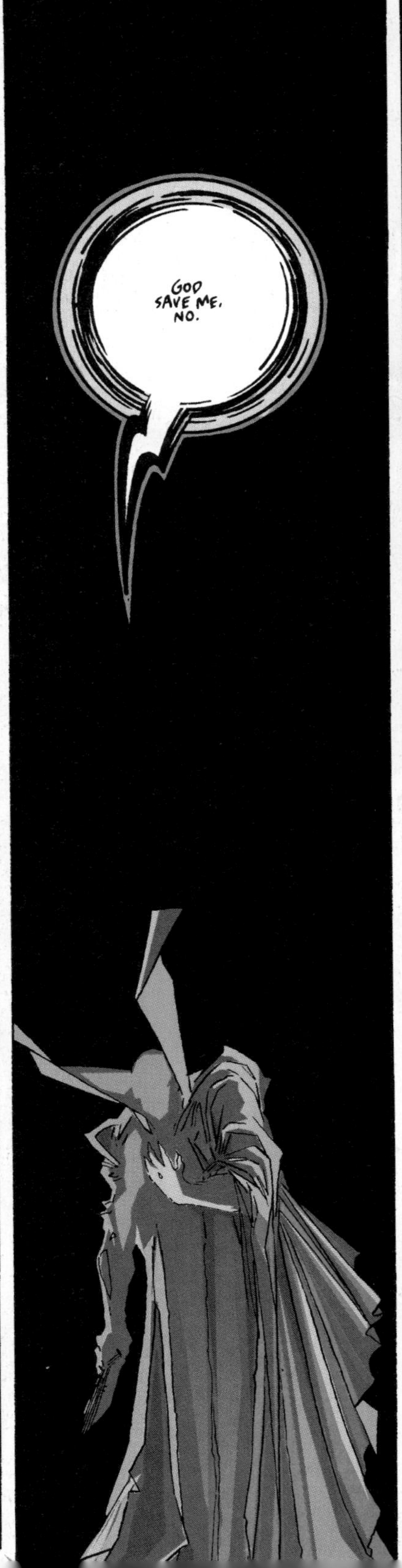
GOD SAVE ME. NO.

BLAKE, W
IT CAN'T BE.

9:4:3:2

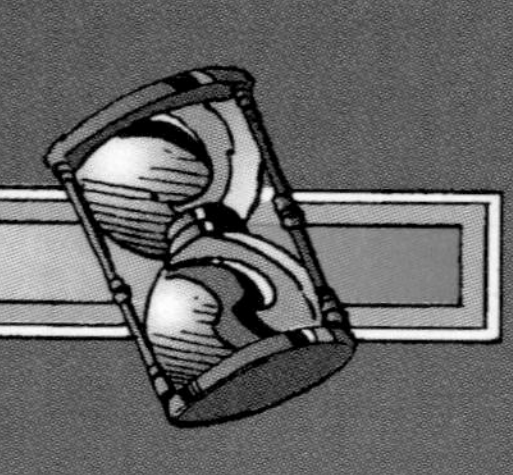

QUEENS, THE NEXT DAY...
A TWENTY-FIVE MINUTE COMMUTE FROM MANHATTAN STANDS A NONDESCRIPT HOUSE. WHITE FENCE. PORCH. THE PERFECT LITTLE HIDEWAY--

--AND THE HOME OF WANDA BLAKE, WIDOW OF LT. COL. AL SIMMONS.

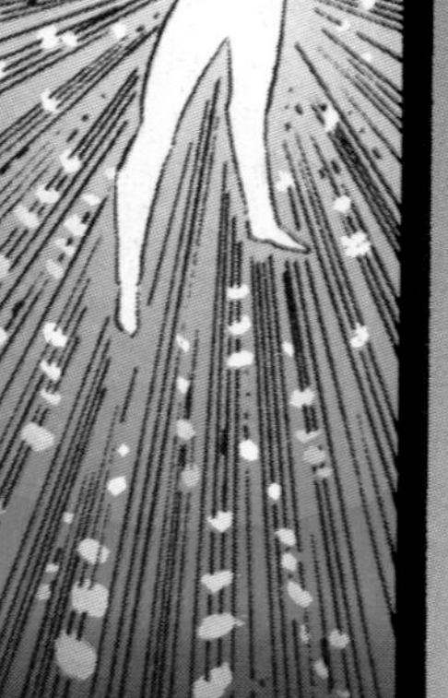
TIME TO CHANGE INTO HUMAN FLESH AGAIN. WISH I COULD LOOK LIKE MY-SELF, BUT THESE POWERS SEEM TO HAVE A MIND OF THEIR OWN SOMETIMES.
I CAN'T EVEN CHANGE MY APPEARANCE. KEEP TURNING INTO THIS DAMN WHITE GUY.
WORSE YET...
...I LOOK LIKE SOME CALIFORNIA BEACH BUM.
AND OF ALL THE HAIR COLORS-- WHY BLONDE?!
THAT'S IT, KEEP JOKING. THEN MAYBE YOUR NERVES WILL SETTLE DOWN.
OR AT LEAST YOUR HANDS WILL STOP SHAKING.

FEEL LIKE SOME STUPID SCHOOL KID GOING OUT ON HIS FIRST DATE. NOW THERE'S A JOKE, WE DATED THREE YEARS AND WERE MARRIED FIVE...
HAVE TO GO SLOW. FEELS LIKE I'VE BEEN GONE ONLY A FEW DAYS, BUT FIVE YEARS HAVE PASSED FOR HER. HOPE SHE'LL REMEMBER.
HOPE I CAN COUNT ON HER.

WELL... HERE GOES EVERYTHING.
BZZZT
BE RIGHT WITH YOU!
GOOD DAY! MAY I HELP YOU?
MY GOD. SHE'S EVEN MORE BEAUTIFUL.
Uh... HELLO... I'M FROM THE... THE...
WHAT'S THE MATTER? IT LOOKS LIKE YOU'VE SEEN A GHOST.
EXCUSE MY APPEARANCE...! I WAS JUST TRYING THIS DRESS ON TO SEE IF IT FITS. BIG BUSINESS PARTY TONIGHT. YOU KNOW THE KIND. LOTS OF PEOPLE. LOTS OF FOOD. MINIMAL FUN. BUT IF I DON'T GO, THEN THE WHOLE OFFICE GETS UPTIGHT.
GRRRRRRRR
SO WHAT DO YOU THINK OF IT?
YOU'RE GORGEO... I MEAN, IT'S GORGEOUS.
SNIFF SNIFF SNIFF SNIFF

THANKS.
ANYWAY, YOU RANG THE BELL. SO WHAT CAN I DO FOR YOU?
SNIFF SNIFF SNIFF SNIFF
ALL RIGHT NOW. YOU'VE ALREADY GONE OVER THIS A DOZEN TIMES. HIT HER WHERE SHE'S GOT A SOFT SPOT.
Uh...
I'M FROM THE S.P.C.A., AND WE'RE GOING AROUND THE NEIGHBOR-HOOD, CHECKING TO SEE IF THE DOGS HAVE BEEN LICENSED. WE'RE HAVING A SPECIAL THIS WEEK WHERE YOU CAN RENEW THE LICENSE FOR TWELVE DOLLARS, OR REGISTER FOR FIFTEEN DOLLARS IF TH
FIRST TIME. ALSO, WE
KNOW IF
MAMA! MAMA!
WHAT?!
WHY YOU GO, MAMA?
EXCUSE ME.
SWEETY, MOMMY HAD TO GET THE DOOR. A MAN WANTS TO KNOW IF YOUR DOGGIE IS OKAY.
A GIRL!!
THE FILE DIDN'T SAY ANYTHING ABOUT A CHILD.
HOW CAN IT BE...
WE COULDN'T...
I THOUGHT SHE COULDN'T...
I'M SORRY. SHE'S ONLY FIFTEEN MONTHS OLD AND STILL AT THAT CLINGY STAGE. EVERY TIME I LEAVE THE ROOM SHE THINKS I'M ABANDONING HER.
SILLY GIRL. MOMMY WOULDN'T LEAVE YOU.
WE ALWAYS WANTED CHILDREN, BUT SOMETHING WASN'T RIGHT. DOCTORS SAID IT WAS NO USE.
BUT IT WAS ME!
GODDAMMIT, IT WAS ME!!
NOW, WHERE WERE WE AGAIN...?

I COULDN'T GIVE HER WHAT SHE WANTED MOST...
TERRY!
TERRY! QUICK!! GET DOWN HERE NOW! I NEED HELP!!
I'M COMING!
MAMA, MAN FALL DOWN! tee-hee-hee
...WHAT I WANTED...
...WHAT...
UNHH
NYNNHH--!
...I THINK HE'S COMING TO.
WHERE AM I? NO! JESUS, THE FILE WAS TRUE! TERRY DID MARRY WANDA...
HEY, BUDDY, TAKE IT EASY NOW.
YOU OKAY?
DO YOU WANT US TO PHONE A DOCTOR OR SOMETHING?
MAYBE I COULD CALL YOUR FAMILY, OR YOUR WIFE...
I DON'T HAVE A WIFE ANYMORE.
SORRY TO HEAR THAT.
SHE MUST HAVE BEEN REALLY SPECIAL.
YEAH... ME TOO. KILLS ME EVERY TIME I SEE HER.

MORE THAN YOU'LL KNOW.
THING IS, I DON'T KNOW WHY I LOST HER.
IT'S OKAY, BUDDY ...
...WANDA LOST HER HUSBAND FIVE YEARS AGO, TOO. KILLED IN THE LINE OF DUTY.
I'M SORRY.
ALL OF US WERE. HE WAS THE BEST FRIEND I HAD.
arf!
BUT SOMEHOW THROUGH THAT TRAGEDY, WANDA AND I FOUND EACH OTHER. TOOK US A LONG TIME, THOUGH.
LIKE A MAN OUT OF TIME.
PARDON?
NOTHING.
SO YOU SEE, WE'VE ALL BEEN THROUGH LIFE'S WRINGER. AND EVEN THOUGH THE HURT DOESN'T COMPLETELY GO AWAY, THE MEMORIES OF GOOD TIMES ARE YOURS TO HOLD ON TO.
SAY, HOW'RE YOU FEELING, ANYWAY?
WELL, IF IT MAKES YOU FEEL ANY BETTER, OUR DOG LIKES YOU... A LOT! SHE WAS MY LATE HUSBAND'S DOG, AND SHE HASN'T WARMED UP TO ANYONE SINCE HE DIED. AS A MATTER OF FACT, SHE HATES EVERY-ONE... EVEN TERRY. YOU MUST HAVE A KIND SOUL.
NOT ANY MORE.
Oh, DON'T BE SILLY!
YOU STRIKE ME AS A VERY STRONG PERSON. TAKE THAT GIFT AND SHARE IT WITH OTHERS. I'M SURE YOUR EX-WIFE DOESN'T WANT YOU TO STOP BEING YOURSELF.
MY WIFE... I MEAN MY EX-WIFE... DOESN'T KNOW ANYTHING ABOUT ME ANYMORE.
IF I TRY TO TELL HER MY FEELINGS, I THINK I'D RUIN HER LIFE. SHE-- SHE SEEMS REALLY HAPPY NOW. I DON'T KNOW WHAT TO DO ABOUT THAT.
SHE'S RE-MARRIED, HAS A FAMILY NOW. EVEN THOUGH I LOVE HER MORE THAN EVER, I DON'T KNOW IF IT'S RIGHT FOR ME TO INVADE THAT HAPPINESS.
SHE'S AS HAPPY AND BEAUTIFUL AS YOU SEEM TO BE.
WHAT A SWEET THING TO SAY. THANK YOU.
YOU'RE WELCOME. SORRY IF I RUINED YOUR DAY.

As night falls, his pain only mounts.
NO!
WHY??
WHY ARE YOU TORTURING ME?! WHAT KIND OF SADISTIC PLEASURE ARE YOU GETTING FROM THIS??
YOU WANT MY SOUL?
THEN COME GET IT!
JUST TRY AND GET IT!!
I WAS GOING TO GIVE IT TO YOU WILLINGLY! DO YOU HEAR!!
I JUST WANTED MY WIFE! CAN'T YOU UNDERSTAND THAT?? I DON'T WANT THESE POWERS... I NEVER ASKED FOR THEM OR ANYTHING ELSE! I ONLY WANTED ONE THING... TO SEE MY WIFE!
YOU COULD HAVE HAD MY SOUL. YOU COULD HAVE HAD ANYTHING!
BUT YOU'VE LIED AND CHEATED FOR THE LAST TIME, I PROMISE YOU!

YOU'VE STOLEN WANDA FROM ME... TAKEN MY FACE, MY VERY EXISTENCE AWAY. AND YOU EVEN HAD TO PROVE IT WAS ME WHO COULDN'T PRODUCE CHILDREN.
YOU KNEW SHE WANTED A CHILD MORE THAN ANYTHING. NOW SHE HAS THAT CHILD-- HOW CAN I ETHICALLY GET IN THE MIDDLE OF THAT?!
IF YOU'RE GOING TO SCREW ME, I'M GOING TO SCREW YOU!
YOU WANT MY SOUL-- THEN COME GET IT! LET'S SEE WHO'S GOT THE POWER!
8:8:2:1
YOU SCUMBAG.
AS IF ON CUE...
YO!
MR. SPAWN-DUDE! REMEMBER ME?? WE DIDN'T GET A CHANCE TO SHARE OUR COMMON INTERESTS.
UH?
LIKE KILLING!
AND MAIMING!
AND SLAUGHTERING!
AND DESTROYING!

ALL THE THINGS YA DID WHEN YA WERE WITH THE GOVERNMENT? REMEMBER?
YOU AND I COULD HAVE A MILLION LAUGHS TOGETHER
HA HA HAHAHAHAHAHAHAHAHAHAHAHAHAHAHAHA

I DON'T KNOW WHO OR WHAT YOU ARE... BUT I GUARANTEE YOU'VE PICKED THE WRONG TIME!
IF YOU'RE FROM THE SAME HELLPIT I CAME FROM... THEN I'VE GOT A MESSAGE TO SEND BACK TO YOUR BOSS!
GOOD! THEY SAID YOU HAD A LOT OF SPUNK!
SO LET'S SEE HOW MUCH HEART YOU HAVE!
GKH!
Hmmm... THAT WAS SURE SIMPLE!
THE MASTER'LL BE PLEASED.

I LIVE TO SERVE THE MASTER.
OBVIOUSLY, NOT ENOUGH.
DON'T KNOW WHY HE WASTED SO MUCH TIME ON THIS GUY. I HEARD HE HAD SOME SPECIAL POWERS.
I'M TIRED OF THE OTHERS ALWAYS BEING AFRAID OF SOMEONE ELSE.
IT'S THE VIOLATOR THEY SHOULD FEAR MOST.
NOT SOME SOFT FLESH-AND-BONES OF A MERE HUMAN!
VIOLATOR.

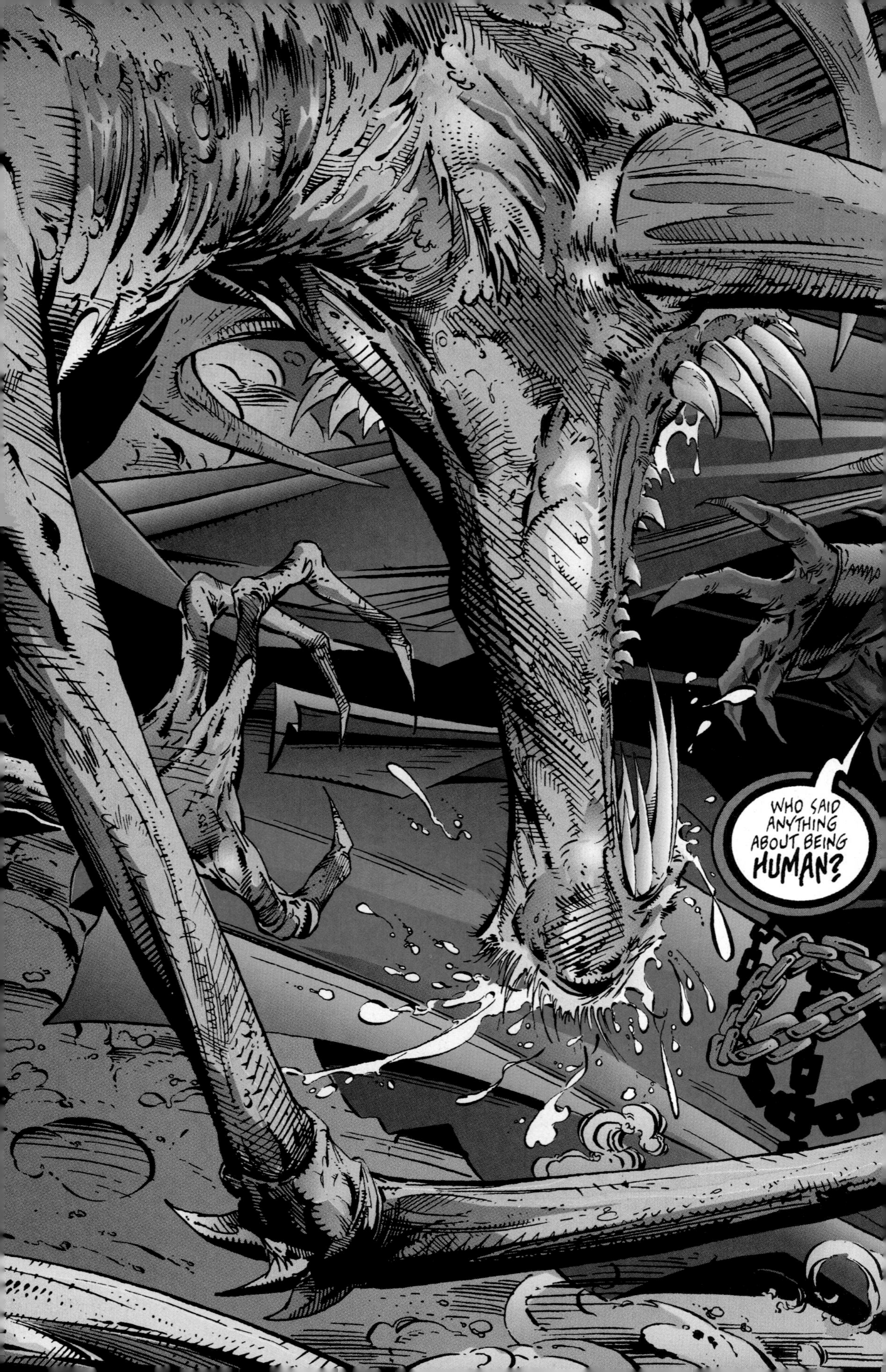
WHO SAID ANYTHING ABOUT BEING HUMAN?

NEXT ISSUE:
ALL HELL BREAKS LOOSE ON EARTH!

4

Q U E S T I O N S

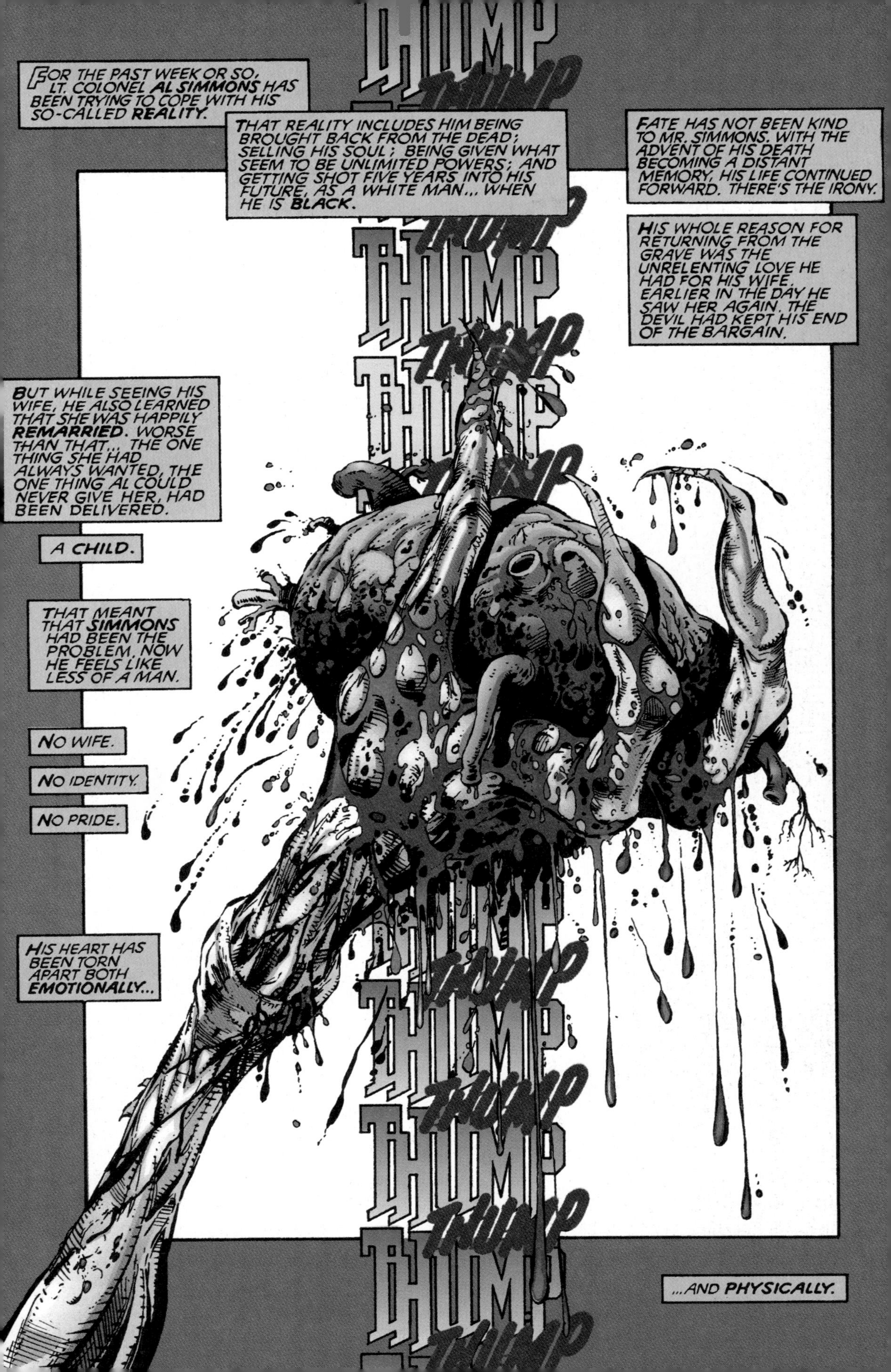
FOR THE PAST WEEK OR SO, LT. COLONEL AL SIMMONS HAS BEEN TRYING TO COPE WITH HIS SO-CALLED REALITY.
THAT REALITY INCLUDES HIM BEING BROUGHT BACK FROM THE DEAD; SELLING HIS SOUL; BEING GIVEN WHAT SEEM TO BE UNLIMITED POWERS; AND GETTING SHOT FIVE YEARS INTO HIS FUTURE, AS A WHITE MAN... WHEN HE IS BLACK.
FATE HAS NOT BEEN KIND TO MR. SIMMONS. WITH THE ADVENT OF HIS DEATH BECOMING A DISTANT MEMORY, HIS LIFE CONTINUED FORWARD. THERE'S THE IRONY.
HIS WHOLE REASON FOR RETURNING FROM THE GRAVE WAS THE UNRELENTING LOVE HE HAD FOR HIS WIFE. EARLIER IN THE DAY HE SAW HER AGAIN. THE DEVIL HAD KEPT HIS END OF THE BARGAIN.
BUT WHILE SEEING HIS WIFE, HE ALSO LEARNED THAT SHE WAS HAPPILY REMARRIED. WORSE THAN THAT... THE ONE THING SHE HAD ALWAYS WANTED, THE ONE THING AL COULD NEVER GIVE HER, HAD BEEN DELIVERED.
A CHILD.
THAT MEANT THAT SIMMONS HAD BEEN THE PROBLEM. NOW HE FEELS LIKE LESS OF A MAN.
NO WIFE.
NO IDENTITY.
NO PRIDE.
HIS HEART HAS BEEN TORN APART BOTH EMOTIONALLY...
...AND PHYSICALLY.
THUMP THUMP THUMP THUMP THUMP THUMP THUMP THUMP THUMP THUMP THUMP

LET'S TRY THAT AGAIN.
BUT THIS TIME, TRY AND DO SOME REAL DAMAGE.

I DON'T BELIEVE IT!
I JUST DON'T BELIEVE IT!
WHO GAVE YOU SUCH POWERS?! SINCE WHEN DID HUMANS BEGIN TO RATE? THEY'VE ALWAYS BEEN TOO FRAGILE FOR THIS! I JUST DON'T BELIEVE IT!
SAY SOMETHING NEW, SCHOOL-BOY.
HE DOESN'T NEED HIS HEART.
THUM THUM THUM THUM
HE DOESN'T NEED A HEART!!
WHAT'S GOING ON?! I THOUGHT I HAD THE POWER. YOU SAID I'D BE STRONGER THAN SPAWN!!

SPAWN CONTINUES HIS SILENCE, FOR WHAT DOES A MAN SAY TO AN OFFSPRING OF THE PIT OF HELL.
THE MASTER AND I ARE GOING TO HAVE WORDS.
MAYBE THE OBVIOUS.
NOT THIS SCUM-SUCKING BAG OF FLESH.
HOW CAN HE SURVIVE WITHOUT HIS BLOODY HEART?! NO ONE WARNED ME. I THOUGHT THIS WAS GOING TO BE AN EASY ASSIGNMENT.
8:6:6:4

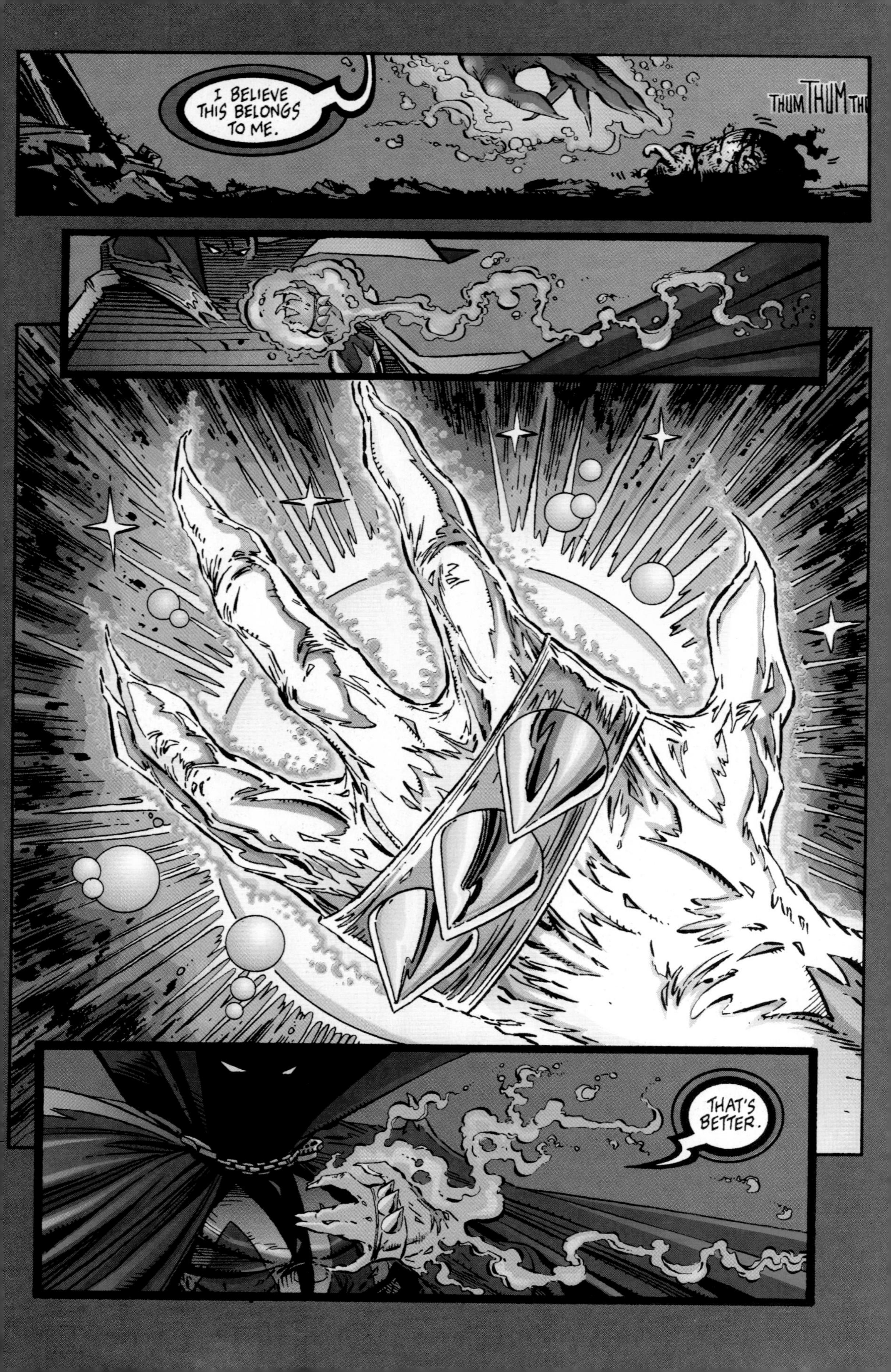
I BELIEVE THIS BELONGS TO ME.
THUM THUM THU
THAT'S BETTER.

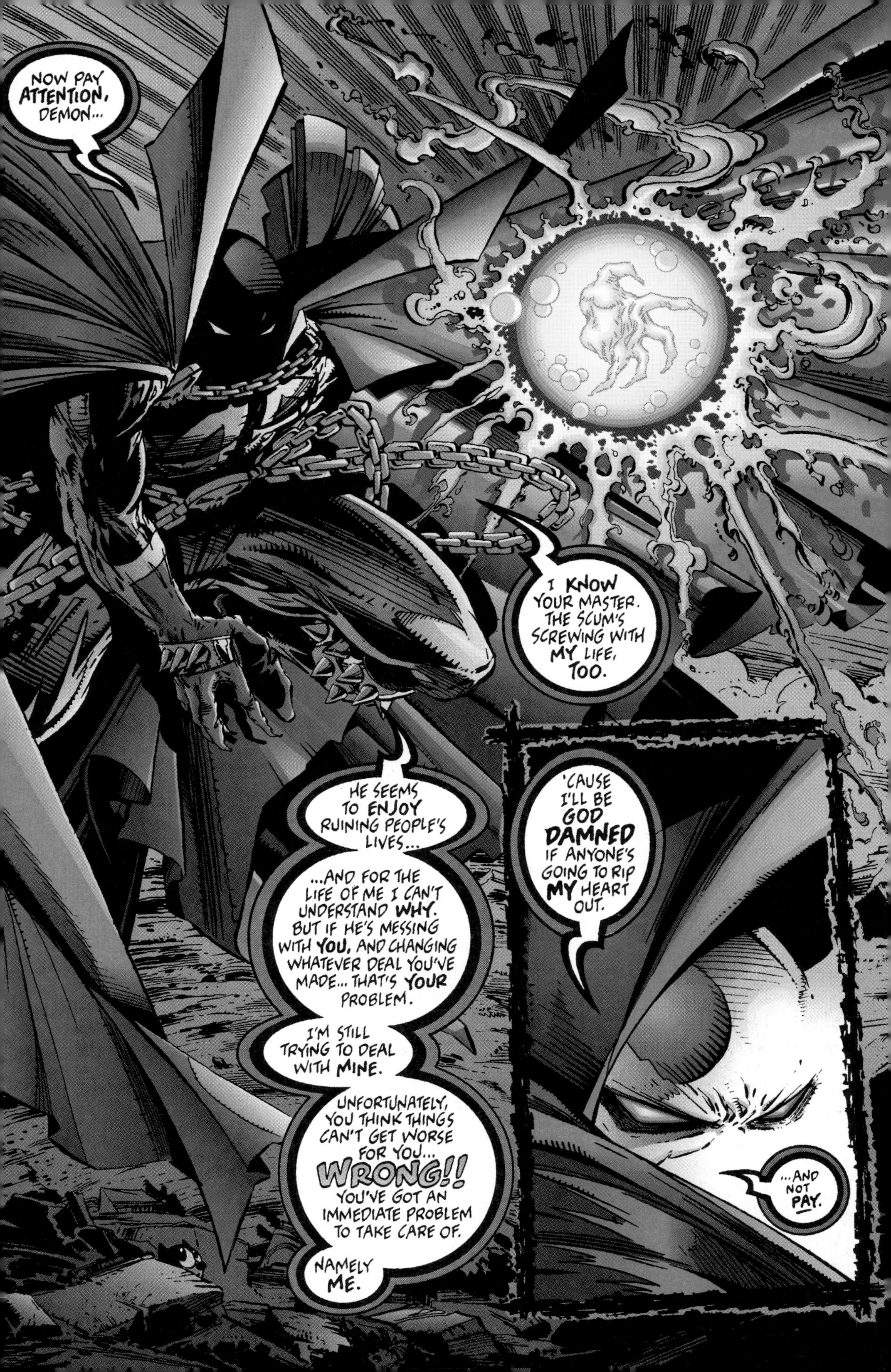
NOW PAY ATTENTION, DEMON...
I KNOW YOUR MASTER. THE SCUM'S SCREWING WITH MY LIFE, TOO.
HE SEEMS TO ENJOY RUINING PEOPLE'S LIVES...
...AND FOR THE LIFE OF ME I CAN'T UNDERSTAND WHY. BUT IF HE'S MESSING WITH YOU, AND CHANGING WHATEVER DEAL YOU'VE MADE... THAT'S YOUR PROBLEM.
I'M STILL TRYING TO DEAL WITH MINE.
UNFORTUNATELY, YOU THINK THINGS CAN'T GET WORSE FOR YOU... WRONG!! YOU'VE GOT AN IMMEDIATE PROBLEM TO TAKE CARE OF.
NAMELY ME.
'CAUSE I'LL BE GOD DAMNED IF ANYONE'S GOING TO RIP MY HEART OUT.
...AND NOT PAY.

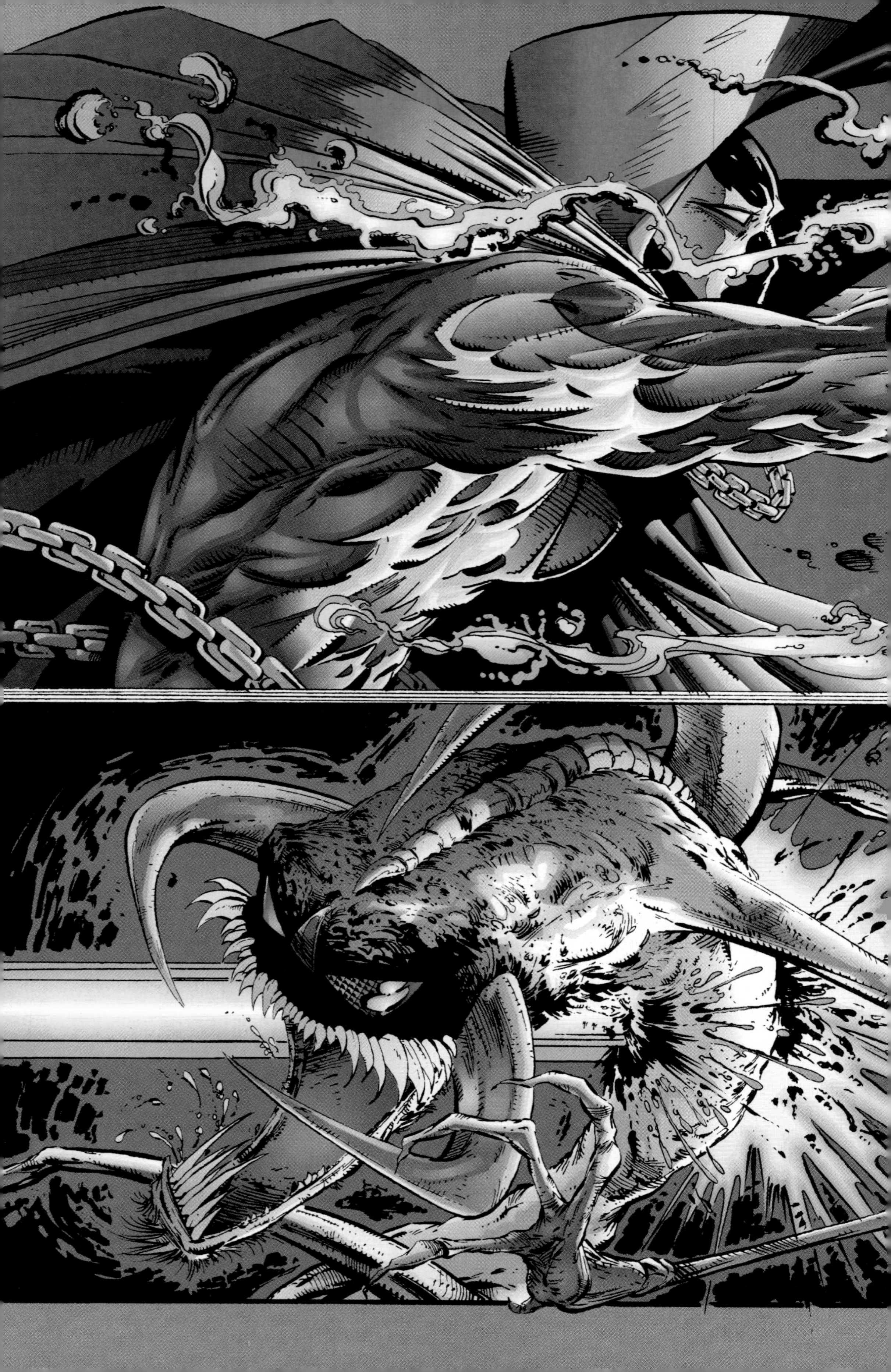

THE FORCE OF SPAWN'S BLAST CARVES A HOLE THROUGH THE VIOLATOR THE SIZE OF A BASKETBALL. FRAGMENTS OF BLUISH, ROTTING CHUNKS VOMIT THEMSELVES IN A HELTER-SKELTER PATTERN. THE BRICK WALLS NOW HAVE A MURAL OF CRIMSON GORE.
AS THE BLOOD RUNS SOFTLY DOWN THE WALL, SPAWN IS TAKEN ABACK FOR A MOMENT. NOT BY THE BLOOD; HE HAS SEEN AND SPILLED FAR TOO MUCH. NOR IS IT THE FORCE OF HIS POWER. IT IS SIMPLY THAT ALL THIS EVEN EXISTS.
HOW... CAN HE REPAIR A DISMEMBERED HEART?
WHY... DOES HE EVEN HAVE SUCH POWERS?
WHEN... IS ALL THE MADNESS GOING TO END?
WHERE... DOES HE GO, NOW THAT HE HAS LOST EVERYTHING?
THE QUESTIONS RICOCHET THROUGH HIS BRAIN... AND THE SCARIEST PART FOR HIM IS THAT HE IS ALMOST GETTING USED TO ALL THE INSANITY AROUND HIM.
KCHKT!

YOU IDIOT!!
YOU'RE NOT THE ONLY ONE THAT CAN SURVIVE AN ORGAN TRANSPLANT! I HAD THE POWER LONG BEFORE YOU STUMBLED UPON IT!
SO WHAT'S YOUR POINT?
MY POINT, DEAR BOY, IS-- IF YOU'RE LOOKING TO PLAY THE OLD EYE FOR AN EYE GAME, YOU'RE A BIGGER FOOL THAN I THOUGHT!
ALLOW ME TO DEMONSTRATE!

LISTEN, I'M NOT HERE TO GAME-PLAY. I'M HERE TO KEEP YOU IN LINE-- MAKE SURE YOU DON'T STRAY.
SO WHAT'S YOUR POINT?
WHY HE'S MAKING SUCH A BIG DEAL OUT OF YOU, I STILL HAVEN'T FIGURED OUT.
BUT UNTIL SUCH TIME, IT'S MY JOB TO SHOW YOU THE ROPES.

JUST HOPE I DON'T STRANGLE YOU WITH THEM!
NOW WOULDN'T THAT BE A PITY.
HAHAHAHAHAHAHA
HA! NICE SHOOTING! YOU'RE SUPPOSED TO HIT THE TARGET, CHUMP.
ZAKT!!
LET ME GIVE YOU A POINTER--
--LIKE THIS!!
CHOMP

TUNCH!
NO! YOU TAKE THIS!
AND THAT!
OW.
ENOUGH!
BIG DEAL! *I* DIDN'T NEED THAT ARM *ANYWAY*.
WHAT ABOUT *YOU*?!
UH!

I gave the both of you far too much credit. It is not necessary to mutilate each other... when neither of you can die...
Like a pair of jealous siblings, you don't realize the two of you are part of the same family.
And like it or not, I'm your DADDY!!
And like a good parent, I can see I need to share some of my insight, so you two boys'll know exactly what's going on.
DESTINY and DAMNATION ...you control neither. So, even though you struggle to make sense of what's happening...
...it doesn't matter because I run both your lives!
GO TO HELL!
BELIEVE ME, SPAWN, HE ALREADY HAS.

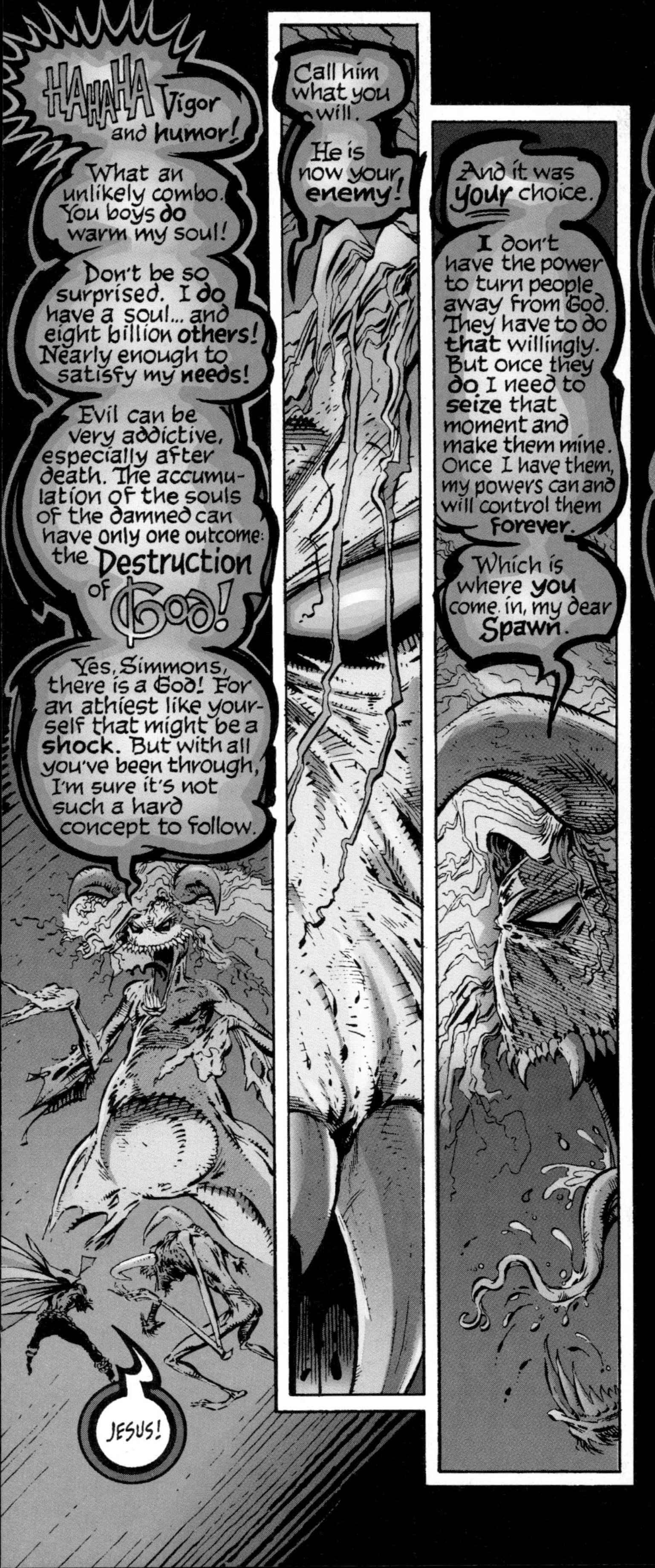
HAHAHA Vigor and humor!
What an unlikely combo. You boys do warm my soul!
Don't be so surprised. I do have a soul... and eight billion others! Nearly enough to satisfy my needs!
Evil can be very addictive, especially after death. The accumulation of the souls of the damned can have only one outcome: the Destruction of God!
Yes, Simmons, there is a God! For an athiest like yourself that might be a shock. But with all you've been through, I'm sure it's not such a hard concept to follow.
JESUS!
Call him what you will.
He is now your enemy!
And it was your choice.
I don't have the power to turn people away from God. They have to do that willingly. But once they do I need to seize that moment and make them mine. Once I have them, my powers can and will control them forever.
Which is where you come in, my dear Spawn.
My army of evil is not quite complete. I need billions more, for the forces of good are naturally quite strong. To ensure my eventual victory, though, I need agents to do my bidding. Your past human life made you the perfect candidate -- young, brash, destructive, ruthless, arrogant... and a hired killer. There's not too many of you around. As one of my agents, you needed powers to set you apart. That was simple. But I'd be a fool to make it limitless.
You're wise enough to have sensed the draining of the power. If not, let me explain. The more you use your energy, the faster you come to a second death. The slower you use it, the less chance you have of stopping evil around you. Either way, I eventually end up owning your soul!
The only choice you have is... how fast you willing to give it?
HAHAHA

hee hee
All this because of some petty little emotion called Love.
You humans are Soooo predictable.
So you see, my spawn from hell-- I can't lose. It's either the depletion of your power--which leads to your death--which leads to losing your soul to the darkness...
...and simultaneously killing the so-called bad guys, which helps build my army that much faster...
OR...
...you do nothing! Just stand by and let the evil and ugliness prosper here on Earth, while your emotions grow colder as you justify to yourself why you needn't do anything to those who prey on the innocent.
Now that you have been fairly warned, let me offer my assistance.
I'll give you the new arm.
No sense you wasting any more power, my child.

HEY!
HOW ABOUT A LITTLE SOMETHING FOR MY EFFORT!
What about me?
LOOK, BOSS, I THINK I DID A HELLUVA JOB HERE!
... KEPT A EYE ON SOME OF THE CRIMINAL ACTIVITY...
...MADE THE COPS THINK THERE'S A LUNATIC ON THE LOOSE...
...EVEN PUT A BIT OF FEAR INTO SPAWN'S HEART.
SPEAKIN' OF WHICH--
--NO ONE WARNED ME OF HIS POWERS WHEN I GOT THIS ASSIGNMENT --!
I MEAN, LOOK AT THIS ARM! NOT A PRETTY SIGHT!
AND THIS HOLE IN MY BELLY--IT'S WORSE THAN A BLOODY ULCER!

Silence!
Gulp
You have failed miserably! It is incompetents like you that make my battle against the God so laborious! I sometimes think that there are traitors among us!
You, Violator, are a sad excuse for Hell!
You, my erratic child, are being grounded!
I made you in my image... told you to keep a watchful eye on Spawn. Prod him if called for.
But you abused those powers, going on a killing spree with no agenda in mind. Now, the New York criminals are being cautious.
Paranoid thieves serve me no purpose!
OOOF
For now, I'm through with the two of you!
HEY! I CAN'T CHANGE FORMS!

Oh GREAT!
JUST GREAT!!
GO AHEAD, KICK ME WHILE I'M DOWN! THIS IS JUST FRIGGIN' PERFECT! I WORK MY BUTT OFF TO TRY AND PLEASE YOU AND WHAT DO I GET FOR MY TROUBLES...
SQUAT, THAT'S WHAT!
THERE'S JUST NO PLEASING SOME PEOPLE!!
BUT THAT'S OKAY. I DON'T MIND BEING SHORT, FAT AND UGLY!
AS A MATTER OF FACT, I KINDA ENJOY IT! SO IF THIS IS THE WORST YOU CAN DO, I'M NOT IMPRESSED!
WHO WANTS TO LIVE IN HELL ANYWAYS. MAKES ME SWEAT LIKE A PIG. AND THIS SPAWN GUY.
PFFFT!!! BIG HAIRY DEAL.
YOU CALL THAT AN AGENT?! DON'T MAKE ME LAUGH.

HMMPF!
THIS SUCKS THE BIG ONE!
WITH THE BATTLE ENDING SO QUICKLY, THE POLICE ARE ONCE AGAIN TOO LATE TO INTERVENE.
THAT SUIT'S SPAWN'S NEEDS, UNTIL HE SORTS OUT THE DIZZYING EVENTS SURROUNDING HIS NEW LIFE, BEING UNKNOWN AND UNDETECTED WILL BE HIS ONLY SOURCE OF COMFORT.
A HAT AND TRENCH-COAT, REMOVED FROM THE BACK OF A CAR, SERVE TO DISGUISE HIM.
HE IS NOW NOTHING MORE THAN A TWO-BIT THIEF, HE THINKS, WANDERING THE LATE-NIGHT STREETS IN SEARCH OF PEACE, OF SOME SEMBLANCE OF SANITY.
POWER.
TO USE OR NOT TO USE; THAT IS THE QUESTION.
IF HE CAN'T DECIDE, MAYBE THE FATES WILL.
ROB, LOOK! IT'S THAT NEW SUPER-HERO!
RIGHT ON, MAN! LET'S CHECK HIM OUT!
COOL! I DIDN'T THINK HE REALLY EXISTED!
I SAW HIM FIRST!
HOW?
H-HOW DID YOU KNOW?

HEY MISTER! WATCH OUT!
Uh?
AWW COOL, MAN! LOOK AT HIM, ERIK!
IT'S THAT DRAGON DUDE FROM CHICAGO!
I TOLD YOU HE WAS RAD!
HE'S BETTER THAN THOSE YOUNGBLOOD! I BET HE COULD TAKE BEDROCK, EASY.
NOT!
BEDROCK'S WAY TOUGH. AIN'T NO ONE CAN TOUCH HIM.
GIMME A BREAK! THE 'ROCK IS A SISSY. HE STILL LIVES AT HOME WITH HIS MOM.
YEAH, WELL, SO DO YOU, HOME-BOY.
BUT I'M NOT A 'BLOOD.
HEROES AIN'T SUPPOSE TO BE NORMAL. THEY'RE SUPPOSE TO BE BETTER.
THAT'S WHY THEY'RE SO FAMOUS.

"BESIDES, WHO WANTS TO BE NORMAL ANYWAY."

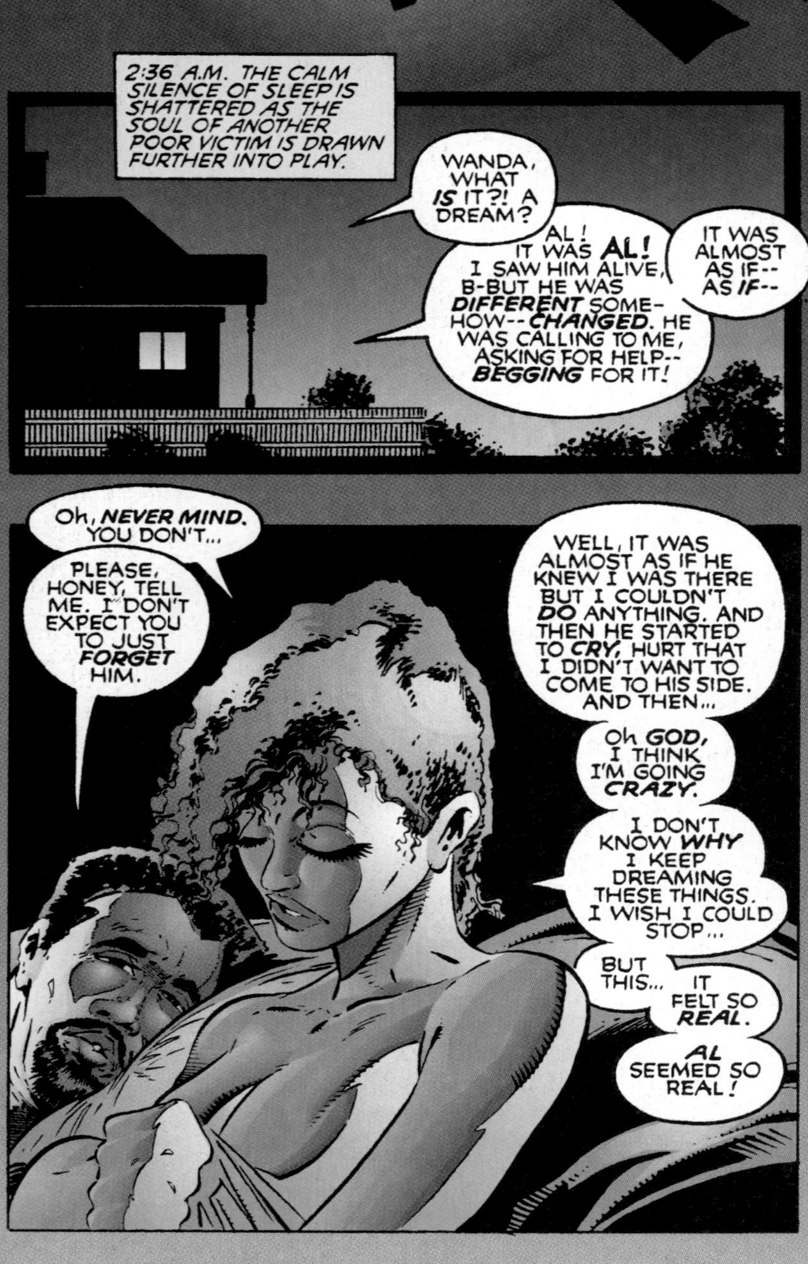

5

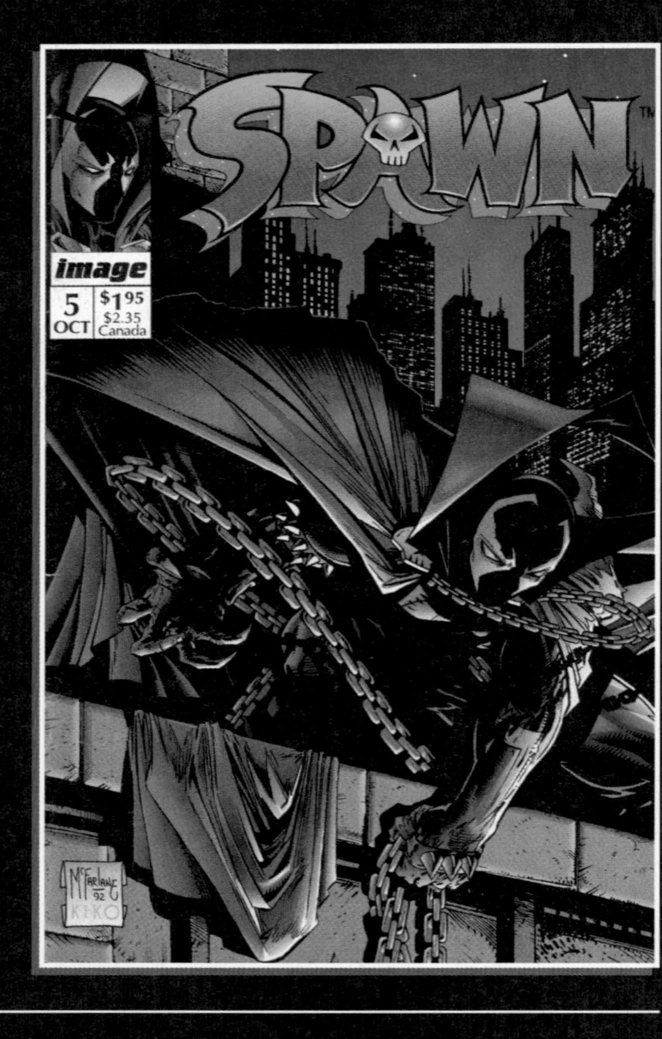

U S T I C E

I'LL BE SORRY TO SEE YOU LEAVING US, BILLY.
EVERYONE HERE AT THE INSTITUTE HAS SO ENJOYED YOUR COMPANY, BUT WE ALL KNEW THIS DAY WOULD COME. WE JUST DIDN'T KNOW THAT IT'D BE SO SOON. YOU MUST BE PLEASED WITH YOUR LAWYER'S EFFORTS. HE SOUNDED QUITE PLEASED THAT THE COURT UPHELD HIS PETITION OF APPEAL, CITING SOME OBSCURE CASE FROM THE 1930's. THOUGH I DON'T PRETEND TO KNOW THAT MUCH ABOUT THE LAW, WE CAN BOTH FEEL VINDICATED. THE SYSTEM DOES INDEED WORK.
IT SADDENS ME TO HAVE TO SAY THAT THIS WILL BE YOUR LAST DAY WITH US. HOW-EVER, WITH THE JUDGE'S REDUCTION OF YOUR TERM ON THAT TECHNICALITY, AND DR. REYNOLDS' TESTIMONY STATING YOUR COMPETENCE, THERE'S NO MORE TO BE SAID. THE SIX AND A HALF YEARS YOU SPENT HERE AT THE INSTITUTE WENT BY FAR TOO QUICKLY.
TOMORROW, YOU BEGIN A NEW LIFE. AN OFFICER WILL PICK YOU UP AND TAKE YOU TO THE COURT HOUSE, TO SIGN THE FINAL PAPERS.
UNFORTUNATELY, I MUST WARN YOU, BILLY. THERE ARE FORCES OUTSIDE THAT DON'T WISH YOU ANY KIND OF HAPPINESS. THEY MIGHT EVEN TRY AND BRING BACK SOME OF YOUR BAD DREAMS. YOU WON'T ALLOW THAT, WILL YOU? WE BOTH KNOW THAT YOU'RE NOT THE SAME PERSON YOU USED TO BE.
YOU ARE CURED, BILLY KINCAID.
OTHERS MAY NOT WANT TO BELIEVE THAT, BUT THE STAFF AND I HAVE ALWAYS BEEN IMPRESSED WITH YOUR MODEL BEHAVIOR. ALWAYS THE GENTLEMAN.
YES, YOUR TIME HERE HAS BEEN SO REWARDING.
SO UNEVENTFUL.
SO THERAPUTIC.
SO CONVINCING.
Uh, SIR, PLEASE KEEP YOUR VOICE DOWN.

BEFORE YOU GO, THE JUDGE WANTED ME TO REMIND YOU THAT YOU'RE NOT TO HAVE ANY CONTACT WITH THE DEAD GIRL'S PARENTS.
I HAVE ASSURED THEM TO PUT THEIR WORRIES ASIDE... AND THAT THEY WILL HAVE YOUR FULL CO-OPERATION.
DO YOU UNDERSTAND, BILLY?
BILLY ?!
YES... WELL... LOOKS LIKE YOU'RE OVERWHELMED BY THE WHOLE PROCEDURE. THAT'S PERFECTLY UNDER-STANDABLE.
I MUST ADMIT THIS WAS ALL RATHER SUDDEN FOR ME, TOO.
BUT WE ARE ALL SATISFIED BY THE END RESULT.
SO, I GUESS THAT JUST ABOUT WRAPS THINGS UP. DR. REYNOLDS AND I WILL HAVE OUR REPORTS AVAILABLE IN THE MORNING.
I'LL SEE YOU TOMORROW AT EIGHT O'CLOCK SHARP.
Uh...
...IS THERE ANYTHING YOU'D LIKE TO SAY, BILLY?
I DON'T CARE HOW SATISFIED EVERYONE IS, THAT MAN'S A FRIGGIN' SICKO! SLAUGHTERED THE KID SO BAD IT TOOK SIX EXPERTS TO FINALLY IDENTIFY THE GIRL.
WE NAILED HIS ASS FOR JUST THE ONE MURDER. I'M NOT HAPPY, TWITCH, BUT IT'S THE ONLY TIME WE CAUGHT 'IM FLAT.
JUST LOOK AT HIS EYES...

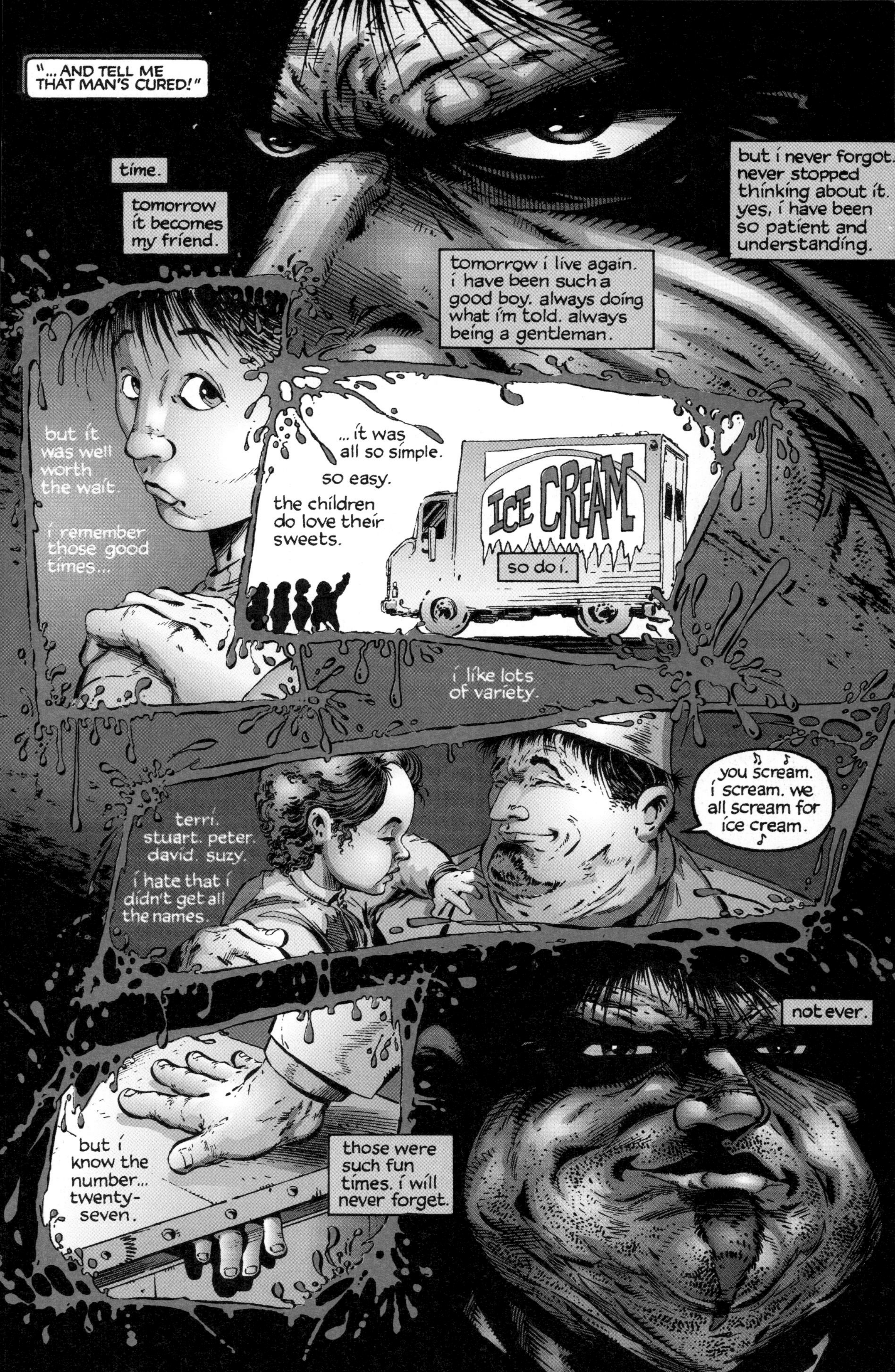
"...AND TELL ME THAT MAN'S CURED!"
time.
tomorrow it becomes my friend.
but i never forgot. never stopped thinking about it. yes, i have been so patient and understanding.
tomorrow i live again. i have been such a good boy. always doing what i'm told. always being a gentleman.
but it was well worth the wait.
i remember those good times...
...it was all so simple.
so easy.
the children do love their sweets.
ICE CREAM
so do i.
i like lots of variety.
terri. stuart. peter. david. suzy.
i hate that i didn't get all the names.
you scream. i scream. we all scream for ice cream.
not ever.
but i know the number... twenty-seven.
those were such fun times. i will never forget.

Ah, BILLY. NICE TO SEE YOU SMILING. GLAD YOU'RE SO HAPPY ABOUT YOUR IMPENDING FREEDOM.
I'LL SAY GOOD-BYE TO THE STAFF FOR YOU.
you scream. i scream. we all scream for ice cream.
Huh?
WHAT THE HELL WAS THAT?!!
JUST A LITTLE RHYME BILLY TAUGHT EVERYONE WHILE HE WAS HERE. RATHER CUTE, DON'T YOU THINK?
I DON'T FIND ANYTHING CUTE ABOUT THAT WALKING BUTCHER!
I ASSURE YOU, DETECTIVE...
...THE PSYCHIATRISTS HAVE ALL AGREED...
SCREW YOUR PSYCHIA-TRISTS!!
THAT MAN'S A FREAK! AND IF YOU THINK THAT SITTING BEHIND LOCKED DOORS FOR SIX YEARS IS A CURE, THEN YOU GUYS ARE EVEN BIGGER IDIOTS THAN I THOUGHT!
WHAT HE DID TO LITTLE AMANDA JENNINGS WASN'T AN ISOLATED EVENT.
OVER TWENTY KIDS DISAPPEARED FROM HIS TOWN.
I DIDN'T SEE THAT IN YOUR REPORT!
YOU DON'T THINK HE'S CURED... YOU'RE JUST TOO DAMNED AFRAID TO BE AROUND HIM ANY MORE!
I'M SORRY YOU FEEL THAT WAY, DETECTIVE-- BUT YOU CAN PUNISH HIM ONLY WHEN HE'S BEEN CONVICTED. YOU ARE FAMILIAR WITH THE CONCEPT OF LAW, YES?
NOW, IF YOU'LL BOTH EXCUSE ME, I HAVE PATIENTS WAITING...
OH, DO ME A SMALL FAVOR, BILLY. I'D LIKE TO SEE YOU CLEAN-SHAVEN TOMORROW. THAT GROWTH IS SO UNFLATTERING.

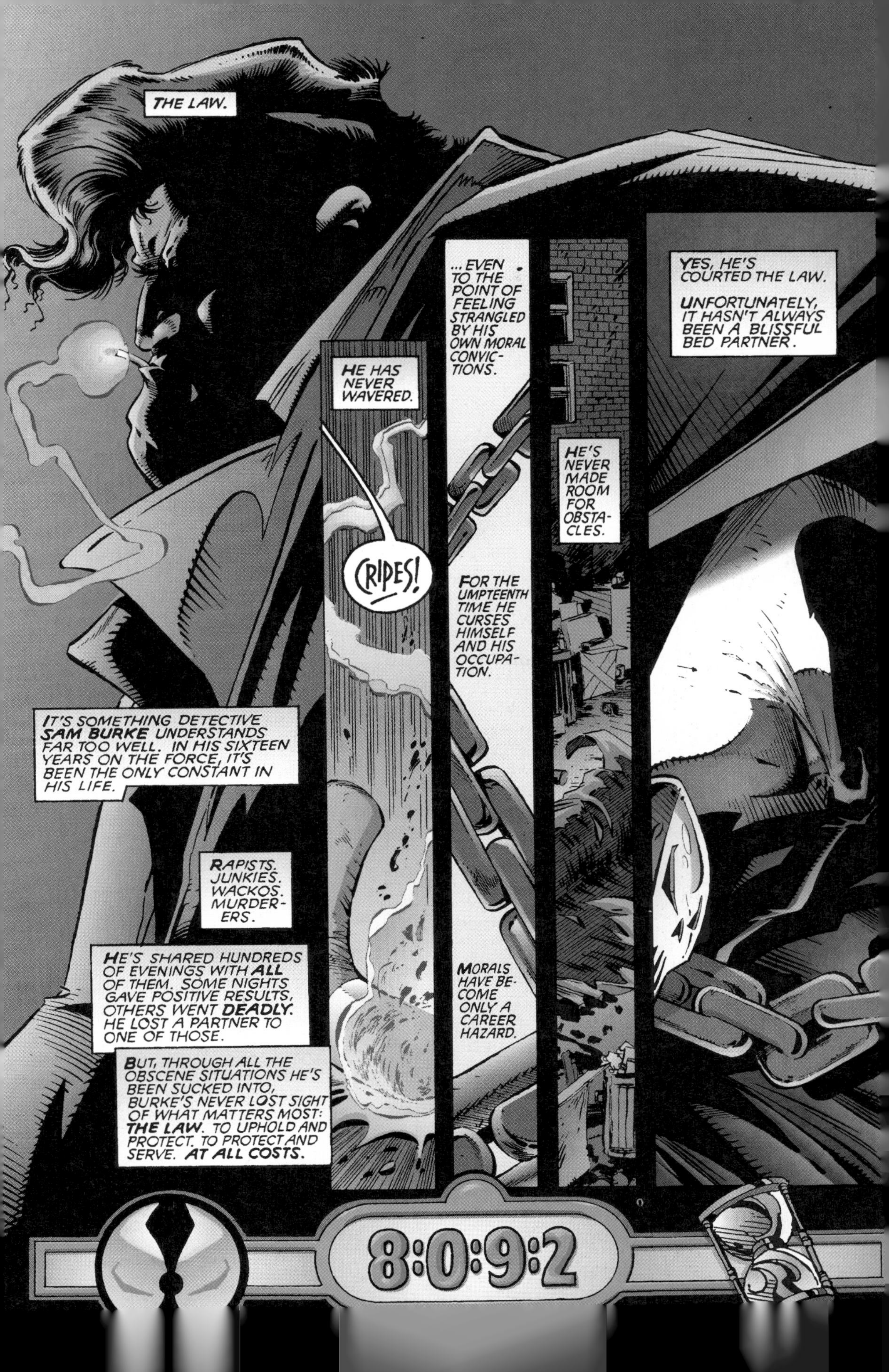
THE LAW.
IT'S SOMETHING DETECTIVE SAM BURKE UNDERSTANDS FAR TOO WELL. IN HIS SIXTEEN YEARS ON THE FORCE, IT'S BEEN THE ONLY CONSTANT IN HIS LIFE.
RAPISTS. JUNKIES. WACKOS. MURDERERS.
HE'S SHARED HUNDREDS OF EVENINGS WITH ALL OF THEM. SOME NIGHTS GAVE POSITIVE RESULTS, OTHERS WENT DEADLY. HE LOST A PARTNER TO ONE OF THOSE.
BUT, THROUGH ALL THE OBSCENE SITUATIONS HE'S BEEN SUCKED INTO, BURKE'S NEVER LOST SIGHT OF WHAT MATTERS MOST: THE LAW. TO UPHOLD AND PROTECT. TO PROTECT AND SERVE. AT ALL COSTS.
HE HAS NEVER WAVERED.
CRIPES!
...EVEN TO THE POINT OF FEELING STRANGLED BY HIS OWN MORAL CONVICTIONS.
FOR THE UMPTEENTH TIME HE CURSES HIMSELF AND HIS OCCUPATION.
MORALS HAVE BECOME ONLY A CAREER HAZARD.
HE'S NEVER MADE ROOM FOR OBSTACLES.
YES, HE'S COURTED THE LAW.
UNFORTUNATELY, IT HASN'T ALWAYS BEEN A BLISSFUL BED PARTNER.
8:0:9:2

AND IN NEW YORK, JEFF PITMAN, ATTORNEY FOR CONVICTED CHILD KILLER BILL KINCAID, WAS FINALLY SUCCESSFUL IN HIS ATTEMPTS TO MITIGATE KINCAID'S SENTENCE. THE ORIGINAL TWENTY-TWO YEAR TERM WAS REDUCED TO TEN YEARS. THAT, COMBINED WITH TIME OFF FOR GOOD BEHAVIOR AND TIME SERVED, MAKE BILL KINCAID A FREE MAN TOMORROW.

IT WAS NEARLY EIGHT YEARS AGO THAT A JOGGER IN NEW YORK CITY FOUND AMANDA JENNINGS' BODY UNDER THE GEORGE WASHINGTON BRIDGE. THE EIGHT YEAR OLD GIRL WAS THE DAUGHTER OF FORMER SENATOR PAUL JENNINGS.

JENNINGS' HIGH-PROFILE EXTRA-MARITAL AFFAIR TARNISHED HIS RE-ELECTION BID A YEAR EARLIER. SOME SOURCES FELT THAT HIS MORE TRADITIONALLY-ORIENTED FORMER SUPPORTERS IN LAW ENFORCEMENT GAVE THE MATTER LESS ATTENTION THAN IT WARRANTED.

BELIEVE ME, IT WAS ***ONE*** TORRID LOVE AFFAIR. SENATOR JENNINGS AND ***MARLA FLEET*** WERE THE TALK OF THE TOWN DURING HIS RE-ELECTION CAMPAIGN. VOTERS DIDN'T WANT TO HEAR ABOUT BUDGETS OR TAXES. THEY WERE MORE INTERESTED IN THE ***STEAMY DETAILS*** OF HOW SENATOR JENNINGS SWEPT THE FORMER ***MISS UNIVERSE*** OFF HER FEET. MIX IN AN ***EXTREMELY*** VENGEFUL WIFE AND THE MEDIA HAD ITSELF A FEAST FOR ***MONTHS***.

THE STORY THAT MADE THE ROUNDS AT THE TIME-- THAT THE ***FORMER*** SENATOR'S ***RAGING*** HORMONES LED TO LESS OF AN INVESTIGATION OF HIS DAUGHTER'S DEATH-- IS TRULY DISTURBING. THESE WAGS IMPLY THAT WHILE JENNINGS WASN'T MUCH LOVED WHILE ***IN*** OFFICE, THE TAWDRY TRUTH BEHIND HIS DOWNFALL MAY HAVE LED TO INADEQUATE INFORMATION REACHING THE INTERESTED PARTIES.

AS A RESULT, BILLY KINCAID RECEIVED A TWENTY-TWO YEAR STRETCH INSTEAD OF THE LIFE SENTENCE WITHOUT PAROLE THAT THE PUBLIC SO DEARLY WANTED.

SURPRISE! SURPRISE!

KIDDIE KILLER KINCAID, FREE TO WALK THE STREETS OF THE BIG APPLE! WE'VE BEEN FAVORED WITH YET ***ANOTHER*** AWE-INSPIRING RULING AS THE COURTS ALLOW THIS CHILD-MURDERER HIS FREEDOM. AFTER PESTERING THE JUDICIAL SYSTEM WITH HIS ***WHINING*** AND ***APPEALS*** THESE PAST FIVE YEARS, KINCAID'S LAWYER FINALLY GOT WHAT HE WANTED-- ANOTHER ***PSYCHO*** READY TO ROAM CENTRAL PARK. OH JOY! OH RAPTURE! I FEEL SAFER ALREADY.

C'MON, FOLKS! I HATE REPEATING MYSELF BUT I'M NOT SURE ANYONE'S ***LISTENING.*** LOOKIT, THE WAY ***I*** SEE IT, KINCAID'S LAWYER DID US ***ALL*** A FAVOR. FOR THE PAST SIX YEARS, BILLY'S BEEN ***HIDDEN*** FROM US, BUT NOW WE HAVE AN OPEN ***OPPORTUNITY.*** I GUARANTEE THAT HE WAS A LOT ***SAFER*** ON THE ***INSIDE***.

MY ONLY WISH IS THAT SOMEONE BREAKS HIS BACK. ***HELLO!*** ARE YOU LISTENING, ***MR. SHADOWHAWK?***

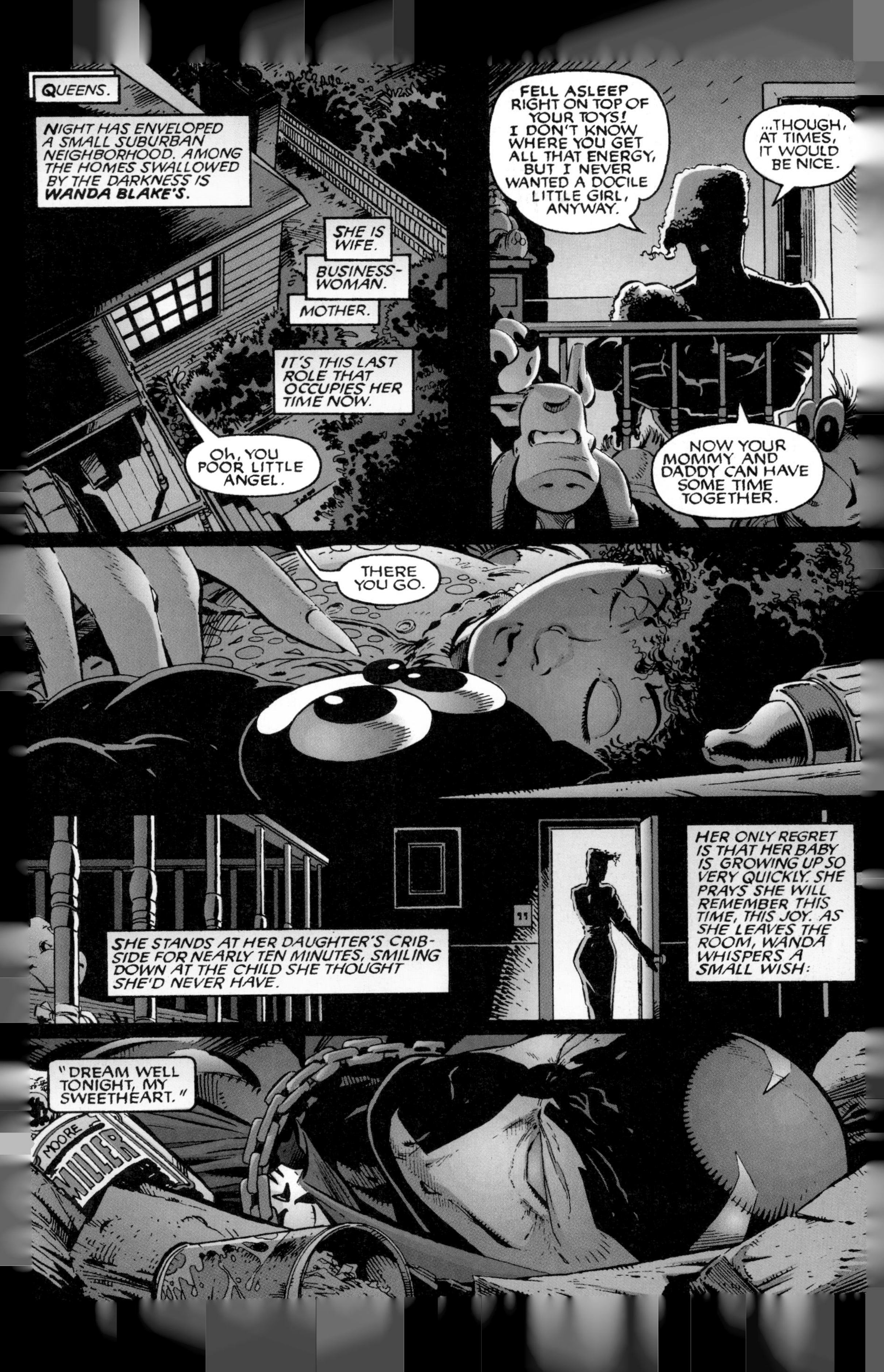
QUEENS.
NIGHT HAS ENVELOPED A SMALL SUBURBAN NEIGHBORHOOD. AMONG THE HOMES SWALLOWED BY THE DARKNESS IS WANDA BLAKE'S.
SHE IS WIFE.
BUSINESS-WOMAN.
MOTHER.
IT'S THIS LAST ROLE THAT OCCUPIES HER TIME NOW.
Oh, YOU POOR LITTLE ANGEL.
FELL ASLEEP RIGHT ON TOP OF YOUR TOYS! I DON'T KNOW WHERE YOU GET ALL THAT ENERGY, BUT I NEVER WANTED A DOCILE LITTLE GIRL, ANYWAY.
...THOUGH, AT TIMES, IT WOULD BE NICE.
NOW YOUR MOMMY AND DADDY CAN HAVE SOME TIME TOGETHER.
THERE YOU GO.
SHE STANDS AT HER DAUGHTER'S CRIB-SIDE FOR NEARLY TEN MINUTES, SMILING DOWN AT THE CHILD SHE THOUGHT SHE'D NEVER HAVE.
HER ONLY REGRET IS THAT HER BABY IS GROWING UP SO VERY QUICKLY. SHE PRAYS SHE WILL REMEMBER THIS TIME, THIS JOY. AS SHE LEAVES THE ROOM, WANDA WHISPERS A SMALL WISH:
"DREAM WELL TONIGHT, MY SWEETHEART."
MOORE
MILLER

I DON'T KNOW WHY MY BLOOD BOILS EVERY TIME I THINK OF KINCAID. YOU'D FIGURE I'D BE OVER THIS GUY AFTER SIX YEARS.
DETECTIVE BURKE
201
BUT I'VE GOTTA TELL YOU, TWITCH, HE DID THINGS TO THE JENNINGS GIRL THAT WERE BEYOND BELIEF... HER TEETH PULLED OUT BY PLIERS, MAGGOTS DROPPED INTO HER CUTS, AND...
...AND...
Ah, HELL. YOU'VE SEEN THE REPORT.
YES, SIR.
AS YOU KNOW, I HAVE QUITE A LARGE FAMILY.
Y' OUGHT TO COME BY THE HOUSE.
MY SEVEN CHILDREN ARE VERY PRECIOUS TO ME. WHAT KINCAID DID IS UNFORTUNATE. HOWEVER, HIS CONSTITUTIONAL RIGHTS MUST BE UPHELD.
YEAH! YEAH!
I KNOW. I GET REMINDED EVERY TIME I WALK THROUGH THAT DOOR!
WELL, THEN, MAY I SUGGEST, SIR, THAT WE SIMPLY KEEP A VERY CLOSE EYE ON MR. KINCAID, FOLLOWING HIS RELEASE.
YOU KNOW THAT CHIEF BANKS TOOK A CHUNK OUT OF ME FOR THAT TRIP WE TOOK TO THE WINDGATE INSTITUTION THIS AFTERNOON. DOESN'T WANT ME TAKING OUT "SOME PERSONAL VENDETTA" ON THE TAXPAYER'S NICKEL. CAN YOU BELIEVE THAT!!
A FRIGGIN' SENATOR'S KID GETS SLICED INTO QUARTER-INCH CUBES AND WE CAN'T BE BOTHERED ?!!
WHAT'S A PSYCHO GOTTA DO TO GET OUR ATTENTION ANYWAYS ?
LIKE OUR FRIENDS IN THE LEGAL PROFESSION, I PRIDE MYSELF ON FINDING LOOPHOLES, SIR...
...SO I WAS WONDERING IF YOU'RE FREE AFTER WORK FOR THE NEXT TWO WEEKS OR SO, IF YOU'D LIKE TO JOIN ME IN MY NEW HOBBY...
MIDNIGHT STAKEOUTS!
JUST A COUPLE OF PALS DOING A LITTLE MALE-BONDING IN THE SAME NEIGHBORHOOD, BY COINCIDENCE, AS A CERTAIN KID KILLER.
WHAT DO YOU SAY, PAL?
TWITCH, I LIKE YOUR STYLE.
THANKS, SIR.

TWO DAYS LATER...
you scream.
i scream.
we both screamed
for ice cream.
MISTER! MISTER!
ALTHOUGH SHE WON'T NOTICE, TODAY LITTLE SHERLEE JOHNSON WILL BE GETTING SERVED BY A NEW VENDOR....
hi! that sure is a pretty dress you have...
...so pretty that you get a free popsicle. go inside the truck and get your favorite.
REALLY?
sure, sure.
take all you want. get the best flavor.
GEE! THANKS!

one.
two.
three.
four.
five.
six.
seven.
eight.
and nine!
i just love doing finger-painting!
it's sooo fun.
GLUE

but what's a party without a few friends?
maybe tomorrow we can go find us a little male friend.
might liven up the place.
what do ya say?
MAMA!
MAMA! MAMA!
WHAT! WHAT! WHAT! SWEETIE.
BOY, ARE YOU FULL OF BEANS TODAY. HOPE YOU WERE A GOOD GIRL FOR MRS. PALMER.
HOW WAS SHE TODAY, PAM?
SHE'S ALWAYS GOOD, WANDA.
IF I HAD MORE KIDS LIKE HER AT THIS DAYCARE IT'D SURE MAKE MY LIFE A WHOLE LOT SIMPLER.
YOU'RE GOING TO HAVE TO GIVE ME THE RECIPE TO THOSE HAPPY PILLS YOU GIVE HER.
I MISS YOU, MAMA.
YEAH, WE'RE VERY LUCKY. SHE'S BEEN SUCH A GOOD BABY FOR US. ALTHOUGH TO TELL YOU THE TRUTH, WHEN I FOUND OUT I WAS PREGNANT, I'D HAVE TAKEN ANYTHING THAT CAME MY WAY.
WELL, YOU'VE BOTH BEEN GREAT PARENTS SO FAR. TERRY HAS BEEN JUST AN AMAZING DAD.

"DAD."
THE NAME TEARS THROUGH SPAWN'S HEART LIKE A BULLET. IT'S A NAME THAT HE SO DESPERATELY WANTED TO BE CALLED DURING HIS LIFE WITH WANDA.
NOW HE KNOWS THAT WILL NEVER HAPPEN. WHAT MAKES IT WORSE IS THAT HE CAN'T BLAME THE DEVIL FOR THIS ONE.
EVEN BEFORE HIS DEATH, HE'D BEEN CURSED.
SO, HE CONTINUES TO WATCH FROM A DISTANCE AS THE WOMAN HE LOVES-- HIS WIFE-- PLAYS GLEEFULLY WITH THE CHILD CONCEIVED BY HER CURRENT HUSBAND.
I'M GONNA GET'CHA!
Hee... MAMA... DON'T... Hee--MAMA
AFTER A TIME, HE RETREATS...
HAHAHAHAHAHAHAHAHAHAHAHAHAHA
OH LOUIE! YOU SLAY ME!
AND THAT AIN'T THE FUNNY PART...
...TO A PLACE WHERE HE SPENDS HIS NIGHTS, LOST AMONG LOST SOULS.
...WHEN JOHNNY CALLED ME THE "DESTRUCTOR OF SOCIETY," I ABOUT PEE'D MYSELF.
TONIGHT, THESE OUTCASTS OF THE WORLD HAVE BANDED TOGETHER FOR COMPANIONSHIP, A FEW LAUGHS, A FEW SLIGHTLY EXAGGERATED STORIES.
SO I SAYS TO HIM-- "JOHNNY, OLD SON, HOW CAN I BRING DOWN SOCIETY WHEN I CAN'T EVEN SPEAK JAPANESE OR FRENCH?!"
WHEN ALL THE CHEAP WINE HAS VANISHED AND THE FIRE HAS STARTED TO DIE OUT...
...THESE TEMPORARY FRIENDS HUDDLE TOGETHER FOR A FEW HOURS' REST...
...TRYING TO ESCAPE THE GHOSTS THAT HAUNT THEM. FOR A SHORT TIME SLEEP IS ALMOST A CURE.

ALMOST.
WHEE-O WHEE-O WHEE-O WHEE-O
CRIPES! DAMN BUMS BLOCKING ANOTHER ALLEY. ALWAYS SLOWING US DOWN!
K-KASSH
KANG
TUNCH!
GOT A ROBBERY IN PROGRESS AND I CAN HARDLY SEE WHERE I'M GOING!
SOMEONE OUGHTTA RUN THESE LOSERS OUTTA TOWN!
JEEZ!
C'MON, GEORGE, SLOW IT DOWN! A BIT! YOU'RE DRIVING LIKE A LUNATIC!
SPKASH
SPATCK
KNCH-KKT

JOEY?
HEY, JOEY, C'MON MAN.
STOP KIDDIN'!
JOEY!
GOD.
HOLY--! LOOK WHAT THEY'VE DONE TO HIM! THOSE DAMN COPS DIDN'T EVEN SLOW DOWN.
PLOWED RIGHT THROUGH WHERE HE WAS LYING.
I TOLD HIM NOT TO SLEEP UNDER THEM BOXES.
BUT YOU KNOW HOW JOEY WAS, YOU COULDN'T TELL HIM NOTHIN'!
THIS AIN'T GOT NOTHING TO DO WITH JOEY!
THEM BLOODY COPS DON'T GIVE A CRAP ABOUT US! WE AIN'T EVEN WORTH BRAKING FOR BEFORE THEY RUN US DOWN!
SUPPOSED T' BE PROTECTING THE LAW--
HA!
THEY BREAK THE LAW EVERY TIME NO ONE'S LOOKIN'--
AND THEY AIN'T PROTECTING ME FROM SQUAT!
THEM BUGGERS CALL IT JUSTICE-- WELL, LOOK AT THIS!
BU H REEL
"BILLY" KINCAID FREED; MURDER CHARGE REDUCED
RUNNING DOWN AN INNOCENT MAN TRYING TO FIND WARM FROM THE WIND... AND LETTING THIS KINCAID FELLOW GO, AFTER KILLING BABIES!
THAT AIN'T JUSTICE, THAT'S NUTS!
KINCAID! FREE!
ALREADY... IT CAN'T... damn! KEEP FORGETTING FIVE YEARS HAVE GONE BY.
GOOD! I WON'T LOSE OUT A SECOND TIME.

I REMEMBER JENNINGS' HIRING ME TO KILL KINCAID. SAID HE COULDN'T STAND TO SEE HIS EX-WIFE SUFFER.
EVEN THOUGH HE WASN'T WITH THE GOVERNMENT ANYMORE, HE KNEW WHAT I WAS ALL ABOUT.
A MILLION BUCKS FOR THE HIT. NO ONE WAS TO KNOW ABOUT IT-- NOTHING I COULDN'T HANDLE.
FIGURED I COULD RETIRE A BIT SOONER, FROM ALL THE GARBAGE I WAS DEALING WITH AT HEADQUARTERS.
WANDA AND I WOULD HAVE BEEN SET FOR LIFE. UNFORTUNATELY, JENNINGS STILL HAD PLENTY OF ENEMIES. INFORMATION
BY THE TIME I LOCATED KINCAID, THE COPS HAD BEAT ME TO HIM.
THE SICK PART WAS THAT KINCAID WAS SMILING MORE BROADLY THAN THE COPS.
I DIDN'T UNDERSTAND THAT. WHY WOULD HE BE LAUGHING?
EVEN DURING HIS TRIAL HE HAD THAT SICKLY SMIRK ON HIS FACE. WHEN THE JUDGE PUT HIM AWAY, HE LAUGHED AGAIN. WHY?
I FOUND OUT TWO WEEKS LATER.
IN AN ABANDONED SHACK IN NORTH-WEST VIRGINIA WERE... REMAINS. MULTIPLE BODIES. ALL KIDS. ALL SO MUTILATED WE NEVER DID GET A FINAL BODY COUNT.
THAT SHACK BELONGED TO BILLY KINCAID.

WE HAD ENOUGH TO GET HIM TEN LIFETIME TERMS. BUT SUDDENLY THINGS STARTED DIS-APPEARING. FILES. PHOTOS. CONTAINERS.
FINALLY, THE SHACK WHERE WE FOUND THE EVIDENCE BLEW UP. NOT BURNED DOWN, BUT BLEW UP! NOTHING WAS LEFT.
OUR PROOF OF UNTOLD DEATHS WAS GONE.
BUT THE REAL KICKER CAME LATER. MY BOSS, JASON WYNN, TOLD EVERY-ONE INVOLVED TO JUST DROP THE CASE --AND THEY DID. NO QUESTIONS ASKED.
IT WAS ONLY ONE OF THE THOUSAND REASONS WHY WYNN AND I FOUGHT. SO I PUT IT ON THE BACK BURNER. BIDING MY TIME.
MEANWHILE, I HA NOTHING TO SHOW FOR MY EFFORT
JENNINGS HAD SOME VERY POWERFUL ENEMIES... PEOPLE WHO WOULD HIRE A PSYCHO TO KILL A LITTLE GIRL.
I COULD HAVE USED THE CASH-- MAN, THE THINGS I WANTED TO GIVE WANDA... INSTEAD, I CAVED IN... TURNED THE OTHER WAY.
York Times
RESURRECTED
SOMETHING TO STOP THIS INSANITY.
"BILLY" KINCAID FREED; MURDER CHARGE REDUCED
SEVEN YEAR OLD GIRL MISSING
I ALWAYS SAID I'D FIND SOME ANSWERS. NOW'S THE RIGHT TIME. I NEED A DISTRACTION FROM THIS CRAZINESS I'VE BEEN GOING THROUGH.
SEVEN YEAR OLD GIRL MISSING
parents said she was playing in the they are in reward

SO IT BEGINS.
A NEW PURPOSE HAS BEEN GIVEN TO THE HELTER-SKELTER LIFE OF **THE SPAWN**. THIS FORMER MERCENARY HAS A BLEMISH ON HIS RECORD. HE MEANS TO CLEAN THAT UP.
IS IT A DECISION BORN OF LOGIC? A DEAD MAN'S AFFAIRS BEING PUT IN ORDER?
NO.
THIS IS THE RATIONALE OF A **HIRED GUN** WHO'S **BACK FROM THE GRAVE**.
WITH ALL THAT'S WRONG IN HIS "LIFE THE ONLY WAY TO TAKE HIS MIND OFF THINGS IS WITH WORK. FOR AN EX-**GOVERNMENT ASSASSIN,** THAT MEANS DANGER. FEAR. DEATH.
HIS ADRENALINE IS PUMPING ALREADY.

KIDS TO WALK UP AND DOWN THE BLOCK AS A LITTLE BAIT FOR OUR GOOD FRIEND MR. KINCAID.
THE MISSUS WOULD KILL ME IF SHE KNEW.
YES, SIR.
IT'S TOO BAD IT TOOK US A COUPLE NIGHTS TO TRACK KINCAID DOWN. THE BUGGER'S PROBABLY BEEN SCOUTING THE NEIGHBORHOOD ALREADY. AT LEAST WE'LL GET SWITCHED TO THE GRAVEYARD SHIFT TOMORROW.
AIN'T GONNA BE A HECK OF A LOT OF KIDS OUT AT TWO IN THE MORNING.
YA KNOW, TWITCH, SOMEHOW THIS WHOLE THING ISN'T QUITE RIGHT. WE'VE GOT A KILLER LIVING FREE, OUT ON A TECHNICALITY, AND I'VE GOT TO SNEAK AROUND TRYING TO KEEP AN EYE ON HIM.
EVEN SENATOR JENNINGS ...
FORMER SENATOR, SIR...
WHATEVER!
EVEN THE FORMER SENATOR JENNINGS DOESN'T SEEM ALARMED BY THIS.
NO PARENTS. NO JUDGES. NO COPS.
NO ONE'S PAYING ANY ATTENTION TO THIS. I'M NOT EVEN MARRIED, LET ALONE A FRIGGIN' PARENT, AND I SEEM THE MOST OUTRAGED BY THIS!
... AND I CAN'T EVEN VENT MY STUPID MORALS.
"BY THE BOOK." MY WHOLE CAREER'S BEEN BUILT ON THOSE THREE WORDS... YET HERE I AM HIDING IN THE SHADOWS.
SIR, ALL WE CAN DO IS LEAD BY EXAMPLE. THAT SOME PEOPLE CHOOSE TO FOLLOW BAD EXAMPLES ISN'T ANYONE'S
FOR EXAMPLE, I HAVE SEVEN CHILDREN. IF ONE OF THEM TURNS OUT TO BE A CRIMINAL, AND THE OTHERS DON'T, WAS I A BAD PARENT?
I'D LIKE TO THINK THE ANSWER IS NO.
IT DOESN'T MEAN I'M PERFECT, BUT I COULD AT LEAST SAY I TRIED MY BEST. NO MORE. NO LESS.
THIS STAKEOUT IS OUR WAY OF DOING OUR BEST.

"WE'RE NOT BREAKING THE LAW, SIR. WE'RE JUST GIVING IT A HELPING HAND."
i hate nights.
no sun. no kids. no fun.
tomorrow i'll go out and play, but i need to find some excite- ment tonight.
now let me think.
um.
um.
HE'S AT IT AGAIN.
IT DOESN'T MATTER WHO HE TAKES. HE DOESN'T CARE WHOSE KID IT IS.
IT COULD BE ANYONES'.
um.
hee. hee. hee.
oh, billy, that's a good one.

EVEN WANDA'S!

TINK
TINK
TINK
wha?!

uh, SIR, LOOKS LIKE WE HAVE A VISITOR.
A 'CAPED' ONE, NO LESS.
A CAPE?!

it seems someone wants to play.
perfect timing.

LET'S GO!
IT'S THAT MAFIA KILLER! WHAT THE HELL'S HE DOING HERE?!!
DON'T TELL ME HE WORKS WITH KINCAID!

come out come out wherever you are...

NO MORE.

HURRY, TWITCH! GET THE DOOR. I'LL COVER.
CRIPES!
THE CHIEF'S GONNA KILL ME!

i...
i...
ice cream...
ice cream...
ice cream...

WHAT THE...!
SWEET MOTHER! WHAT'S HAPPENING HERE?!!
CHECK THE HOUSE! NOW!
A QUICK SEARCH REVEALS EVIDENCE OF ANOTHER CHILD'S DEATH.
DAMMIT! THIS IS ALL WRONG.

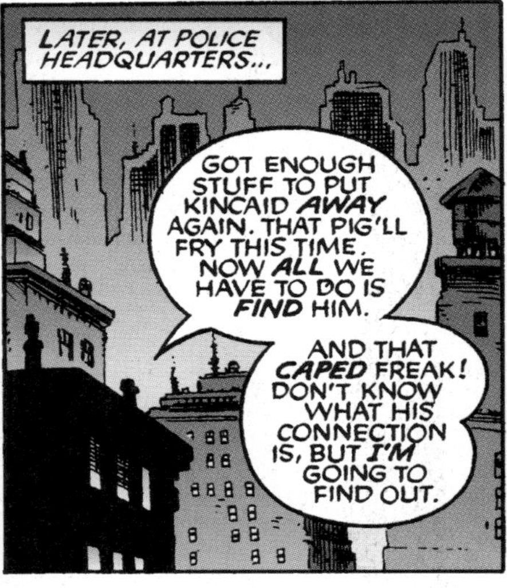
LATER, AT POLICE HEADQUARTERS...
GOT ENOUGH STUFF TO PUT KINCAID AWAY AGAIN. THAT PIG'LL FRY THIS TIME. NOW ALL WE HAVE TO DO IS FIND HIM.
AND THAT CAPED FREAK! DON'T KNOW WHAT HIS CONNECTION IS, BUT I'M GOING TO FIND OUT.

NOW, WE JUST HAVE TO GET THE CHIEF TO CONSENT TO LETTING US HUNT KINCAID DOWN. CIRCUMSTANTIAL EVIDENCE DOESN'T REALLY THRILL HIM.
WHAT IF THE CHIEF DOESN'T GO FOR IT...? ARE WE ON OUR OWN AGAIN, SIR?
NO! WE DO THIS BY THE BOOK! I ALREADY BENT THE RULES ON OUR STAKE-OUT.

I CAN'T MAKE ANY MORE EXCEPTIONS.

FORTUNATELY, SOME CAN.
BOYS SCREAMED AND GIRLS SCREAMED SO I MADE HIM SCREAM AND SCREAM AND SCREAM...

"QUESTIONS" PART ONE

Todd McFarlane – *story, pencils & inks*
Tom Orzechowski – *letters*
Steve Oliff – *colour*
Wanda Kolomyjec – *editor*

"QUESTIONS" PART TWO

Todd McFarlane – *story, pencils & inks*
Tom Orzechowski – *letters*
Steve Oliff, Reuben Rude and Olyoptics – *colour*
Wanda Kolomyjec – *editor*

"QUESTIONS" PART THREE

Todd McFarlane – *story, pencils & inks*
Tom Orzechowski – *letters*
Steve Oliff, Reuben Rude and Olyoptics – *colour*
Wanda Kolomyjec – *editor*

"QUESTIONS" PART FOUR

Todd McFarlane – *story, pencils & inks*
Tom Orzechowski – *letters*
Steve Oliff, Reuben Rude and Olyoptics – *colour*
Terry Fitzgerald – *editor*

"JUSTICE"

Todd McFarlane – *story, pencils & inks*
Tom Orzechowski – *letters & editor*
Terry Fitzgerald – *story consultant*
Steve Oliff, Reuben Rude and Olyoptics – *colour*